**DATE DUE**

| | | |
|---|---|---|
| NOV 2 3 1988 | | |
| DEC 2 1 1988 | | |
| DEC 5 1988 | | |

D0768988

**POINT LOMA NAZARENE COLLEGE**
*Ryan Library*
3900 Lomaland Drive, San Diego, CA 92106-2899

Call Number             Accession Number

152.3                  191627
B615

THE BIOLOGICAL FOUNDATIONS OF GESTURES

# The Biological Foundations of Gestures: Motor and Semiotic Aspects

# NEUROPSYCHOLOGY AND NEUROLINGUISTICS

a series of books edited by **Harry A. Whitaker**

BRUYER:
*The Neuropsychology of Face Perception and
Facial Expression*

KELLER/GOPNIK:
*Motor and Sensory Processes in Language*

NESPOULOUS/PERRON/LECOURS:
*The Biological Foundations of Gestures*

VAID:
*Language Processing in Bilinguals: Psycholinguistic
and Neuropsychological Perspectives*

152.3
B615

# THE BIOLOGICAL FOUNDATIONS OF GESTURES:

## Motor and Semiotic Aspects

Edited by

**JEAN-LUC NESPOULOUS**
*Universite de Montreal*
**PAUL PERRON**
*University of Toronto*
**ANDRÉ ROCH LECOURS**
*Universite de Montreal*

 LAWRENCE ERLBAUM ASSOCIATES, PUBLISHERS
1986    Hillsdale, New Jersey                London

POINT LOMA NAZARENE COLLEGE
191627
RYAN LIBRARY

Copyright © 1986 by Lawrence Erlbaum Associates, Inc.
All rights reserved. No part of this book may be reproduced in
any form, by photostat, microform, retrieval system, or any other
means, without the prior written permission of the publisher.

Lawrence Erlbaum Associates, Inc., Publishers
365 Broadway
Hillsdale, New Jersey 07642

**Library of Congress Cataloging-in-Publication Data**

The Biological foundations of gestures.

"The present volume is the outcome of a symposium
on Gestures, Cultures and Communication, held in May
1982 at Victoria College, University of Toronto.
This conference . . . which took place during the Third
International Summer Institute for Semiotic and
Structural Studies, was organized by the Toronto
Semiotic Circle''—Introd.
Includes bibliographies and indexes.
1. Gesture—Physiological aspects—Congresses.
2. Gesture—Psychological aspects—Congresses.
3. Neuropsychology—Congresses. 4. Motor ability—
Congresses. 5. Semiotics—Congresses. 6. Communica-
tive disorders—Physiological aspects—Congresses.
I. Nespoulous, Jean-Luc. II. Perron, Paul.
III. Lecours, André Roch. IV. International Summer
Institute for Semiotic and Structural Studies (3rd :
1982 : Victory College, University of Toronto)
V. Toronto Semiotic Circle. [DNLM: 1. Kinesics—
congresses. 2. Motor Activity—congresses.
BF 637.C45 B615 1982]
QP360.B563 1986      152.3      86-2174
ISBN 0-89859-645-9

Printed in the United States of America
10  9  8  7  6  5  4  3  2  1

# Contents

# List of Contributors

**André Ali-Chérif,** Clinique Neurologique, Groupe de Neuropsychologie Expérimentale et Clinique, C.H.U. Timone, Marseille, France.

**Daniel Beaubaton,** C.N.R.S. Institut de Neurophysiologie Expérimentale et Clinique, C.H.U. Timone, Marseille, France.

**Joan C. Borod,** Aphasia Research Center, Boston V.A. Medical Center, and Neurology Department, Boston University Medical School and Psychiatry Department, Bellevue Hospital Center and New York University Medical School.

**Michéle Brouchon,** Laboratoire de Neuropsychologie Humaine, EHESS Département de Neuropsychologie, C.H.U., Timone, Marseille, France.

**Pierre Desaulniers,** Laboratoire Théophile-Alajouanine, Centre hospitalier Côte-des-Neiges, Montréal, Québec, Canada.

**Pierre Feyereisen,** Research Associate of the National Fund for Scientific Research, University of Louvain, Belgium.

**Cheryl Gibson,** Department of Psychology, University of Waterloo, Waterloo, Ontario, Canada.

**Yves Joanette,** Laboratoire Théophile-Alajouanine, Centre hospitalier Côte-des-Neiges & Faculté de Médecine, Université de Montréal, Montréal, Québec, Canada.

**Adam Kendon,** Visiting Fellow, Department of Anthropology, Research School of Pacific Studies, Australian National University; formerly Visiting Professor of Anthropology, Connecticut College.

**Marcel Kinsbourne,** Behavioral Neurology Department, Eunice Shriver Center for Mental Retardation, Waltham, Massachusetts, U.S.A.

**Elissa Koff,** Aphasia Research Center, Boston V.A. Medical Center, and Neurology Department, Boston University Medical School; and Psychology Department, Wellesley College.

**Dominique Labourel,** Laboratoire de Neuropsychologie et de Rééducation du Langage, Hôpital Neurologique, Lyon, France.

**Yvan Lebrun,** Department of Neurolinguistics, School of Medicine V.U.B., Brussels, Belgium.

**André-Roch Lecours,** Laboratoire Théophile-Alajouanine, Centre hospitalier Côte-des-Neiges & Faculté de Médecine, Université de Montréal, Montréal, Québec, Canada.

**Chantal Leleux,** Department of Neurolinguistics, School of Medicine, V.U.B., Brussels, Belgium.

**Michael Mair,** Resident Surgical Officer, Moorfield Eye Hospital, London, United Kingdom.

**Jean-Luc Nespoulous,** Laboratoire Théophile-Alajouanine, Centre hospitalier Côte-des-Neiges & Département de Linguistique, Université de Montréal, Montréal, Québec, Canada.

**Marjorie Nicholas,** Aphasia Research Center, Boston V.A. Medical Center, and Neurology Department, Boston University Medical School.

**Marjorie Perlman,** Aphasia Research Center, Boston V.A. Medical Center, and Neurology Department, Boston University Medical School.

# The Biological Foundations of Gestures:
# Motor and Semiotic Aspects

# In Memoriam

# Paul Ivan Yakovlev
# 1894–1983

André Roch Lecours

> **Those who knew him will cherish their memories of the kind, sensitive, gentle man who was a trusted and loyal friend, adviser, mentor, confidant, and constant source of inspiration.**
>
> —*Thomas Kemper, 1984.*

Turetz (Russia) is situated at 55.22 degrees North and 29.15 degrees East of the Greenwich meridian, **at the median point of a line separating the Orient from the Occident.**[1] It is there, in the wealthy domain of his maternal grandfather, that Paul Ivan Yakovlev is born on December 15 (Julian calendar) or 28 (Gregorian calendar) of the year 1894. As an aristocrat, his mother speaks French with members of her family (Russian is a language one should speak with servants or at the market, but not with one's kins); his father is a retired imperial army officer. Paul is very young when his mother dies and he is only 9 years old when, at his father's death, he goes to live in Wilno with his mother's younger sister, a widow (with three daughters), who is the director of a private gymnasium for girls.

As an adolescent, he decides that he will become a philologist and historian, or else a painter and a sculptor. But time passes and he changes his mind about his future: He thinks of his paternal grandfather, who has been a military surgeon, and he starts considering medicine as a career. An artist **has to be a genius or else one isn't worth while . . . but in medicine all you have to do is read**

---

[1]Direct quotes from Paul Yakovlev, printed in bold, are from interviews led by Marjorie LeMay, Thomas Kemper, or the author.

1

**books, remember it all and you know all the answers.** In 1914, he obtains his baccalaureate from the Classical Gymnasium of Wilno. He is 21 years old, in 1915, when he is awarded a Sir Jacob Wylie Fellowship[2] and enters the Saint Petersburg Imperial Academy of Military Medicine, with the intention of becoming a psychiatrist (**a doctor who would manipulate the soul, make it happier, healthier**).

During the period when Saint Petersburg is becoming Petrograd before it becomes Leningrad, Paul Yakovlev (Fig. 1) grows less and less interested in unleashing **the secrets of the psyche** and more and more interested in **what was**

---

[2]J. Wylie: of Scottish origin, the founder of the Saint Petersburg Imperial Academy of Military Medicine, was physician to Catherine the Great and Surgeon General of the Russian armies until his death in 1834.

called in those days organic psychiatry, in which everything had to have a mechanical explanation. He studies histology with Alexandre Maximov, who is scholarly, with diligence of presentation; organic chemistry with Alexandre Borodine, who keeps his grand piano in his laboratory at the Academy; and physiology with Vladimir Mikhailovitch Bekhterev, the founder of Russian neurology, who remains active although he has recently retired, and later with Ivan Petrovitch Pavlov, a most impressive man whose lectures on conditional reflexes are indeed fascinating, and whose extremely antipsychology orientation is a topic of passionate discussions among students of the Academy. This is a troubled period, but young Yakovlev has great masters and he is soon convinced that his own life can only be devoted to the acquisition of scientific knowledge.

During the summer vacations of 1916 and 1917, Paul Yakovlev serves as a stretcher-bearer in the Imperial Army. Then comes the October Revolution. Thereafter, the Academy is no longer "Imperial" though it still is a medical school, and a good one. In 1919, Petrograd falls prey to famine, typhus, Spanish influenza and civil war: People around Paul Yakovlev, especially the young people, are terrorized and confused. At the end of the year, Trotsky's Red Army needs physicians: the students of the Academy therefore receive their diplomas 6 months ahead of time, on December 25. Paul Yakovlev is aware that Russia cannot, in the foreseeable future, provide him with the opportunity to carry on with his scientific education. Moved by a powerful feeling of instinctive biological survival and after consulting with Maximov, he takes the decision to act accordingly. On the morning of December 27, he and a Polish colleague, Trachinski, pretending that they have been charged with a public health mission, board a train heading for the Finnish border where local (Finns and White Russians) as well as English, American, and German troups are closely watching the movements of the Trotskist army. In order to avoid having to present their manufactured . . . certificate and to answer the questions of the red army inspector, the police, the inspector controlling the passports, the two friends move from one wagon to the next till they find themselves on the crowded rear platform of the train. Alongside the railroad tracks, there are snowy woods and, beyond the woods, the Gulf of Finland, frozen solid. In spite of bitter cold winds, Paul Yakovlev and his friend persuade one another that the Gulf constitutes the shortest and safest route out of Russia. Twenty kilometers or so before the border, in the middle of the night, dressed with several layers of clothes, they slip off the slow moving train and they start walking in the snowstorm. Beside their certificates and diplomas, they are carrying black bread, bacon, a revolver, a compass, 800 Imperial Rubles and white blankets. The latter are used whenever the generators of searchlights are heard and beams ripple too close (one then flops down, covers oneself, and hopes one has become invisible). At one point, Trachinski extirpates a bottle from his bag: It contains a (pinkish) mixture of laboratory alcohol and something else (cocaine?): Paul Yakovlev's companion has stolen the ingredients at the Academy on Christmas Eve and the concoction now turns out to be of the greatest help. When the sun rises, on December 28, the day of Paul Yakovlev's 25th anniversary, the two reach the shore and seek safety inside empty barrels near a deserted cement factory; a dog passes by, sniffs at the terrorized fugitives, and wanders on: a stray dog that has long learned that minding one's own business is now one of the behaviors making one's survival more likely. With night coming, Yakovlev and Trachinski resume their outing toward destiny. At dawn, on December 29, as they emerge from the snowy bushes bordering on the Gulf, the two companions are arrested by Finnish guards. One of them, unbelievably, recognizes Paul Yakovlev from a previous visit to Petrograd. This makes things easier but the pair is nonetheless sent to Coventry: The Finns will accept Russian refugees only when sure that they are not attacked by typhus or some other dreadful disease. The two survive quarantine, shake hands, and part forever. Trachinski's plan is to go and study butterflies in Siam.

Paul Yakovlev spends a few months in Finland, making a little money in Helsingfors (now Helsinki) at one time and in Aabo (now Turku) at another time. He then decides that the day has come for him to find a place where he can return to his scientific quest: Given the interest that he has in psychic disturbances resulting from brain damage, and also given the advice of his professors in Petrograd, his target is the private clinic which Hermann Oppenheim has opened in 1890, after having been denied Westphal's succession by the Prussian Secretary of Education, and which has progressively outclassed the Charité as the international center of clinical neurology in Berlin (Weil, 1970). Paul Yakovlev therefore presents himself at the German embassy with his Academy diploma and a few letters of recommendation written by his Russian professors: But Oppenheim has died earlier in 1919, before Yakovlev's protectors dated, wrote and signed their letters, and the recommendee is now suspected of counterfeiting. As these events require reflexion and reorientation, Paul Yakovlev decides to stay in Helsingfors a little longer. Until March 1920, he works in the port where his job is to inspect a cargo of Swedish matches (''Vulcan'') that have been damaged by sea water: For a few months, he hand-picks boxes—dry matches on one side and wet ones on the other—while pondering various scenarios: Germany being excluded, where to go next? France and the Salpêtrière: After all, he is quite fluent in French and he has read everything that Charcot and his disciples and successors have written.

In April, Paul Yakovlev boards a ship to England. In London, as in the other great capitals of Western Europe, it is generally believed that Bolchevism will not survive and the Russian embassy has remained faithful to the Tzar: There, refugees can easily trade Rubles for Sterling. Paul Yakovlev can survive and, after having by chance discovered—while taking a walk through the streets of London—the existence and seat of the British-Russian Brotherhood Society, he even is able to earn an extra hundred Pounds or so writing reports on the state of public health in Russia since the Fall of 1917. October the fourth, 1920, is the day of the first commercial flight between London and Paris: Paul Yakovlev, too poor to buy a ticket, feels considerable frustration, but this same day, he procures a place on the boat-train that travels from London to Paris via Dover and Boulogne.

In Paris, more precisely in the Latin Quarter, near the Pantheon, Paul Yakovlev rents a room in Madame Bourdon's boarding house. Of Madame Bourdon, he was later to say, with obvious fondness and gratitude, that she was very strict as to monthly payments but acted in a motherly manner with the **petits métèques** from Haiti, Paraguay, and Mexico who were then her guests and, especially, with this Russian **petit métèque** who, whatever the hour of day or night, paced back and forth his limited private space above the entresol dining room (**Monsieur Yakovlev, vous êtes un maniaque**). A few days after his arrival in Paris, Paul Yakovlev rings at Charles Richet's[3] door and tells him that he comes on behalf of a Cambridge colleague, Professor Daniel Gardner; he explains that he has met and befriended Gardner in London and he presents Richet with a letter of recommendation which Gardner has recently written for him. Richet is favorably impressed and he introduces the young Russian physician to a dearest friend, Madame Abrikossov, one of the last of Charcot's students, who has retained friendly relationships with the Salpetriere. Soon thereafter, Paul Yakovlev becomes a "stagiaire étranger" at the "Clinique des maladies du système nerveux" where, following Fulgence Raymond and Joseph Jules Dejerine, Pierre Marie has recently assumed Jean-Martin Charcot's chair.

At the Faculty, it is decided that Paul Yakovlev's medical studies are valid but that, in order to fulfill local requirements, he will have to recommence internship in obstetrics, pediatrics, gynecology and . . . infectious diseases. The candidate happily complies, agreeing that, at least for three out of four, these requirements appear to be reasonable in view of the fact that he has graduated from a military institution.

When Pierre Marie retires and yields Charcot's chair to Georges Guillain, Paul Yakovlev goes to work at the Pitié, next door to the Salpêtrière, with Joseph François Félix Babinski: He has found the man who will guide him in his doctoral research and thesis, and whom he will forever consider as his Mentor. It is at la Pitié that Paul Yakovlev begins to develop an interest for the effects of sensory disturbances on motor behavior; he becomes involved in discussions concerning cerebral lesions leading to paraplegia in flexion, a problem which one of his colleagues, Théophile Alajouanine,[4] is studying in the context of his doctoral research.

Babinski knows that his new student is poor and he finds him a job: Paul Yakovlev will work as an "interne de nuit" (night resident), in a fashionable Neuilly Sanatorium, where most "patients" are politicians in need of temporary

---

[3]Nobel prize in medicine and physiology, 1913, for his discovery of anaphylaxis.
[4]Who succeeded Guillain in 1947; Lhermitte, Lecours, & Signoret, 1981.

invisibility, rich American addicts taking a detoxication cure, and so forth. Accomodations are exceptionally good and emergencies infrequent: The place is excellent for one who has an appointment in a large university hospital (la Pitié, then Sainte-Anne) and has to spend after-duty hours studying and writing a doctoral dissertation. The latter, which is entitled "Association pithiato-organique" and therefore witnesses to one of Babinski's major preoccupations in those days, is published at the end of 1924—one year after Alajouanine's—by the Presses Universitaires de France. Paul Yakovlev defends it publicly on January the eighth, 1925; the board of examiners is presided by Professor Charles Achard and comprises Professors Jean Athanase Sicard, Henri-Claude, and Balthazar.

At this point, Paul Yakovlev would consider in very positive terms the prospect of pursuing his career in France. But this would mean having to take French citizenship, which in turn would mean waiting several years and regressing for a time to high school level training and examinations: This scenario is readily excluded, as well as a few others. After a trip to Berlin, in 1923, he has concluded, for various reasons, that his professional perspectives are no better in Germany than in France. Moreover, he has renounced the idea of returning to Russia, where **dust had not settled after all.** On the other hand, he is corresponding with Alexandre Maximov, who has migrated to the United States in 1921 and is now teaching at the University of Chicago: Maximov now insists that the land of opportunity for an ambitious scientist is no longer Western Europe but the United States of America. Moreover, Paul Yakovlev has had, as a patient in Neuilly, an American physician from Providence, Rhode Island; this colleague has introduced him to an attaché of the American embassy in Paris; the attaché has an influential uncle who is an archbishop somewhere in Ohio; consequently, soon after defending his dissertation, Paul Yakovlev is offered an extra quota American passport on the basis of his **exceptional professional qualifications.**[5] He accepts without hesitation, packs his books, his brand new diploma from the University of Paris and a few other things and, on March 15, 1925, he boards a ship leaving le Havre for New York. In April, he becomes the assistant of a neurologist who is practicing in Providence; the newspapers tell of (nothing less than) an **eminent collaborator of Babinski** who has traveled all the way from Paris to Providence in order to complete his neurological training with a famous local practitioner. But the eminent collaborator finds it difficult to live on $20.00 a month and, above all, his idea of being a neuroscientist is indissociable from that of obtaining an appointment in a university of renown: Boston is the place where he would like to be.

At the Boston City Hospital, Stanley Cobb, William Lennox, and Tracy Putnam have developed a major interest in epilepsy. Cobb and Lennox are preparing a monograph on the subject and a young enthusiastic competent polyglot neurologist who can review the foreign literature is a highly desirable collab-

---

[5]**Which I must admit were flimsy indeed,** was later to add Paul Yakovlev.

orator. Paul Yakovlev's salary increases from $20.00 to $150.00 a month: He serves in the outpatient clinics of the hospital and, as a Harvard research fellow in neurology, he reads and takes notes. The review is completed in June, 1926, and, in July, he begins to work in Palmer, Massachusetts, as a neurologist and neuropathologist of the Monson State Hospital for the epileptics. He has established good contacts within the Harvard Neurological Unit at the Boston City where, for several years, he will spend at least one week every month: He considers himself the Harvard **liaison man** at Monson. His research career has begun and his first American paper—"Epilepsy and Parkinsonism"—will soon be published in the New England Journal of Medicine (1928).

In the Fall of 1931, Paul Yakovlev borrows one thousand dollars and travels to Paris, then to Bern where the very first international meeting entirely devoted to neurology is taking place. This is for him the occasion to meet again with a man who has had a most decisive influence on him: Pavlov, who has serenely begun his 9th decade, has traveled to Switzerland for the occasion. Harvey Cushing is also there to report on the more than one thousand cases of brain tumor on which he has operated, and no doubt to insist on the necessity of surgical treatment for patients with pituitary adenoma (now 78, retired and living on the Côte d'Azur, Pierre Marie, whose studies of acromegalia have become classical although **he has missed the adenoma,** has not made the trip).

After the meeting, Paul Yakovlev takes the train to Zurich where he will spend 7 months working with Mieczyslaw Minkowski (at von Manakow's Hirnanatomisches Institut) and acquiring a Masters degree in neuroanatomy. Once in Zurich and as the result of Minkowski's intervention, he reclaims the (thanks God intact) anatomical specimen he has brought in his luggage, but has been forced to leave at the Swiss border in the interest of avoiding the needle probing procedure of a zealous customs officer searching for smuggled diamonds. The specimen is the brain of a 2-year-old boy whom he has observed at Monson and whose autopsy he has performed. Remembering the Dejerines' way of preparing brains in gapless serial sections, Paul Yakovlev plans to learn the technique in Minkowski's laboratory. He travels back to New England in March, 1932, with heavier luggage: He brings back the slides of the first specimen of the Yakovlev Collection (a case of what he will call **schizencephaly** in a classical publication yet to come). Later that Spring, Paul Yakovlev receives an appointment as "Assistant in Neurology" at Harvard Medical School. He then weds Mary McQuaid and spends his honeymoon in Montreal, a city he knew quite well as the result of a few **gambolling expeditions during the prohibition years.** Back home again, he starts making plans to build his first giant microtome: modeled after a smaller one, designed and built several years previously by Milton and Robert Goddard.[6] Paul Yakovlev remains at Monson until 1938, gathering materials for his Collection (for instance, two cases of paraplegia in flexion of cere-

---

[6]Robert Goddard: the inventor of the rocket.

bral origin; Kemper, 1984), researching and publishing on topics such as neurosomatic deterioration in epilepsy, the anatomoclinical correlations of myoclonus in epilepsy, decerebrate rigidity, congenital ectodermoses, hepatolenticular degeneration, paradoxical tendon reflexes.

Paul Yakovlev's "official baptism in Harvard Neurology" (Livingston, 1973) comes in 1938 when he leaves Monson for the Fernald State School where, in 1941, the "Assistant in Neurology" graduates to "Instructor in Neurology", and where he remains until 1947, pursuing essentially the same type of research: The giant microtome is perfected; new specimens are collected and prepared in serial sections. Topics already approached are further studied and new ones are tackled: tuberous sclerosis (and "brain stones"), the plantar reflex "as a criterion of endurance" preceded by "locomotion and the plantar reflex" in mental deficients as opposed to normals (Paul Yakovlev remembers what he has learned with his French mentor), porencephalies (some of the most spectacular specimens of the Collection), Morquio's disease, Hallervorden-Spatz' disease, carbon monoxide poisoning, hydrocephaly, and so forth. In 1942, his postgraduate seminars in neurology and psychiatry, of which he later claimed that they were "the beginning of continued education system in medicine" (Kemper, 1984), are published by the Waltham State Metropolitan Hospital (with the support of the Rockefeller Foundation). With Roy Dennis Halloran, Paul Yakovlev even publishes a "Course in military neuropsychiatry" (1942) and later, with Harry Solomon, a "Manual" of the same (1944).

Paul Yakovlev thereafter spends 4 years at the Middletown State Hospital and at the Yale University Medical School as a Clinical Associate Professor of Neurology (1947–1951). He develops a training program which becomes very popular among Connecticut physicians, including residents and Faculty members. The first trinity paper—telencephalon impar, semipar, totopar; endokinesis, ereismokinesis, telokinesis (see Chapter 1 of this book)—is published in 1948; it is followed by publications on Heller's syndrome, various types of brain malformations, the anatomical substratum of seizures, and so forth. The Yale venture comes to an end due to divergences with **the local pundits of psychoanalysis.**

"Harvard knows a good man when it sees one, especially a man who has previously served Harvard and who is 'farmed out,' so to speak, at another prestigious school. So Harvard invites Paul to 'come home' " (Livingston, 1973): In 1951, he is appointed as a Clinical Professor of Neuropathology, Harvard Medical School. He thereafter continues his research: the fronto-pontine bundle, fronto-thalamic projections, paraplegia in flexion (a tip of the hat to Théophile Alajouanine), meningo-facial angiomatosis, the cytology of the geniculate nuclei, the "crowbar skull," leukodystrophies, the connections of the temporal lobe in man, cerebral calcifications, brain anatomy in mental retardation, the limbic nuclei of the thalamus and the connections of the limbic cortex, the cingulate gyrus and its cortico-cortical connections, stereotaxis, handedness, myelinogenesis, Parkinson's disease, cerebral infarctions in the human fetus, the decussation of the bulbar pyramids, the development of the corpus callosum, and so forth: Paul Yakovlev is enjoying his Collection. In 1951, Paul Yakovlev is elected President of the American Association of Neuropathologists. In 1954, with Marcus Singer, he publishes an atlas of the human brain in sagittal sections and, in 1974, with Jay Angevine and E. L. Mancall, an atlas of the human cerebellum.

Between the time of publication of the two atlases, Paul Yakovlev has been appointed consultant in neuropathology at the Peter Bent Brigham Hospital (1954), at the Children's Medical Center (1956), and at the Massachusetts General Hospital (1961). He has become a Professor Emeritus (1961), the Curator of the Warren Anatomical Museum (1961), he has traveled the world over,[7] and he has become a living legend (Fig. 2). Year after year, he has been the respected fatherly and inspiring mentor of students and scholars from all over the world (in Derek Denny-Brown's words, "he has acted as a catalyst on generations after generations of neurologists and psychiatrists"); he has taught clinical neurology, neuropathology, neuroembriology, neuroanatomy; he has explained the importance of seeking relationships between brain maturation and the emergence and differenciation of behaviors, in humans and in other animals; he has invited everyone for cheese and vodka at 21 Addington Road, Brookline; he has frightened everyone with his very particular manner of driving beat-up cars through the streets—and two tunnels—of Boston; and he has earned both the indefectible friendship and the admiration of most. He lost neither when he relocated the Collection at the Eunice Kennedy Shriver Research Center, Fernald State School, in 1969, and, in 1974, at the Armed Force Institute of Pathology of the Walter Reed Medical Center.

The Yakovlev Collection[8]: more than 1000 whole brains embedded in celloidin and prepared in gapless serial sections (27 tons of glass; Haleem, 1984); brains of humans, monkeys, dolphins and other animals; normal brains and pathological ones; foetal brains, young brains, adult brains, senescent brains. The giant microtomes have been put to good use. And, with the Collection, the personal library: some 2000 books and 5000 reprints. Altogether, a material that

---

[7]Including to his homeland. Paul Yakovlev's first trip back to Russia took place in 1958, in the context of a U.S. scientific exchange mission to the U.S.S.R.; while in Leningrad, 39 years after he had left Saint Petersburg, a hostess wondered where on earth could an American scholar have learned to speak Russian exactly the way her grandmother used to. Several other voyages to Russia followed thereafter: Renting a car in Paris and driving alone to Leningrad was something he utterly enjoyed during the sixties. His travels to Russia included a period of several months of scientific work in Moscow, in 1978, as well as a farewell trip, in 1979, at the age of 83.

[8]"There is no other collection of neuroanatomical material in serial sections consistently fixed, embedded, cut, stained and mounted to such exacting standards . . . the Yakovlev Collection is an irreplaceable reference material, patiently collected over a period of 42 years" (Denny-Brown, 1972, quoted by Kemper, 1984).

has proven tremendously useful in the past and should remain available, now that Paul Yakovlev has died, on June the 16th, 1983, to be used by generations to come.

## REFERENCES

Denny-Brown, D. (1972). *P. I. Yakovlev, M.D.,* unpublished.

Haleem, M. (1984). Paul Ivan Yakovlev (1894–1983). In J. D. Balentine (Ed.), *Newsletter* (pp. 2–3). The International Society of Neuropathology, Charleston, So. Carolina.

Kemper, T. (1984). Paul Ivan Yakovlev (1894–1983). *Archives of Neurology, 41,* 536–540.

Lhermitte, F., Lecours, A. R., & Signoret, J.-L. (1981). Theophile Alajouanine (1890–1980). *Brain and Language, 13,* 191–196.

Livingston, R. B. (1973). *Presentation of a portrait of Paul I. Yakovlev to Harvard Medical School,* unpublished.

Weil, A. (1970). Hermann Oppenheim (1858–1919). In W. Haymaker & F. Schiller (Eds.), *The founders of neurology* (pp. 492–495). Springfield, IL: Thomas.

# Introduction

Jean-Luc Nespoulous
Paul Perron
André Roch Lecours

The present volume is the outcome of a symposium on Gestures, Cultures and Communication, held in May 1982 at Victoria College, University of Toronto. This conference, one of a series of five colloquia which took place during the Third International Summer Institute for Semiotic and Structural Studies, was organized by the Toronto Semiotic Circle. It grew out of an earlier meeting, held in 1980, during the first International Summer Institute, on the Neurological Basis of Signs in Communication Processes, whose proceedings were published in 1981 by the Toronto Semiotic Circle.

The purpose of the 1982 conference was to explore the biological basis of gestures by bringing together investigators working mainly in the fields of anthropology, neurophysiology, neuropsychology and psycholinguistics. A range of important studies on gestural activity was presented in an attempt to deduce from behavioral observations, fundamental issues on the cerebral organization underlying those behaviors. After the symposium, it became apparent that it would be fruitful to investigate and develop further several topics which had been discussed in detail by the participants. Thus, this volume includes revisions of six of the delivered papers prepared by the main speakers as well as three chapters written by the respondants after the conference. Retaining a biological perspective, the editors also invited six other contributors to submit chapters on gestures in areas which only had been touched upon during the meeting.

## I. Gestural behavior: Definition

Whereas consensus is often reached as to what could be labeled verbal behavior (its definition, its basic components, its boundaries), this is hardly the case for gesture. Lack of consensus seems primarily to originate from intrinsic ambiguities related to the problem of defining, in the entire spectrum of *motor activity,* those activities which properly can be identified as *gestures.* This ambiguity and fundamental difficulty is, in fact, present in dictionary definitions of gesture, as well as in those proposed by various contributors to this volume. Thus, if one consults the *Lexis* dictionary (1977), gesture is defined in the following way: "Movements of body parts, particularly of the arms, the hands or the head conveying, or not conveying, meaning," whereas the *Oxford English Dictionary* (1951) defines gesture as "significant movement of limb or body . . . expressing feeling and/or evoking response from another and/or conveying intention." An examination of the above definitions clearly shows that the former, which is not systematically linked to the transmission of information to another person and incorporates at one and the same time specifically semiotic activities, is more extensive than the latter which limits gesture to semiotic and intentional behavior.

## II. Typology of Gesture

Much in the same way that decisions must be taken concerning the extension of the general definition of gesture, questions related to its typology and classification must also be addressed. For example, it is necessary to select the categories or subcategories of behavior to be examined. In this volume two of us, J.-L. Nespoulous and A. R. Lecours (Ch. 2) distinguish between two classes of gestures: those having an obvious communicational intent and those related to practical actions. Moreover, they underscore the necessity, within the context of a *neurosemiotics*—whose aim would be to study the mutual relationships between brain and semiotic activity in man—of exploring *both areas* of investigation concurrently: an analysis of the former type of gestures (i.e., gestures having a communicational intent) enabling one to undertake important research in *semiotic individual behavior* (e.g., deaf patients employing a code such as the American Sign Language, or normal subjects' gestures accompanying speech); the analysis of the latter type of gestures (i.e., gestures involved in practical actions) leading to the study of *nonsemiotic behavior*—but nonetheless learned—used in everyday life (e.g., hammering nails or brushing one's teeth). Adam Kendon, on the other hand, proposes a more restrictive definition of gesture: "The word 'gesture' serves as a label for that domain of visible action that participants routinely separate out and treat as governed by an acknowledged communicative intent" (Ch. 1).

Yet, even in the case of definitions of gesture that are rather extensive, the dichotomy "semiotic *vs* non-semiotic" raises several complex problems. A non-semiotic act—and examples abound in daily life as well as in literature—can become "semiotized" either by means of an explicit original convention between participants (in John le Carré's *Smiley's People,* carrying a briefcase in the left hand indicates that the operation is ready to begin), or by the receiver alone (in François Rabelais' *Gargantua,* a character Gymnast, exercising simply for health reasons, is surprised by soldiers and thought to be possessed by the devil). In addition to the above fundamental dichotomy (semiotic *vs* nonsemiotic), other classificatory avenues must be explored in the study of gesture, such as: autonomous *vs* nonautonomous gestural behavior (Kendon Ch. 1); opaque *vs* iconic gestural forms (Nespoulous & Lecours, Ch. 2), keeping in mind more external properties such as manual *vs* facial, mono-manual *vs* bi-manual. . . . Along these taxonomical lines (and others of course), decisions are to be reached in each and every study as to the scope and the limits of the analysis to be undertaken: Should investigation include—even if they are separated out—all types and subtypes of human motor activity or should it bear only on some specific categories of gestural behavior?

## III. Methodological Aspects

After various alternatives have been considered and solutions proposed concerning definitions and typology, other questions must be addressed which are essentially related to the analysis of gestural data. As a matter of fact, methods of investigation are bound to vary according to the stated objectives and to the nature of gestural behavior studied. For instance, the analysis of a corpus of American Sign Language (Lebrun & Leleux, Ch. 13) obviously does not present the same problems as those raised when observing the earliest gestural behavior of neonates (Trevarthen, Ch. 8), or again, when studying mimogestuality accompanying discourse (Kendon, Ch. 1 and Labourel, Ch. 15).

Nonetheless, there do exist methodological issues of a general nature which necessarily crop up whenever one attempts to account for a given instance of gestural behavior. A minimal number of four methodological approaches can be envisaged to elucidate such behavior:

—a first approach would deal with the *microanalytical exploration of the gestural behavior.* Its aim would be to study, in the most exhaustive manner possible, the unfolding of the motor act without prejudging the value, the function, or possible content of each microsegment so analyzed. This "phonetics" of gesture can be extremely unwieldy to manipulate but it clearly has the advantage of not prematurely projecting interpretations on the object studied. Frequently ethologists, working on animals or man (Cosnier, 1977), resort to such a method, not knowing a priori what is, or is not, pertinent for the comprehension of the behavioral system whose structure they are attempting to describe and evaluate (Pike, 1967).

—A second approach, which is also microanalytical, often borrows its descriptive apparatus from *structural linguistic models.* This is the course adopted by Birdwhistell (1970), Signoret & North (1979) in their study of apraxia, and

Stokoe (1980) in his work on A. S. L. Based on the postulate of the "double articulation," the usefulness of this approach seems to be less and less pertinent as one moves away from highly codified and structured systems of gestural communication such as A.S.L. (Bouissac, 1973).

—A third approach, of a decidedly *macroanalytic nature,* consists in identifying from the onset "behavioral patterns" and describing them in "ordinary language": "The subject takes out a cigarette, lights it, puffs on it while looking to the left." In his work on mimogestuality, Cosnier (1977) adopts this very method founded on the study of cinematographic documents. So do Scheflen (1973) in work on psychiatric interviews, and Montagner (1974) in a study done on nursery-age children in situations of social interaction (see Bouissac [1973] for a critical review of this issue).

—A last approach, described by Cosnier as the *functional method,* makes use, rather early on in the descriptive procedure, of preestablished typological grids (Labourel, Ch. 15), grouping gestural behavior according to its nature and function (Nespoulous & Lecours, Ch. 2). Although presented separately here, grids and methods are not mutually exclusive and nothing prevents an investigator from beginning a study using micro- or macroanalysis, and then concluding by having recourse to functional analysis regrouping various behaviors into homogeneous (if possible) categories.

Only when the aforesaid preconditions have been met, and explicit controlled choices of a theoretical and methodological nature have been made, can the systematic study of gesture be safely undertaken. It is therefore within this problematical domain of theory and methodology that the following contributions, each mapping out areas in the mosaic of gestural studies, should be situated. The *biological* foundations of gesture—the main topic of this volume—cannot be established unless the above distinctly *semiotic* problems have been resolved (at least in part), thus opening the way to a yet-to-come integrated neurosemiotic approach.

The research reported in this volume seeks to clarify three other interrelated domains linked to the biological study of gesture: the neurological substratum of gestures and motor activity in general; issues concerned with developmental theories of gesture, and pathological manifestations of gestural behavior and their relationship to neurological substratum.

## THE NEUROLOGICAL SUBSTRATUM OF
## GESTURES AND MOTOR ACTIVITY

Marcel Kinsbourne establishes a classification of gestures different from those suggested by the two previous authors. Various types of gestures and orienting are identified and specific brain activation motivating them is localized and mapped out. Although it is possible to approach each gesture or gesture type neuropsychologically, the author indicates that there seems to be no unit upon which to base a neuropsychology of gesture in the way there exists a neuropsychology of language.

In his chapter, P. Feyereisen proposes that two competing hypotheses may account for righthand advantage in manual activity during speaking: hemispheric specialization for the control of sequencing movements, or left hemisphere activation during speech. As far as unilateral brain damage is concerned, neither specific impairment of manual activity, nor the influence the type of aphasia has on gesture production, have been observed. Though no evidence exists for a common cerebral mechanism underlying speech and gestures, critical experiments analyzing interference between verbal behavior and right hand activity still remain to be done. In addition, the conditions in which lateral differences occur have not yet been assessed. But more particularly, aphasiology offers the opportunity to test specific hypotheses about the relationship between language and gestures.

For M. Brouchon, Y. Joanette and M. Samson, over the last 2 decades, a better understanding of the mechanisms underlying visually guided movements has been achieved giving rise to a descriptive model which assumes a clearly defined sequential organization. A first phase, corresponding to the limb's transport to the object, is completed by a second phase corresponding to the object manipulation. The first phase itself is viewed as consisting of two sequential components: a pre-programmed projection of the arm towards the object, which is achieved through a *feedforward* system guided by *peripheral* vision, followed by a final adjustment permitting the hand to make contact with the object, which is achieved through a *feedback* mechanism guided by *central* vision. Yet, given the integrity of the previously referred to mechanisms involved in visually guided movements, there still can be differences in visuo-motor behavior according to the portion of space or—"field"—in which the stimulus is located. Distinction between "prehension" and "locomotory" fields in target location are fundamental for the study of "normal" and brain-damaged subjects with partial lesions. The study concludes that the ultimate goal of a visually guided movement—*reaching* in *prehension* field versus *indicating* in *locomotory* field—could determine the gesture in itself.

In their study, M. Poncet, D. Beaubaton, and A. Ali-Chérif note that the presence of ipsilateral motor control of axial and proximal limb movements has been demonstrated in both animals and man. In animals, investigations of visuo-motor performance following induced lesions of optic chiasma and corpus callosum highlight the mechanisms of this control. Work on the organization of corticospinal pathways has permitted to address the problem of its anatomical basis. In man, the study of motor disturbances subsequent to division of the cerebral commissures and the analysis of apraxic deficits secondary to focal brain lesions has suggested the existence of such ipsilateral motor control. Human split-brain studies run into the difficulty of sending visual information to a single hemisphere for a sufficiently long lapse of time, hence the impossibility of thoroughly studying visuo-motor performances. However, the presence, in a patient, of lateral hemianopia associated with full callosal disconnection syndrome offers a unique model to study, unrestrained, the motor capacities of the only sighted hemisphere.

Examining video and audio tape material of two interactors, M. Mair investigates the neurological basis of facial movements and voice frequency. Rather than focus on the production of gesture per se, his micro-analysis of interaction shows the remarkable detail and precision of the interlocking of motor output among interacting subjects. The timings are so rapid and so coordinated that the conjoined brains which turn them out actually modify each other's output as it is produced. The synchronies observed have neurological substrata that can be deduced through the description of the visual system and its timings. Final questions are raised about the nature of the faculty of "projection" or "intention" which mobilizes the biological system.

## DEVELOPMENTAL THEORIES OF GESTURE

The analysis carried out by C. Trevarthen of videotapes and films reveals complex regulations in the hand movements of newborns. Throughout infancy hands express subtle shades of motivation, movements in communication being distinctive both in form and perceptual regulation from those to grasp and manipulate objects. A large corpus of still photographs of interactions between infants and mothers and of play with objects is reviewed. Changes in hand movement are related to principal developmental milestones. Evidence is presented that hand gestures are organized, from early months, to express the infant's awareness of persons, orientation of interest and emotional state. Strong evidence for innate lateralized cerebral (including subcortical) control of gestural expressions comes from signs of consistent asymmetry in hand movements of infants. [Changes in hand preferences for different tasks indicate growth and complementary cognitive functions in the two hemispheres. Such an evidence suggests that (a) innate hemispheric asymmetry is first concerned with intersubjective communication; assymmetries in manipulative skill may be secondary, and that (b) learned culturally significant hand skills have an asymmetric cerebral localization linked to language].

Reviewing various models constructed by developmental theorists to account for the relationships existing between movement and knowledge of the world in infants, S. Segalowitz (Ch. 9) points out that some theorists (e.g., Piaget) suggest that the movements of the young infant are the means by which the child constructs knowledge of his world; others (e.g., Trevarthen, Bower) that the existence of coordinated movements in this period indicates rather that some cognitive structures of communication already exist and do not have to be constructed. The latter position gathers support from the viewpoint that there is evidence for cerebral functional asymmetries for language-related perception in early infancy, and that therefore a "pre-organized" language system is a strong possibility. In this chapter, it is argued that such a system would, in fact, look quite different from what has been proposed, that the neurological basis for it would not be the left hemisphere, and that the evidence on early coordination of movements would indicate rather that such activity is not part of a more global communication system. Attempts to build such an integrated model are premature at present.

In the next study, C. Gibson and S. Segalowitz stress that, despite normal nonverbal intelligence, deaf children generally do not achieve a reading proficiency beyond a fourth grade level. Attempts to account for this deficit point to reduced vocabulary and delayed language acquisition. The possibility is explored that it is the salience of spatial information for them that creates not only a counterproductive bias, but also an upper limit on their ability to extract verbal information. Moreover, when deaf children attempt to learn a language system, the visual modality carries the most consistent and compelling information. This is true for speech reading, sign language, pantomime, and gesture, but discussion here is restricted to sign language. Two readily identifiable components of sign language which may have an important influence on the development of competence in a verbal language system are the symbolic dimension and the spatial component. These aspects are examined from a developmental perspective, especially with respect to the role of hemispheric asymmetries in cognitive functioning.

## PATHOLOGICAL MANIFESTATIONS OF GESTURAL BEHAVIOR AND NEUROLOGICAL SUBSTRATUM

Fundamental issues concerning the identification, the definition and classification of apraxic gestures and their relationship to neurological substratum are raised in A. R. Lecours, J.-L. Nespoulous and P. Desaulniers's chapter. From a clinical point of view, the model inherited from Leipman at the beginning of the 20th century has not been sufficiently problematized. The said model does not account for the different clinical manifestations of apraxia. Moreover, Leipman's classificatory model, based on connection theory, is in fact essentially hermetic, since, for example, if ideational apraxia is diagnosed then there is said to be a problem with the program, and if there is a problem with the program then there is ideational apraxia.

In his chapter, E. Roy examines disorders in performing limb praxis and action sequencing tasks as they reflect disruption in conceptual and production processes underlying action. The conceptual processes or system is thought to provide an abstract representation of action and involves three types of knowledge: (a) that relevant to objects and their functions; (b) that relevant to actions (e.g., hammering) into which objects (e.g., a hammer, a shoe) become incorporated and (c) that relevant to the serial ordering of actions in a sequence. The production system encompasses perceptual-motor functions for organizing and executing actions and is linked at higher levels with the conceptual system. The performance of actions is thought to involve a delicate balance between higher processes which demand attention and those, at lower levels, which are much more autonomous. To further understand the principles underlying the performance of actions, comparisons are made between types of errors seen in apraxia with those seen in normality.

The dozen cases of communication disorders following cerebral injury in adult deaf people which have been reported over the years are extensively reviewed by Y. Lebrun and C. Leleux. The symptoms noted in the cases are diagnosed in order to find out about the ways communicative skills can be disturbed by brain damage in deaf signers. The study shows that: writing and fingerspelling, in the same brain-injured patient, may be disturbed differently; reading is often the least impaired, or the best recovered, verbal skill; and the expressive modality which is the best preserved, is often, but need not be necessarily, the earliest or the preferred means of expression of the patient premorbidly. Knowledge of aphasia in hearing subjects also helps in the understanding of the physiopathology of acquired disorders of communication in deaf people since, in right-handed signers, acquired disorders of communication are conspicuously more frequent after left than after right cerebral injury, just as is aphasia in hearing people; and like aphasic impairments signing disorders cannot be said to result from apraxia.

The effects of unilateral brain damage on the facial communication of emotion are investigated by J. Borod, E. Koff, M. Perlman, and M. Nicholas. In addition, they relate facial emotional expression to other facial behaviors, e.g., apraxia, mobility, and paralysis. They begin with a review of the neuroanatomical and behavioral data in this area and they describe the procedures and findings in their study. Facial emotion was examined in 42 adult subjects (right brain-damaged, left brain-damaged, normal controls) under posed and spontaneous elicitation conditions. Videotaped while communicating positive and negative emotions, the subjects' facial expressions are rated for responsivity, accuracy, intensity, and asymmetry. These ratings are subjected to statistical analysis and results for each subject group are presented. The same subjects are also examined on measures of bucco-facial apraxia, hemiface mobility, and facial paralysis; performance on these measures are presented and correlated with the facial emotional expression data. The chapter concludes with discussion regarding the overall findings with special attention to issues such as: (1) the role of the right versus left hemisphere in facial behaviors: (2) distinctions between volitional and automatic motor responses; (3) experimentally induced versus clinically-observed emotional behavior; (4) controlling for demographic factors (e.g., age) in studies of facial communication involving neurological populations; and (5) the possible relationship between expression and perception in communicating emotion.

In the final chapter, D. Labourel observes six aphasic patients from an ethological standpoint and studies the meaning of gestures and mimics in a communicative situation. A typology is proposed based on the different functions given by Jakobson (1960) in his communicative diagram. A classification of gestures and mimics during spoken exchange is established on three levels: reference, situation, and speech. The results show that the quantity and the type of gestures and mimics vary greatly from one patient to another and that this variation does not seem to be clearly correlated to the fluent or nonfluent characteristic of the type of aphasic observed. The main function of mimics and gestures also varies according to the situation and the aim of the communication. Apraxia, the question of laterality for gestures and brain dominance are discussed. Functional analysis of gestures and mimics indicates some ambiguities and the possibility of compensation for a verbal deficit by means of preserved mimogestuality is linked to several factors. In most cases, the gestural deficit is found not to be as serious as the verbal deficit.

The issue of gesture is on the threshold of remarkable developments and once again moving to playing an important role in the study of human communication. This obviously raises many questions about the nature of language itself and man's extraordinary capacity for expression. It is hoped that the chapters presented from such varied perspectives and diverse disciplines will contribute to the mapping out of potential directions of pluridisciplinary investigation in an area in which research has been largely dormant and too long neglected. If this is so, then the volume on the biological foundations of gesture will have served its purpose.

## REFERENCES

Birdwhistell, R. L. (1970). *Kinesics and context.* Philadelphia: University of Pennsylvania Press.

Bouissac, P. (1973). *La mesure des gestes.* The Hague: Mouton.

Cosnier, J. (1977). Communication non-verbale et langage. *Psychologie Médicale, 9–11,* 2053–2072.

Jakobson, R. (1960). Closing statements: Linguistics and Poetics. In T. A. Sebeok (Ed.), *Style in language,* Cambridge, MA: MIT Press.

*Lexis* (1977). Paris: Larousse.

Montagner et al. (1974). Approche étho-physiologique des communications non-verbales chez le jeune enfant. *Bulletin d'audiophonologie, 5,* 211–242.

*Oxford Dictionary of English* (1951). Oxford: Clarendon.

Perron, P. (Ed.). (1981). *The neurological foundations of signs in communication processes.* Toronto, Toronto Semiotic Circle.

Pike, K. L. (1967). *Language in relation to a unified theory of the structure of human behavior*. The Hague: Mouton.

Scheflen, A. E. (1973). *Communicational Structure*. Bloomington: Indiana University Press.

Signoret, J.-L. & North, P. (1979). *Les apraxies gestuelles*. Paris: Masson.

Stokoe, C. W. (1980). Sign language and sign languages. *Annual Review of Anthropology, 9*, 365–390.

# THE NATURE AND
# FUNCTION OF GESTURES

# 1 Current Issues in the of Gesture

## Adam Kendon

## INTRODUCTION

The study of gesture has a long history. The earliest books devoted exclusively to it appeared at the beginning of the 17th century. In the 18th century, especially in France, gesture was looked upon as having great relevance for the understanding of the natural origin of language and the nature of thought. Condillac and Diderot, in particular, wrote about it quite extensively. In the 19th century, gesture continued to command serious attention. Edward Tylor and Wilhelm Wundt both dealt with it at length. They believed that its study would throw light upon the transition from spontaneous, individual expression to the development of codified language systems. For much of this century, however, the study of gesture appears to have languished. The question of language origins, which has always provided an important justification for its study, fell into disrepute. Psychology neglected gesture because it seemed too much connected with deliberate action and social convention to be of use for the understanding of the irrational or to be easily accommodated in terms of behavioristic doctrine. It has been neglected by linguists because it has seemed too much a matter of individual expression. In any case it could not be accommodated into the rigorous systems of phonology and grammar with which linguists were preoccupied. Even the growth of interest in what came to be known as "nonverbal communication" did not stimulate the study of gesture as one might have expected. This was because the preoccupation here has been with how behavior functions communicatively in the regulation of interaction and in the management of interpersonal relations. Gesture is too much a part of conscious expression and too closely connected with the verbal for it to be of central relevance here.

Lately, however, things have begun to change. A revival of interest in speculation about the evolution of language, and in particular Gordon Hewes' discussions of the gestural origins theory, the discovery that chimpanzees can be taught sign language and the development of the linguistic study of sign language itself, have all created a climate in which the study of gesture once again seems to be important. The interest that linguists have been showing in how language is used in interaction has led to a realization that, from a functional point of view, spoken utterances often only work because they are embedded in contexts of other forms of behavior, including gesture. Psychology has lately restored higher mental processes to center stage in the array of topics it considers important, and so gesture, as a form of symbolic expression, is suddenly seen to be of interest.[1]

## DEFINING GESTURE

One should begin with the question of definition. What is a gesture? A modern definition of gesture (as given in the Oxford English Dictionary, for instance) is that it is a movement of the body, or any part of it, that is considered as expressive of thought or feeling. This is an extremely broad definition. At first sight, it would seem to include practically everything that a person might do. However, a brief consideration of how the word is commonly used shows that the word gesture refers to only certain kinds of bodily movements that are considered expressive of thought or feeling.

As commonly understood, gesture refers to such actions as waving goodbye, or giving the thumbs up signal, or thumbing the nose at someone. It includes pointings and pantomimes that people sometimes engage in when they are too far away from one another to talk (or where talk would interfere). It includes the head waggings and arm wavings of vigorous talk, as well as the movements a person may improvise to convey something for which his words seem inadequate. However, there are other kinds of action which, though expressive, seem less appropriately called gesture. For example, we would not say of someone who was weeping that he was engaged in gesture or, if we did, this would probably imply that the weeping was "put on," that it was a show or a performance, and that it was not wholly genuine as an expression of emotion. More-

---

[1]Kendon (1982) expands the argument of these paragraphs. Bulwer (1644/1974) is the first book in English to be devoted to gesture exclusively. Angenot (1973) discusses a number of French works of the same period. Condillac's discussion of gesture is in his *Essay on the Origin of Human Knowledge* (Condillac 1754/1971). Diderot discusses gesture in his *Lettre sur les Sourds et Muets* (Diderot 1751/1916). Gesture and sign language is dealt with at length in Tylor (1878) and Wundt (1900/1973). For an account of the decline of interest in the question of language origins, see Stam (1976). For a discussion of recent revival of interest in it, see Hockett (1978). Hewes' discussions include Hewes (1973, 1976). For the teaching of sign language to apes see Hill (1978) for a recent review. Sebeok and Umiker-Sebeok (1980) is a useful anthology.

over, the term gesture is not usually applied to the movement
when they are nervous, such as hair pattings, self-grooming
ments, and the repetitive manipulations of rings or necklaces ι
accoutrements. In ordinary interaction, such movements are
regarded, or they are treated as habitual or involuntary and, althou͟          ͮ    ͮ
often revealing, and may be read by others as symptoms of the individual's
moods or feelings, they are not considered as gestures as a rule.

Further, there are many actions that a person must engage in if he is to
participate in interaction with others which, again, though they may be quite
revealing of the person's attitudes and feelings are not regarded as gesture because they are regarded as being done for the practical necessities of interaction,
and not for the sake of conveying meaning. Consider the movements that a
person in interaction must engage in to establish, to maintain, or to change his
distance and orientation in respect to the other participants. The distance a person
may establish between himself and his partner in interaction may often be taken
as an indication of his attitude towards them or of his understanding of the nature
of the interaction that is taking place. Such spatial and orientational movements
are not considered as gestures, however, for they are treated as being done, not
for their own sake, but for the sake of creating a convenient and appropriate
setting for the interaction. Even when someone seems to edge closer to another
than the other expects, or when they sit far off and do not move up, despite the
far reaching consequences that may sometimes follow, such actions are not yet
considered gestures if, as is usually the case, they are done in a way that
subordinates them to actions that must be done merely to maintain such spatial
and orientational arrangement as is essential for the carrying out of a conversation.[2]

It can also be said that pratical actions are not normally considered gestures
even when such actions play a part in social interaction. For example, when
people have conversations they may also engage in such activities as smoking or
drinking or eating. The actions required for such activities may sometimes be
used as devices to regulate the social interaction. People who meet for talk over
coffee and a cigarette may vary the rate at which they drink up their coffee or
smoke their cigarette as a way of regulating the amount of time to be spent in
conversation. Lighting a cigarette or re-lighting a pipe can often be elaborated as
a way of "buying time," as when a person needs to think a little before he
replies. Yet, despite the communicative significance such activity undoubtedly
may have, it is not typically treated as intended to communicate anything. To
spend time getting one's pipe ready to light up is to take "time out" of a
conversation, it is not to engage in a conversational move or turn, even though it
may play a part in structuring the moves or turns of which the conversation is
composed.

---

[2]For a discussion of the role of spacing and orientation in interaction see Kendon (1973, 1977).

191627

The actions of smoking, or of any practical action, may be performed in ways that can be highly expressive, however. There are many different ways in which smoke may be exhaled, for example—in a thin and elegant jet, in untidy clouds, directed at people or away from them. One may wave one's cigarette about in elaborate balletic movements; one may stub it out with force or with delicacy. Practical actions, thus, may become embellished with flourishes to the point that their expressive dimension may be openly recognized. As this happens, they come to take on the qualities of gesture.

If practical actions can be given some of the qualities of gesture, it is also possible to observe that gestures may sometimes be disguised so that they no longer appear as such. It has been reported that in Germany there is a gesture in which the forefinger touches the side of the head and is rotated back and forth. It is used to mean "he's crazy" and it is regarded as a grave insult. Its use has been the cause of fights and one may be prosecuted for performing it in public. A surreptitious version of it has appeared, however, in which the forefinger is rotated in contact with the cheek. In this version the gesture is performed in such a way that it could be mistaken for scratching the cheek or for pressing a tooth that was giving discomfort. Likewise, in Malta, the gesture known as the Italian Salute or the *bras d'honneur* is regarded as so offensive that one can be prosecuted for performing it in public. Apparently, the Maltese have evolved a way of performing this gesture in such a way that it could be mistaken for a mere rubbing of the arm, and not as a gesture at all. In this version, the left arm is held straight with the hand clenched in a fist, while the right hand gently rubs the inside of the left elbow (see Morris, Collett, Marsh, & O'Shaughnessy, 1979).

Such examples are of interest because they make it clear that participants are able to recognize, simply from the way in which the action is performed, whether it is intended as a communicative action or not. Apparently, for an action to be treated as a 'gesture' it must have features which make it stand out as such. Such features may be grafted on to other actions, turning practical actions or emotional displays into gestures. Such features may also be suppressed, turning movements from gestures into incidental mannerisms or passing comfort movements.

A few years ago, I conducted a study to explore the question of how ordinary perceivers perceive actions.[3] I wanted to find out whether or not people did consistently recognize only certain aspects of action as belonging to gesture. In this study twenty people were each shown, individually, a film of a man giving a speech to a fairly large group of people. The film had been made among the Enga, who live in the Western Highlands of Papua New Guinea. The people who watched the film were all Caucasian, English-speaking Australians and none of them were students of psychology or of any other behavioral science. The film was about four minutes in length and I showed it without sound. I asked each

---

[3]Partially reported in Kendon (1978).

person to tell me, in his own words, what movements he had seen the man make. Each subject was allowed to see the film as many times as he liked and, in discussing his observations, I was careful to use only the vocabulary that he himself proposed. The aim was to find out what movements the subjects picked out in their descriptions and to find out what different sorts of movements they identified.

In the course of the film, the man who was speaking engaged in elaborate movements of his arms and head, he walked forward, he manipulated the handle of an axe he was holding, he tugged at his jacket, he touched his face and nose. All subjects, without exception, first said that they saw movements which they said, were deliberate, conscious, and part of what the man was trying to say. All subjects also said that they saw some other movements which, they said, were just natural, ordinary, or movements of no significance. Thus, not only was a sharp distinction drawn by all twenty people between 'significant' movements and other movements. All twenty mentioned these 'significant' movements first and only later, and sometimes only after some probing, did they mention that they had seen some other movements.

When asked to indicate where these different movements were seen to occur, all subjects were able to do this without any hesitation, and there was very considerable agreement as to which movements were considered a "significant" part of what the man was trying to say and which were "natural" or "ordinary" or of no significance. Thus, thirty seven movement segments were commented on. In all cases, a majority of subjects assigned them to either the "gestural" or the "natural" category, and there were only four segments in respect to which more than five out of the twenty subjects differed from the majority in how these movements were to be assigned.

A consideration of the characteristics of the movement segments selected as part of the orator's deliberate expression as compared to those selected as "natural" or "ordinary" or of "no significance" allows us to arrive at some understanding of the features of deliberately expressive movement, as compared to other kinds of movement.

Deliberately expressive movement was movement that had a sharp boundary of onset and that was seen as an *excursion,* rather than as resulting in any sustained change of position. Thus, for limb movements, those movements in which the limb was lifted sharply away from the body and subsequently returned to the same position from which it started, where seen as deliberately expressive. In the head, rotations or up–down movements were seen as deliberately expressive if the movements were rapid or repeated, if they did not lead to the head being held in a new position, and if the movements were not done in coordination with eye movements. If they were, then, the observers would say that the man was engaged in changing where he was looking and this was considered different from movements that were part of what he was saying. Movements of the whole body would be regarded as part of the man's deliberate expression if it was seen as *returning* to the position from which it began, and not resulting in a sustained change in spatial location or bodily posture.

Movements that involved manipulations of an object, such as changing the position of an object, were never seen as part of the man's expression. They were usually referred to, if noticed at all, as "practical." Movements in which the man touched himself or his clothing were also never regarded as part of deliberate expression. These movements were, by almost all subjects, completely overlooked at the outset, and dismissed as "natural" or "nervous" or "of no importance" when they had their attention drawn to them.

These twenty observers were doing what all of us normally do in our dealings with others. Like all of us, they were attending to the behavior of another in a highly differentiated way, and what stood out for them, what was most salient and worth reporting, were those movements which shared certain features which identify them, for the observer, as deliberate and, in this case, intended as communicative. Just as a hearer perceives speech whether comprehended or not as 'figure', no matter what the 'ground' may be, and just as speech is always regarded as fully intentional and intentionally communicative, if movements are made so that they have certain dynamic characteristics they will be perceived as 'figure' against the 'ground' of other movement, and such movements will be regarded as fully intentional and intentionally communicative. We may recognize a number of features that a movement may have—features which, for the sake of a name, shall be referred to as the features of manifest deliberate expressiveness. Any movement a person produces may share these features to a lesser or greater degree. The more it does so, the more likely is the movement to be given privileged status in the attention of another and the more likely is it to be seen as part of the individual's effort to convey meaning. What are normally called 'gesture' are those movements that partake of these features of manifest deliberate expressiveness to the fullest extent. They are movements at the extreme end of the scale, so to speak. The word 'gesture' serves as a label for that domain of visible action that participants routinely separate out and treat as governed by an openly acknowledged communicative intent.

I say "openly acknowledged communicative intent" because, as the discussion of smoking or of the illegal German and Maltese gestures showed, it is possible to engage in movements deliberately for the interactional effects they may have, but to do so in such a way that they will *not* be treated as deliberately communicative. Indeed, this is done all the time, and our ability to do this, and our willingness to treat the behavior of others as if it may be differentiated in this way, is an important component of our abilities to engage in daily interaction adequately.[4]

---

[4]Compare also Goffman's (1963) distinction between "given" information and information "given off."

It is worth noting, in this connection, that whereas it is possible to produce a movement which is ambiguous in its deliberate expressiveness, it is not possible to do this with speech. One either says something or one does not. If something is said that can't quite be made out, it yet remains that *something* undoubtedly was said and the partner in an interaction has the right to challenge and to ask "What did you say?" Gestures are rarely challenged. Movements which might or might not be gestures can be made, but very rarely is one allowed to make noises that might or might not be speakings. It would be most interesting to know whether this also is true in sign language interactions. In a sign language interaction, can movements be produced which might or might not be signings, or is there a way in which certain movements are always assigned to intentional discourse, while other movements are permitted the sort of ambiguity that is permitted for the movements made by speakers? It seems possible that when, for sign language users, all expression must be in one modality, it is more difficult to engage in the kind of 'unofficial' communication that is routine for hearing interactors. Perhaps this is why it is often said that deaf signers are so 'open' to one another in their conversation and give expression to their feelings so readily.[5] They are so because they have no choice. They cannot, as speakers can, draw the kind of sharp distinction between definite, deliberate utterance, and something that can vary in its definite deliberateness that the availability of both speech and gesture permits.

Now although, as suggested, it is possible for people to modify their performance of gestural acts so that they do not look like gestures and although they can add features to nongestural actions to give them some of the character of gestures, this remains a capacity of performance that interactants make use of in their management of behavior or in interaction. It does not alter the proposal that participants effectively operate with one another in terms of a notion of bodily movements that are clearly part and parcel of the individual's openly acknowledged intention to convey meaning. It is to this that the term 'gesture' is applied. An approach has been proposed to an understanding of how that term may be defined which comes at it from the point of view of the participant in interaction. It was said that *gesture* is behavior that is treated as intentionally communicative and that such behavior has certain features which are immediately recognizable. It was also said that there are other aspects of behavior which have other characteristics which, as a result, are seen as "incidental" or "practical" and which are treated as quite distinct from "gesture" notwithstanding the role they can be

---

[5]Compare discussion in Washabaugh (1981). He there proposes a distinction between "presence manipulating" and "meaning-exchanging" communication processes. He suggests: ". . . the multichanneled visual communications, such as those used by many deaf persons, are of a sort which tips the balance more toward presence-manipulating processes and away from meaning-exchanging processes" (p. 248). Here we suggest that this is in part because, in the medium of "gesture" it is possible to blur the boundary between intendedly communicative action and unintendedly communicative action.

shown to play, and are often deliberately employed to play, in the organization of interaction.

It would appear, then, that participants perceive each other's behavior in terms of a number of different systems of action—the deliberately communicative or gestural, the postural, the practical, the incidental and, perhaps, although this was not explored specifically, the emotional. There is also reason to suppose that these different streams of action are produced under the guidance of different systems of control. Actions that are treated as 'gestural', it appears, are intimately associated, in their production, with the actions of spoken utterance while actions that are treated as belonging to other functional systems appear to be differently produced.[6] It is here, indeed, that neurological investigation could provide much useful information. A number of studies of aphasia have appeared in recent years that have explored the relationship between impairment of spoken language abilities and impairment of certain aspects of gesture—in particular, the ability to produce and to recognize pantomimes.[7] The evidence from these studies seems to suggest a rather close association between such gestural abilities and abilities with spoken language. What these studies have much less frequently addressed is the extent to which the overall interactive competence of brain-damaged patients is impaired. A few authors have pointed out that aphasics are often capable of dealing quite well with all the regulatory aspects of interaction—they can maintain an appropriate spacing and orientation, they recognize when it is their turn to make a conversational move. Their impairment lies in their ability to mobilize speech and gesture to produce coherently meaningful units of utterance. Duffy and Buck (1979) have shown, for instance, that left hemisphere damaged aphasics, while impaired in their abilities to produce and to recognize pantomimes in proportion to the degree of their impairment in verbal language, are not significantly different from normals or, indeed, from right hemisphere damaged patients, in their production of appropriate and coherent facial expressions of affect. Katz, LaPointe, and Markel (1978) have reported a study in which they have shown that aphasics show little impairment in those aspects of behavior that communicate emotional states, attitudes, relative status in the interaction, and regulation of turn-taking. Foldi, Cicone, and Gardner (1982) have reached a somewhat similar conclusion. All of this supports the view that gesture is indeed to be distinguished from emotional expression, and from those aspects of behavior that serve in the structuring and regulation of face-to-face interaction. A possibility worth further exploration, then, is that as

---

[6]See Meyer (1976) for discussion of the different neurological foundations for emotional expression and voluntary action. Kimura's (1976) studies suggest the intimacy of the relationship between the control of speech and the control of gesture.

[7]See, for example, Goodglass and Kaplan (1963), Duffy, Duffy and Pearson (1975), Pickett (1974), Duffy and Duffy (1981), Gainotti and Lemmo (1976). Peterson and Kirshner (1981) is a recent review.

*percipients,* we differentiate the behavior of others into a number of different action systems and attend to them differentially, accordingly; as *actors* we organize and produce behavior also in terms of a number of different systems; and that systems of action as produced, and systems of action as perceived, are mutually coordinate.

## TYPES OF GESTURE

If the notion of **gesture** is to embrace all kinds of instances where an individual engages in movement whose communicative intent is paramount, manifest, and openly acknowledged, it remains exceedingly broad. Most who have written on the subject in recent years have offered classifications, suggesting various types of gesture. There is much variation in the terms employed, as one might expect. However, a review of these classifications suggests fundamental agreement. All writers recognize that gesture may function as utterance autonomously, independently of speech, and most have proposed a special class of gesture to cover this. There is also recognition that gesture that occurs in conjunction with speech may relate to what is being said in a variety of ways. Thus, most draw a distinction between speech-associated gesturing that somehow provides a direct representation of some aspect of the content of what is being said, and gesturing that appears to have a more abstract sort of relationship. Efron (1941/1972), for example, distinguishes as "physiographic" those speech-related gestures that present a sort of picture of some aspect of the content and he terms "ideographic" those speech-related gestures which, he says, are "logical" in their meaning and which portray not so much the content of the talk as the course of the ideational process itself. More recently Freedman (1972) distinguishes "representational gestures" from nonrepresentational or "speech primacy gestures"; Wiener, Devoe, Rubinow, and Geller (1972) distinguishes "pantomimic" gestures from "semantic modifying and relational gestures," and McNeill and Levy (1982) distinguish "iconic" gestures, "metaphoric" gestures and gestures which seem to be related only to the rhythmic structure of the speech, which he has termed "beats." Gestures of this sort have also been recognized by Efron (1941/1972) and by Ekman (1977) under the term of "batons."

For the purposes of this paper the following distinctions are made. All gesturing that occurs in association with speech and which seems to be bound up with it as part of the total utterance is referred to as *gesticulation.* The particular kinds of relationship between gesticulation and the speech it is associated with are discussed on their merits, and no classification of this is attempted in advance. Gestures which are standardized in form and which function as complete utterances in themselves, independently of speech, are referred to as *autonomous gestures* (this includes those forms that are quite often referred to today as *emblems*). It must also be recognized that under certain circumstances gesturing can come to be organized into what is referred to as a *gesture system* and, in circumstances where complete generality of communicative function is required, we observe the emergence of *sign languages*.[8]

One further distinction. It is to be noted that the main concern of those who have dealt with gesture has been with what might be called its discourse or propositional functions. However, it should be recognized that there are many kinds of gesture that function in the management of interaction. For example, there are gestures of greeting, of request, command, assent, and refusal. Kaulfers (1931) has proposed that gestures functioning in this way should be treated separately. There are some grounds for thinking that such gestures may differ in their developmental history from gestures of discourse. They may emerge earlier and they may be related to somewhat different functional capacities from those that serve to represent the contents of discourse. Gestures of this sort shall not be further explored here. However, attention should be drawn to this distinction and one should attempt to examine any neurological evidence to support it. For example, do left hemisphere damaged aphasic patients, showing impairment in their pantomimic abilities, also show impairment in their abilities to deal with gestures of interactional management, or can they function as well with these gestures as they can with the posturings, positionings, and other features of behavior in a social encounter which serve in its regulation as an interactional event, regardless of the actual contents of the utterances that are exchanged?

It is worth noting, incidentally, that in conversational contexts, at least, gestures of interactional management are done mainly with the head and face, rarely with the hands. Thus, gestures of assent and refusal and those gestures by which a listener lets the speaker know how what he is saying is being received are done mostly with the head. In the speaker, the head may be used in gestures of assent and negation which may accompany speech. It may also be used in pointing. Otherwise, its gesticulatory role appears to be largely confined to discourse segmentation functions. The face may also play a role in discourse segmentation, but it also serves in the representation of content, although it is

---

[8]The phenomena of sign languages are beyond the boundaries of gesture although no sharp distinction can be drawn. Once gesture becomes completely autonomous as an instrument of communication, because it must now depend upon itself for its own discourse contexts, it undergoes processes of change which lead it to becoming organized along language-like lines. Autonomous gestures, for example, are equivalent in function to complete utterances and are not to be equated with "signs" in a sign language even though, in some cases, a sign language may have taken over forms that are used in the non-sign language using community as autonomous gestures. Washabaugh (personal communication) reports this for the sign language used by the deaf of Providence Island. What is notable is that in such a case, when adopted into a sign language, autonomous gestures become "lexicalized" in their function and are no longer used as complete acts of utterance on their own. For recent work on sign language see Klima and Bellugi (1979), Wilbur (1979), Stokoe (1980), Lane and Grosjean (1980). For accounts of Providence Island sign language see Washabaugh (1980a, 1980b) and Washabaugh, Woodward, and DeSantis (1978).

restricted largely to the representation of content of particular sorts, mainly content that has to do with feelings and with social role.[9] In a preliminary study in which the gesturing of people telling the story of Little Red Riding Hood was examined, it appears that when the story teller takes the role of the Grandmother, of Little Red Riding Hood, or of the Wolf, and utters their words in their voices, the face is used in consistently different ways to portray the different characters, but hand gestures are not used. Events that are narrated, on the other hand, are often accompanied by hand gestures. These are used to depict actions and also to portray the spatial structuring of situations. It can be expected that head and face gesturing have somewhat different functions from forelimb gesturing—although much more work is needed before this can be affirmed with much confidence.

## GESTICULATION

Gesture, at least of the propositional or discourse sort, is widely regarded as being somehow closely related to spoken utterance, although the nature of this relationship has been interpreted in a number of different ways. The view developed here supposes that gesture, like speech, serves as a vehicle for the representation of meaning. Gesture comes to be closely associated with speech because it is being used for the same purposes. It does seem that one should begin by thinking of the individual who proposes to produce an utterance as wanting to make some meaning available for others. Accordingly, a unit of action is organized that will do this. In organizing such a unit of action the individual will make use of whatever vehicles for meaning representation there are available. These include spoken language, but also included is the possibility of representing meaning through visible action, which is here called gesture. The individual may have available to him a variety of conventionalized forms, already highly coded with established shared meanings, or he may not, in which case he may have to resort to the production of improvised forms of action. On this view, it will be seen that gesture is viewed as a *separate* vehicle for the representation of meaning, quite independent of speech, but that it comes to be closely associated with speech because it is employed, along with speech, in the service of the same intentions. Gesture and speech are, thus, partners in the same enterprise, separately dependent upon a single set of intentions. Their close association does not come about because one is somehow a byproduct of the other. It arises because they are being employed simultaneously in the service of the same overall aim.

---

[9]Head and face gesturing has received very little systematic attention. Birdwhistell (1970) reports on some different kinds of headnods and their functions. Work in the experimental tradition on headnods is reviewed in Rosenfeld (1978). For facial gestures see discussion in Ekman (1979). Sherzer (1973) and Smith et al. (1974) provide analyses of lip pointing and tongue showing, respectively.

In developing this view, recent studies of gesticulation, recent studies of the development of gesture in children, and some of the recent neurological work are examined. Then, some observations on how participants in conversational interaction make use of gesture are discussed.

If one observes manual gesticulation in a speaker, it is possible to show how such movements are organized as *excursions,* in which the gesticulating limb moves away from a rest position, engages in one or more of a series of movement patterns, and is then *returned* to its rest position. Ordinary observers identify the movement patterns that are performed during such excursions as "gestures." They see the movement that precedes and succeeds them as serving merely to move the limb into a space in which the gesture is to be performed. A *Gesture Phrase* may be distinguished, thus, as a *nucleus* of movement having some definite form and enhanced dynamic qualities, which is prececed by a preparatory movement and succeeded by a movement which either moves the limb back to its rest position or repositions it for the beginning of a new Gesture Phrase.

If the flow of gesticulatory activity is thus analyzed into its component Phrases and these phrases are plotted out on a time-based chart against a time-based transcript of the concurrent speech it is found that there is a close fit between the phrasal organization of gesticulation and the phrasal organization of the speech. For example, if the flow of speech is segmented into Tone Units (which are phonologically defined syllabic groupings united by a single intonation tune), it is usually found that there is a Gesture Phrase to correspond to each Tone Unit.

A Tone Unit, as mentioned, is a phonologically defined unit of speech production. However, it matches quite closely units of speech that may be defined in terms of units of content or "idea units." The association between Gesture Phrases and Tone Units arises because Gesture Phrases, like Tone Units, mark successive units of meaning. Gesture Phrases are not, thus, by-products of the speech production process. They are directly produced, as are Tone Units, from the same underlying unit of meaning. There are several observations that can be adduced to support this. Thus, it is found that Gesture Phrases are often begun in advance of the Tone Unit to which they are related and they are often completed before the Tone Unit's completion. The "stroke" of the Gesture Phrase never follows the nucleus of the Tone Unit. Thus, Gesture Phrases must be organized at the same time as Tone Units, if not a little in advance of them. Further, when there is a disruption in the flow of speech *within* a Tone Unit, this typically occurs before the production of the nucleus, that is, before the production of the high-information word. Such disruptions are often attributed to some failure in the process of word retrieval. If a Gesture Phrase is in progress at the moment of such a disruption one finds that the Gesture Phrase is not interfered with, it continues to completion with perfect coherence. In such cases, it is possible to see how the 'idea' is fully available and is serving to govern the production of gesture, although there has been an interruption in speech production. Sometimes, both speech and gesture are interrupted, of course, and one may observe an individual producing a succession of incomplete gesture phrases at the same time as he produces a succession of incomplete phrases of speech. In these cases, however, disruption is at a deeper level, for here the ideas to be expressed have not yet been organized.

So far, I have been quoting from my own investigations (Kendon, 1972, 1975, 1980). Recently McNeill (1979) and McNeill and Levy (1982) have published studies of gesticulation which are closely in accord with these observations. However, McNeill's work is much more extensive and he has approached his analysis from a slightly different point of view. In one analysis, he examined what he called gestures (defined in a way that is quite similar to my notion of the Gesture Phrase) in terms of the relationship they exhibited with the conceptual structure of the concurrent speech. He found a close fit between the occurrence of a gesture and the occurrence of a speech unit expressing whole concepts or relationships between concepts. In further analyses, McNeill (1979) reports that the "peak" of the gesture (that is to say, the most accented part of the movement which I call the "stroke") coincides with what was identified as the conceptual focal point of the speech unit. McNeill has suggested that each new unit of gesture, at least if it is of the sort that can be considered reprsentational of content, appears with each new unit of meaning. Each such gesture manifests, he suggests, a representation of each new unit of meaning the utterer wishes to present.

In conclusion, these studies of how gesticulation is related to the speech it accompanies indicate that it is organized separately, but brought into coordination with speech because it is being employed in the service of the same overall aim. The detailed rhythmic coordination of gesticulation with speech arises at the level of the organization of the execution of motor acts. The forms that gestures assume are organized directly from original conceptual representations in parallel with linguistic forms, but independently of them.

Studies of the development of gesture in children should now be considered. From what has been done so far it appears that the child's capacity to make use of gesture expands in close association with growth in his capacity for spoken language. However, the way in which children use gesture appears to be different from the way it is used by adults. It seems that, in adults, gesture is used in relation to speech in a much more precise and specialized way. It appears that, with age, there is an increase in the degree to which the two modalities are coordinated.

Recent longitudinal studies of social interaction of the very young with their mothers show that the gestured actions which provide the first evidence of the ability of the child to engage in language-like communication, far from being replaced as the capacity for speech emerges, expand, and elaborate. Bates (1979) is quite explicit on this point. In summarizing her longitudinal study of twenty-four children between the ages of 9 and 14 months, she writes: "Our findings do not support a model of communicative development in which preverbal communication is replaced by language.'' Language and gesture, she says, ''are related via some common base involving both communication and reference'' (p. 112). As this common base develops the capacity for using both gesture and speech develops. A similar conclusion has been reached in other longitudinal studies. Wilkinson and Rembold (1981) write for instance, that ''as children become more aware of grammar and more facile at expressing it verbally, they also become more skilled in expressing grammar gesturally.'' (p. 184)[10]

Studies of gesture in older children have, for the most part, concentrated on the evidence this can provide about changes in the child's capacities for symbolization and they do not address the question of the spontaneous employment of gesture in relation to speech. There are four recent studies that do, however. Each has been conducted independently of the others and they all appear to suggest a very similar picture. See, for example, a study by Freedman (1977), of changes in gesturing with age as children provide definitions of common words; studies, by McNeill (in press) and by Wiener (1972) and his students, of gesturing in children of different ages as they retell the story of an animated cartoon they have watched; and a study, by Evans and Rubin (1979), of children between the ages of 5 and 10 years as they explained to an adult the rules of a simple game they had just been taught. Evans and Rubin looked at the nature of the gestures the children employed, and the role these gestures played in making the explanations intelligible.

Taken together, these four studies are consistent with one another in a number of respects. All agree in noting an increase in gesticulation with age. All of them indicate, however, that there are important changes in the kinds of gesticulation that occur and in the way these gesticulations are related to speech. There appears to be a shift away from elaborate enactments or pantomimes, which serve instead of speech, towards a use of gesture that is more selective and which is much more closely coordinated with what is being said in words. Thus, Freedman described how the 4-year-old, as he attempts to offer a definition of a word such as ''hammer,'' may first pantomime the use of the hammer before attempting a verbal definition. A 10-year-old gestures elaborately while he is talking as if, as Freedman puts it, he ''surrounds himself with a visual, perceptual and imagistic aspect of his message.'' The 14-year-old, on the other hand, uses gesture selectively, usually only in relation to specific words, with which the gesture is highly coordinated. Likewise, McNeill describes how children under the age of 8 enact whole scenes and that they do not relate their words and gestures. In adults, in contrast, ''iconic'' gestures tend to be precisely coordinated with spoken units of meaning. Furthermore, these gestures become more symbolic in the adult, serving as signs of actions or events. There is no attempt, as there is in the child, to engage in total reenactments.

---

[10]See also Lock (1978, 1980), Clark (1978), Bullowa (1979) and, for example, Bruner (1978).

These studies suggest, thus, that the employment of gesture for the representation of meaning increases in its elaborateness as the child gets older, but that at first it is used separately from speech. Later, as the child's command of speech develops, gesture comes to be used in conjunction with it. It is as if there is an increasing convergence and coordination between the two originally separate forms of expression.

Analyses of how gesticulation is organized in relation to speech and analyses of changes in how gesture is used by children both are compatible with the view that gesture and speech must be considered separate representational modes which may nevertheless be coordinated and closely associated in utterance because they may be employed together in the service of the same enterprise. Recent neurological studies can also be cited to support this view. As mentioned earlier, there are a series of reports available which show that in left hemisphere damaged patients there is a good correlation between degree of impairment in speech usage and comprehension and degree of impairment in ability to both produce and comprehend pantomimic gestures. Furthermore, as recent studies by Cicone et al. (1979), and Delis et al. (1979) have shown, gesticulation is also altered in cases of aphasia in ways that are quite parallel to the alterations in speech. However, there are also reports of left hemisphere damaged patients in which, although there is impairment in aural aspects of language, reading ability, and pantomimic ability are not impaired. It is in these patients, apparently, that it may be possible to show that training in use of some form of gesture language such as American Sign Language may be beneficial (e.g., Skelly, 1979, and Peterson & Kirshner, 1981). These reports suggest that visual symbolic abilities are neurologically separable from aural symbolic abilities. It is possible to impair one, but not the other. However, because so often both are impaired to the same degree, this indicates that the two kinds of abilities are separately subsumed under a more general function.

## FUNCTIONS OF GESTURE

What gesture may be used for should now be considered. If, as suggested, gesture is employed for the same purposes for which speech is employed, this is meant in a very broad sense. By this is meant that gesture and speech are both employed in the task of the production of patterns of action that may serve for others as representations of meaning. It does not mean that they serve this task in the same way. When speech cannot be used, circumstances may make it possible for it to come about that gesture can be organized to do all of the things that speech can do. Where speech is available, then we find that gesture and speech are employed differentially, in complementary roles, speech serving one set of communicative functions, gesture another.

Gesture and speech are very different from one another. In particular, because gesture employs space as well as time in the creation of expressive forms, where speech can only use time, the way in which information may be preserved in the two media is very different. Furthermore, it seems likely that important differences may arise from the fact that gesture is a visual medium, where speech uses sound. This may mean that the impact of gesture on a recipient may sometimes be very different from the impact of speech.

Given these different properties, we may expect that, where both modes of expression are available, they will be employed to service different components of the overall aim of the utterance. A specific example, which comes from a collection of instances of gestural usage that I have been maintaining for some time now, for the purposes of developing a more systematic understanding of how speakers employ gesture, will serve as illustration.

As many are no doubt aware, the *New York Times,* on Sundays, is very large and heavy. This always surprises an Englishman, when he sees it for the first time, for Sunday newspapers in Britain are very much thinner. An Englishman, long resident in the United States one Sunday moriming at a railroad station fell into conversation with a compatriot who had only arrived the week before. In the course of exploring his reaction to things American the resident Englishman said: "Have you seen the *New York Times?*" Precisely in association with "seen the" the speaker first placed his two hands forward, palms facing one another, he then placed them one above the other, palms facing downwards, thereby depicting a thick oblong object. The newly arrived Englishman laughed in response and immediately commented on the enormous size of the paper.

There are two things to note about this example. First of all, the sentence "Have you seen the *New York Times?* is fully formed grammatically and it is semantically perfectly acceptable. Yet we could not understand the way it was responded to here unless we had access to the gesture associated with it. Thus, to understand the meaning of the utterance in this situation, speech and gesture must be considered together. Furthermore, it will be noted that the gesture was performed exactly over the words "seen the." It must be seen that the gesture was thus an integral part of the entire utterance plan from the very first. The utterance, in its construction, thus, had both verbal and gestural components.

The gestural component, it will be seen, was the component by which the size and shape of the *New York Times* was referenced. Obviously, this could have been done verbally—the speaker could have said, "Have you seen how big the *New York Times is.*" Here, however, the reference was made to the size of the newspaper by gesture. By employing gesture for this purpose the speaker was able to refer to just that aspect of the Sunday *New York Times* which always surprises an Englishman. This surprising feature is a visual feature, and by using the same modality of sense perception that his recipient used when he first encountered it, he thereby provides him with a depiction that will remind him quite directly of that first surprising moment. It would appear, thus, from this example, that not only was the utterance planned as an integrated unit with gestural and verbal components but that, further, there was a differentiation of function between these two components, a differentiation of function that must also have been part of the utterance plan.

There are many other ways in which gesture concurrent with otherwise coherent speech may be used. For example, it may be used to disambiguate possibly ambiguous words. Thus, in a context where the word "Minolta" could have meant either a still camera or a movie camera, as the speaker said, "You could do it with your Minolta," over the word "Minolta" he provided a gestural enactment of holding a camera and pressing the shutter, thereby making it clear that it was the still camera he had in mind. In another example, someone is discussing some photographs he had seen with another, who, on a different occasion, had seen the same display. The speaker said, "I liked the one of the window." As he said this, he moved his extended finger in an arc in front of him, and this served to establish that it was a photograph of a window in a curved structure that he was referring to. A father, home from work, talking with his wife in the living room about what the children had done that day, said: "They made a cake, didn't they?" As he said "cake" he tilted his head to his left, in the direction of a window overlooking the garden where, earlier in the day, the children had made a cake of mud. In all of these examples, as with the *New York Times* example, the meaning conveyed by the gesture could as easily have been conveyed in words. The speakers could have said, "You could do it with your Minolta one oh one"; "I like the one of the window in the curved building"; "They made a cake in the garden, didn't they?"

However, in each case a component of the meaning of the total utterance was assigned to gesture for representation. In the *New York Times* example it appears that reference to size and shape was assigned to gesture to evoke the listener's response to a visual surprise. In the Minolta example, employing gesture to disambiguate a word may have served to economize on the time available for the speaker's turn. Meaning components of utterances may get assigned to gesture for various reasons. Thus, it seems that the utterer is able to employ gesture and speech together, but in a differentiated way, each modality playing a role complementary to the other in the production of a well-designed utterance.

In other examples, it can be observed how a gestural element is used in alternation with speech. In these cases we may see how it does duty as if it were a spoken element. Slama-Cazacu (1976) drew attention to this and used the term "mixed syntax" to refer to it. Birdwhistell (1970), in his discussion of what he has called "kinesic markers," has also drawn attention to it and Sherzer (1973), in his analysis of the use of the pointed lip gesture among the Cuna Indians of

Panama has shown how this gesture would often be used to stand in for deictic words or for labels for objects or places being referred to. He argued that it should be given a place in the lexicon of the spoken language. Many instances of this can be drawn from my own collection, and in many cases it is possible to see how the substitution of a gestural element for a spoken element served well in the circumstances in which the utterance was being used. Thus, there are examples of people repeating part of what they have just said gesturally because a momentary increase in ambient noise made their speech inaudible or because, in another example, their recipient failed to understand them because he was unfamiliar with the accent with which they spoke. In other cases, one may observe gesture standing in for a spoken element where no established spoken element is available. Thus, a videotape of a student choreographer working with a small troupe of dancers shows how she frequently uses partial enactments of the movement patterns she wants her dancers to employ as if they were verbal labels. Later, the movement patterns in question acquire verbal labels and then she no longer uses enactments in this way.

In yet other cases, one may observe gesture being used as an alternate for speech within an otherwise spoken utterance where there is some question of the propriety of what is to be said. One of the properties of gesture seems to be that it can be treated as somehow less official, less a full-fledged way of saying something than can speaking. This was alluded to much earlier in discussing the definition of gesture and it may have something to do with the fact that gestures may be varied in their explicitness in a way that speech cannot. In one of my best examples of "mixed syntax," a host suggests to a guest, too early in the evening, that it is time for him to drive him home. He says to the guest, after offering him a second cup of coffee, but declining to pour one for himself, "I was up much too late last night, so maybe we oughta/GESTURE/"—for the gesture putting up his two index fingers and holding them parallel to one another, moving them together in an up-down movement in the direction of the door. In another example, a boy came to ask his father for something he was afraid his father would not let him have, and to refer to it he used a gesture instead of naming it.

These few examples must suffice to make the point that gesture, as it is used by speakers, is not more primitive than speech, it is not used only for emotional purposes, it is not a mere by-product of the speech production process, it is not a mere paralinguistic decoration we can easily do without, and it is not in any way 'redundant' or merely illustrative. On the contrary, gesture is employed by speakers as a complement to speech, serving in cooperation with it in the elaboration of a total utterance. Often it is used in this way with considerable sophistication, the utterer displaying a clear understanding of the relative merits of the communicational properties of the two media of expression he has at his disposal.

These anecdotes will suffice to make this point, but careful systematic exploration is badly needed here. Yet, surprisingly, almost nothing has been done.[11] There are doubtless many reasons for this. However, the following difficulties encountered should be mentioned. First, people, on the whole, are highly skilled in adapting the organization of their utterances to the nature of the communication situation. This means that a simple experimental approach to the study of the communicative value of spontaneous gestural usage by speakers is quite difficult to devise, for by altering the access speakers can have to gestures, one finds they adjust readily what they say—this is why observations on conversations on the telephone or conversations in the dark can prove nothing. Second, as the survey of anecdotes makes clear, the functions of gesture are extremely diverse. This subject cannot be approached with any simple hypotheses about what functions gesture has. At this stage, a natural history of gestural usage is what is needed, a natural history that would rely upon the careful analytic description of numerous recorded examples.

The view of gesture put forward in this chapter has a number of implications. First, it should lead to some dethronement of spoken language. That is to say, it should lead to a view in which spoken language forms are regarded as no 'deeper' than other forms by which meaning may be represented. As Teodorrson (1978) has suggested in a recent discussion, spoken language is but one kind of manifestation or to use his term "delological" form of the representational process. There is no doubt that spoken language has been elaborated into a communicative code of extraordinary flexibility and generality. However, this is an elaboration that has come about because spoken language has been chosen as the instrument for main use, so to speak. As the phenomena of primary sign languages make it clear, gesture can also be elaborated into a flexible and functionally general communicative code to a degree that is quite comparable to spoken language, if circumstances are appropriate. Among the circumstances required, it should be noted, is the existence of a communication community in which gesture, rather than speech, is the main modality, and it is further important that such a community be fairly large and that it persist through time. In the past, there has been much discussion about the limitations of sign languages. It is my belief that these are, in principle, no more limited than spoken languages. Hitherto communities of sign language users that are large enough and that have persisted for long enough have not been available for study. As the brief history

---

[11]Studies which bear on the question of how speakers use gesture communicatively include Cohen and Harrison (1973), Cohen (1977) and Graham and Heywood (1976). Studies of the significance of gesture for recipients include Graham and Argyle (1975), Walker and Nazmi (1979), Riseborough (1981), Sherzer (1973), Birdwhistell (1970) and Slama-Cazacu (1976). These studies are reviewed in Kendon (1983).

of American Sign Language makes clear, such languages can be elaborated, given enough time, and given a large enough community of users.[12]

Second, the view of gesture advocated here should have important implications for theories of mental representation. It is seen that since gestural expressions are fully integrated with spoken aspects, they must be planned for together at the outset. This means that, however ideas are stored in our heads, they must be stored in a way that allows them to be at least as readily encoded in gestural form as in verbal form. The issue of the mental representation of ideas has been the subject of some debate recently. There are those who maintain that ideas are represented in an abstract propositional format that is the same as the format used to encode verbal information (e.g., Pylyshyn 1973). On the other hand, there are those who believe that the representation of ideas is modality specific and that visual ideas are encoded in terms of structures that are spatial and that are analogous transforms of the things they represent (e.g. Shepard, 1978). In a review of these positions Anderson (1978) concluded that, at the present time, it will not be possible, using the techniques available in experimental psychology, to decide whether all ideas are encoded propositionally or whether they may be encoded "pictorially" as well. Either hypothesis, he argues, accounts equally well for current experimental findings.[13] Here it is suggested that the observation that gesture is deployed as an integral part of utterance shows that any theory of representation that gives primacy to a representational format modeled on spoken language structures will not do. A close examination of how gesture and speech are deployed in an utterance makes it clear that meanings are not transformed into gestural form by way of spoken language formats. They are transformed directly and independently. Thus such meanings, however they are stored, are stored in a way that is separate from the formats of spoken language, however abstractly these may be conceived.

In conclusion, let me point out that space has not permitted me to discuss all topics of importance. In particular, cultural differences have not been discussed (but see Kendon, 1984). It is widely supposed that there are large cultural differences, and this seems to be the case. Surprisingly, there is still only one study that has documented this in any detail: Efron (1941/1972) made detailed comparisons between the gesticulatory styles of Southern Italians as compared to East European Jews. One of his most interesting findings was that whereas the Southern Italians made extensive use of 'pictorial' gestures—to the extent that, as Efron put it, it was almost as if the speakers illustrated their talk with slides—the Jewish speakers used gestures that were quite abstract in their relationship to the content of their speech. What this suggests is that, for both groups, gesticulation was used extensively in talk but that the cultures differ in the kinds of

---

[12]For the history of the development of American Sign Language and the conditions which have promoted its growth see Woodward (1978) and Lane (1980).

[13]I refer here to discussions by Pylyshyn (1973), Shepard (1978).

information it is relied upon to provide. Experimental studies by Graham and Argyle (1975) and by Walker and Nazmi (1979) have shown that Italians do rely upon gestures for information about the visual appearance of things to a greater extent than do British people. The survey of autonomous gestures in Europe recently published by Morris and his colleagues (1979) also shows clearly that, in Southern and Mediterranean Europe, there is a much richer repertoire of such gestures than in the North. Cultures differ, it would seem, not only in the extent to which they employ gestures but also in the sort of information they rely upon gestures to provide. Detailed comparative field studies on gestural usages are badly needed here, if this point is to be pursued. To the best of my knowledge, none have been undertaken.

There are many issues of great interest concerning the phenomena of autonomous or emblematic gesture that were not discussed. What can be said about the messages such autonomous gestures are employed to convey? An informal analysis of some of the available published lists from several different cultures suggests that the range of communicative functions for such gestures is relatively restricted (e.g., Kendon, 1981). Once again, however, no data exist that would allow us to say anything about the circumstances of their use. Of great interest would be case studies of the origins of such gestures and how such gestures become established. What are the processes of formalization that they undergo?

Comparisons between autonomous gestural forms between one culture and another also need to be undertaken. Although a number of lists exist—lists from France and Italy, from Columbia in South America, from Kenya, Arabic culture, Iran and India, no one has attempted a systematic comparison.[14] Such a comparison might be quite revealing, for it would throw light on the question of the "universality" of such gestures. Ekman (1977) has proposed, for example, that gestures that refer to bodily activities—eating, sleeping, and the like—are more likely to be similar to one another worldwide than are gestures that refer to other things. This is because gestures that refer to bodily activities are derived from enactments of those activities, and there is much less possibility for variation in how such enactments might be formalized than there is, for instance, for the enactments of manipulatory patterns associated with objects.

In this chapter the view was expressed that we are on the threshold of a new era in the study of gesture and that this study will have important consequences for our understanding of representational processes, of the nature of language, and for the ways in which different expressive modalities are exploited in the organization of communication in interaction. My purpose here has been to review some of the recent work that bears on these issues. The *philosophes* of 18th Century Paris were not mistaken in their appreciation of the significance of

---

[14]Gesture lists for France, Italy, Colombia, Kenya, North African Arabic, and Iran are given in Wylie (1977), Munari (1963), Efron (1941/1972), Saitz and Cervenka (1972), Creider (1977), Barakat (1973) and Sparhawk (1978), respectively.

gesture. Gesture, it seems, is of great interest precisely because it can be seen, on the one hand, how it is a manifestation of a spontaneous mode of representation of meaning but how, on the other, such manifestations can become standardized and transformed into arbitrary symbolic forms. The study of gesture allows us to look both ways, so to speak. It allows us to look inward toward the processes of mental representation, on the one hand, and outward to the social processes by which communicative codes become established on the other. Gesture stands at the point at which individual efforts at meaning representation fuse with the processes of codification. As such, it is invaluable for the study of the central communicative processes of the human species.

## REFERENCES

Anderson, J. R. (1978). Arguments concerning representations for mental imagery. *Psychological Review, 85,* 249–277.

Angenot, M. (1973). Les traités de l'éloquence du corps. *Semiotica, 8,* 60–82.

Barakat, R. A. (1969). Gesture systems. *Keystone Folklore Quarterly.* 14, 105–121.

Barakat, R. A. (1973). Arabic gestures. *Journal of Popular Culture, 6,* 749–792.

Bates, E. (1979). *The emergence of symbols.* New York: Academic Press.

Birdwhistell, R. L. (1970). *Kinesics and context.* Philadelphia: University of Pennsylvania Press.

Bruner, J. S. (1978). Learning how to do things with words (pp. 62–84). In J. S. Bruner & A. Garton (Eds.), *Human growth and development.* Oxford: Clarendon Press.

Bullowa, M. (Ed.). (1979). *Before speech.* Cambridge: Cambridge University Press.

Bulwer, J. (1944/1974). *Chirologia, or the natural language of the hand . . . Whereunto is added chrionomia or the art of manual rhetoric.* (J. Cleary, Ed.). Carbondale and Edwardsville: Southern Illinois University Press.

Cicone, M., Wapner, W., Foldi, N., Zurif, E., & Gardner, H. (1979). The relation between gesture and language in aphasic communication. *Brain and Language, 8,* 324–349.

Clark, R. A. (1978). The transition from action to gesture (pp. 231–257). In A. Lock (Ed.), *Action, gesture and symbol: The emergence of language.* London: Academic Press.

Cohen, A. A. (1977). The communication functions of hand illustrators. *Journal of Communication, 27,* 54–63.

Cohen, A. A., & Harrison, R. P. (1973). Intentionality in the use of hand illustrators in face-to-face communication situations. *Journal of Personality and Social Psychology, 28,* 276–270.

Condillac, E. B.de (1756/1971). *An essay on the origin of human knowledge: Being a supplement to Mr. Locke's essay on the human understanding.* Translated from the French by Thomas Nugent. Gainesville, Florida: Scholars Reprints and Facsimiles.

Creider, C. (1977). Towards a description of East African gestures. *Sign Language Studies, 14,* 1–20.

Delis, D., Foldi, N. S., Hamby, S., Gardner, H., & Zurif, E. (1979). A note on temporal relations between language and gestures. *Brain and Language, 8,* 350–354.

Diderot, D. (1751/1916). Letter on the deaf and dumb. Translated and edited by H. Jourdain in *Diderot's philosophical works.* Chicago: Open Court Publishing Company.

Duffy, R. J., & Buck, R. A. (1979). A study of the relationship between propositional (pantomime) and subpropositional (facial expression) extra verbal behaviors in aphasics. *Folia Phoniatrica, 31,* 129–136.

Duffy, R. J., & Duffy, J. R. (1981). Three studies of deficits in pantomimic expression and pantomimic recognition in aphasia. *Journal of Speech and Hearing Research, 46,* 70–84.

Duffy, R. J., Duffy, J. R., & Pearson, K. (1975). Pantomimic recognition in aphasics. *Journal of Speech and Hearing Research, 18,* 115–132.

Efron, D. (1941/1972). *Gesture and environment, etc.* New York: Kings Crown Press. Republished as *Gesture, race and culture.* The Hague, Mouton.

Ekman, P. (1977). Biological and cultural contributions to bodily and facial movement (pp. 39–84). In John Blacking (Ed.), *The anthropology of the body.* London: Academic Press.

Ekman, P. (1979). About brows (pp. 169–201). In M. Von Cramach, K. Foppa, W. Lepenier, & D. Ploog (Eds.), *Human ethology: Claims and limits of a new discipline.* Cambridge: Cambridge University Press.

Ekman, P., & Friesen, W. (1969). The repertoire of nonverbal behavior: Categories, origins, usage and coding. *Semiotica, 1,* 49–97.

Evans, M. A., & Rubin, K. H. (1979). Hand gestures as a communicative mode in school aged children. *Journal of Genetic Psychology, 135,* 189–196.

Foldi, N. S., Cicone, M., & Gardner, H. (1982). *Pragmatic aspects of communication in brain damaged patients.* Unpublished manuscript.

Freedman, N. (1972). The analysis of movement behavior during clinical interviews (pp. 152–172). In A. Siegman & B. Pope (Eds.), *Studies in dyadic communication.* Elmsford, NY: Pergamon Press.

Freedman, N. (1977). Hands, words and mind: On the structuralization of body movements during discourse and the capacity for verbal representation (pp. 109–132). In N. Freedman & S. Grand (Eds.), *Communicative structures and psychic structures: A psychoanalytic approach.* New York and London: Plenum Press.

Gainotti, G., & Lemmo, M. (1976). Comprehension of symbolic gestures in aphasia. *Brain and Language, 3,* 451–460.

Goffman, E. (1963). *Behavior in public places.* New York: The Free Press of Glencoe.

Goodglass, H., & Kaplan, E. (1963). Disturbance of gesture and pantomime in aphasia. *Brain, 86,* 703–702.

Graham, J. A., & Argyle, M. (1975). A cross cultural study of the communication of extra verbal meaning by gestures. *International Journal of Psychology, 10,* 56–67.

Graham, J. A., & Heywood, S. (1976). The effects of elimination of hand gestures and of verbal codability on speech performance. *European Journal of Social Psychology, 5,* 189–195.

Hewes, G. W. (1973). Primate communication and the gestural origins of language. *Current Anthropology, 14,* 5–24.

Hewes, G. W., (1976). The current status of general theory of language origin. *Annals of the New York Academy of Sciences 280,* 482–504.

Hill, J. (1978). Apes and language. *Annual Review of Anthropology, 7,* 89–112.

Hockett, C. F. (1978). In search of Jove's brow. *American Speech, 53,* 243–313.

Jancovic, M. A., Devoe, S., & Weiner, M., (1975). Age related changes in hand and arm movements as non-verbal communication: Some conceptualizations and an empirical exploration. *Child Development, 46,* 922–928.

Katz, R. C., Lapointe, L. L., & Markel, N. N. (1978). Coverbal behavior and aphasic speakers. In R. H. Brookshire (Ed.), *Conferences on clinical aphasiology: Collected proceedings 1972–1976.* Minneapolis: BRK Publishers.

Kaulfers, W. V. (1931). Curiosities of colloquial gesture. *Hispania, 14,* 249–264.

Kendon, A. (1972). Some relationships between body motion and speech: An analysis of an example (pp. 177–210). In A. Seigman, Ed. *Studies in dyadic communication.* New York: Pergammon Press.

Kendon, A. (1973). The role of visible behavior in the organization of face-to-face interaction. In M. von Cranach and I Vine (Ed.), *Movement and social communication in man and chimpanzee* London: Academic Press.

Kendon. A. (1975). Gesticulation, speech, and the gesture theory of language origins. *Sign language studies, 9*, 349–373.

Kendon, A. (1977). *Studies in the Behavior of Social Interaction* Lisse: Peter de Ridder.

Kendon, A. (1978). Differential perception and attentional frame: Two problems for investigation. *Semiotica, 24*, 305–315.

Kendon, A. (1980). Gesticulation and speech: Two aspects of the process of utterance (pp. 207–227). In M. R. Key (Ed.), *Nonverbal communication and language*. The Hague: Mouton.

Kendon, A. (1981). Geography of gesture. *Semiotica, 37*, 129–163.

Kendon, A. (1982). The study of gesture: Some observations on its history. *Recherches Semiotique/Semiotic Inquiry, 2*, 45–62.

Kendon, A. (1983). Gesture and speech: How they interact. In J. Wieman & R. Harrison (Eds.) *Nonverbal interaction*, Beverly Hills, CA: Sage Publications.

Kendon, A. (1984). Did gesture have the happiness to escape the curse at the confusion of Babel? In A. Wolfgang (Ed.), *Nonverbal behavior*, Lewiston, NY: C. J. Hogrefe.

Kimura, D. (1976). The neural basis of language *qua* gesture (pp. 145–156). In H. Whitaker & H. A. Whitaker (Eds.), *Studies in neurolinguistics* (Vol. 2). New York: Academic Press.

Klima, E., & Bellugi, U. (1979). *The signs of language*. Cambridge, MA: Harvard University Press.

Lane, H. (1980). A chronology of the oppression of sign language in France and the United States. In H. Lane & F. Grosjean (Eds.), *Recent perspectives on American sign language*. Hillsdale, NJ: Lawrence Erlbaum Associates.

Lane, H., & Grosjean, F. (Eds.). (1980). *Recent perspectives on American sign language*. Hillsdale, NJ: Lawrence Erlbaum Associates.

Lock, A. (ed). (1978). *Action Gesture and Symbol: The Emergence of Language*. London: Academic Press.

Lock, A, (1980). *The guided reinvention of language*. London: Academic Press.

McNeill, D. (1979). *The conceptual basis of language*. Hillsdale, NJ: Lawrence Erlbaum Associates.

McNeill, D. (in press). Iconic gestures of children and adults. In A. Kendon (Ed.), *Approaches to gesture*. Special issue of *Semiotica*.

McNeill, D., & Levy, E. (1982). Conceptual representations in language activity and gesture. In R. J. Jarvella & W. Klein (Eds.), *Speech, place and action: Studies in deixis and related topics*. Chichester: Wiley.

Meyer, R. E. (1976). Comparative neurology of vocalization and speech: Proof of a dichotomy. *Annals of the New York Academy of Sciences, 280*, 745–757.

Morris, D., Collett, P., Marsh, P., & O'Shaughnessy, M. (1979). *Gestures: Their origins and distribution*. London: Jonathan Cape, New York: Stein and Day.

Munari, B. (1963). *Supplemento al dizionario Italanio*. Milan: Muggiani.

Peterson, L. N., & Kirshner, H. S. (1981). Gestural impairment and gestural ability in aphasia: A review. *Brain and Language, 14*, 333–348.

Pickett, L. (1974). An assessment of gestural and pantomimic deficit in aphasic patients. *Acta Symbolica, 5*, 69–86.

Pylyshyn, Z. W. (1973). What the mind's eye tells the mind's brain: A critique of mental imagery. *Psychological Bulletin, 80*, 1–24.

Riseborough, M. G. (1981). Physiographic gestures as decoding facilitators: Three experiments exploring a neglected facet of communication. *Journal of Nonverbal Behavior, 5*, 172–183.

Rosenfeld, H. (1978) Conversational control functions of nonverbal behavior. In A. W. Seigman & S. Feldstein (Eds.), *Nonverbal behavior and communication*. Hillsdale, N. J.: Lawrence Erlbaum Associates.

Saitz, R. L., & Cervenka, E. J. (1972). *Handbook of gestures: Columbia and the United States.* The Hague: Mouton.

Shepard, R. N. (1978). The mental image. *American Psychologist, 33,* 125–137.

Sebeok, T. A. & Uniker-Sebeok, J. (Eds.). (1980). *Speaking of Apes.* New York and London: Plenum Press.

Sherzer, J. (1973). Verbal and nonverbal deixis: The pointed lip gesture among the San Blas Cuna. *Language and Society, 2,* 117–131.

Skelly, M. (1979). *Amerind gestural code based on universal American Indian hand talk.* New York: Elsevier.

Slama-Cazacu, T. (1976). Nonverbal components in message sequence: 'Mixed syntax' (pp. 217–227). In W. C. McCormack & S. A. Wurm (Eds.), *Language and man: Anthropological issues.* The Hague: Mouton.

Smith, W. J., Chase, J., & Lieblich, A. K. (1974). "Tongue showing: A facial display of humans and other primate species. *Semiotica, 11,* 201–246.

Sparhawk, C. M. (1978). Contrastive identificational features of Persian gesture. *Semiotica, 24,* 49–86.

Stam, J. H. (1976). *Inquiries into the origin of language: The fate of a question.* New York: Harper and Row.

Stokoe, W. C. (1980). Sign language and Sign languages. *Annual Review of Anthropology, 9,* 365–390.

Teodorrson, S. T. (1980). Autonomy and linguistic status of non-speech language forms. *Journal of Psycholinguistic Research, 9,* 121–145.

Tylor, E. B. (1878). *Researches into the early history of mankind.* London: John Murray.

Varney, N. R. (1978). Linguistic correlates of pantomime recognition in aphasic patients. *Journal of Neurology, Neurosurgery and Psychiatry, 41,* 546–568.

Walker, N., & Nazmi, M. K. (1979). Communicating shapes by words and gestures. *Australian Journal of Psychology, 31,* 137–147.

Washabaugh, W. (1980a). The organization and use of Providence Island sign language. *Sign Language Studies, 26,* 65–92.

Washabaugh, W. (1980b). The manu-facturing of a language. *Semiotica, 29,* 1–37.

Washabaugh, W. (1981). Sign language in its social context *Annual Review of Anthropology. 10,* 237–252.

Washabaugh, W., Woodward, J., & DeSantis, S., (1978). Providence Island sign language: A context dependent language. *Anthropological Linguistics, 20,* 95–109.

Wiener, M., Devoe, S., Rubinow, S., & Geller, J. (1972). Nonverbal behavior and nonverbal communication. *Psychological Review, 79,* 185–214.

Wilbur, R. (1979). *American sign language and sign systems.* Baltimore, MD: University Park Press.

Wilkinson, L. C., & Rembold, K. L. (1981). The form and function of children's gestures accompanying verbal directives (pp. 175–190). In P. S. Dale & D. Ingram (Eds.), *Child language: an international perspective.* Baltimore: University Park Press.

Woodward, J. (1978). Historical bases of American Sign Language. In P. Siple (Ed.), *Understanding language through sign language research.* New York: Academic Press.

Wundt, W. (1900/1973). *The language of gestures.* The Hague: Mouton. (Translation of *Völkerpsychologie: Eine Untersuchung der Entwicklungsgesetzevon Sprache, Mythus und Sitte.* Vol. I, 4th Ed., Part I, chap. 2. Stuttgart: Alfred Kröner Verlag, 1921).

Wylie, L. (1977). *Beaux gestes: A guide to French body talk.* Cambridge, MA: The Undergraduate Press.

# 2 Gestures: Nature and Function

Jean-Luc Nespoulous
André Roch Lecours

> *Originally, our hands were nothing but pincers used to hold stones; Man's genius has been to turn them into the daily more sophisticated servants of his thoughts as a homo faber and as a homo sapiens.—André Leroi-Gourhan, Gesture and Speech, 1964–1965*

If André Leroi-Gourhan's quotation clearly lays emphasis upon the sophistication of manual activity in man, it insists as well upon the fact that, with his hands, man acts as a homo faber as well as producing signs, even if his basic semiotic system as a homo signidex remains in most cases oral language . . . in most cases but not in all cases: Several papers in the present volume focus on nonverbal semiotic behaviors of both (a) aphasic patients trying—when possible—to make up for their verbal deficits through spontaneous and untaught gestural activity, and (b) deaf-mutes using Sign Language as their basic semiotic system. Leroi-Gourhan's quotation raises a most important question, by setting forth the twofold nature of gestural activity in man . . . a question which definitely becomes a crucial problem for whoever decides to enter upon the study and the analysis of human gestural behaviors.

Indeed, if the linguist can approach the study of an oral or written corpus without bothering about the nature or the status—which is always *symbolic*—of the elements he wants to analyze, the task of the semiotician analyzing gestures is much different and far more difficult. If any verbal sign corresponds nicely to the classical *stat aliquid pro aliquo*, things are rather different when one observes gestural activity in man . . . different in that gestures are not systematically used semiotically; they are not always abstract distanciated behaviors used to convey meaning or bear reference.

Good definitions of gestures in dictionaries mention—just like Leroi-Gourhan's quotation—this twofold nature of gesture. Here is one example: gestures—''movements of body parts, particularly of the arms, the hands or the head, conveying (or not) meaning.'' However, even when it is merely and unambiguously an *act*, gestural behavior is not to be considered as innate. In such a case, gestures have to be learned and integrated by the child—through successive attempts—in very much the same way as linguistic signs have to be learned and integrated. Both types of gestures—differing perhaps from some universal behaviors—belong to human culture and thus vary a lot from one social environment to another. Pathological observations, moreover, reveal that if verbal behaviors can be disturbed due—among other things—to brain damage (within the context of so-called *aphasia*), gestural behaviors—both acts and symbols—can be similarly disturbed due, once again, to brain lesions (within the context of so-called *apraxia*).

Despite such a parallelism in both acquisition and pathology, gestures appear to be more difficult to apprehend than linguistic signs, the semiotic status of which is obvious straight from the beginning. Things get even more complex when one realizes that an originally practical gestural behavior—an act, in other words—can be turned into a symbol through the setting up of a specific, and often unprecedented, convention:

> *Example:*   When I light up my cigarette, you will show the cashier your gun and ask him for his money.

This phenomenon, which will be called *semiogenesis,* after Tardy and others, leads to the consideration of the existence of three basic types of gestural behavior:

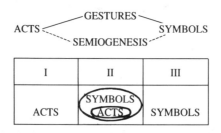

If such semiogenesis relies upon common agreement of human subjects involved in one specific semiotic intercourse, it may sometimes occur in only one of the interlocutors, the receiver, for instance, who can interpret *semiotically* an *act* accomplished by someone else.

*Example:*    Noticing the fact that someone lit up his pipe during verbal intercourse, someone else present in the environment may interpret this act as indicating the smoker's uneasy feeling about what is said or done around him.

This basic trinity is far from being sufficient to account for the large variety of gestural behaviors. It is here only to emphasize the fact that gestures do not all share the same degree of distanciation—from undistanciated acts to distanciated symbols.

Other dichotomies can of course be used to differentiate basic types of gestural behavior. A few of them are briefly mentioned before presenting (a) some problems raised by the analysis of gesture, on the one hand; and (b) some more sophisticated typologies of gestures, on the other hand.

## BASIC DICHOTOMIES

Apart from the *act-symbol dichotomy,* three other dichotomies appear to be useful for whoever attempts to define different types of gestures.

### Opacity vs. Transparency

These terms are self-evident from a general semiotic perspective and need no explanation within the context of this volume.

It is, particularly, useless to linger over what can be called the myth of *transparency* of gestures, a myth which can be linked to that of *universality.* If some gestures do have more cross-cultural extension than most linguistic signs, it remains that cultural differences are far from negligible. If some gestures can indeed be thought to have been somewhat transparent at some stage of their social history, their diachronic evolution turned them into more and more opaque segments (we are referring here to so-called symbolic gestures and not, of course, to acts).

Within the context of American Sign Language, Klima & Bellugi (1974) emphasize the fact that, despite their marked iconic origin, "few signs are so clearly transparent in their iconicity that a nonsigner can guess their meaning without some additional cues." A topic such as arbitrariness—as opposed to iconicity—in American Sign Language particularly, has also been extensively dealt with by authors such as Frishberg (1975) and Markowicz, from Gallaudet College in Washington (1979).

Another important dichotomy might lead us to differentiate *gestures as elements of an autonomous semiotic system* (as in the case of American Sign Language) on the one hand, and *gestures as partial elements of multisemiotic activity,* often primarily based on oral language, on the other. This dichotomy will be evoked later on and Yvan Lebrun and Dominique Labourel (this volume) provide us with observations on these two types of gestural behavior.

A third dichotomy has to do with *intentionality* of gestural activity. Like many dichotomies, this one is not particularly easy to handle. In a standard presentation, we should oppose:

1. clearcut *centrifugal* behaviors, clearly directed towards an interlocutor, and

2. other behaviors – *centripetal,* this time, insofar as they are not aimed specifically at anyone, which, of course, does not prevent anyone from interpreting them when observing them. In other words, in the latter case, even though such gestures were not originally devised *intentionally* to convey any meaning to someone else, they can be interpreted by any receiver who perceives them. Yet, centrifugal and centripetal behaviors as defined by means of the concept of intentionality (if such a definition can ever be set forth rigorously) must not be confused with *physically* centrifugal and centripetal activities, even though correlations between the two are highly likely.

Joaquin Sousa-Poza and Robert Rohrberg (1977) analyzed so-called body-bound movements and nonbody-bound movements in a semistructured interview, involving two communicative tasks—the one being "person-oriented," the other "non-person-oriented." Both tasks were *intentionally centrifugal* in the respect that, in both cases, the subjects had to speak to someone else. They found that the more person-oriented the communicative task was,[1] the more frequent body-focused movements were (body-bound movements overlap with Ekman & Friesen's *self-adaptators,* 1969), a result which the authors interpreted as a reflection of the degree of uncertainty of the speaker, revealing at the same time the difficulties of underlying speech-programming activities (much in the same way as hesitation pauses may reveal underlying ongoing cognitive activity). Frequency of such body-bound movements was much lower when the subjects were involved in more descriptive and less-committing communicative tasks ("Would you describe your hometown to me?").

Among other things, Sousa-Poza's study emphasizes the fact that, when involved in centrifugal activity (a verbal communicative task, for instance), the speaker may at the same time produce other types of behaviors which, perhaps, are not intentionally centrifugal even though the interlocutor will perceive them and, no doubt, interpret them in many cases. However, the problem remains— when attempting to analyze the continuum of multileveled semiotic behavior— of differentiating rigorously, if possible, those elements that are clearly intentional and directed towards the interlocutor from those elements that are unintentional. Again, the receiver perceives both types of elements and will often be led to interpret them all. This important, although difficult, point is reconsidered later.

---

[1] "What were your experiences during the worst time you ever remember having in your life?"

Other dichotomies which have been used by different authors interested in gestural behavior could be mentioned but we will only focus on two main points which seem important for any semiotician involved in the study of gesture:

— the first point has to do with methodological problems raised by the analysis of gestural activity.
— the second point, as already mentioned, will bear on several attempts which have been made in the literature to classify gestures into different behavioral categories.

## THE ANALYSIS OF GESTURAL BEHAVIOR

Semiotic analyses of gestures are many. They vary according to:

(a) The aims the semioticians want to achieve through such an analysis.
(b) The level or levels of gestural behaviors such semioticans consider to be relevant in relation to these aims.

In what follow, Louis Hjelmslev's basic model is used to present different avenues of investigations on gestures. When studying language, Hjelmslev, advocating the existence of some type of isomorphism between the *expression level* and the *content level,* splits up both these levels into *formal* and *substantial* sub-levels. The level of linguistic form—akin to Saussure's *Langue*—has to do with abstract linguistic elements to which can be attributed stable, objective, social value; whereas the level of linguistic substance has to do with concrete and thus variable manifestations of specific subjective features.

Four levels can thus be distinguished:

| E | | D |
|---|---|---|
| N | Substance of Content | E |
| C | | C |
| O | Form of Content ⎤ | O |
| D |            ⎥ De Saussure's ''Langue'' | D |
| I | Form of Expression ⎦ | I |
| N | | N |
| G | Substance of Expression | G |

On the basis of Hjelmslev's paradigm, different approaches to gestural analysis can be devised:

## Analysis of the Substance of Gestural Expression

Within this analysis, gestures are described as movements or sets of movements, without their semiotic value or function being taken into account. Such an approach is thus very much akin to that used by phoneticians when they analyze speech signals. Although basically concerned with physical and motor aspects of gestural activity, this type of approach is of paramount interest as a first stage of the analytical process. Phonology cannot develop properly without a preliminary phonetical analysis; the reverse, of course, being equally true: what would phonetics be without any formal and general underlying model (provided by phonology)?

## Analysis of the Form of Gestural Expression

When going over the bridge existing between substance anf form, one crosses the Saussurian border existing between *La Parole*—or individual speech acts which do vary immensely from one speaker to another and even from one speaker at a given moment to the same speaker at another given moment—and *La Langue*—social system of stable values, shared by the members of a given linguistic community. Within this *formal* analysis—"formal" in Hjelmslev's and Saussure's terms (*"la langue est une forme et non une substance"* CLG.)—the aim which is assigned to the semiotician is not to describe in detail gestural substance but rather to focus upon those substantial elements which do have a function—a discriminating and oppositional function, that is—within the context of a given cultural community. In doing so, some substantial features can be discarded as nonpertinent and only those features which do belong to the structure of the social system under study are retained.

As previously mentioned, such a study of the form of gestural expression requires to a certain extent a preliminary analysis of gestural substance. And it leads to the inventory of abstract, invariant formal gestural segments, segments or target-segments which are shared by anyone belonging to the same cultural community, whatever substantial differences and variations may be observed across subjects and over time.

## Analysis of the Form of Gestural Content

Such an analysis obviously cannot be dissociated from the previous one insofar as both the formal signifier and the signified—in Saussure's terms—stand as both sides of a same sheet of paper, since it is impossible to tear up its recto without tearing up the verso at the same time. Thus, through both—and largely simultaneous—formal analyses, within the context of so-called *semiology of communication,* we can derive the inventory of gestural segments (with both their signifier and their signified) characteristic of a given cultural community. A study of this type was carried out by Birdwhistell within the context of kinesics.

## Analysis of the Substance of Gestural Content

At this level of analysis we enter the domain of the so-called *semiology of signification,* the aim of which is to apprehend—as much as possible—through the gestures produced, the subjectivity of the individual. And here again, in the same way as with the analysis of the substance of expression, we are confronted with important cross-individual differences and variations, hence the difficulty of rigorous analysis at this level. To sum up, the possible complementarity of all four abovementioned levels should be accentuated. Of paramount importance in the analytical process is to know (a) at which level one is situated when setting forth a specific observation and (b) when one changes one's level of observation.

A last comment: It is one thing to build up a gestural inventory of formal segments, it is another to account for the dynamic organization of gestural activity within the context of a particular gestural act. Obviously, any type of gestural analysis must account for both of these—static and dynamic—dimensions. Moreover, when gesture is used together with verbal behavior, the analysis must also account for the *interactions* existing between the different semiotic channels used by the subject and not treat them separately.

## GESTURAL TYPOLOGIES

Of course, classifications of gestures depend on the type or level of analysis which has been selected in the description of the corpus and various different typologies have been proposed by different authors. The purpose here is not to review them all but to concentrate on two—and only two—ways of approaching that classificatory problem:

1. A first tentative typology has to do with the degree of arbitrariness of the link existing between the gestural segment on the one hand, and the referent on the other. This first approach appears to be relevant, particularly because opacity and transparency vary largely from one gestural form to another.

This sort of typology is thus primarily based upon the intrinsic nature of gestures within the context of a given semiotic system.

2. The second tentative typology to be presented has to do with functional values of gestural segments within the context of actual semiotic acts. Such a typology is primarily based upon the extrinsic nature of gestures; it refers to semiotic uses rather than to intrinsic abstract characteristics of gestural segments.

Evidently both typologies are complementary. Both classifications were used in an attempt to account, for the nonverbal—gestural—activity of an aphasic patient (Nespoulous, 1979). We focus on *general properties* of such typologies since D. Labourel presents extensive work on gestural behavior *among aphasics* (see Ch. 15).

### Gestures and Arbitrarity

This first tentative typology leads to the consideration of the existence of three basic categories of gestures:

(a) arbitrary gestures;
(b) mimetic gestures;
(c) deictic gestures.

### Arbitrary Gestures

These are gestures which—at least within the context of *synchronic* observation—cannot be interpreted without being *learned,* on account of their *opacity.*

Such gestures are not that common in the cultural setting we live in but they do exist. They can be used and understood—once learned—without any complementary verbal information, a reason which led such authors as Cosnier (1977) and Dahan (1977), from Lyon (France), to call them *quasilinguistic* gestures since they can be used *instead of speech* on occasion even if, most of the time, they are produced together with verbal strings.

It appears that such gestures can be either *referential* or *modalizing:*

—referential when they do refer to actors, actions, objects, circumstances, etc., constituting the texture of the message the individual wants to convey.
—modalizing when they bear more specifically witness to the individual's opinion about what he is saying or doing (Nespoulous, 1980).

An example of referential gestural behavior is the case of the aphasic patient we have been observing (Nespoulous, 1979). When the patient wanted to tell us what his wife's occupation was (namely "bank clerk"), realizing that the required lexical item was not accessible to him, he attempted to produce a periphrase the main element of which (from an informative point of view) was clearly a gesture "when people have XXX, they go there" (XXX = conventional gesture for "money").

As examples of modalizing gestures in the behavior of the same patient, we can cite many instances of gestural activity through which he expresses—without any ambiguity—his satisfaction or, more often, his dissatisfaction concerning the nature of his speech production:

— shrugging his shoulders to denote: "I don't know"
— letting both arms fall against his legs (with a sigh) to denote: "I can't find the right word"

These gestures are frequent in the behavior of aphasic patients and they are certainly frequent in the behavior of normal subjects too. Contrary to what happens with referential gestures, modalizing gestures can be difficult sometimes to interpret outside the context in which they have been produced.

### Mimetic Gestures

These are as well gestures produced in the absence of the referent; but, in this second case, the relationship *gestural segment/referent* is no longer arbitrary but *transparent.*

Such gestures, characterized by their *iconicity,* can be created by the individual—if necessary—as semiotic intercourse goes on (with variable accuracy from one subject to another). They are not very frequent in everyday conversation among normal speakers but the patient we observed produced a lot of them whenever, in his attempts to substitute gestures for inaccessible lexical items, he did not find in his pre-existent gestural stock any conventional segment he could use.

Most of the time such newly coined gestures are of *great amplitude.* They very often require both hands and, sometimes, even the whole body. Such an amplitude seems to be necessary, and even essential on account of the newness of this type of behavior. Following Wundt (1973), it can be said that the more strictly codified, conventional—socially integrated, that is—a gesture is, the weaker its amplitude; on the contrary, gestural amplitude will increase with the newness of the segments coined by the individual.

An example is another sample taken from the above-mentioned interview with an aphasic patient. Trying to explain that, if the situation of the French economy is not very good, it is not very good either in the United States, he behaves as follows:

— "We . . . here" and, after putting his left forefinger on his right hand, he draws a fictive line—first ascending, then descending; from right to left—which ends when his left hand happens to be in perfect symmetry with his right hand. Then, he says: "They . . . over there."
— In order to be sure that we understood which country he was referring to, he produces another gesture sketching New York's skyscrapers.
—Finally he raises his arms towards the sky, then lets them fall against his hips, thus denoting the "hopelessness" of the economic situation there too.

Following Wundt, the existence of, at least, two subtypes of mimetic gestures can be considered:
—*strictly mimetic gestures,* on the one hand. In this first case, the main lines of an object or the main stages of an action are drawn in space with—at least—the forefinger.

As an example of this, our aphasic patient, in order to mention the fact that his doctor had advised him to go for a walk every day, attempted to simulate walking by repetitive movements of both arms (the patient was sitting on a chair).

In this first subgroup of mimetic gestures, there is obviously an *analogical relationship* between the gestural segment and its referent.

Again according to Wundt, *connotative gestures* are a second subtype of mimetic gestures. Here we find gestures representing in space one of the secondary features of the object: Wundt's basic example of the representation of a goat by its beard. Our patient's representation of New York by its skyscrapers seems to fall within this second subcategory. In such a case, there seems to be a *metonymical relationship* between the gestural segment and its referent.

### Deictic Gestures

By definition deictic gestures cannot be used without the object referred to being present in the situation in which semiotic behavior takes place. Contrary to what happens in both previous classes of gestures, there *would* not be any *distanciation* allowed in this case. Obviously, each gesture should be transparent within a given context.

|                    | ARBITRARY | MIMETIC | DEICTIC |
|--------------------|:---------:|:-------:|:-------:|
| DISTANCIATION  :   |    +      |    +    |    −    |
| TRANSPARENCY   :   |    −      |    +    |    +    |

Our patient used a few gestures of this type during his interview which, by the way, took place in an "asepticized" consulting room, in a hospital (the richer the environment a speaker is in, the more likely he is to use such deictic behaviors).

These behaviors seem to fall within three different subcategories:

*1. Specific Deictic Gestures.*    In this first case, the individual points at one particular object with the purpose of referring to *this particular* object. In this case, there is indeed no distanciation whatsoever between gesture and referent.

> *Example:*    our patient pointing at a pencil because he wants to use it to draw an object he cannot name.

Our impression is that gestures and/or glances pointing at the interlocutor fall as well within such a sub-category.

*2. Generic Deictic Gestures.*    In this second case, the individual points at an object to evoke the *whole* class of items the object belongs to (and not *this* particular object).

> Example:    our patient pointing at a newspaper on a table in the consulting room to answer our question: "What did you read before your accident?"

*3. Deictic Gestures Referring to the Function of the Object.*

> *Example:*    our patient pointing at an armchair to answer our question: "What do you do after lunch?"

Obviously, deictic gestures in all three subcategories do not have, strictly speaking, any intrinsic content. Only the situation within which they are produced can help us in interpreting them. They constitute—in the same way as verbal deictic items (demonstrative, for instance)—highly polyvalent elements, "shifters," in Jakobson's (1963) terms, which take their semiotic value both from the whole semiotic context and from the extrasemiotic situation.

## Gestures and Functions

Just like verbal strings, gestures can have different functions and if we use for gesture—to begin with—such a functional framework as the one proposed by Roman Jakobson for language, it may even be the case that *one gesture* can have *several functions* at the same time (on account of the fact that Jakobsonian functions are not all situated at the same level). If we accept the following rearrangement of Jakobson's functions of language:

| LEVEL | FUNCTION |
|---|---|
| Goal of discourse | —conative (centrifugal)<br>—non-conative (centripetal) |
| Establishing contact | —Phatic |
| Discourse itself | —Referential<br>—Expressive<br>—Aesthetic |
| Explicating of discourse | —Metalinguistic |

it is thus possible to say that the following gesture—used by one particular individual (a driver, for instance) to indicate to his fellow-traveller on his right that he wants him to give 25 cents to pay the toll on a motorway—is at the same time *conative, phatic* and *referential:*

— *conative* because, through gestural behavior, the driver wants his friend to give him 25 cents.
— *phatic* in this respect that, without any contact between the driver and his friend, the semiotic behavior would have been a failure.
— *referential* in that the gesture bears reference to one specific concept within the context of one specific cultural community.

Here, we come across one of the most common problems raised by typologies: the nonexclusiveness of categories. This problem was already encountered in the first basic classification we proposed and it is found here again when dealing with functional categories of gestures (in fact, in our first typological attempt, an iconic element or behavior at the same time could be deictic—or indiciary in Peirce's terms—and symbolic. E.g., the noise made by a plane is (a) iconic (metonymically representing the plane itself); (b) indiciary (indicating, for instance, the proximity of an airport) and (c) symbolic (of the economic power of a city, for example) . . .

Despite all these problems, a few functional typologies of gestural behavior can be found in the literature and I will end my "introductory remarks" by presenting one of them very briefly, namely that set forth by Jacques Cosnier, in Lyon (France). His classification is somewhat heterogeneous (some subclasses, in fact, seem to be based on the nature of gestures rather than on their function) but it has the advantage of being fairly extensive (it has proved to be quite handy in many works carried out under his supervision, like the one presented in the present volume by Dominique Labourel). Once again, when analyzing the typological framework of one particular author, it can be noted that the more homogeneous it is, the less extensive it is and vice versa.

### Quasilinguistic Gestures

The main characteristic of these gestures—as already mentioned—is that they can be used in the absence of any verbal behavior, even though they are often produced together with speech. Cosnier and Dahan found 200 such gestures in French and Italian subjects. In the French inventory, 40% of these gestures are used to express a feeling and 60% bear reference to actions or objects (such as "to drink"; "to eat" . . .)

### Coverbal Gestures

Coverbal gestures are gestures the function of which is (1) to illustrate ongoing verbal behavior (illustrative); or (2) to express personal emotions related to verbal behavior (expressive) or (3) to lay emphasis upon specific verbal elements within discourse (paraverbal).

*Illustrative Gestures.* Several subtypes of illustrative gestures can be evidenced:

— *deictic:* pointing at an object which is the referent of one of the lexical items to be found in the subject's speech.
— *spatiographic:* outlining the spatial configuration of the referent of one of the lexical items.
— *kinemimic:* outlining the action referred to by one of the lexical items.

— *pictomimic:* outlining some formal properties of the referent of one of the lexical items (big vs. small . . .).

*Expressive Gestures.*    Here Cosnier classifies mainly facial expressions of emotions (He indeed groups together both facial expressions and hand gestures within the context of the analysis of what he labels "mimogestualité.") As far as I can tell, the difference between this sub-type of coverbal gestures and expressive quasilinguistic gestures mentioned above might have something to do with the fact that the former cannot be interpreted without speech whereas the latter can.

*Paraverbal Gestures.*    Paraverbal gestures are head or hand movements accompanying speech intonation and stress.

## Gestures Governing Social Interaction

These behaviors constitute basic pragmatic elements of interaction strategies. They can be subdivided into:

1. *phatic,* involving gestural and/or visual activity (glances)
2. *regulatory,* such as nods, the aim of which is to indicate that one is carefully listening to what is being said.

Dahan convincingly demonstrated that the absence of regulatory gestures in the behavior of the listener could lead the speaker to interrupt his speech or to produce incoherent discourse.

## Metacommunicative Gestures

Cosnier here refers to gestures that indicate the speaker's opinion about what he is saying. Such gestures could certainly be called *modalizing* gestures and they can sometimes go as far as contradicting the meaning conveyed by the verbal strings (Nespoulous, 1980).

## Extracommunicative Gestures

These are gestural behaviors which, according to Cosnier, are deprived of any semiotic value.

1. body movements related to comfort, such as crossing one's legs, for instance.
2. *"autistic"* gestures: scratching, finger-tapping, nail-biting . . .
3. *manipulations:* smoking a cigarette, folding of paper . . .

Regarding these gestures, it should be emphasized that if they are not intentionally produced to convey any specific meaning, some specific meaning will sometimes be attributed to them by anyone who perceives them (cf. supra). Even though oral language remains undoubtedly man's basic semiotic system, semioticians, linguists, sociologists, anthropologists, neuropsychologists and others cannot avoid taking into consideration human gestural activity, for culture not only floods into man verbally but it pervades the entirety of his behavior. This is already obvious when one observes so-called "normal individuals" but it is all the more obvious when one considers such individuals as the ones Dominique Labourel and Yvan Lebrum refer to: aphasics (at least some of them) and deaf-mute signers.

*Car, à côté de la culture par mots, il y a la culture par geste.*

(Antonin Artaud)

## REFERENCES

Cosnier, J. (1977). Communication non-verbale et langage. *Psychologie Médicale, 9*(11), 2033–2049.

Dahan, G., & Cosnier, J. (1977). Sémiologie des quasi-linguistiques français. *Psychologie Médicale, 9*(11), 2053–2072.

Ekman, P., & Friesen, W. (1969). The repertoire of nonverbal behavior: Categories, origin, usage and coding. *Semiotica, 1*, 49–98.

Frishberg, N. (1975). Arbitrariness and iconicity: Historical change in American sign language. *Language, 51*, 696–619.

Jakobson, R. (1963). *Essais de linguistique générale.* Paris: Editions de Minuit.

Klima, E. S., & Bellugi, U. (1974). Language in another mode. In E. H. Lenneberg (Ed.), *Language and brain: Developmental aspects.* Neurosciences research program bulletin, *12*(4), 539–550.

Labourel, D. (1981). *Approche éthologique de la communication chez six aphasiques.* Thèse pour le Doctorat de 3ème Cycle, Université de Lyon II.

Markowicz, H. (1979). La langue des Signes: Réalité et fiction. *Langages, 56*, 7–12.

Nespoulous, J.-L. (1979). Geste et discours. Etude du comportement gestuel spontané d'un aphasique en situation de dialogue. In *Etudes de Linguistique Appliquée, 36*, 100–121.

Nespoulous, J.-L. (1980). De deux comportements verbaux de base: Référentiel et modalisateur. De leur dissociation dans le discours aphasique. *Cahiers de Psychologie, 23*, 195–210.

Sousa-Poza, J. F., & Rohrberg, R. (1977). Body movement in relation to type of information (person- and non-person oriented) and cognitive style (filed dependence). *Human Communication Research, 4*(1).

Wundt, W. (1973). *The language of gestures.* The Hague: Mouton.

# THE NEUROLOGICAL
# SUBSTRATUM OF GESTURES
# AND MOTOR ACTIVITY

# 3 Brain Organization Underlying Orientation and Gestures: Normal and Pathological Cases

Marcel Kinsbourne

From the point of view of neuropsychology there are no gestures. In other words, gestures are not a coherent category. By this I mean that there is no center for gestures in the brain, there is no form of brain damage which selectively abolishes the ability to gesture. Rather, different kinds of gestures are differentially affected in different circumstances, never primarily but always as part of a more general, underlying processing deficit. That is important because to my mind the brain is the touchstone of the biological reality of categories. In the case of language the brain tells us that category is real because there are parts of the brain which subserve language, and one can suffer a selective language loss. Gestures cannot be compared to language in that way. They comprise bits and pieces of different behaviors which we have chosen so to name. The same applies to semiotics. There is no brain center for semiotic behavior. There is no lesion which strips acts of meaning or of signaling value, leaving their representations preserved in the brain. So we are dealing with categories which are useful abstractions but do not delineate packages of the mind. Rather than define gesture, which for these reasons is a sterile thing to do, we shall discuss a variety of behaviors which people have called gestures.

First, I would like to present a classification of gestures. It will not be the same as A. R. Lecours' (this volume), but only because a different description better serves my present purpose. No one taxonomy is best. A particular taxonomy may be useful for the points one wishes to make. One may first distinguish between movements serving the homeostasis of the body (Yakovlev's ereismokinetic level), and movements pointed toward external space. And the latter are divided into the obvious sequential elements of orienting toward, locomoting to, and then instrumentally acting upon whatever is there (Kinsbourne,

1978a). Gestures are not inherently instrumental, although an instrumental act can be turned into a gesture secondarily. Movement toward is not a gesture, but orienting has some properties of gesture, turning of the head and eyes and pointing toward something. This, Donne called the "mystic language of eye and hand." Movements that serve homeostasis include scratching and rubbing, self-touching movements. When investigators videotape people in conversation, they distinguish between free-moving gestures and self-touching gestures. That distinction is useful, for they seem to serve different purposes or have different roles. Self-touching gestures, for instance, have been shown to be left lateralized, at least while emotional issues are being addressed (Fesio & Crescenzi, 1982; Ruggieri, Celli, & Crescenzi, 1982). Free-moving gestures have been shown to be right lateralized (Kimura, 1973), though perhaps also particularly in emotional circumstances, reciprocal with self-touching by the left hand (Fesio et al., 1982; Ruggieri et al., 1982).

Self-touching gestures may serve the purpose of moderating exessive activation in the brain (Kinsbourne, 1980). They are particularly notable when people are anxious, embarrassed, nonplussed. For example, the universally understood gesture of scratching one's head while one puzzles over a difficult question, I interpret as serving the function of holding in check the surge of arousal that occurs when one looks for a solution to a problem. When a person is in a brain state that involves a high level of nonspecific activation, when there is anxiety, frustration, uncertainty how to respond, he will tear at himself in one way or another, scratch, smooth his hair, straighten his tie. This type of gesture is totally different from what is discussed in A. Kendon's chapter (this volume). There is an analogy between these movements and displacement activities in the animal world, which are movement routines that animals undertake when their primary goals are unattainable. A cat sees a reward but cannot reach it because of an electrified floor which would give it a foot shock. So the cat suddenly starts grooming when grooming was presumably not on its mind. Or a bird, in similar circumstances, pecks at a grain which is not there. In states of high arousal which cannot be discharged by appropriate action, a repetitive movement routine is substituted which is familiar, highly practiced but adaptively irrelevant, at least for external purposes. This is a movement which does not instrumentally affect anything, or signal anything, but discharges activation in some part of the brain. Some electrophysiological studies of animals in displacement situations have indeed found certain indices of arousal in the brain to be high when the displacement activity begins and to subside as it continues.

This interpretation of movements which are self-touching or repetitive or both and not instrumentally adaptive is important in certain cases of pathology. When people do this it is not always possible to interpret the adaptive purpose of what they do unless one knows the state their brains are in. That is particularly the case in people who are psychotic or mentally retarded. There one sees a variety of bizarre behaviors which are bizarre because, they are movement sequences

which are not normally undertaken; or not normally undertaken under the particular prevailing circumstances. A retarded person might wave his hand across a
light, causing it to flicker, occasionally sending him into a minor seizure, a
momentary lapse of consciousness. Or he might launch into head banging, or
spinning and whirling around. Or a person may do something we all do, such as
uttering a sentence, but, unlike the rest of us, not do it to communicate with
anyone. An autistic individual might repeat what is said to him, or utter a jingle
he heard on television. If the listener assumes that this was meant to inform
someone of something, he would be puzzled about what the message was. The
echoing statement is not in principle different from the whirling or the flapping.
They are all devices, using different output mechanisms, to diminish excessive
arousal. These so-called stereotypic or manneristic gestures tend to occur when
something novel has happened. Given damaged and unstable homeostatic control
of activation level, even what is for the rest of us a very minor change might
constitute a flood of information hard to resolve for a damaged and limited mind,
causing a surge of central activation and precipitating the patient into a compensatory "displacement" routine. That is the extreme case; but we all, under
circumstances of tension, anxiety, and uncertainty exhibit twitching, finger
drumming or otherwise repetitive behavior. These gestures, although of course
they have signaling value in that other people observing them can infer what is
going on, do not have a signaling purpose primarily. We distinguish between
these gestures which are homeostatic in function and the following ones.

Gestures can be subdivided into those which have a primary purpose, are used
specifically to do something. are instrumental; those that are part of a more
extensive movement routine and partake of the purpose of that more extensive
routine; and those that are spin-offs, secondary to some other purpose. There are
systematic gestures, constituting a language. There are also sporadic gestures,
expressions, grimaces which have conventional meaning. There are also articulatory gestures such as noises, so-called "prosodic grunts," which are in the
same family: "ah ha! hm!" etc., and are widely crossculturally understood.
There is no worthwhile neuropsychology of these articulatory gestures and they
will not be discussed here.

Then there is a gesture integrated with other forms of conveying meaning. In
his chapter. A. Kendon gives elegant examples of the integration of verbal and
gestural communication, not redundantly, as for instance when one makes a
point with his voice, and points with his finger to make the point, but rather as in
his example, "Have you seen the *New York Times?*" where the work "New
York Times" is one item of information, while the gesture alerts the recipient to
the attribute that is being considered. I suspect that gesture is used to supplement
the verbal communication when it is the more economical way of transmitting
the information being conveyed. To determine under which circumstances people gesture rather than describe verbally one may consider what language is good
and what it is bad for. Language is good for making specific points in isolation

and one after the other: point after point after point. Words are inefficient for describing spatial relationships, and simultaneous relationships such as comparatives. You might refer to a small child and that child could be of any size within a wide range. If a gesture is added, one can specify in one economical movement more precisely how small that child was. It would take many words and some thought to match the gesture in terms of a verbal statement.

In general, gestures are used in those circumstances in which one gesture is worth a thousand words, just like a picture is sometimes worth a thousand words. The examples A. Kendon gives were exact instances of that point. Thus, a turn of the head tells one immediately which person is being referred to or where that person is, in contrast to a description in terms of points of a compass or numbers on an imaginary clock face, which is quite cumbersome. One further consequence follows. When gestures are used to convey information more economically than words they are predicated on right hemisphere functioning. The right hemisphere is thought to be more specialized for the depiction and recognition of the simultaneous relations between items, concurrently existing relationships (Kinsbourne, 1982). One would suppose that it is the right hemisphere which formulates the thought process of which the gesture is an instantiation. If that were ture, one could then predict that the kind of use of gesture described by Kendon, would be lost in certain cases of right hemisphere damage.

Kendon also mentions in his chapter a dictum of John Anderson. There is a debate between those who think it possible for analogue processes representing continuous change to occur in the brain, and those who claim that representation is exclusively propositional, amodal. The latter is a vacuous position since all that is involved is a propositional notation in terms of which anything can be noted. This tells us nothing about how the brain works. Kendon quotes Anderson as having concluded that it is impossible to determine whether representation is by image or propositional. We disagree.

Lempert and I studied a mental rotation task (Lempert & Kinsbourne, in preparation). It involves a grid, like a tic-tac-toe, a three by three matrix, with notations in two of the nine cells. The subject is asked to represent where those notations would be located if they were rotated by a specified number of degrees. We recorded latency and accuracy of making that judgment. The finding of interest with regard to the nature of representation is that we found in five successive studies using variants of the basic paradigm, that right-handed people can mentally rotate more rapidly clockwise than counterclockwise. In one study we studied left-handers. They did not exhibit a difference between clockwise and counterclockwise rotation. That outcome is something which a propositional mental representation cannot represent. Biological biases of this kind can easily be explained on an analogue representational basis.

The second category, in which the gesture is part of a coordination of movements and it is the total coordination of movements that has adaptive significance shall now be examined. An example of this is selective orienting, which in its fully fledged manifestation is turning of the head, of the eyes, pointing, swivelling of the body. Thus orienting is an incipient approach, the individual being posed to approach a point. This orienting behavior is truly important, not only in terms of the disposition of attention to the right and left of center, but also for the development of speech and communication (Kinsbourne & Lempert, 1979). Its origins can be traced in very small people.

One of the few things that newborn babies do is to turn their heads. If one puts a newborn baby on its back, the baby will not remain on its back, at least not completely. The head will be turned to one or the other side. That is a very constant finding. The head will more often be turned to the right than to the left (Gesell & Ames, 1950). That preponderance of turning to the right holds only for those children both of whose parents are right-handers (Liederman & Kinsbourne, 1980). It is not true of those children who have one left-handed parent. In the newborn baby just the head turns, but over a month or 2 months orienting develops into a richer gesture, in that when the head and eyes turn, the same-sided arm extends and the mouth opens. This is known to neurologists as the "asymmetric tonic neck reflex," which is the rudiment for turning attention and poising for action in one direction (Kinsbourne, 1978b). As the child develops, the direction of preponderant head and eye turning is found to be the side of the longer grasp of an object (Caplan & Kinsbourne, 1976), and the side of the hand with which the child more often reaches to grasp (Hawn & Harris, 1979).

Then comes pointing. Pointing in its adult form involves a differential extension of the index over the other fingers. As such it is not within the repertoire of the very immature motor system. A baby will flap its hand toward something and one cannot tell whether that flap represents a deictic movement or an attempted grasp. Perhaps one can make the inference that if the object is a long way away and the baby can tell that it's a long way away and nevertheless flaps toward it, that it's a deictic or indexical gesture. But these inferences are not secure. However, by 8 or 9 months pointing occurs which is specific and unmistakable, pointing towards distant things together with orienting, opening of the mouth, widening of the pupils, an alerting of the individual.

Pointing has two aspects of interest (Lempert & Kinsbourne, 1985). One is that it is preferentially accompanied by vocalizing, first babbling and then speaking. The other is that it is not necessarily communicative in intent. There is a paradox. Even a very young baby has a communicative repertoire which is remarkably rich (Bruner, 1975). Yet when a child behaves in ways like those which grown-ups use for communication, that is not necessarily why the child is doing it. The child clearly can communicate and the child points, like we do when we point something out to another. Yet, it cannot be assumed that the child is pointing anything out to anybody. There are numerous reports of children pointing at things when there is no other person present in the room. I interpret initial pointing as part of orienting. Pointing out and checking that the other is also looking at what one is pointing out becomes possible a few months later.

Early naming is mostly naming of things which are present in the environment, concrete, vivid perceptually and to which the child points while he names. I suggest that the naming, like the pointing, also initially is part of selective orienting and is not yet communicative in intent (although again the child soon realizes the communicative potential inherent in uttering the name.) So pointing and naming are initially indexical and only later symbolic. Further, when children can name quite flexibly they still very frequently point at what they are naming, even when the pointing conveys no additional information. Only with further maturity does the speech act become dissociable from the naming/pointing, orienting synergism out of which the speech act grows. However, this is not to say that the synergism disappears. Synergisms never disappear. They become more readily inhibited but they can still be elicited in certain circumstances in the adult. Thus, the tonic neck reflex can be demonstrated even in the grown-up when turning the head against great resistance. The orienting that goes with naming or with a verbal proposition can be illustrated by anecdote in adults. You are sitting around the table in a committee. Tom, before he left the room, had made a point. You say, "as Tom has reminded us." As you say this everybody's eyes flicker to the spot where Tom was sitting, to an empty chair. They gain nothing from looking at an empty chair, but they are orienting automatically to where the person was when they again hear something that he had said.

Once maturity is achieved, the orienting that goes with the naming can be suppressed, but the neural "wiring" is still there. Whether the response tendency is suppressed is as much a cultural matter as a biological one. Like gesture in general, it represents an overflow of brain patterned activity. There is perhaps as much difference between the British and the Apache brain as the British and the Italian. But the British and the Apaches would not permit any movement to reveal the turbulent state of their minds, whereas stereotypical Italians act out, even to excess, their feelings, however minimal they may be. That is a culturally determined matter.

What then is the brain basis of this orienting? The neuropsychological syndrome, which to my mind is most eloquent in explaining it to us, *unilateral neglect* of space and of person (Kinsbourne, 1977). This syndrome is bizarre. The patient has had a stroke. The right posterior part of the brain is severely damaged. He is lying in bed. You approach him from the left. You are ignored. (However high your status or critical your mission.) If you approach the person from the right, his attention is as if magnetically drawn to you, even more than one would expect. The person does not make spontaneous exploratory head-turning gestures to the left. If you present the person with a display, such as an open newspaper, you can see how an orienting gesture to one end of the display precedes any attempt to read (although it takes perceptible time for the head and eyes to pass across that page). If you then ask the person what he saw, he proves to be oblivious of all that expanse of print over which his gaze passed. Instead he reads some words at the right margin which by themselves make no sense. When you ask him why he makes no sense when he reads he says "Well, my eyes aren't very good, I should be wearing my glasses" or make some other not very illuminating comment. The orienting is more than a turning, it has something to do with awareness. What we see is an imbalance in the orienting tendencies. There are opponent systems in the hemispheres. One controls turning to the right, the other turning to the left. If one is incapacitated the other one overreacts, the system swings to its extreme like a see-saw and attention is skewed to one side of visual space, auditory space and personal space. The person ignores the left side of their body, but not exactly down the middle. How can we formulate this rather extensive problem in attention and intention? They neither intend to nor have attention toward things to the left side of what's there, including their own body. Moreover, they have a variety of cover stories to explain their distorted behavior. "What's this arm?" "It's a monkey." "It's your arm, Doctor." etc. We can only suppose that what we have here isn't just an imbalance in relation to one's schema of both personal and extrapersonal space. Perhaps when one intends a movement one plans it by some internal representation which designates its goal in space. That planning itself requires a shift of attention in the direction of intended movement. If you cannot shift your attention there, how can you intend and move there?

This lateral orienting has profound implications not only for where you're looking, where your head is pointing, but also for what you notice, what you experience. There are many minor forms of this and one occurs when there is not so much gross damage of each hemisphere but separation between them. Some years ago, Trevarthen and I studied several split brain patients (Kinsbourne, 1974; Trevarthen, 1974). We could show a minor form of their attention imbalance simultaneously in the two hemispheres. Each hemisphere would attend rather little to the same side of space. That gives some clue about what the corpus callosum really does.

The neglect phenomenon is very much biased towards neglect of left with right hemisphere lesions. It is much more subtle and less frequent after left hemisphere lesions. I have thought of two reasons why this might be.

The first one is that the neglect phenomenology is established in a dyadic interaction. An experimenter or a clinican confronts and interacts with the patient and the patient manifests his or her neglect. Conversation goes on, as well as implicit verbalization. If the person is right-handed, the left hemisphere is presumably the language hemisphere and it will be activated by the interaction with the clinician. It will therefore suppress the right hemisphere through inhibition. Thus, any impairment of the right hemisphere will be exacerbated by the verbal interaction making the neglect worse. But if the left hemisphere is damaged, the verbalization will alleviate it and, and tend to redress that imbalance (Kinsbourne, 1970). There is experimental evidence for this. Heilman and Watson (1978) had neglect patients look at a surface with numbers of items on it. The patients had to cross out the items. They would miss some items on the left. The measure for neglect was how many items were missed. They used two kinds of items, letters and scribbles, nonverbal shapes. The imbalance hypothesis predicts that there would be more severe neglect for letters than scribbles. Given the letters, they would activate the left hemisphere and further suppress the right, whereas when the material was spatial, the opposite would be the case. The difference in degree of neglect was in fact found.

The second reason why there may be a preponderance of neglect after right hemisphere lesion has to do with the rightward turning bias that was mentioned earlier, that is found even in newborn babies. There is evidence that all things being equal right-handed humans turn right (Ludwig, 1932). They do not just use their right hand, they turn right, they swivel their attention right. They walk to the right rather than to the left if either were feasible in principle. That leads on to a type of model that Denenberg (1981) has written about in relation to his ingenious experiments with rodents and lateralized brain lesions. He has pointed out that the interaction between the hemispheres need not be equal and opposite. In fact he has cited experimental evidence that it is not. One hemisphere may actively suppress the other and the other hemisphere put up a barrier against that force, but not itself exerting counteractivity. In consequences, if the hemisphere that is the barrier is damaged then the force is released and attention swings to the opposite side of space. This is what happens when the right hemisphere is damaged. If the hemisphere that exerts the force is damaged the barrier does not swing, but attention remains centered. We should conceive of a number of cybernetic interactions which are, if not complex in engineering terms, at least more so than the rudimentary information flow models that we customarily use.

A third category of gestures comprises tell-tale gestures, spin-offs of behavior. They illustrate the fact that the brain is all connected up and that focal patterned activity tends to overflow into other parts of the brain and to have repercussions on the status of those effector organs which can resonate with that pattern (Kinsbourne & Hicks, 1978). Let me operationalize this concept. If a person has in their mind a shape or a movement they are apt to move their arm in a way that is consistent with the flow of what they are thinking of, not necessarily deliberately to show the other person how it looks, but as an overflow of the activity. For example, you might say: "I think you have to make a distinction here." And you make the gesture of putting one thing on one side and one on the other. That gesture is automatic. In your mind you are forming a representation of a distinction and your hand makes the appropriate gesture as an overflow of what is in your mind. This kind of overflow can also be observed with eye movements, and there have been studies that have people imagine, look in their mind's eye at, say, a staircase, and the subjects show zigzag movements of the eyeballs as if they were ascending a staircase. Of course when one centrally represents a staircase there is nothing external to look at to explain the changes in eyeball position. There is an internal scan overflowing into external scan. Such overflow is particularly obvious in the immature individual to the point that thought process and physical movement appear to be one and the same in the baby. One can read off the baby's state of mind from the baby's posture and movements.

One can read something else off the gestures of the eyes and the gestures of the hand. Over and beyond their patterning one can also read off something about laterality. In which direction is the gaze, which hand is moving? First the gaze. There are two streams of investigation in the psychological literature pertinent to turning as it reflects thinking. One was initiated by Day (1964) and has been followed up by Bakan (1969) and many other investigators. It concerns an interindividual difference. While some people solve problems they tend to look to the right, while others tend to look left. It is argued that this is an index of their cognitive style, their style of thinking about the issue. Here is a gesture of the third type, a spinoff, a tell-tale clue of what is happening in this apparently not so black box.

The other way of looking at right versus left eye movement, which is within the individual, is the one that I first presented (Kinsbourne, 1972). It too has accumulated a considerable literature (Ehrlichman & Weinberger, 1978). When the person is given the task of thinking in words, they look to the right. When thinking spatially, they look up and to the left. Here lateral gaze is used as an index of which hemisphere the person uses in relation to different tasks, in contrast to the previous case, where which hemisphere different people use given a fixed task was studied. In fact, we are not merely observing lateral eye movement, we are observing turning, lateral orienting. In my original study, I looked at head and eye movement and found them equally indicative. As one thinks about a verbal problem one's head turns right, and one's eyes turn right. Measuring the head movement is just as revealing as measuring the eye movement. Subsequently, investigators have immobilized the head, so that it could not move, and concentrated on gaze. We have here a way of roughly estimating the balance of activation between the hemispheres. The extent to which they are both activated is indexed by upward gaze, the extent to which one hemisphere rather than the other is activated, by contralateral gaze.

In this paradigm for exploring for what each hemisphere is specialized, in addition to confirming that in verbal thinking a right-handed person will look to the right, and in spatial thinking to the left, Schwartz, Davidson, and Maer (1975) have discovered that, given negatively affective material to think about, people look left, whereas given neutral material, they look right. There is additional evidence for left hemisphere activation during the experience of positive affect (Reuter-Lorenz & Davidson, 1981). There are apparently orthogonal balances between negative and positive affect and verbal and spatial thinking. One can attempt the *tour de force* of integrating them. One can think of the right hemisphere as establishing the context, setting figure in ground, setting the framework, stipulating the relationships between the point of focal attention and other points. With respect to emotion, perhaps the left hemisphere focuses on a single point, oblivious of everything else. And to be happy surely is to oblivious of what is really going on. Whereas the right hemisphere takes into account what is going on, making its owner miserable.

In the area of investigation that treats right versus left looking as an individual variable, there exists a complex literature which is hard to interpret. Each individual study seems flawed and yet there is some coherence across outcomes. The suggestion is that people who tend to look right while thinking about problems are concrete, materialistic, analytic in their cast of mind. People who tend to look left are more inner directed and given to using imagery in representation rather than words. One of our studies will illustrate this (Gerdes & Kinsbourne, 1974). Undergraduates about to have dental extractions were sitting anxiously in the waiting room. We measured their heart rate, elicited right versus left looking tendencies by a standard set of questions, and asked them to tell us how they felt and why. The results were as follows. The right lookers tended to overdescribe their anxiety as indexed by their heart rate and projected the reasons for how they felt outward. The left movers were more apt to underverbalize their anxiety and refer it inwardly. They would internalize the situation. A provocatively parallel finding emerges from Bear & Fedio's (1977) study of temporal lobe epileptics. The left-sided cases (presumably activated on that side by subthreshold epileptic discharges) rated themselves more seriously handicapped, whereas to observers the right-sided cases appeared worse off.

Finally we shall consider gesturing while speaking. Kimura (1973) showed that people gesture more with the right than with the left hand when speaking but not more with one or another hand when they are thinking in spatial terms. For her, this was indicative of some basic link between articulation and hand movement on the output or praxic side of information transmission. A perplexing aspect of this study was that, in 15 minutes, the subjects would make as few as three gestures. However, Dalby et al. (1980) did a more ecologically valid study of the same phenomenon, judging sidedness of gestures of public speakers holding forth. He too reported a predominance of right-handed gestures during speaking. However, one must make some distinctions here. There is the gesture Kendon described which complements the flow of information. There is also the gesture that emphasizes or accentuates the flow of information. So you may have the movement that says: "It goes like this" (indexical or descriptive) or the movement that says "now-you-listen-to-me-young-man" (punctuating).

In a study relative to this kind of distinction, subjects were shown pictures of complex scenes or listened to descriptions of them over 15 seconds (Kinsbourne & Sewitch, 1972). They then made up a brief story elaborating on that scene or that description. (Whether they looked at the picture or heard it described made no difference to the outcome, so I shall collapse them in my account.) We wanted to look for any preponderance of right versus left versus bilateral gestures while the people told their stories. The finding was in one sense unrevealing in that there was no right-left difference. There was a lot of bilateral movement, than Kimura found. This is presumably because we had free flowing conversations. We also had two independent judges rate each recorded gesture on a 3-point scale, as abrupt or discontinuous, free-flowing, or intermediate between the two. The findings were: abrupt movements preponderated in the right hand; free-flowing movements preponderated in the left hand, and the intermediate category showed no lateral preponderance. This pilot study suggests that the right hand preponderance of movement occurs not during any speech, but specifically when the speech is of analytic rather than of descriptive type. If the speech attempts to represent matters that cannot be easily described in words there might be more left-handed gestures. We chose those complex pictures and stories to elicit this phenomenon. It does not contradict Kimura's data, it looks at a different aspect of the behavior. But contrary to Kimura's interpretation, it does show that the gestures are not necessarily tied to the speech output. The gestures represent what is going on in the mind, by tapping the pattern of brain activation. If the behavior consists primarily of speech act after speech act, then the gesture will follow the speech act. But if the main cognitive transaction is to imagine something, and speech is secondary to what is being imagined, then the gestures go along with the imagining and not with the speech. It is not a mere output linkage. The gestures do represent, in a simplified way, the person's state of mind, not necessarily because he wants them to, but even automatically, by an overflow of activation within the highly linked nervous system.

Instead of explicitly discussing the neuropsychology of gesture and orientation, I have argued that gesture and orientation are not coherent concepts neuropsychologically. There is no lesion that is so placed in the brain as to impair the package of phenomena that we label gesture the way a lesion can be placed to impair the package of phenomena we label language. There is no gesture territory like there is a language territory. Gesture is a compendium word for a variety of biologically different phenomena. But though there is no unitary neuropsychology of gesture one can nevertheless approach each gesture type neuropsychologically.

## REFERENCES

Bakan, P. (1969). Hypnotizability, laterality of eye-movements and functional brain asymmetry. *Perceptual and Motor Skills, 28*, 927–932.

Bear, D., & Fedio, P. (1977). Quantitative analysis of interictal behavior in temporal lobe epilepsy. *Archives of Neurology, 34*, 454–467.

Bruner, J. S. (1975). The ontogeny of speech acts. *Journal of Child Language, 2*, 1–19.

Caplan, P. J., & Kinsbourne, M. (1976). Baby drops the rattle: Asymmetry of duration of grasp by infants. *Child Development, 47*, 532–536.

Dalby, J. T., Gibson, D., Grossi, V. & Schneider, R. D. (1980). Lateralized hand gesture during speech, *Journal of Motor Behavior, 12*, 292–297.

Day, M. E. (1964). An eye-movement phenomenon relating to attention, thought and anxiety. *Perceptual and Motor Skills, 19*, 443–446.

Denenberg, V. H. (1981). Hemispheric laterality in animals and the effect of early experience. *The Behavioral and Brain Sciences, 4*, 1–49.

Ehrlichman, H., & Weinberger, A. (1948). Lateral eye movements and hemispheric asymmetry: A critical review. *Psychological Bulletin, 85*, 1080–1101.

Fesio, R. V,, & Crescenzi, C. A. (1982). Gesturing and self contact of right and left halves of the body: Relationship with eye contact. *Perceptual and Motor Skills, 55*, 695–698.

Gerdes, E. P., & Kinsbourne, M. (1974). Alternative strategies of reporting state anxiety and their cerebral basis. *Journal Supplement Abstract Service. Catalogue of Selected Documents in Psychology, 4*(15).

Kinsbourne, M. (1980). Do repetitive movement patterns in children and animals serve a dearousing function? *Journal of Developmental and Behavioral Pediatrics, 1*, 39–42.

Kinsbourne, M. (1982). Hemisphere specialization and the growth of human understanding. *American Psychologist, 37*, 411–420.

Kinsbourne, M., & Hicks, R. F. (1978). Functional cerebral space: A model for overflow, transfer and interference effects in human performance. In J. Requin (Ed.), *Attention and performance VII* (pp. 345–362). Hillsdale, NJ: Lawrence Erlbaum Associates.

Kinsbourne, M., & Lempert, H. (1979). Does left brain lateralization of speech arise from right-biased orienting to salient percepts? *Human Development, 22*, 270–275.

Lampert, H., & Kinsbourne, M. (1985). The possible origin of speech in lateral orienting. *Psychological Bulletin, 97*, 62–73.

Lempert, H., & Kinsbourne, M. (in preparation). An asymmetry in mental rotation.

Liederman, J., & Kinsbourne, M. (1980). Rightward motor bias of newborns depends on parental right-handedness. *Neuropsychologia, 18*, 579–584.

Ludwig, W. (1932). *Das Rechts-Links-Problem im Tierreich und beim Menschen*. Berlin: Springer.

Reuter-Lorenz, P., & Davidson, R. J. (1981). Differential Contributions of the two hemispheres to the perception of happy and sad faces. *Neuropsychologia, 19*, 609–613.

Ruggieri, V., Celli, C., & Crescenzi, C. A. (1982). Self contact and gesturing in different stimulus situations: Relationships with cerebral dominance. *Perceptual and Motor Skills, 54*, 1003–1010.

Schwartz, G. E., Davidson, R. J., & Maer, F. (1975). Right hemisphere lateralization for emotion in the human brain: Interactions with cognition. *Science, 19*, 286–288.

Sewitch, D., & Kinsbourne, M. (1972). *Laterality of gesture during verbal description of pictures.* unpublished manuscript.

Trevarthen, C. (1974). Functional relations of disconnected hemispheres with the brain stem, and with each other: Monkey and man. In M. Kinsbourne & W. L. Smith (Eds.), *Hemispheric disconnection and cerebral function*. Springfield, IL: CC Thomas.

# 4 Lateral Differences in Gesture Production

Pierre Feyereisen

Two lines of thought converge to suggest that some insights into the brain mechanisms underlying speech may be gained from a study of gestures. One is the idea that verbal and nonverbal systems do not constitute separate communication modes, specialized in the transmission of rational and emotional information, respectively; human communication could better be conceived as a multichannel process where meaning is represented either by words or gestures (A. Kendon, Ch. 1). The other is a modification in the conception of hemispheric specialization, which substitutes for the verbal/nonverbal dichotomy more "functional" dichotomies such as serial/parallel and analytic/holistic. In this perspective, the left-hemispheric advantage in verbal tasks arises from a specialization of that hemisphere in sequential, analytical, or high-resolution processes. In both cases, a shared property of language and gestures is stressed: both are able to convey meaning, and both do it by way of motor activity (articulation or gesticulation). Thus, researchers have begun to look for common cerebral mechanisms, and data have been collected in two areas: in the lateral differences in hand movements of normal subjects and in the manual activity of unilaterally brain-damaged subjects.

However, the relevance of these studies for the knowledge of control mechanisms underlying speech and gestures remains unclear. Different interpretations of the data may be offered. The studies reviewed here show that evidence for a common cerebral basis in the control of oral and manual movements is still lacking and that more precise models describing both the specificity and the commonalities of language and gestures are needed.

## LATERAL DIFFERENCES IN MOVEMENTS DURING
## SPEECH OF NORMAL SUBJECTS

### Kimura's Observation

Kimura (1973) first reported that right-handed subjects made more gestures with the right hand than with the left when speaking. The reverse was noted in left-handers, with the additional observation that the total manual activity (both hands summed) in these subjects was twice the activity of right-handers. No lateral differences or "hyper-activity" of left-handers were observed in self-touching movements. In fact, lateral differences for self-touching appeared when the subjects solved verbal and nonverbal problems, but in these cases the preferred hand was the ipsilateral hand to the presumably involved hemisphere. From these observations Kimura concluded, first that there is a common system for the control of both gestures and speech and that this system for most people is primarily located in the left hemisphere and, second, that there is a difference in the cerebral organization of self-touching movements and gestures. A closer inspection of the data indicating a link between speech lateralization, as measured by the dichotic test, and hand preference for gestures shows that no lateral differences in gestures emerge in left-handers with right-ear superiority. From this observation, Kimura discussed a two-factor explanation of asymmetry: Both speech lateralization and hand preference play a role for each hand respectively. Kimura rejected this model because it cannot account for the high incidence of right-hand gestures in left-handed subjects with a left-ear advantage, and she assumed instead a more bilateral representation of language in left-handed subjects.

Several studies confirm Kimura's observations. Ingram (1975) observed three groups of right-handed children (at the ages of three, four and five) and noted a right-hand preference for gestures irrespective of age and sex, but no lateral difference appeared in self-touching. No left-handed subjects were considered in that study. Dalby, Gibson, Grossi, and Schneider (1980) tried to replicate Kimura's findings in more natural settings. They observed professors during lectures and student dyads in informal situations. The subjects were classified as right- or left-handed according to their score in a handedness questionnaire. A significant movement lateralization by movement type interaction was noted: In both the teachers and the students, more gestures were made by the right hand, but no lateral differences appeared for self-touching movements. The subjects' handedness factor was not analyzed because of a lack of speech lateralization data and the small size of the sample of left-handers. Additional observations on speech behavior (Kimura & Humphrys, 1981; Moscovitch & Olds, 1982; Sousa-Poza, Rohrberg, & Mercure, 1979) also confirm the preference for right-hand gestures in right-handers, with qualifications that are discussed below. Thus, the global superiority of the right hand in gesturing seems to be well-established.

However, no study since the pioneering work of Kimura (1973) has replicated her observations on left-handers and the interpretation problems they raise.

## Do Hands and Mouth Show a Similar Right-Side Advantage?

Analysis of other motor asymmetries, which are not related to the handedness factor, could clarify the question. Unfortunately, a link in lateral differences for hand and mouth movements during speech has not yet been found. Moreover, contradictory results have been published concerning mouth asymmetry itself. The first studies in this area followed the observations of Sackheim and Gur (1978) and Campbell (1978) that, in evaluating chimeric composites, the left hemiface was judged as more expressive than the right. Some authors have assumed a right-hemispheric mediation in the control of emotional expressions (see reviews by Sackheim & Gur, 1982 and by Campbell, 1982). If such an interpretation is valid, one would expect a reduced left-hemiface advantage for nonemotional movements. Such a result was obtained by Graves, Goodglass, and Landis (1982), who observed a wider opening of the right side of the mouth during speech. The fact that such an asymmetry does not appear in women in a picture description task was interpreted as reflecting the greater sensitivity of these subjects to the emotional content of the picture. No sex effect was observed in a word-naming task. In Cacioppo and Petty's (1981) study, lateral differences were qualified by significant task influences. Emotional and nonemotional facial movements were elicited in spontaneous conditions (reading a mathematics text-book or a sad story) and in voluntary conditions (the task was "to feign an expression of someone lost in thought on a difficult problem" or of someone grieving). The most noticeable asymmetry favored the right hemiface, which was judged as more expressive in the voluntary pose for thoughtfulness. However, the hypothesis that emotional factors play a critical role in facial assymetry was ruled out by two observations of the copying of meaningless movements. First, Koff, Borod, and White (1981) observed a left-hemiface superiority in judging which side has the greater facility in making three unilateral mouth movements. Second, Campbell (1982) recorded facial movements in two situations: saying the alphabet and performing facial "gymnastic" exercises. The evaluators reported a greater mobility of the left hemiface in the exercise condition only. In the speaking condition, the judgments did not differ in function of the normal or mirror-reversed presentation of the picture. A left-hemiface superiority is consistent with the broader spatial/sequential dichotomy, according to which there would be a right-hemispheric superiority in controlling the positioning of bodily segments. A left-hand advantage has been observed in executing finger flexion movements (Kimura & Vanderwolf, 1970) and in copying hand postures on children (Ingram, 1975). Another interpretation of the left-hemiface superiority would be that it has benefited from greater practice due to a lateral bias in emotional expression.

## Interpretation Problem: Motor Sequencing versus Left-hemispheric Activation

Discussions about the possible influence of instigation conditions (spontaneous versus voluntary movements) and of the emotional factors are related to another problem in interpreting Kimura's findings of lateral differences in manual activity during speaking. Two explanations of the observed asymmetries may be proposed: First, there is a left-hemisphere superiority in the control of a complex motor sequence, and second, right-hand gesturing is due to left-hemispheric activation during a verbal task. Kimura (1976) suggested the first interpretation is integrating facts of various natures: association between speech lateralization and manual skills, observations of apraxic disorders following left-hemispheric lesions, and disturbances of manual communication in deaf subjects with left-sided cerebral damage. As regards manual activity during speaking, the qualitative aspects of gestures were analyzed by automatically recording rotation and flexion-extension movements of the forearm (Kimura & Humphrys, 1981). The mean number of changes per movement was computed to compensate for the right-hand advantage in gesture frequency. In both spatial dimensions, it was noted that the number of direction changes was greater for right-arm movements. This could account for the results obtained by Sousa-Poza et al. (1979) and replicated by McNeill and Levy (1982); in concrete conversations (describing one's hometown or daily work), only "representational" movements were lateralized. However, in more abstract conversations analyzed by Sousa-Poza et al., the reverse was true, and only nonrepresentational movements were more often produced with the right hand. It is reasonable to assume that, in concrete descriptions, gestures with a referential content are morphologically more complex than others, but one might suspect a bias in classification of gestures as representational since the chance for a gesture to be seen related to the verbally expressed meaning is greater for concrete and figurative contents than for more abstract ones. Such a bias would explain why more nonrepresentational movements are observed in conversations about abstract subjects, as noted by Sousa-Poza and Rohrberg (1977).

According to the activation hypothesis, the observed lateral differences are unrelated to the sequential complexity or representational value of the gesture, and asymmetry does not depend on variables specifically bound to motor control as in eye shift toward the right in verbal problem solving (Ehrlichman & Weinberger, 1978; Kinsbourne, 1972), or in mouth asymmetry during spontaneous speech (Graves et al., 1982). Hand preference in gestures would simply indicate relative hemispheric involvement in the control of verbal expression. According to this interpretation, a greater right-hemispheric participation in the task is reflected in increased left-hand gesturing and thus in reduced asymmetry. Such an interpretation was given by Kimura (1973) for the left-handers' activity.

If the right hemisphere predominates in emotional behavior, one would also expect a higher left-hand activity during emotional content processing. Moscovitch and Olds (1982) observed subjects conversing about emotional experiences and compared hand gestures with and without simultaneous facial expression: in right-handers, the right-hand advantage was slightly reduced when accompanying a facial expression, and there was a significant difference in the probability of right- and of left-hand gestures being associated with facial expression (38% vs. 58%). The absence of lateral differences in gestures of deeply depressed subjects (Ulrich, 1980; Ulrich & Harms, 1979) could be a related phenomenon, but this result is difficult to interpret, since two variables were confused: emotional behavior and a sampling bias in favor of left-handers in the population (see the review of Flor-Henry, 1979). Emotional influence, however, is not restricted to speech-related movements. Ruggieri, Celli, Crescenzi (1982) observed a predominant left-hand activity in self-touching movements during the discussion of intimate topics and a right-hand advantage for these movements with neutral topics. Surprisingly enough, reversed asymmetries were noted when speech-related movements were considered, so the implications for differential hemispheric involvement are unclear from that study. An economical explanation would be that the hand engaged in self-touching movements is the non-gesturing hand, but Feyereisen's (1977) observations did not confirm such an hypothesis. On the contrary, the hand chosen for the self-touching movements was the previously active hand in task relevant activities (gestures and object manipulation).

Sousa-Poza et al. (1979) noted a personality influence on the lateralization of gestures: "field-dependent" subjects, whose hemispheric functioning is assumed to be less asymmetrical than in "field-independent" subjects (but see Bruyer, 1982a, for a critical review), did not show a right-hand preference in manual activity during speaking.

A problem with this "activation" hypothesis is explaining why self-touching movements are not influenced by hemispheric involvement. Some speculations on the gestural origins of language were offered, and a programmed linkage between skilled hand movements and verbal behavior was suggested. The results of Sousa-Poza et al. (1979) showing greater asymmetry for representational movements in concrete descriptions would also be unclear in an activation model if we assume a right-hemispheric involvement in imagery (Bruyer, 1982b). An association of gestures with intonational aspects of speech would lead in the same way to a reduced left-hemispheric advantage. Moreover, gesture lateralization has been shown to be influenced by situational factors. In observing mothers pointing, Murphy and Messer (1977) noted that pointing was done with the arm furthest away from the baby irrespective of which side of the baby the mother was seated. A critical control would be to examine the behavior of the other hand to see if there is any inhibition by care-taking activities, such as touching, holding and adopting protective postures. In the absence of these data, the fact that bias in attention toward the right-side favors left-hand movements is an intriguing finding as far as the activation hypothesis is concerned.

Not enough data have been collected to choose among the different interpretations. More particularly, there is as yet no evidence concerning the critical properties of gesture production leading to asymmetrical control. Some of the hypothetical dimensions are sequential in nature (opposing complex gestures to spatial positioning, to simple movements, to self-touching movements and to facial movements), referential versus emotional content, bias in attention, and association with prosody or with imagery. Of course, these aspects are not independent of each other, and demonstrating an experimental dissociation is not an easy task.

## Interference: Speech/Gesture Relationships

Another contrast between the activation and the motor control model is the possibility of interference. In an information processing model, one may conceive that gestures and speech are concurrent behaviors, competing for the limited resources of the central nervous system. If gestures and speech both demand attention in motor sequencing, interference would then be observed as with a tapping test while speaking (Kinsbourne & Cook, 1971). The more speech uses the limited capacities of the system, the less there is available for gestures. For example, gestures might occur during automatized verbal utterances or during silent pauses, and fluent speech would be associated with reduced gesturing (sharing-time phenomena). On the other hand, one might consider manual activity as an automated process characterized by such properties as unavoidability, little awareness and resistance to modification. By definition, automaticity implies an absence of interference. According to the activation hypothesis, the more the left hemisphere is working, the more right-hand gesturing will occur and thus an absence of interference is predicted even if the formulation of the hypothesis does not assume automaticity.

Unfortunately, strict measures of processing load are unavailable and indirect measures raise methodological problems. On the one hand, speech tempo and task difficulty are not independent factors, and their influence cannot be dissociated in natural speaking conditions: The more difficult the task, the more frequent are the dysfluencies, and thus the more time is available for gestures. Thus, observation of hand activity in different tasks must control speech output variations. On the other hand, it is not clear that verbalization is more attention-demanding than lexical searching or sentence programming: thus, gesture occurrence during a pause could be viewed either as a time-sharing phenomenon or as a cue for a heavy processing load.

Critical experiments examining distribution of resources between language and gestures as a function of lateral differences have not yet been done. If the relationships between language and gestures are analyzed without reference to the question of laterality, a complex picture emerges and methodological problems preclude any firm conclusions. On the one hand, observations of hand movements in bilingual subjects show that fewer gestures are produced when speaking the dominant language. Differences in fluency are eliminated by computing a gesture-to-word ratio. In spite of cultural differences favoring gesture production in their own language, French students use more gestures when describing their living room in English (Sainsbury & Wood, 1977). The effect is more marked when the English description comes first, i.e., when there is maximal encoding difficulty. The same result was noted by Marcos (1979) in Spanish-English and English-Spanish bilinguals: in both groups, more nonrepresentational movements were produced in the nondominant language. Gestures are not affected by the level of imagery of the topics (giving opinions about love versus describing a movie). These results are consistent with an automatic activation model. On the other hand, attempts to manipulate the linguistic complexity of the message have not shown similar effects on gesture production. In the study of Baxter, Winters, and Hammer (1968), familiarity with the conversation topics as assessed by a pretest, did not influence motor activity, but did interact with the cognitive style of the subjects. Thus, the effect differs according to individual characteristics. Cohen and Harrison (1973) asked subjects to explain how to reach a given place, but the ease or difficulty of the task did not affect the mean number of gestures. In these two studies the negative results were not qualified by an analysis of the speech output, so we do not know whether the subjects were more fluent or not in the easy tasks than in the difficult ones. Cohen (1977) replicated his former experiment and, with another measure of gestural activity, observed a significant effect of task difficulty: a complex task, requiring three or four decision points, elicited longer verbal utterances and more movements per second than a simple one. Yet, if difficulty is marked by longer speaking time and increased gestural activity, one cannot explain the previously observed negative results when the absolute number of gestures was considered. Moreover, it is difficult to conclude that Cohen's results were due to higher processing load rather than reduced speech rate.

Relationships between speech rhythm and body movements have been analyzed in pilot studies, and again the results are contradictory. The first studies assumed a common association of gestures and verbal dysfluencies to the speaker's level of anxiety (Boomer, 1963). But in an experimental manipulation of speech tempo, Boomer and Dittmann (1964) failed to confirm an association between pauses and gestures: speeding up or slowing down the verbal rate by specific instructions did not influence the number of movements per minute, but a movement per word computation seemed to show a relative increase of gesticulation in the nonfluent condition. When the temporal association between head, hand, and foot movements and verbal utterances was more precisely analyzed, the movements were found to be related to the rhythmic characteristics of the utterance (Dittmann, 1972; Dittmann & Llewellyn, 1969). More movements were observed than expected in the beginning of the phonemic clauses, i.e., during the first word of a verbal unit whose end is marked by a juncture (final syllable stretching and pause) and to which only one stressed word belongs. When dysfluent clauses were considered, movements also frequently occurred after a hesitation pause. The combined effects of starting position, hesitation, and lengthened speaking time led to an increased gestural rate in nonfluent clauses. Other kinds of dysfluencies (e.g., sentence change, repetition, and stuttering) have been reported to follow instead of to anticipate gesture production, but inappropriate statistical analysis casts doubt on the results (Ragsdale & Silvia, 1982). In these studies, motor manifestations were assumed to reflect the speaker's encoding difficulties and to be directly related to processing load. However, replication of these observations is desirable because of methodological problems such as high interindividual variability, no distinction between kinds of movements, no reported comparison of gesture occurrence during pauses and vocalization, and insufficient details about the procedure.

Butterworth and Beattie (1978) proposed a more complex answer to the question of the relationships between hesitations and gestures. Verbal utterances were segmented in alternating planning and execution phases, differing by the amount of pauses. Gestures more often accompanied verbalizations during the hesitant planning phase, but during the execution phase, a greater gesture-per-second ratio was observed during hesitations. In total, more gestures occurred during execution phases. Moreover, the morphology of the gestures differed according to the occurrence time: representational gestures were more often observed during hesitations, especially in the execution phases, but nonrepresentational movements were more frequent during vocalizations, especially in the planning phases. Thus, Butterworth and Beattie showed that the activation and the interference models are not really incompatible. Since more gestures were observed during execution phases and more nonrepresentational movements during vocalizations, there is evidence for the arousal properties of speech. The more complex gestural representations during hesitations and reduced movements rate during planning phases could reflect resource allocation between gestures and speech. As a matter of fact, Butterworth and Beattie's work is an attempt to form an information processing model of the relationships between language and gestures, since different levels of processing were distinguished in the gestural and verbal productions. Extension of these observations in the analysis of lateral differences could be decisive for the interpretation of the superiority of right-hand gesturing.

To conclude this review of studies on gesture and language in normal subjects, it may be stated that we need more data about poorly documented phenomena and that the studies of lateral differences in perceptual processes have not yet been very fruitful for the analysis of motor asymmetries. In recent years, conceptions about lateral differences have evolved from an assumption that hemispheric specialization depends on the nature of the stimulus to more functional dichotomies, where lateral advantages emerge from the modes of processing (Bertelson, 1982; Bradshaw & Nettleton and open peer commentary, 1981). Thus, according to task demands, the right or the left hemisphere would be favored, irrespective of the verbal or nonverbal nature of the stimulus. Looking at behavioral asymmetries as a tool to analyze cognitive organization, the information processing approach seems to have little to say about gestures. Most of the studies on lateral differences have been conducted on the receptive side where the input to the system is known and can be manipulated in such a way that it becomes possible to trace the flow of information. Levels of processing are more difficult to identify when the output is the result of an elaboration upon a signal imprecisely defined as "plan" or "intent" (however, see Paillard, 1982 for stages in motor control, and Garrett, 1980, and Butterworth, 1980, about levels in language production). Some conceptions about hemispheric specialization (for example, Moscovitch, 1979; Sergent, 1982) that distinguish stages in extracting information from the input do not seem directly relevant for the explanation of the lateral differences in hand movements. In fact, we do not know very much about the mechanisms of gesture production, even outside the domain of lateralization. Thus, initial indication of a right-hand advantage in manual activity during speaking has brought no new insights into the cerebral correlates of verbal behavior, but instead raises several problems: What is the relative contribution of the different explanatory factors: speech lateralization, handedness, or more situation-dependent factors like seating arrangement? Are the right side of the face and the right hand controlled by similar mechanisms? Is right-hand preference due to left-hemisphere superiority in the control of motor sequences or to its activation during speech? Does right-hand activity result from an automatic process or from interference between concurrent activities? Many of these problems may be analyzed in terms of the consequences of unilateral brain damage. Observation of the behavior of the aphasic or the right-hemisphere damaged subject is likely to bring some new arguments about these issues and to allow a description of the relationship between language and gestures.

## GESTURE PRODUCTION AFTER UNILATERAL BRAIN DAMAGE

### Historical Perspective: Disorders in Gesture Production

Influence of hemispheric processing on gestural activity was traditionally examined in the context of apraxia (Feyereisen & Seron, 1982). The significant association between disturbances of language and of purposive movements in left-hemispheric lesions has been interpreted either as reflecting a more general deficit of the symbolic function (Duffy & Duffy, 1981; Duffy & Liles, 1979), or due to the superiority of the left hemisphere in motor sequencing or, more precisely, in the control of successive positioning in rapidly changing motor configurations (Kimura, 1977, 1982). These hypotheses about the nature of a single mechanism whose disruption could economically explain verbal and gestural impairments are difficult to reconcile with several known facts. The gestural deficit correlates with the severity of aphasia, as assessed by the WAIS performance score (Goodglass & Kaplan, 1963), the PICA (Duffy & Duffy, 1981; Pickett, 1974), the Token Test (De Renzi, Motti, & Nichelli, 1980), and the syndrome of global aphasia (Kertesz & Hooper, 1982). Thus, some milder aphasic cases are able to communicate by gestures better than by words (Davis, Artes, & Hoops, 1979). On the other hand, training in use of gestural communication has little impact on word retrieval in aphasics (Drummond & Rentschler, 1981). Another dissociation between language and gestures is that global aphasics may improve their ability to communicate by gestures better than by words (Helm-Estabrooks, Fitzpatrick, & Barresi, 1982; Peterson & Kirshner, 1981). Furthermore, dissociations between different kinds of gestural deficits have been observed. Hécaen (1978) noted that in homogeneous groups of patients, scores for gestural description of objects and for expressive gestures are not correlated. The problem with this study, however, is that computing a single correlation for the whole sample would probably lead to another conclusion stressing the severity effect. Kimura (1982) reported nonsignificant correlations between oral and manual movements, and suggested that anterior and parietal localizations of left-hemispheric lesions play different roles in motor control. Kolb and Milner (1981) also noted a differential impact of frontal and parietal lesions on oral and manual movements. Lastly, Heilman, Rothi, and Valenstein (1982) distinguished different kinds of ideomotor apraxia according to the subject's performance in the visual discrimination of gestures.

Thus, studies of apraxia encounter problems similar to those shown in studies of lateral differences in gestures: beyond the fact that the left hemisphere shows a global superiority in the control of purposive movements, there is no evidence of common mechanisms underlying speech and gestures. The association between aphasia and ideomotor apraxia might be in some cases fortuitous (for example, large lesions could disrupt logically distinct processes). The most promising perspectives seem to be in elaborating specific models instead of global explanations for all the observed left-hemisphere advantages.

Recently, it has been suggested that observations on manual activity during speaking in aphasic subjects could generate new insights into the question. If movement characteristics and conditions of elicitation are critical factors in the analysis of cerebral correlates of gesture production, there would be an advantage in examining current hypotheses about motor control for this particular kind of movement. Moreover, data so collected may be more directly compared to observations on lateral differences in normal gesture production. Two types of investigation have been conducted: quantitative studies on gestural production in aphasics and semiotic analysis of these gestural representations.

## Manual Activity During Speaking in Aphasic Subjects

The observation of aphasics offers two major points of interest: first, the effects of left-hemispheric lesions on verbal and gestural behavior allow us to test the hypothesis of common cerebral basis with little inference and, second, the diversity of aphasic disturbances permits us to identify more specific components of the language production system (conceptual representation, lexical search, syntactic encoding, output short-term memory, articulation) that might be related to gesture production. Several pilot studies on small populations address these issues.

Goldblum (1978) observed manual activity in four groups: aphasic, left-lesioned without aphasia, right-lesioned, and normal subjects. Anterior and posterior lesions were distinguished for each of the brain-damaged groups. The dependent variable was the number of movements divided by the number of words. No statistical analysis was made, but visual analysis of data suggests a greater gesture-to-word ratio in the anterior aphasic group. Of course, this result could be due to reduced verbal fluency as well as to increased gestural activity. Goldblum also noted that in left-lesioned subjects, unlike the behavior of normal and right-hemisphere lesioned subjects, unilateral movements were more frequently done by the left hand, even if no motor impairment of the right hand was detected in a muscular strength test. Another study by Cicone et al. (1979) compared two anterior and two posterior aphasics to four normal subjects. This time, the dependent variable was the total number of gestures during the observation period (nine segments of 15 seconds each per subject). More movements were observed in posterior than in anterior aphasics, but if the left hand only is considered, the difference becomes negligible. A quantitative analysis by Feyereisen (1983) with several measures of gestural behavior showed an increase of the manual activity in fluent and nonfluent aphasics as compared to normal subjects. No statistical difference between the aphasic groups was apparent, but the small size of the sample made a Type II error likely, i.e., accepting the null hypothesis of equality when in fact it is false. Moreover, large interindividual variations can obscure group effects. As far as manual preference is concerned, no lateral advantage was observed in fluent aphasics, but nonfluent aphasics who have motor deficits used the left hand more often. Thus, in none of these studies was there a noticeable impairment of the gestural production in the aphasic groups, and no clear differences between the kinds of aphasia were observed. Taken together, these results do not argue for a common cerebral basis underlying speech and gestures; the hypothesis of a nonverbal impairment parallel to the verbal deficit is not confirmed, and verbal fluency is not shown to be a critical factor in the explanation of gesture production. Moreover, no lateral differences appeared in manual activity of left-hemisphere lesioned subjects without motor deficit, and a compensation by the left hand was observed in the cases of hemiplegia. However, controls for complexity of these movements, as measured by the automatic recording technique of Kimura and Humphrys (1981) have not yet been carried out.

Regarding the representational value of gestures the studies of both Goldblum (1978) and of Cicone et al. (1979) demonstrated a higher proportion of iconic movements in the anterior aphasic group. Cicone et al. also found analogs to the characteristics of fluent speech in gestural productions: posterior aphasics executed more complex gestures (i.e., sequences of several motor units), but their message was less understandable than that of other groups (higher proportion of unspecified gestures). These results were interpreted either as reflecting more preserved lexical knowledge in the anterior group, or as due to the influence of more elaborated syntactic frames in the production of nonrepresentational gestures in posterior aphasics. However, even if hand movements are activated during speech attempts in aphasic subjects, as shown by Feyereisen (1983), these subjects do not seem to exploit the resources of the gestural mode of communication as deaf-mute subjects do. Two explanations may be proposed: aphasics might be focused on the previously mastered verbal language, or the primary function of gestures might not be a referential one. In fact, the representational value of gestures was never precisely assessed. Most authors distinguish iconic and batonic gestures and find them occurring in almost equal proportions in normal subjects (see the data presented by Butterworth & Beattie, 1978; Cicone et al., 1979; McNeill & Levy, 1982). But, iconicity is defined as a relationship between the form of the gesture and the verbal content, and thus an impoverished or paraphasic speech output may influence the classification of the movements. Apart from this methodological problem, some authors (e.g., Mehrabian, 1972) have stressed the expressive value of gestures. Hand movements can be interpreted as cues of the relationship between the speaker and his utterance (involvement, competence, etc.). Gestures also intervene in the regulation of speaking turns: the listener is less likely to interrupt the conversational flow if the speaker is gesticulating (Duncan & Fiske, 1977). Nespoulous (1979) and Labourel's (1982) analyses of gestures by aphasics suggest that gestures could fulfill different functions simultaneously, and not only refer to figurative contents (forms, qualities, actions, space, time, number, etc.).

One problem for a model of gesture production is accounting for the rhythmic and referential properties of gestures (Rimé, 1983). On the one hand, gestures are able to convey the same kind of information as words do. Butterworth, Swallow, and Grimston (1981) argued from the normal appearance of gestures in a case of jargonaphasia and from significant association between gesture interruptions and hesitations or neologisms that the locus of word finding difficulties for this subject was less in the semantic than in the phonological representation of the lexical item. On the other hand, Kendon (1972, 1975) proposed the hypothesis that gesticulation makes visible the organization of speech, linking the sentences that express the same idea and separating different ideas in the same utterance. Such a role would be independent of the representational qualities of the movements. Delis et al. (1979) raised a related issue in their analysis of complex sentences produced by two Wernicke's aphasics. It was noted that gestures began simultaneously with the proposition more often when the main and embedded clauses were semantically discontinued than when they were linked. These very preliminary observations could hardly be viewed as providing decisive empirical data about gesture-production mechanisms. Their interest is rather in a shift of perspective: the research no longer tends to concentrate on common superordinate mechanisms but to analyze interactions between gestures and language. Aphasiology has become the field of natural experimentation where the consequences of selective linguistic impairment may be observed.

In such a perspective, personal observations on the nonverbal behavior of aphasics have been conducted to test hypotheses about the influences of speech disturbances on motor manifestations. Increased gestural activity in both fluent and nonfluent aphasics and the association between gestures and gaze aversion support the hypothesis that hand movements reflect speech encoding difficulties (Feyereisen, 1983; Feyereisen & Lignian, 1981). A problem with such a conception is that the specific influence of agrammatism, defective phonological representation, and word finding difficulties are not specified. The existing data do not show many differences in gestural production in relation to aphasia types. However, reanalysis of the data suggests a possible dissociation between frequency and duration of gestures (defined as morphological changes within a movement). Fluent aphasics tend to produce numerous gestures of short duration, and nonfluent aphasics tend to hold their hands in a raised position during long hesitation pauses. Gesture frequency and mean duration do not correlate across subjects, and thus an increase in manual activity can be due to different mechanisms. On the other hand, gaze aversion during the central part of a speaking turn is more often observed in nonfluent than in fluent aphasics, which is consistent with the conception of gaze aversion as a way of reducing processing load. In these studies, nonverbal behavior is assumed to reflect covert mental operations. Impaired oral production would be disrupted in some automatic processes and thus the task would be more demanding than in normal subjects. According to this hypothesis, increased gestural production would be due to higher activation of the speech control mechanisms.

Whatever the state of the art, manual activity during speaking seems to constitute a particular motor behavior requiring specific explanations. We have no evidence for a common mechanism controlling manual and oral gestures in the observed cases of articulatory deficits. There is also no reason to assume similar contributions of the left hemisphere to co-verbal gestures and to performances in standard tests of apraxia. Yet, because the current observations of manual activity are restricted to milder cases and exclude global aphasia to which ideomotor apraxia is often associated, there is no opportunity to demonstrate a dissociation between the two kinds of movements. On the other hand, possible impairment of the spontaneous gestural activity without apraxia in cases of right hemispheric, frontal, or subcortical damage has not yet been documented. But, contemporary perspectives on motor control (e.g., Paillard, 1982) do not facilitate amalgamating the different manifestations in unitary explanations. We hope that showing lateral differences in gesture production may help us to establish the required behavioral taxonomy and to distinguish levels of processing in previously undifferentiated phenomena.

## CONCLUSIONS

Analysis of lateral differences in gesture production and observation of manual activity during speaking in aphasic subjects lead to an apparent paradox: on the one hand, right-hand preference is assumed to reflect a predominant left-hemisphere control for these movements, but, on the other hand, aphasia originating from left-hemisphere lesions does not disrupt gestural activity. As a matter of fact, the seemingly contradictory findings are consistent with the hypothesis according to which right-hand gestures reflect the left hemisphere load in speech processing.

The difficulty with such an explanation is that it does not account for the patterning of the movements, i.e., their morphological complexity and possible representational value. Not enough data have been gathered on these issues. The extent to which and the conditions in which gestures can convey precise meanings are still unknown. In normal subjects, analysis of the processes in gesture interpretation is greatly underdeveloped relative to the numerous studies analyzing the decoding of facial expressions or visual behavior. The temporal association of gestures and speech is also a poorly documented phenomenon, especially in aphasic subjects. In addition to replications of important pilot studies on normal gestural activity, we need more detailed descriptions of the conditions in which lateral differences appear. From such a perspective, new insights may be gained by bringing together separate fields: the information processing approach to lateral differences, aphasiology, and the experimental analysis of gesture production. Indeed, the position we have adopted in this paper is that explanations of the observed behavioral asymmetries depend on the knowledge of how manual activity is controlled and of how it interacts with verbal expression. A clear interpretation of the plain fact of a right-hand advantage would be premature until we analyze the processes of translating thoughts into words and movements.

## REFERENCES

Baxter, J. C., Winters, E. P., & Hammer, R. E. (1968). Gestural behavior during a brief interview as a function of cognitive variables. *Journal of Personality and Social Psychology, 8,* 303–307.

Bertelson, P. (1982). Lateral differences in normal man and lateralization of brain function. *International Journal of Psychology, 17*, 173–210.

Boomer, D. S. (1963). Speech disturbance and body movement in interviews. *Journal of Nervous and Mental Disease, 136*, 263–266.

Boomer, D. S., & Dittmann, A. T. (1964). Speech rate, filled pause and body movement in interviews. *Journal of Nervous and Mental Disease, 139*, 324–327.

Bradshaw, J. L., & Nettleton, N. C. (1981). The nature of hemispheric specialization in man. *The Behavioral and Brain Sciences, 4*, 51–91.

Bruyer, R. (1982a). Est-il utile d'établir une connexion entre la neuropsychologie et le concept de dépendance à l'égard du champ? *Cahiers de Psychologie cognitive, 2*, 91–98.

Bruyer, R. (1982b). Neuropsychologie de l'imagerie mentale. *L'Année psychologique, 82*, 497–512.

Butterworth, B. (1980). Some constraints on models of language production. In B. Butterworth (Ed.), *Language production, Vol. 1: Speech and talk* (pp. 423–459). London & New York: Academic Press.

Butterworth, B., & Beattie, G. (1978). Gesture and silence as indicators of planning in speech. In R. Campbell & P. T. Smith (Eds.), *Recent Advances in the Psychology of Language: Formal and Experimental Approaches* (pp. 347–360). New York: Plenum Press.

Butterworth, B., Swallow, J., & Grimston, M. (1981). Gestures and lexical processes in jargonaphasia. In J. Brown (Ed.), *Jargonaphasia* (pp. 113–124). New York & London: Academic Press.

Cacioppo, J. T., & Petty, R. E. (1981). Lateral asymmetry in the expression of cognition and emotion. *Journal of Experimental Psychology: Human Perception and Performance, 7*, 333–341.

Campbell, R. (1978). Asymmetries in interpreting and expressing a posed facial expression. *Cortex, 14*, 327–342.

Campbell, R. (1982). The lateralization of emotion: A review. *International Journal of Psychology, 17*, 211–229.

Campbell, R. (1982). Asymmetries in moving faces. *British Journal of Psychology, 73*, 95–103.

Cicone, M., Wapner, W., Foldi, N., Zurif, E., & Gardner, H. (1979). The relation between gesture and language in aphasic communication. *Brain and Language, 8*, 324–349.

Cohen, A. A. (1977). The communicative functions of hand illustrators. *Journal of Communication, 27*(4), 54–63.

Cohen, A. A., & Harrison, R. P. (1973). Intentionality in the use of hand illustrators in face-to-face communication situations. *Journal of Personality and Social Psychology, 28*, 276–279.

Dalby, J. T., Gibson, D., Grossi, V., & Schneider, R. D. (1980). Lateralized hand gesture during speech. *Journal of Motor Behavior, 12*, 292–297.

Davis, S. A., Artes, R., & Hoops, R. (1979). Verbal expression and expressive pantomime in aphasic patients. In Y. Lebrun & R. Hoops (Eds.), *Problems of aphasia* (pp. 109–123). Lisse: Swets and Zeitlinger.

Delis, D., Foldi, N. S., Hambi, S., Gardner, H., & Zurif, E. (1979). A note on temporal relations between language and gestures. *Brain and Language, 8*, 350–354.

De Renzi, E., Motti, F., & Nichelli, P. (1980). Imitating gestures. A quantitative approach to ideomotor apraxia. *Archives of Neurology, 37*, 6–10.

Dittmann, A. T. (1972). The body movement-speech rhythm relationship as a cue to speech encoding. In A. W. Siegman & B. Pope (Eds.), *Studies in dyadic communication* (pp. 135–151). New York: Pergamon.

Dittmann, A. T., & Llewellyn, L. G. (1969). Body movement and speech rhythm in social conversation. *Journal of Personality and Social Psychology, 11*, 98–106.

Drummond, S. S., & Rentschler, G. J. (1981). The efficacy of gestural cueing in dysphasic word-retrieval responses. *Journal of Communication Disorders, 14*, 287–298.

Duffy, R. J., & Duffy, J. R. (1981). Three studies of deficits in pantomimic expression and pantomimic recognition in aphasia. *Journal of Speech and Hearing Research, 24,* 70–84.

Duffy, R. J., & Liles, B. Z. (1979). A translation of Finkelburg's (1870) lecture on aphasia as 'asymbolia' with commentary. *Journal of Speech and Hearing Disorders, 44,* 156–168.

Duncan, S., & Fiske, D. W. (1977). *Face-to-face interaction: Research, methods and theory.* Hillsdale, NJ: Lawrence Erlbaum Associates.

Ehrlichman, H., & Weinberger, A. (1978). Lateral eye movements and hemispheric asymmetry: A critical review. *Psychological Bulletin, 85,* 1080–1101.

Feyereisen, P. (1977). Préférence manuelle pour les différents types de mouvements accompagnant la parole. *Journal de Psychologie normale et pathologique, 74,* 451–470.

Feyereisen, P. (1983). Manual activity during speaking in aphasic subjects. *International Journal of Psychology, 18,* 545–556.

Feyereisen, P., & Lignian, A. (1981). La direction du regard chez les aphasiques en conversation: Une observation pilote. *Cahiers de Psychologie Cognitive, 1,* 287–298.

Feyereisen, P., & Seron, X. (1982). Nonverbal communication and aphasia, a review: II Expression. *Brain and Language, 16,* 213–236.

Flor-Henry, P. (1979). Laterality, shifts of cerebral dominance, sinistrality and psychosis. In J. Gruzelier & P. Flor-Henry (Eds.), *Hemisphere asymmetries of function in psychopathology* (pp. 3–19). Amsterdam-New York-Oxford: Elsevier-North Holland.

Garrett, M. F. (1980). Levels of processing in sentence production. In B. Butterworth (Ed.), *Language production* (Vol. 1, pp. 177–120). London & New York: Academic Press.

Goldblum, M. C. (1978). Les troubles des gestes d'accompagnement du langage au cours des lésions corticales unilatérales. In H. Hécaen & M. Jeannerod (Eds.), *Du contrôle moteur à l'organisation du geste* (pp. 383–395). Paris: Masson.

Goodglass, H., & Kaplan, E. (1963). Disturbance of gesture and pantomime in aphasia. *Brain, 86,* 703–720.

Graves, R., Goodglass, H., & Landis, T. (1982). Mouth asymmetry during spontaneous speech. *Neuropsychologia, 20,* 371–381.

Hécaen, H. (1978). Les apraxies idéomotrices: Essai de dissociation. In H. Hécaen & M. Jeannerod (Eds.), *Du contrôle moteur à l'organisation du geste* (pp. 343–358). Paris: Masson.

Heilman, K. M., Rothi, L. J., & Valenstein, E. (1982). Two forms of ideomotor apraxia. *Neurology (Ny), 32,* 342–346.

Helm-Estabrooks, N., Fitzpatrick, P. M., & Barresi, B. (1982). Visual action therapy for global aphasia. *Journal of Speech and Hearing Disorders, 47,* 385–389.

Ingram, D. (1975). Motor asymmetries in young children. *Neuropsychologia, 13,* 95–102.

Kendon, A. (1972). Some relationships between body motion and speech: An analysis of an example. In A. W. Siegman & B. Pope (Eds.), *Studies in dyadic communication* (pp. 177–210). New York: Pergamon.

Kendon, A. (1975). Gesticulation, speech, and the gesture theory of language origins. *Sign Language Studies, 9,* 349–373.

Kertesz, A., & Hooper, P. (1982). Praxis and language: the extent and variety of apraxia in aphasia. *Neuropsychologia, 20,* 275–286.

Kimura, D. (1973). Manual activity during speaking—I. Right-handers. II. Left-handers. *Neuropsychologia, 11,* 45–50; 51–55.

Kimura, D. (1976). The neural basis of language qua gesture. In H. Whitaker & H. A. Whitaker (Eds.), *Studies in neurolinguistics* (Vol. 2, pp. 145–156). New York & London: Academic Press.

Kimura, D. (1977). Acquisition of a motor skill after left hemisphere damage. *Brain, 100,* 527–542.

Kimura, D. (1982). Left-hemisphere control of oral and brachial movements and their relation to communication. *Philosophical Transactions of the Royal Society of London, 298B,* 135–149.

Kimura, D., & Humphrys, C. A. (1981). A comparison of left-and right-arm movements during speaking. *Neuropsychologia, 19,* 807–812.

Kimura, D., & Vanderwolf, C. H. (1970). The relation between hand preference and the performance of individual finger movements by left and right hands. *Brain, 93,* 769–774.

Kinsbourne, M. (1972). Eye and head turning indicate cerebral lateralization. *Science, 176,* 539–541.

Kinsbourne, M., & Cook, J. (1971). Generalized and lateralized effect of concurrent verbalization on a unimanual skill. *Quarterly Journal of Experimental Psychology, 23,* 341–345.

Koff, E., Borod, J. C., & White, B. (1981). Asymmetries for hemiface size and mobility. *Neuropsychologia, 19,* 825–830.

Kolb, B. & Milner, B. (1981). Performance of complex arm and facial movements after focal brain lesions. *Neuropsychologia, 19,* 491–503.

Labourel, D. (1982). Communication non-verbale et aphasie. In X. Seron & C. Laterre (Eds.), *Rééduquer le cerveau* (pp. 93–108). Bruxelles: Mardaga.

Marcos, L. R. (1979). Nonverbal behavior and thought processing. *Archives of General Psychiatry, 36,* 940–943.

McNeill, D., & Levy, E. (1982). Conceptual representations in language activity and gesture. In J. Jarvella & W. Klein (Eds.), *Speech, place and action* (pp. 271–295). New York: Wiley.

Mehrabian, A. (1972). *Nonverbal communication.* Chicago: Aldine.

Moscovitch, M. (1979). Information processing and the cerebral hemispheres. In M. S. Gazzaniga (Ed.), *Handbook of behavioral neurobiology,* Vol. II: (pp. 379–446). *Neuropsychology.* New York: Plenum Press.

Moscovitch, M., & Olds, J. (1982). Asymmetries in spontaneous facial expressions and their possible relation to hemispheric specialization. *Neuropsychologia, 20,* 71–81.

Murphy, C. M., & Messer, D. J. (1977). Mothers, infants and pointing: A study of a gesture. In H. R. Schaffer (Ed.), *Studies in mother-infant interaction* (pp. 325–354). New York and London: Academic Press.

Nespoulous, J.-L. (1979). Geste et discours: Étude du comportement gestuel spontané d'un aphasique en situation de dialogue. *Etudes de Linguistique Appliquée, 36,* 100–121.

Paillard, J. (1982). Apraxia and the neurophysiology of motor control. *Philosophical Transactions of the Royal Society of London, 298B,* 111–134.

Peterson, L. N., & Kirshner, H. S. (1981). Gestural impairment and gestural ability in aphasia: A review. *Brain and Language, 14,* 333–348.

Pickett, L. W. (1974). An assessment of gestural and pantomimic deficit in aphasic patients. *Acta Symbolica, 5,* 69–86.

Ragsdale, J. D., & Silvia, C. F. (1982). Distribution of kinesic hesitation phenomena in spontaneous speech. *Language and Speech, 25,* 185–190.

Rimé, B. (1983). Nonverbal communication or nonverbal behavior? Toward a cognitivo-motor theory of nonverbal behavior. In W. Doise & S. Moscovici (Eds.), *Current studies in European experimental social psychology* pp. 85–135. Cambridge: Cambridge University Press.

Ruggieri, V., Celli, C., & Crescenzi, A. (1982). Self-contact and gesturing in different stimulus situations: relationships with cerebral dominance. *Perceptual and Motor Skills, 54,* 1003–1010.

Sackheim, H. A., & Gur, R. C. (1978). Lateral asymmetry in intensity of emotional expression. *Neuropsychologia, 16,* 473–481.

Sackheim, H. A., & Gur, R. C. (1982). Facial asymmetry and the communication of emotion. In J. T. Cacioppo & R. F. Petty (Eds.), *Social psychophysiology.* New York: Guilford Press.

Sainsbury, P., & Wood, E. (1977). Measuring gesture: Its cultural and clinical correlates. *Psychological Medicine, 7,* 63–72.

Sergent, J. (1982). The cerebral balance of power: Confrontation or cooperation? *Journal of Experimental Psychology: Human Perception and Performance, 8,* 253–272.

Sousa-Poza, J. F., & Rohrberg, R. (1977). Body movement in relation to type of information (person- and nonperson-oriented) and cognitive style (field dependence). *Human Communication Research, 4,* 19–29.

Sousa-Poza, J. F., Rohrberg, R., & Mercure, A. (1979). Effects of type of information (abstract-concrete) and field dependence on asymmetry of hand movements during speech. *Perceptual and Motor Skills, 48,* 1323–1330.

Ulrich, G. (1980). Lateralization of hand-movements in patients with affective psychoses during an interview situation: an attempt at a physiological interpretation. *Psychological Research, 41,* 249–258.

Ulrich, G., & Harms, K. (1979). Video-analytic study of manual kinesics and its lateralization in the course of treatment of depressive syndromes. *Acta psychiatrica Scandinavica, 59,* 481–492.

# 5

# From Movement to Gesture: "Here" and "There" as Determinants of Visually Guided Pointing

Michèle Brouchon
Yves Joanette
Madeleine Samson

Study of gestural organization within the central nervous system has benefited considerably from at least two sets of knowledge in the last 2 decades. The first one is the now accepted distinction between two visual systems: one devoted to spatial vision, and the other to identification of objects (Held, 1968; Schneider, 1969; Trevarthen, 1968). The second concerns, on the one hand, results obtained in the current quest for central nervous pathways involved in each of these visual systems and, on the other hand, the current progress in the related physiology of motor control (Mishkin, Ungerleider, & Macko, 1983).

The problem of spatial vision has been studied through a set of observable sequential operations involving each component of the eye-limb system in a purposeful movement. These operations are detecting, orienting to, locating, and reaching a visual object. It can be argued, though, that these operations can be distinguished according to the (spatial) field in which they occur. In fact, these operations can occur either in immediate surroundings in which manual reaching and grasping are achieved without locomotion, or in the visual field outside of direct manual reaching and grasping in which visually guided locomotion and throwing are probably the most usual spatial actions. Such a descriptive approach of spatially oriented behaviors has generally led to a postulate that these are only attainable by reference to an internal map where the spatial relationships between extracorporal space and body space are stored (Paillard, 1971). This model of a spatial internal map is generally represented as a correlation storage of the spatial cues between the sensory input, the motor command and the movement re-afferences.

The hypothesis of a central nervous system constituting a spatial map in terms of the nature of the action to be achieved in a given field is supported by different experimental data. Behavioral observations dealing with the development of the visually guided behavior in kittens have emphasized that the building-up of a locomotory spatial map would be relatively independent of, and a prerequisite for, the acquisition of a reaching map (Hein & Diamond, 1973; Hein & Held, 1967; Held & Hein, 1971). In another area, studies of cellular activity in the posterior parietal lobes of awake monkeys provided neurophysiological data supporting the hypothesis of a dissociation between the immediate surrounding space and a locomotory space. In this respect, one can cite the studies of both Hyvarinen and Poranen (1974), and Mountcastle, Lynch, Georgopoulos, Sakata, and Acuna (1975) each of whom have identified in the posterior part of the parietal lobes (Voght's areas 7a and 7b) different classes of neurons the firing activities of which correspond to different components of the eye-limb system. The interesting point here is that neurons of all of these categories—including a visual one—were reported to fire only when the stimulus was rather close to the monkey, within its reaching field, and ceased to discharge when the object was in that portion of space out of its reaching field.

Both these facts suggest that, at least in animals, actions in the immediate neighborhood of the body (pericorporal)—the reaching field—would be stored in, and referred to, a different internal map than similar actions directed towards the more distant environment (extracorporal). Moreover, they give some evidence that the posterior parietal cortex may be an area in which the spatial mapping of the reaching field is achieved (Brouchon, 1982; Brouchon, Labrecque, & Roll, in preparation). This hypothesis of different spatial maps, according to the field (intracorporal, pericorporal or extracorporal) in which an action is to be achieved, raises the question of the equivalence of actions in different fields or, in other words, the question of the relationship between their respective goals.

Defining the location of the goal of a motor act is a problem which is still quite complex and vague in the current studies of the physiology of motor control. Following the previous distinction between automatic and voluntary movements, which implies that the goal is defined in terms of hierarchy according to the degree of intention involved in the achievement of a motor act (Berstein, 1967), a more pragmatic definition was provided during these last two decades. In the current literature on motor control, the goal of an action is usually defined as to the attainment of a movement's final position (Bizzi, 1980). Such a definition has the advantage of yielding observable events accompanying reaching. It thus allows its description in terms of time, force, velocity, and directions of the processing involved. It must be pointed out, however, that such a descriptive approach quite often associates attainment of a goal with the activation of different afferent and efferent systems. In other words, this model of the physiology of motor control has shown a term-to-term correspondence between the pattern of motor command and the motor output itself.

At the same time, it neglects the question of the environmental regulation of movement and so fails to distinguish teleological questions concerning the organism's intended goal.

Referring to Bernstein's theory of the physiology of activity, we assume the nonunivocality of the relationship between the pattern of motor command and the observable motor output. Such an assumption means that different motor outputs can be related to a single goal and so to the same pattern of action, and reciprocally, that two similar motor outputs could express the reaching of two different goals according to interaction between environmental constraints and the internal representation of the action.

In the present work, we suppose that two similar pointing movements of the hand to a visual target, involving at the biomechanical level the same afferent and efferent components, could represent two different goals and so correspond to two different gestures depending on the target location in the visual space. A reaching gesture to a target located in immediate surroundings becomes an indicating gesture when the same target is situated in a further field, out of reach of the outstretched arm.

In order to test the specificity of the cerebral maps that process the spatial information involved in these two gestures, we have analyzed and compared in two different tasks—a reaching task and an indicating task—the temporal and spatial performances of a normal subject and of brain-damaged patients whose spatial organization is impaired.

## METHODOLOGY

### Experimental Set-Up

*Reaching.*    Subject is seated at a pointing table (Fig. 5.1), head supported in a chin-rest. An array of 11 light-emitting diodes (LEDs) is situated on a plate 10 cm below, at a distance of 50 cm from the eyes. This array comprises one central

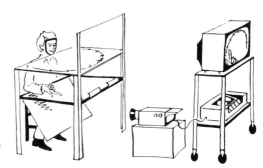

FIG. 5.1. Reaching set up; see comments in text.

LED flanked by 10 target LEDs, one at each of 5, 10, 20, 40 and 55 degrees on either side of the median line. This array has an arc-shape such that each of the LEDs is at the same distance from the eyes. The subject's pointing hand is laid down on a resting pad, 25 cm below the plate. The task consists in touching with the index finger of that hand, one of the 10 target LEDs as it is turned on. Reaching performances were videotaped (Fig. 5.1). These recordings were subsequently analyzed in spatial and temporal terms, with the use of an electronic editing unit.

*Indicating.*   The purpose of this set-up was to reduplicate as much as possible the physical conditions of the reaching set-up but, this time, for the purpose of eliciting a measurable indicating task. As in for reaching the subject is seated, chin supported on a chin-rest (Fig. 5.2). In front of him is an array of 11 LEDs situated at eye level on an arc-shaped wall, 300 cm (3 meters) from eyes. The array of LEDs is disposed similarly to that in the reaching task, that is, one central LED flanked by 10 target LEDs one at each of 5, 10, 20, 40 and 55 degrees on either side of the median line. The subject's pointing hand is resting on a resting pad 25 cm below the eye-LEDs plane. Indicating was performed by the index finger of the pointing arm as it out-stretched toward the target. In order to render the indicating gesture measurable, a laser beam was used to extend the indicating index (Fig. 5.2). This laser beam was visualized as a 0.5 cm diameter spot on the arc-shaped wall in the direction indicated by the index finger. Indicating performances were videotaped and then analyzed with the use of an electronic editing unit.

### Experimental Protocol

Subject is instructed to reach for or to indicate with the index finger, as quickly and as accurately as possible, any of the 10 target diodes that would be turned on.

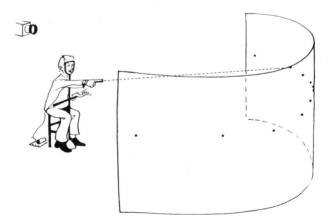

FIG. 5.2.   Indicating set up; see comments in text.

Each target diode is turned on 5 times in a random fashion. After each trial, reaching or indicating, subject is instructed to bring his hand back to the initial position on the resting pad. Such a series of reaching or indicating trials is obtained independently (a) for each hand, and (b) in two different conditions, namely a *closed-loop* and an *open-loop* condition. In the reaching task, the open-loop condition is obtained by replacing the plexiglass top part of the pointing table (Fig. 5.1) which lies between subject's eyes and hands, by an opaque screen. Thus, subject still can see the array of target LEDs but has no visual feedback of the actual position of his hand. In the indicating task, the open-loop condition is obtained by turning the laser beam on for a fraction of a second at the end of the indicating gesture, the subject being briefly blindfolded by screens which fall in front of both eyes at the instant the laser was turned on. Thus, he has no visual feedback of the actual position of the indicated point as opposed to the closed-loop condition in which the laser beam is constantly turned on.

The use of these two conditions, closed and open-loop, permitted to distinguish between the two basic components of the actualization of a reaching or indicating movement; that is, (a) the motor program itself corresponding to the initial phase of the movement which is present in both the closed *and* open-loop conditions, and (b) the visually controlled final adjustment which is present *only* in the closed loop-condition.

In both the reaching and indicating tasks, two spatial measures have been calculated for each trial. The first spatial measure is the *distance error* which is defined differently for reaching than for indicating. In reaching, distance error is the difference between 50 cm, which is the distance at which are situated the target LEDs, and the actual distance at which the target LED was pointed with reference to the position of the eyes. This distance error in the reaching task is related to eventual hypermetric or hypometric pointings. In indicating, distance error is measured as the vertical distance between the eyes—target LEDs level—and the actual pointed level. The second spatial measure is the *angular error* which, contrary to the distance measure, is identically defined for reaching and indicating. The angular error is the number of degrees separating the angular position of the target LEDs (5, 10, 20, 40 or 55 degrees on either side of the median line) and the angular position of the reached or indicated point.

Temporal measures were obtained only in the reaching task. The first temporal measure is the *reaction time* (RT) defined as the time lapse between the turning on of the target LED and the initiation of the reaching movement. The second temporal measure is the *transport time* (TT) defined as the time lapse between the initiation of the reaching movement and its completion, corresponding to the actual reaching itself.

## Subjects

We here report the reaching and indicating performances of three subjects, one control and two brain-lesioned subjects.

The control subject ("Control") is a 27-year-old right-handed, female graduate student without any past history of central or peripheral nervous system disease.

The first brain-lesioned subject (Mrs. Cos.) is a 46-year-old woman who presented an intracerebral haemorrage in the right parieto-occipital area, 7 months before testing. Despite the fact that she was a left-hander, the resulting neuropsychological semeiology was consistent with such a lesion site in a right "non-dominant" hemisphere: a visuo-motor incoordination ("optic ataxia") using either hand, a left spatial neglect, a visuo-constructive deficit and a spatial type alexia-agraphia without any distinctively aphasic signs. The only neurological sign present was a discret left inferior homonymous quadranopia. A CT-scan showed an area of reduced density including the right parieto-occipital area, and the uppermost posterior part of the right temporal lobe.

The second brain-lesioned subject (Mr. Arm.) is a 31-year-old right-handed man who had brain anoxia consecutive to a cardiac arrest 9 months before testing. Even though he showed no neurological signs, he presented a quite complex neuropsychological semeiology that could have been the reflection of some bilateral parieto-occipital dysfunction. Among these signs were an important visuo-motor incoordination ("optic ataxia") with an also important spatial disorientation which manifested itself through signs such as a visuo-constructive deficit, a dressing apraxia, a reflexive apraxia, and ideomotor apraxia, and an autotopoagnosia. He also had an aphasic and spatial type alexia-agraphia. Despite the importance of these clinical signs, there was no abnormal image on the CT scan.

## RESULTS

Difference in the etiology, and difficulties in defining the precise extent of the lesions have led us to analyze the results subject by subject, for each target, each hand, each hemifield, and both loop conditions. The absence of significant differences in pointing to targets of different eccentricity in a given hemifield has permitted us to sum up the performances hemifield by hemifield. Among the spatial errors defined previously, only the angular error is reported here since it is the only one to be defined identically in both the reaching and indicating tasks.

### Reaching Task—Angular Errors

*Control.*   In the closed-loop condition (Fig. 5.3), the errors are not significantly different from 0, whatever the reaching hand and the target's hemifield. In the open-loop condition (Fig. 5.3), performances differ significantly from those achieved in the closed-loop condition. The mean error is situated between 1° and 4° depending on the hand and target's hemifield combination. In each condition, though, the angular errors represent a systematic over-shoot of the reaching

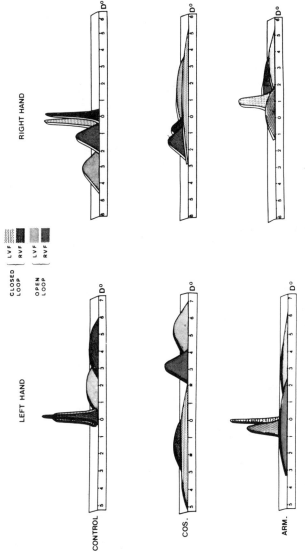

FIG. 5.3. Angular errors in the reaching task for control and both brain-damaged subjects: each curve represents the mean error in the attempt at reaching any of the targets led in a given hemifield (LVF or RVF), in a given condition (closed or open-loop) for a given hand. Maximal width of curves represents one standard deviation. See comments in text.

hand. This effect is increased in the hemifield contralateral to the reaching hand, as well as for the left hand.

*Mrs. Cos.*    With the hand contralateral to the lesion (Fig. 5.3) the errors in closed-loop and open-loop conditions are significantly different from 0 ($p <$ 0.5); but, they differ also from each other ($p < 0.001$) whatever the hemifield considered.

With the hand ipsilateral to the lesion the angular errors remain significantly different from 0 ($p < 0.05$), but do not differ from each other in either hemifield, although they are increased in the left hemifield contralateral to the lesion.

These results suggest that in this right parietal brain-damaged patient, the terminal adjustment in the reaching task is strongly impaired for each hand in the whole visual field; whereas the deficit of the initial plan of movement is limited to the hand and the visual hemifield contralateral to the lesion.

*Mr. Arm.*    In this patient (Fig. 5.3) the errors in closed-loop condition differ significantly from 0 ($p < .05$) for each hand and each hemifield except in the left hand/left hemifield combination. They are the greatest in the right hand/right hemifield condition. However these angular errors are different from those reported in the open-loop condition ($p < 0.05$), except in the right hand/right hemifield combination.

The pattern of errors observed in this patient suggests that both motor components of the visual-manual loop are affected in different ways for each hand in the whole visual field.

### Chronometry of the Reaching Task

*Control.*    RTs for control subject average 250 ms with a small standard deviation (Fig. 5.4). There is no significant difference between RTs measured for different hands, for different hemifields (LVF or RVF) or in different conditions (closed or open-loop).

As far as the TTs are concerned, they only show a significant increase ($p < 0.05$) in the closed-loop condition—whatever the hand or the hemifield—which can be explained by the presence of the final adjustment of the reaching gesture in this condition.

Such results are in total accord with those reported in numerous works bearing on the chronometry of motor control in man (Posner, 1982).

*Mrs. Cos.*    In this subject, RTs are, in general, significantly longer than those reported in the control subject ($p < 0.01$) even though they are somewhat shorter for RVF than for LVF targets, with the exception of the closed-loop condition using the left hand (Fig. 5.4).

With regards to TTs, they are also generally longer than those reported in the control subejct ($p < 0.01$), but the usual increase in the closed-loop condition,

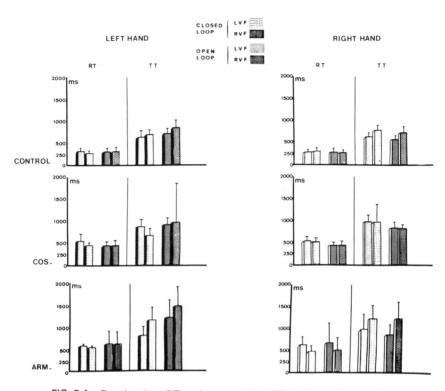

FIG. 5.4.   Reaction time (RT) and transport time (TT) in the reaching task for control and both brain-damaged subjects. Each column represents the mean value (RT or TT) for all reading attempts in a given hemifield (LVF or RVF), in a given condition (closed or open-loop) for a given hand. See comments in text.

reported in our control subject as well, is not to be found (Fig. 5.4). In fact, RTs in the closed loop condition for LVF targets using the left hand are even shorter in the open-loop condition for the same situation. In the other situation, TTs in the closed-loop condition are not significantly different from those seen in open loop, but they are much more dispersed (Fig. 5.4). This lack of TT increase in the closed-loop condition is linked to the impairment of the final adjustment of the reaching gesture evidenced in the angular error analysis.

*Mr. Arm.*   In this subject, RTs are significantly longer than those reported in our control subject ($p < 0.01$) even though the RT values are much dispersed (Fig. 5.4). Curiously though, RTs, for the right hand are shorter in the closed than in the open-loop condition.

TTs are also much longer than those of the control subject ($p < 0.01$) with an important dispersion (Fig. 5.4). These TTs also show significant increase in the closed-loop condition ($p < 0.05$) which probably indicates the presence in this subject of a more important final adjustment of the reaching gesture.

These results clarify those of the angular error analysis. In fact, the general increase of RTs mostly in the open-loop condition as well as the presence of an increase of TTs in the closed-loop condition may reflect an impairment in the motor programming of the reaching gesture. This impairment is partly compensated by the use of a visually based feedback mechanism.

### Indicating Task—Angular Errors

*Control.*    In the closed-loop condition (Fig. 5.5) whatever the pointing hand or the target's hemifield, the errors are not significantly different from 0 ($p < 0.05$), but are similar to the performances achieved in the reaching task.

In the open-loop condition (Fig. 5.5) the angular errors are characterized by a very important dispersion on either side of the physical position of the target. These results are strikingly different from those described earlier in the reaching task in which systematic errors were reported.

*Mrs. Cos.*    In the closed-loop condition (Fig. 5.5), the performance does not differ significantly from 0 ($p < 0.05$) except in the left hand/right hemifield condition. In the open-loop condition (Fig. 5.5), angular errors show, as in the control subject, a very large dispersion without any systematic effect.

In the indicating task, unlike the reaching task, we observe in this patient the presence of the final adjustment portion of the movement, which does not differ from the one reported in controls, at least in three out of four conditions.

*Mr. Arm.*    In the closed-loop condition (Fig. 5.5), the performances are rather similar to those obtained with Mrs. Cos.; that is an adequate final adjustment of the pointing which does not differ from 0 ($p < 0.05$) except in the left hand/right hemifield condition.

In the open-loop condition, dispersion of the errors is more important for the left hand than for the right. With the latter hand, the pattern of errors shows some systematic effect quite similar to the one observed in the same patient in the reaching task.

### DISCUSSION

From the above analysis comparing intra- and interindividual performances as well as spatial and temporal parameters we may conclude the following:

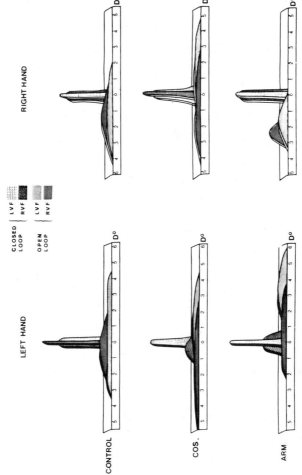

FIG. 5.5. Angular error in the indicating task for control and both brain-damaged subjects: each curve represents the mean error in the attempt at indicating any of the targets—LEDs in a given hemifield (LVF or RVF), in a given condition (closed or open-loop) for a given hand. Maximal width of curves represents one standard deviation. See comments in text.

1. The pattern of the spatial performances is strongly different in the reaching versus the indicating task for all subject.

In the open-loop condition, the large dispersion of errors in the indicating task, even for the normal subject, compared to the systematic and the symmetrical errors achieved in the same condition in the reaching task, probably reveals a difference in the spatial control processes involved in first part of these two gestures. Moreover, the sizeable impairment of the terminal adjustment in the reaching task, expressed in the closed loop condition by the large errors in both patients, and the absence of this fault in the indicating task, suggest that the internal representation of the action may determine separate processing of the spatial information involved in each component of motor act, even though both are dependent on feedback control.

2. The specificity of the posterior parietal areas in the processing of spatial information involved in the motor act achieved in the reaching space, previously demonstrated in monkeys by single cell recordings, in confirmed by our results.

3. The evidence of the specificity of internal models distinguishing the spatial information involved in the reaching and indicating gestures, failed to explain the intra- and interindividual variations of the spatial and temporal performance patterns presented by the patients in the reaching task. In this task, Mrs. Cos. and Mr. Arm.'s performances are significantly different according to the arm and the hemifield concerned. Such a fact is inconsistent with the idea of a single central process working independently of the peripheral sensory and motor structures. It suggests that control mechanisms for the processing of spatial characteristics of the gesture take into account the parts of the body by which those gestures are achieved.

These data, although fragmentary, give some empirical support to the idea that when different goals are assigned to a movement, the processing of the spatial information involved in guiding the motor act changes. In other words, the ultimate intention of action can determine not only the elaboration and the execution of the movement but also, at least in part, the processing of the perceptual cues associated to the movement. In this way a movement of prehension may be transformed into an indicating gesture.

## REFERENCES

Bernstein, N. A. (1967). *The coordination and regulation of movements*. Oxford: Pergamon Press.
Bizzi, E. (1980). Central and peripheral mechanisms in motor control. In G. E. Stelmach & J. Requin (Eds.), *Tutorials in motor behavior*. Amsterdam: North Holland.
Brouchon, M. (1982). Behavioral space organization in brain-damaged patients. *Neuroscience, 7*, 33.

Brouchon, M., Labrecque, R., & Roll, R. (in preparation). Balint's syndrom revisited: A Case report.

Hein, A., & Diamond, R. (1973). Locomotory space as a prerequisite for acquiring visually guided reaching in kittens. *Journal of comparative and physiological psychology, 81,* 394–398.

Hein, A., & Held, R. (1967). Dissociation of the visual placing response into elicited and guided components. *Science, 158,* 390–392.

Held, R. (1968). Dissociation of visual functions by deprivation and rearrangement. *Psychologische Forschung, 31,* 338–348.

Held, R., & Hein, A. (1971). Movement-produced stimulation in the development of visually-guided behavior. *Journal of comparative and physiological psychology, 56,* 872–876.

Hyvarinen, J., & Poranen, A. (1974). Function of the parietal association area 7 as revealed from cellular discharges in alert monkeys. *Brain, 97,* 673–692.

Mishkin, M. Ungerleider, L. G., & Macko, K. A. (1983). Object vision and spatial vision: Two cortical pathways. *Trends in Neurosciences, 6,* 414–417.

Mountcastle, V. B., Lynch, J. C., Georgopoulos, A., Sakata, H., & Acuna, C. (1975). Posterior parietal association cortex of the monkey: command functions for operations within extrapersonal space. *Journal of Neurophysiology, 38,* 871–908.

Paillard, J. (1971). Les déterminants moteurs de l'organisation de l'espace. *Cahiers de Psychologie, 14,* 261–316.

Posner, M. (1982). Cognitive neuroscience: Toward a Science of synthesis. In J. Mehler, S. Walker, & A. Garret (Eds.), *Perspectives on mental representation.* Hillsdale, NJ: Lawrence Erlbaum Associates.

Schneider, G. (1969). Two visual systems. *Science, 163,* 895–902.

Trevarthen, C. (1968). Two mechanisms of vision in primates. *Psychologische Forschung, 31,* 299–337.

# 6

# IPSI-Lateral Motor Control Study in a Total Callosal Disconnection Syndrome with Lateral Homonymous Hemianopia

Michel Poncet
Daniel Beaubaton
André Ali-Chérif

The presence of ipsilateral motor control of axial and of proximal limb movements has been demonstrated in both animals and man. In animals investigations of visuo-motor performance following induced lesions of optic chiasma and corpus callosum highlighted the mechanisms of this control (Brinkman & Kuypers, 1972, 1973; Downer, 1959; Gazzaniga, 1969; Paillard & Beaubaton, 1974). The work of Kuypers (1964) and Lawrence and Kuypers (1968a, 1968b) on the organization of corticospinal pathways has permitted to address the problem of its anatomical basis. In man, the study of motor disturbances subsequent to division of the cerebral commissures (Gazzaniga, Bogen, & Sperry, 1967) and the analysis of apraxic deficits secondary to focal brain lesions (Geschwind, 1975) has allowed to suggest the existence of such an ipsilateral motor control. Human split-brain studies run into the difficulty of sending visual information to a single hemisphere for a sufficiently long lapse of time, hence the impossibility of thoroughly studying visuomotor performances. The presence of lateral homonymous hemianopia associated with a full callosal disconnection syndrome offers from this viewpoint a unique model which allows the investigator to study, unrestrained, the motor capacities of the only sighted hemisphere.

## OBSERVATION

Liliane S. was left-handed, left-footed, and left-eyed. Her parents and siblings were right-handed. At the age of 14½ she underwent surgery for a hematoma occupying the anterior portion of the corpus callosum. The rostral half of the corpus callosum was sectioned and the hematoma removed. A second and third intervention were performed 3- and 5-weeks later in order to evacuate and treat a left anterior frontal abcess. The results of neurological and neuropsychological examinations undertaken 15 months after surgery have been reported in detail elsewhere (Poncet, Ali Chérif, Choux, Boudouresques, & Lhermitte, 1978). Neurological examination only evidenced the presence of right homonymous hemianopia without sparing of the macula. A C.T. scan showed hypodensities in the left frontal region, left paramedian region, and left medial occipital region. These hypodensities were compatible with the presence of a vascular lesion involving all or almost all of the corpus callosum fibers. Neuropsychological examination showed a total callosal disconnection syndrome characterized by the absence of all information transfer between the right and left occipital, right and left parietal and right and left temporal regions (Poncet et al., 1978). The existence of a right homonymous hemianopia, associated with a syndrome of total callosal disconnection, represents a very adjusted model for the study of motor control exerted by right hemisphere on upper limbs. The left hemisphere was deprived of all visual input from the retino-striate and callosal routes. The right hemisphere was the only sighted hemisphere and it can be argued that this hemisphere performed alone all motor tasks requiring processing of visual information.

The visuo-motor capacities were explored by the following test situations. (1) Designation of colored disks. The patient is shown a color and must subsequently choose the corresponding disk from an array of five colored disks. The required response is, in a first condition, a global movement of the upper limb and in a second condition, a discrete finger movement, the wrist being held still. (2) Imitation of gestures executed with either the entire upper limb or the fingers alone. (3) Filmed observation of finger prepositioning in the grasping of objects of various sizes and shapes. All tasks were performed correctly with the left upper limb; designation with fingers, imitation of gestures with fingers and manual prepositioning were successfully executed. With the right upper limb, only gestures involving proximal muscles (shoulder and elbow) could be executed. Gestures involving wrist or fingers could not be performed. In the designation task with the fingers, there was a tendency for the patient to use the whole hand and she would rarely succeed in moving a single finger. Imitations of gestures with the right wrist or fingers were highly imperfect whereas the same hand performed these movements without error on verbal command. When the patient tried to grasp an object, no prepositioning of the right hand was observed; only at the moment of contact did the hand adapt itself to the object's shape.

Clinical examination of motor performances on tests requiring the processing of visual information confirms the presence of ipsilateral motor control of the upper limb which only acts on the proximal musculature and not on the wrist and the hand. Indeed the right hemisphere, which is the sole recipient of visual input in such tasks, exerts control over the musculature of the whole left upper limb and over the proximal portion only of the right upper limb's musculature. In order to study more systematically the question of the motor control exerted by the right hemisphere on the right upper limb a series of experiments has been conducted.

## METHODS

### Apparatus

The subject was seated, facing a vertical panel which supported a grid-patterned printed circuit. This circuit automatically supplied the rectangular coordinates of the point of the panel first contacted by the finger. A mirror, or a glass, oriented at 45° was fixed between the panel and the subject's head. This procedure was used in order to either prevent or allow the subject to visually guide the movement of her limb towards the targets. The visual targets consisted of four diodes (5 mm) which either lit up directly on the vertical panel or, when the mirror was in place, on a horizontal panel placed at the top of the armature. In the latter case the virtual image of the targets was projected on the vertical panel. A circular metal lever (4 cm dia.) was located under the vertical panel, at a distance of 40 cm from the center of the printed circuit. This constituted the starting point of each trial.

### Procedure

Each trial began with the subject's hand at the starting point, which had the effect of closing an electrical circuit. After an unpredictable delay of either 0.5 or 1.0 sec, one of the stimuli was presented for a duration of 1 sec. After each response the subject moved her hand back to the starting position for the next trial. Five different experimental tasks were completed over two sessions. The overall experiment consisted of 16 blocks of 64 trials.

### Tasks

*1. Visual Reaction Time Paradigm.*    The subject was required to leave the starting point as quickly as possible at the appearance of a visual signal on the panel. The reaction time (RT) was measured as the interval between the stimulus onset and the release of the lever. Four conditions were tested, resulting from the combination of two variables: limb side (left vs. right) and limb part (proximal vs. distal). The subject was indeed required to release the starting point by either lifting up her whole forearm (proximal condition) or lifting up her index finger, without any movement of the forearm (distal condition).

*2. Auditory Reaction Time Paradigm.* In this task the same procedure as described above was used. The only difference was the replacement of the visual signal by a tone (1000 HZ for 0.5 sec.).

*3. Bilateral Visual Reaction Time Paradigm.* With both hands resting on separate levers, upon presentation of a visual signal the subject had to lift simultaneously her right and left index fingers (distal condition) or her right and left forearms (proximal condition). The RTs were separately recorded for each limb.

*4. Pointing Movement.* After an unpredictable delay one of the four visual targets was lit up. The subject was required to remove her hand from the starting lever and to reach the visual target on the panel with the index finger. Instructions emphasized both accuracy and speed of responses. Four situations were investigated, resulting from the combination of two variables: limb (left vs. right) and visual condition (with or without visual feedback). Depending on whether a mirror or a glass was inserted between the subject's eyes and hand, she could or could not visually guide her own movement. Of course in both conditions the target was visible.

Three main dependent variables were analysed in this task. Movement latency (L) was defined as the time interval between target presentation and release of the lever. The movement time (MT) expressed the interval between the beginning of movement and the first contact of the finger with the panel. Spatial accuracy was estimated by calculating pointing error (E) as the distance between target position and the mean coordinates of the pointing distribution.

A supplementary analysis was made of the hand movements. A camera placed to the side of the subject recorded the hand trajectories at a film speed of 80 frames per sec. The displacement curve of the index finger could thus be plotted as a function of time. Using differential calculus, curves of velocity and instantaneous acceleration could subsequently be derived. These curves made it possible to determine the values and latencies of the characteristic parameters of trajectory: peak of initial acceleration, peak of maximal velocity, and first peak of deceleration.

*5. Pointing With a Stylus.* In order to minimize the involvement of distal musculature, the subject was required to point at the visual target with a stylus.

## RESULTS

### 1. Visual Reaction-Time

The data presented in Table 6.1 and Fig. 6.1 show that the RTs obtained with the left and right limbs were not statistically different from each other when the

TABLE 6.1

Reaction Times Collected in Experiments 1, 2, and 3

REACTION TIMES

| LIMB PART | DISTAL | | | DISTAL | |
| LIMB | LEFT | RIGHT | | LEFT | RIGHT |
| --- | --- | --- | --- | --- | --- |
| VISUAL | 367.06 ($\pm$16.92) | 517.93 ($\pm$61.33) | | 330.46 ($\pm$21.78) | 342.82 ($\pm$19.3) |
| | | t=4.65 (*p*<.01) | | | t=.83 (NS) |
| AUDITORY | 322.95 ($\pm$34.98) | 335.93 ($\pm$34.63) | | 339.21 ($\pm$39.16) | 305.90 ($\pm$47.) |
| | | t=.52 (NS) | | | t=1.06 (NS) |
| BILATERAL | 359.16 ($\pm$34.39) | 484.16 ($\pm$47.46) | | 344.03 ($\pm$33.06) | 353.76 ($\pm$37.33) |
| | | t=4.18 (*p*<.01) | | | t=.42 (NS) |

Note. The mean values in each condition are indicated with the confident limits at *p*=.05. The differences between left and right limbs are submitted to students t test.

**REACTION TIME**

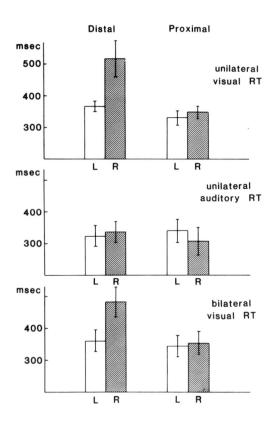

FIG. 6.1.   Mean reaction times (RT) corresponding to the left (L) and right (R) limbs. The two experimental conditions (distal vs proximal movements) are compared in three tasks: unilateral, visual or auditory, RT and bilateral visual RT. Each histogram corresponds to the mean of 64 trials. The averaged values are shown with their confidence limits at $p = 0.05$.

responses were performed by the proximal parts of the limb (movement of the forearm). However, when the distal parts were involved (movement of a single finger), the right hand RTs were found to be 150 msec longer than the left hand RTs, a statistically significant difference.

### 2. Auditory Reaction-Time

When a sound was used as signal, no significant differences in RTs were observed for both limbs and for proximal and distal responses (Table 6.1 and Fig. 6.1).

### 3. Bilateral Reaction-Time

The results presented in Table 6.1 demonstrate a fair synchronization of both arms when the proximal parts were involved. The left limb preceded the right one in 68% of trials by an average time of 9 msec which was not statistically significant. For distal responses, it was found that the left finger preceded the right finger on 91% of trials by an average time of 125 msec, a statistically significant difference.

### 4. Pointing Movement

*Latency.*    Table 6.2 and Fig. 6.2 show that the latency of the pointing response was not affected by the involved limb or the visual conditions. Compared to similar proximal responses of the reaction time paradigm, a slight increase (about 40 msec) of the latencies was observed.

*Speed.*    Table 6.2 and Fig. 6.2 show the average values of movement times (MT), expressing the duration of the pointing responses, in the four experimental situations. In the normal visual condition (visual feedback), a statistically significant increase in MTs appears for the right limb relative to the left limb. The right limb MTs were longer than the left limb MTs by 282 msec. However, the suppression of visual information about the moving limb (no visual feedback) did not cause a similar difference. An overall slowing of the movement execution was observed in this condition.

Cinematographic analysis of movement under visual feedback condition revealed some striking differences between the behavior of the two limbs. First, the occurrence of characteristic peaks (acceleration, deceleration, maximal velocity) was always delayed for the right limb relative to the left limb. Second, examination of the acceleration curves (Fig. 6.3) of the left hand moving to the vicinity of the target shows a regular curve with two well-defined positive and negative peaks. This pattern contrasts with the irregular curve of the right limb, which describes a "discontinuous" movement characterized by successive acceleration-deceleration phases. Third, as shown in Fig. 6.4, the dramatic increase in movement duration for the right limb could result from the lengthy duration of finger positioning, a few centimetres away from the target.

*Accuracy.*    The only factor affecting the terminal accuracy of the pointing response is obviously the visual condition. Suppression of the visual movement cues bring about significant spatial errors (Table 6.2, Fig. 6.2). This effect does not interact with the limb variable. It is worth noting the fair accuracy of both limbs in the visual feedback condition.

### 5. Pointing with a Stylus

When the fingers were set in a grasping posture the parameters of the pointing movement did not differentiate the performances of the two limbs. Table 6.2 shows that the latency, speed and accuracy of the right and left limbs are comparable.

## DISCUSSION

Quantitative studies of motor performances in this patient presenting a callosal disconnection syndrome, associated with a right lateral homonymous hemi-

TABLE 6.2

Latencies, Movement Times, and Errors Observed in Pointing Tasks (Experiments 4 and 5)

POINTING MOVEMENTS

| Visual Conditions | VISUAL FEEDBACK | | NO VISUAL FEEDBACK | |
| --- | --- | --- | --- | --- |
| Limb | Left | Right | Left | Right |
| LATENCY | 381.69 (±22.58) | 367.01 (±18.76) | 368.45 (±16.86) | 346.26 (±20.19) |
| | | t=.98 (NS) | | t=1.65 (NS) |
| MOVEMENT TIME | 367.77 (±10.16) | 649.81 (±30.81) | 529.61 (±27.37) | 537.15 (±29.72) |
| | | t=17.04 ($p < .01$) | | t=.37 (NS) |
| ERROR | 5.91 (±.80) | 6.13 (±.60) | 33.43 (±3.33) | 34.08 (±3.30) |
| | | t=.85 (NS) | | t=.27 (NS) |

POINTING WITH A STYLUS

| Limb | Left | Right | | |
| --- | --- | --- | --- | --- |
| LATENCY | 345.31 (±28.54) | 324.63 (±19.33) | | |
| | | t=1.06 (NS) | | |
| MOVEMENT TIME | 654.74 (±12.39) | 668.84 (±15.78) | | |
| | | t=.98 (NS) | | |
| ERROR | 7.07 (±.70) | 6.25 (±.33) | | |
| | | t=.68 (NS) | | |

Note. The mean values in each condition are given with the confident limits at $p=.05$. The differences between left and right limbs are tested by student's t.

POINTING MOVEMENT

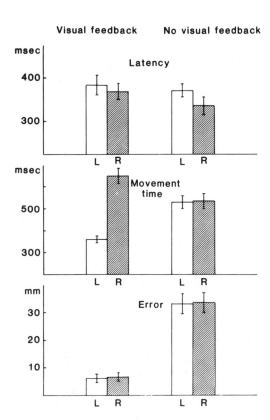

FIG. 6.2. Data obtained in the pointing task. The latencies, movement times and spatial errors for the left (L) and right (R) limbs and compared in two experimental conditions: with the presence of a visual feedback (left part) or without visual feedback (right part). Each histogram corresponds to the average of 64 trials with the confidence limits at $p = 0.05$.

anopia, lead to consider the question of the control exerted by each hemisphere on upper limbs. Our data are particularly revealing with respect to the initiation and execution of either proximal or distal movements according to the involved hemisphere.

## Initiation of Motor Responses

The major finding of the reaction-time tasks consisted in the considerable delay in motor initiation when the patient had to respond to a visual stimulus by a movement of a single finger of the right hand. By contrast, responses involving the proximal parts are triggered as quickly in the right arm as in the left arm. The existence of a right hemianopia, along with previous clinical testing (Poncet et al., 1978), suggests that the right hemisphere only is able to process the visual information, at least to initiate and control a motor command. Therefore, the

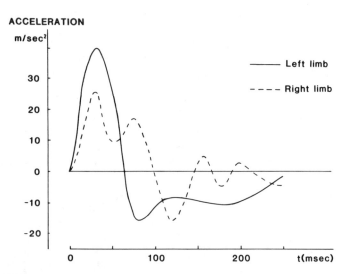

FIG. 6.3.   Kinematic analysis of two hand trajectories obtained with the left (full line) and right limb (dashed line). The curves correspond to the instantaneous accelerations, in the first part of the pointing movement (250 msec).

impairment of the right hand could reflect a defect in the ipsilateral control of distal movements. In all these experiments the control exerted by the right hemisphere on the proximal parts of the ipsilateral limb, as well as on the whole contralateral limb is fairly adequate. It is noteworthy that the use of an auditory input results in a striking improvement of the right hand's reaction time. Indeed in this case, the bilateralization of sensory input induces a control of the right extremities by the left hemisphere, which implies an adapted contralateral command.

These data are consistent with studies (Kuypers, 1964; Lawrence & Kuypers, 1968a, 1968b; Brinkman & Kuypers, 1972, 1973) demonstrating a hemispheric control of the ipsilateral limb restricted to the proximal musculature through the ventro-medial cortico-spinal descending pathways. Reaction time experiments made in split-brain monkeys provided evidence for a slight privilege of the contralateral hemisphere-hand combination over ipsilateral combination (Beaubaton & Requin, 1973). The same type of advantage was observed in human subjects with callosal agenesis (Jeeves, 1969). More recently, Di Stefano et al. (1980) studied the reaction time of normal subjects to visual signals presented in the right or left visual fields. They observed faster responses with the arm ipsilateral to the visual stimulus (contralateral hemisphere-hand control), provided the responses were made unilaterally. This relatively small advantage (2 msec) was absent in bilateral responses involving proximal joints. Analogously, the present study shows that the right-left hand differences were reduced in

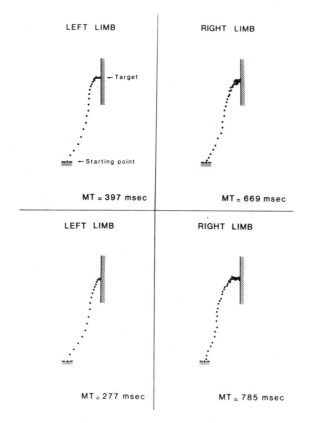

FIG. 6.4.    Trajectories of the pointing hand, from the starting point to the visual target. Two examples for each limb are represented. The total movement duration (MT) is indicated. Each dot corresponds to the position of the hand, obtained from a single cinematographic frame. The time interval between two consecutive dots is 12 msec.

bilateral responses of the distal joints. It must therefore be recognized that the synchronization and the engagement of both hemispheres in organizing motor commands compensates for the impairment of the right hand. A question may be put forward, even for unilateral responses, as to the mechanisms responsible for a possible ipsilateral control of distal parts. In spite of a significant increase in RT, the possibility remains of an initiation of the right hand movements by an hypothetical ipsilateral command. But two interpretations may account for the involvement of the contralateral command, both in agreement with a "cross-cuing" hypothesis as proposed by Gazzaniga (1969, 1970). The first one is a possible role of subcortical nervous structures in the processing of visual information (Trevarthen, 1968). In split-brain subjects, the existence of a bilateral distribution of visual cues through subcortical pathways can explain some control exerted by the "blind" hemisphere (Beaubaton, Paillard, & Grangetto, 1979). In the present case, the left "blind" hemisphere could, through this pathway, be informed about the occurrence of a visual event and trigger, with a substantial delay, a movement in the contralateral hand. The second explanation again involves a cross-cueing mechanism, bringing into play the proprioceptive information. The right "sighted" hemisphere could initiate a muscular contraction in the right proximal parts which, by a subcortical transfer, would inform the left hemisphere about the stimulus occurrence. The possibility therefore exists of a contralateral command in order to initiate movements in the distal segments, while each hemisphere can bilaterally trigger motor activities in proximal body parts. This last point is corroborated by the lack of any right-left difference in the latencies of goal-directed movements in the pointing task (Experiment 4), which mainly involved proximal joints in the response initiation.

## Execution and Control of Ongoing Movements

Once the movement has been programmed and triggered, one has to determine what are the characteristics of the organized response, in terms of velocity and spatial accuracy, and what is the role of the hemispheres in correcting the ongoing trajectory and insuring a precise positioning with respect to the target localization. An analysis of the variables related to the execution of a pointing task shows a significant decrease in velocity (i.e., an increase in MT) when the patient was visually controlling the right limb's movements. Yet, this slow response is performed with perfect accuracy. The main consequence of hemispheric disconnection is therefore a temporal disturbance of the right limb, without a disturbance in spatial capacity. Further, the results obtained in absence of visual feedback indicate a bilateral impairment in both speed and accuracy. Imprecise pointing responses are characteristic of "no visual feedback" conditions. They express the lack of final correction of the movement in order to ensure correct hand placement. The accompanying decrease in velocity in both hands may correspond to a general worsening in motor control. The suppression of visual cues could lead to a search for other sensory cues, resulting in a slowing of execution speed. All in all, these data clearly indicate an impairment in movement kinematics when only the right "sighted" hemisphere is controlling the ipsilateral limb. In their studies on dyspraxia following division of cerebral commissures in man, Gazzaniga et al. (1967) stressed that the worst performances were observed in hemispheric control of the homolateral hand, and particularly of individual finger movements. Similar conclusions were formulated in split-brain studies in monkeys (Brinkman & Kuypers, 1973). Other workers reported visuo-motor deterioration in ipsilateral command, even for movements not involving the distal musculature (Keating, 1973; Beaubaton et al., 1979). Such impairments were therefore attributed to the inefficacy of visual correction of hand position in the vicinity of the target and not exclusively to the lack of control of finger movements. In other words, after commissurotomy, the "target seeing" hemisphere would be able to use positional cues to trigger the program for the ballistic part of an ipsilateral pointing movement, but not to insure the error correcting mechanisms, in the final part of the trajectory. Such a hypothesis appears to be contradictory with the fair accuracy of the right hand, observed in the present experiment. In fact, the apparent contradiction can be resolved by taking into account the possibility of speed-accuracy trade-off. The imprecise ipsilateral pointing, observed in previous studies, seems to be associated with very fast responses for both limbs (Paillard & Beaubaton, 1974). Conversely, in the present experiment, the nature of the task could have emphasized spatial requirement at the expense of speed. The accuracy of the right hand would therefore be related to the supplementary time spent in the execution phase.

Moreover, the analysis of movement kinematics may help to qualify the ipsilateral motor impairment. The discontinuous nature of acceleration patterns and the overall slowing of the right limb is suggestive of attempts to correct the hand's trajectory. Particularly revealing, in this respect, is the long lasting approach phase. When the right limb was used, a considerable amount of the total time expenditure took place in the last five centimeters, near the target. The question therefore arises as to whether the difficulties in the final approach were strictly due to a defective visuo-motor coordination affecting the whole limb or rather by an impaired control of distal segments. The fact that the execution of pointing responses with a stylus held in hand (Experiment 5) brought about identical performances for the two limbs, in terms of duration and accuracy, suggests a specific impairment when distal adjustments are needed.

The overall data are indicative of a possibility by the "sighted" hemisphere to trigger at a proper time, muscular activities in the proximal parts of the ipsilateral limb and to insure a correct goal-oriented response. However, the ipsilateral control of finger movements is poorly executed. The initiation of these movements is longer than with a contralateral hemisphere-hand pairing, and the difficult selection of appropriate finger position impairs the harmonious time-course of the trajectories.

## ACKNOWLEDGMENTS

We wish to thank Jean-René Duhamel who reviewed the translation of the manuscript.

## REFERENCES

Beaubaton, D., & Requin, J. (1973). The time course of preparatory processes in split-brain monkeys performing a variable foreperiod reaction-time task. *Physiology and Behavior, 10,* 725–730.

Beaubaton, D., Paillard, J., Grangetto, A. (1979). Contribution of positional and movement cues to visuomotor reaching in split-brain monkey. In Steele, Russel, Van Hof, & Barlucchi (Eds.), *Structure and function of cerebral commissures* (pp. 371–384). London: Pergamon Press.

Brinkman, J., & Kuypers, H. G. J. M. (1972). Split-brain monkeys: Cerebral control of ipsilateral and contralateral arm, hand and finger movements. *Science, 176,* 536–539.

Brinkman, J., & Kuypers, H. G. J. M. (1973). Cerebral control of contralateral and ipsilateral arm, hand and finger movements in the split-brain rhesus monkey. *Brain, 96,* 653–674.

Di Stefano, M., Morelli, M., Marci, C. A., & Berlucchi, G. (1980). Hemispheric control of unilateral and bilateral movements of proximal and distal parts of the arm as inferred from simple reaction time to lateralized light stimuli in man. *Experimental Brain Research, 38,* 197–204.

Downer, J. L. de C. (1959). Changes in visually guided behavior following mid sagittal division of optic chiasma and corpus callosum in monkeys (Maccaca mulatta). *Brain, 82,* 251–259.

Gazzaniga, M. S. (1969). Cross-cuing mechanisms and ipsilateral eye-hand control in split-brain monkeys. *Experimental Neurology, 23,* 11–17.

Gazzaniga, M. S. (1970). *The bisected brain.* New York: Appleton-Century-Crofts.

Gazzaniga, M. S., Bogen, J. E., & Sperry, R. W. (1967). Dyspraxia following division of the cerebral commissures. *Archives of Neurology, 16,* 606–612.

Geschwind, N. (1975). The apraxias: Neural mechanisms of disorders of learned movement. *American Scientist, 63,* 188–197.

Jeeves, M. A. (1969). A comparison of interhemispheric transmission times in acallosal and normals. *Psychonomic Sciences, 16,* 245–246.

Keating, E. G. (1973). Loss of visual control of the forelimb after interruption of cortical pathway. *Experimental Neurology, 41,* 635–648.

Kuypers, H. G. J. M. (1964). The descending pathways to the spinal cord, their anatomy and function. *Progress in Brain Research, 11,* 178–202.

Lawrence, D. G., & Kuypers, H. G. J. M. (1968a). The functional organization of the motor system in the monkey. I. The Effect of bilateral pyramidal lesions. *Brain, 91,* 1–14.

Lawrence, D. G., & Kuypers, H. G. J. M. (1968b). The functional organization of the motor system in the monkey. II. The effect of lesions of the descending brainstem pathways. *Brain, 91,* 15–36.

Paillard, J., & Beaubaton, D. (1974). Problemes poses par les controles moteurs ipsilateraux après déconnexion hémisphérique chez le singe. In F. Michel & B. Schott (Eds.), *Les syndromes de disconnexion calleuse chez l'homme* (pp. 137–171). Colloque International de Lyon.

Poncet, M., Ali-Chérif, A., Choux, M., Boudouresques, J., & Lhermitte, F. (1978). Etude neuropsychologique d'un syndrome de déconnexion calleuse totale avec hémianopsie latérale homonyme droite. *Revue Neurologique, 134,* 633–653.

Trevarthen, C. (1968). Two mechanisms of vision in primates. *Psychologische Forschung, 31,* 300–337.

# 7 The Eye in the Control of Attention

Michael Mair

## INTRODUCTION

Some years ago, I persuaded two students to talk to each other for half-an-hour while I was recording their moving faces on videotape, and their voices on audiotape. I have been working with these records ever since, at first by means of transcriptions of the movements of their noses and of the fundamental frequency of their voices, latterly by seeking to understand something of the neurological basis of those movements. In focusing on something so restricted—just the product of that half-hour—I would appear to have "caught the lot," to have confronted the entire brain basis of interactive behavior as it was manifested in those fragments. We do not, of course, have a complete story, but must skim, hovercraftlike, over the surface of our subject, dipping down into patches where there is detail known, trying to cover the territory without losing sight of the two faces on the screen, flashing their eyes in their interactive dance. They were caught forever just at the advancing edge of time, leaving behind a story, a text which they had made together, controlling how it turned out by movements of voice, face, head, and eye; making the future into the past via the present, albeit the "specious present" of William James's description. Like two projectors, their brains through their eyes seemed to stab into time, putting form on the world just ahead, negotiating that form with their movements; leaving it organized behind them, irretrievably, as their shared text.

Do eyes project vision onto the world? Greek theorists believed just that— that something streamed out from the eye (Blakemore, 1977, p. 65). Although we no longer accept this, we still have no theory to explain the generation of visual experience. We can say, as might Trevarthen, that we see because we look

123

and that the movements of the eyes are a manifestation of intention. He might say of my interactors that what they were doing should be understood in terms of shared intentionality. The microanalysis of interaction demonstrates the extraordinary detail and precision of the interlocking of motor output among interacting beings. The overall thesis of this paper is that these timings are so fast and so coordinated that the conjoined brains which turn them out are actually modifying each others' output as it is produced. I shall seek to demonstrate that the synchronies that William Condon (Condon & Ogston, 1967) and others have observed do in fact make sense neurologically, and I do this primarily by describing the visual system and its timings. I finish with a speculation about the nature of the faculty of "projection" or "intention," which mobilizes the biological system.

## THE EYE

I will spare the reader the actual dimensions of the eyeball—everybody being aware that we have two of them, each roughly spherical, with a lens system, a sensory surface called the retina, and a nerve connecting it to the brain. The lens system delivers a real, inverted image of the viewed scene to the retina, and this is worth stressing because some authors (Gibson, 1979, p. 61) occasionally seem to suggest that a retinal image is somehow not necessary to sight. It is true that *what we see* has only a very indirect relationship to the image, but quite a lot is in fact known at least about the first stages in processing, and it starts with the image. Leonardo was the first to get direct evidence of the reality of this (See Fig. 7.1). The illustration shows how he saw the image by peeling off layers from the back of an ox eye. Blakemore whimsically suggests that it may have been the discrepancy between this upside-down, distorted patch and the experience of sight which led him to doubt! Subsequent knowledge would surely have led him to despair—the retinal image is almost certainly the last representation of the world in the visual system that is at all "imagelike."

Each retina has an area of about 10,000 square degrees, and has a complex structure. Embryologically, the retinae are the pushed in tips of brain stalks (see Fig. 7.2), and this unique origin for a sensory surface has a number of sequelae, one being that in its layers processing of the image goes on, that is done in the spinal cord or brain stem for other senses, such as touch, hearing, and taste. The receptor units (rods and cones) are particularly fine grained at a patch of retina corresponding to the "line of sight," the fovea (see Fig. 7.3), where they are also limited to one type (cones). Note the geometricality of the array, and this principle of architectural order is maintained throughout, although by the time we get to the association areas in the brain, we have little idea of what the order is doing for function.

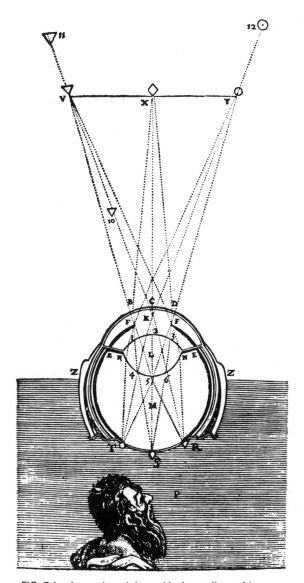

FIG. 7.1.  Leonardo and the upside down, distorted image.

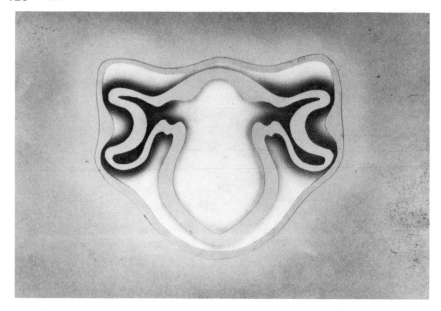

FIG. 7.2. "The Retinae are the pushed in tips of brain stalks". Diagramatic representation (Stylised transverse section)

Figure 7.4 shows some dimensions of this crucial patch of the back of the eye which sees detail. Most of the fibres in the optic nerve serve this patch, and the primary sensory area in the brain also is disproportionately committed to it, a phenomenon known as "cortical magnification." But in fact, about 70% of the cells in the retina make horizontal connections, and the similarity of this set up to the *grain* of photographic emulsion ends at the outer receptor layer. In common with other senses, the unit of sensation is a "center/surround" receptive field, mediated by these horizontal connections. It is the innermost layer of the retina, the ganglion cells, whose processes go to the brain, and these are of many types, with many different *receptor field* characteristics. What the brain gets is a very highly coded signal. Before we leave the retina, it will be instructive to look inside a receptor unit (see Fig. 7.5) where again we see a very geometrical arrangement of membranous sacs. It is said that a single quantum of light can cause a response in a photoreceptor, because of an amplifier mechanism afforded by this internal chemical anatomy, and that a mere half-dozen quanta distributed over a few square millimetres can reliably produce sensation.

## THE CORTEX

Above the retinae, there is a complicated exchange of fibres from the two eyes and the result is that the visual world is neatly divided by a vertical line down the

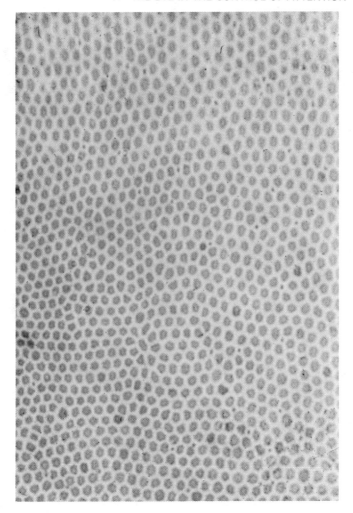

FIG. 7.3.   Foveal cones, cross section.

middle so that the inputs from the left-hand halves of both retinae go to the left hemisphere, and from the right-hand halves to the right hemisphere. In describing the visual system, one must always remember the further inversion produced by the optics of the eye, so it is the right half of the visual scene which goes to the left hemisphere, and vice versa.

From this crossover (the chiasm), the optic tracts, as the nerves are then known, continue to the lateral geniculate nuclei of the thalamus, but a small side branch has been given off to noncortical structures in the roof of the mid-brain, the superior colliculi, which are mentioned later. In the geniculates we encounter

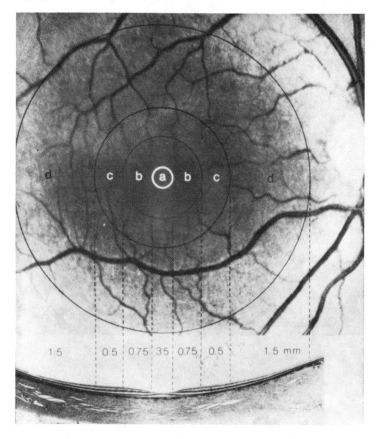

FIG. 7.4.   Macula dimensions (a) Foveola .35 mm (b) Fovea 1.85mm (c) Macula 2.85 mm (The margins of these areas are arbitrarily demarcated.)

a geometrical array, and a systematic interleaving of the contributions from the two eyes. And in the visual cortex as well, we have more geometric patterns in the extraordinary system discovered by Hubel and Wiesel (1979). Whereas up until now the *center surround* principle has been maintained in the way single cells are excited, in the cortex the incoming information is rearranged so that most of its cells respond not to spots of light but to specifically orientated line segments. It appears that the entire cortex, including this primary visual cortex, is subdivided functionally by fine vertical partitions into patches about one millimeter apart (Mountcastle, 1979), and that a multilayered structure is also present throughout. For most of these systems, little is known of their anatomical connections or functions in a precise way, but Hubel and Wiesel have shown that in the visual cortex the columnar arrangement analyses orientation systematically and also alternates a predominance of control between the eyes (Hubel & Wiesel,

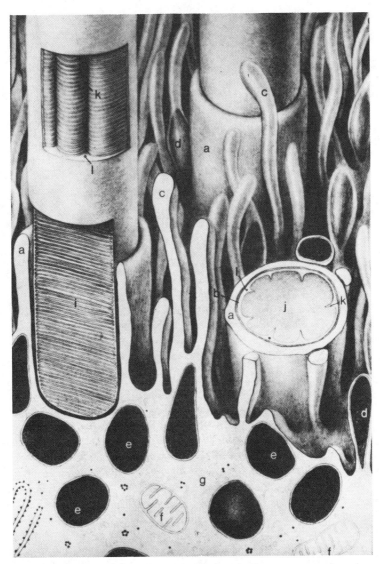

FIG. 7.5.   Single retinal receptors—an artist's impression. (The labeled structures are cellular organelles 'k' indicates the stacks of membranous sacks.)

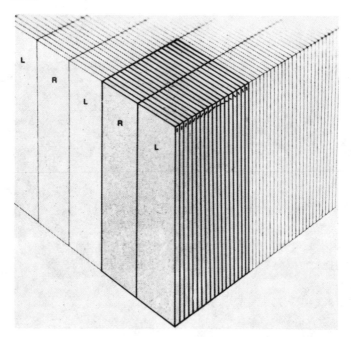

FIG. 7.6.   Schematic diagram from Hubel and Wiesel (1979) of eye dominance columns, showing change in preferred orientation of stimuli with depth in the column. (The alternating 'R' and 'L' strips represent eye dominance columns).

1979). Figures 7.6 and 7.7 are two of their schematic diagrams of these columns, and Fig. 7.8 shows how they imagine that a simple line stimulus to one eye excites the resultant highly ordered matrix.

Hubel and Wiesel talk of their columns being like *machines,* each analyzing the pattern that falls on its patch of retina. "Why," they ask, "should evolution go to the trouble of designing such an elaborate architecture?" They speculate that it may deal with the problem of portraying more than two dimensions on a two-dimensional surface. I return to this *dimension problem* again at the end of the chapter, when I speculate on what may be involved in generating and decoding four-dimensional movement shapes, such as we have in gestures. We must note, however, that beyond their meticulous work there is no clear picture as yet emerging about what happens next in visual processing. Even in the visual cortex, we have the claims of many authors that it is not simple line orientation *features* that are being isolated out, but that instead the retina/cortex system is a frequency analyzer performing a Fourier analysis of the visual scene (Campbell & Robson, 1968). There is some evidence that it is spatial frequencies at particular orientations that the single cells are responding to. The hypothesis has its most daring exponent in Karl Pribram, and he supposes that the visual system is making holograms, albeit *multiplex* holograms. It is difficult to comment on the

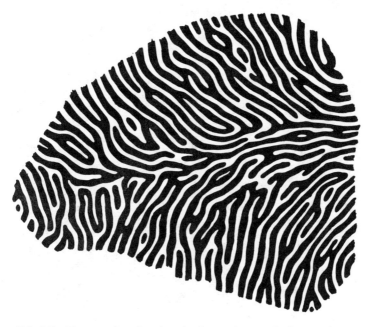

FIG. 7.7.    The patterning of monkey visual cortex into eye dominance columns, those dominated by one eye being black, the other eye white. (This is also a schematic representation but at a larger scale and shows the interleaving patterns on a monkey visual cortex, stained to differentiate the alternating eye dominance.)

appropriateness or otherwise of these hypotheses without considerable mathematical knowledge, but some sort of mathematical transformation of the visual image does seem likely, and it is true that the basic *building block* of perception does seem to be the center-surround field. A hologram hypothesis is superficially appealing as we confront some aspects of higher visual processing. Particularly, it is clear that the concept of *receptor field* loses out to a looser concept of *image analysis* in some of the association areas. Single cells in, for example, the supero-temporal cortex, appear to respond when the stimulus is anywhere in an area including the foveal region of both retinae! We seem to be getting such diverse reports of the repertoire of single cells that there is almost, to pun mercilessly, a *cell for all reasons*. Nobody has tried it with a grandmother's face yet, but particular faces, even particular configurations on individual faces, have been reported as giving unique responses (Perratt, Smith, Milner, Jeeves, & Rogers, 1982). Binocular cells have been found which fire only when something is coming straight at the observer, not if it will pass him by. There is a great multiplication of visual areas, such as Zeki's (1977) color areas, areas implicated in producing size constancy, an area in the posterior parietal cortex linking vision and touch, some cells which fire according to perceived color (rather than absolute wavelength), etc.

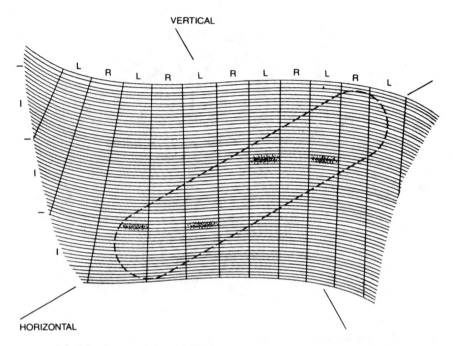

VERTICAL

HORIZONTAL

FIG. 7.8.   Descartes' despair! What a line might "look" like in terms of the topography of stimulation it elicits in the cortex. (A line of a particular orientation is presented to one eye, and excites only those cells sensitive to its orientation.)

So, our brief review of this aspect of the visual system has become anecdotal. How does all this relate to *Attention,* which we think of as regulating sensory input? Before leaving the cortex to consider something of the role that subcortical structures may play in *attention,* we must consider two well-documented phenomena which are clearly related to this. First are the syndromes of *Inattention,* and second, the phenomenon of *Sensory suppression.*

## INATTENTION AND SUPPRESSION

It is one thing not to see because of damage to the eye or to the visual cortex, but another to deny it, and to continue to behave as if sighted. Critchley quotes (1979) what must be the first report of this, from the Roman author Seneca writing of his wife's old nursemaid. "The silly old woman doesn't even know she is blind. She keeps asking the house keeper to change her living quarters, saying her apartments are too dark."

We saw how a *topographical* concept had gone over to an *image analysis* concept beyond the primary sensory cortex, and it is damage to these higher association areas which typically gives the *inattention* or *neglect* syndrome, particularly the parietal cortex. When the condition affects body sensation, the opposite side of the body is just lost to its owner's consciousness, hanging loosely, and such patients may even insist that it belongs to someone else. When the visual field is affected, we appear to have a kind of *black hole* in sight. The defect may be complete or bilateral, or so subtle as to be only revealed by rigorous testing. In such a test, a patient who may successfully count the number of fingers that an examiner is holding up on the affected side may have this ability obliterated by the simultaneous presentation of fingers to count on the unaffected side—an impairment of attention with preservation of *sight*. Such people may protect their disability with circuitous arguments, providing the speech areas in the left cortex are intact. A similar imperative to *make sense of experience* has been noted in split brain experiments, where the right brain has not the competence to say what it knows, and so the left brain makes something up.

Sometimes the subject will *internally complete* a missing portion of the visual field. That we can all do this is easily demonstrated by a simple and well-known experiment. If we roll up a piece of paper into a tube and look through it with one eye at, say, the wall, and then hold a hand in front of the other eye without obscuring the *tunnel* view of wall seen by the first eye, we will see *through* the hand. The brain simply turns off the area of retina obscured by the hand, and completes the hole with the vision of the wall seen by the other eye. This is *suppression* and also completion.

Both *inattention* and *suppression* are about the interaction of attentional mechanisms with raw sense data. In both cases, the raw sense data are there at the retinal level, but lost; in the first case by a damage to association areas, in the second by a turn off at some as yet unidentified site. It is instructive to discuss a condition in which the latter almost universally occurs—squint—for the light it throws on the nature of visual attention.

Figure 7.9 is a diagram of eyes out of alignment, and it shows the two possible end results of this mishap. The first, the superimposition of two images, is called *confusion*. Clinician Fells (1979) points out that reports of this are very rare indeed. The reason for this is that there is suppression of the crucial *line of sight* patch of retina. This leaves perception of the line of sight image of the fixing eye doubled by a fainter and blurred image whose position is very informative to the clinician about the nature of the neuromuscular defect which has given the squint. But usually, and especially in the juvenile onset squinter, the hole in sight (*scotoma*) of the deviating eye also includes the patch of retina which receives the double image, and then the subject sees a unitary visual world once more (Pratt-Johnson & MacDonald, 1976).

The explanation usually given for these effects is teleological—and tautological as well. Suppression occurs to get rid of confusion and diplopia. But what would be wrong with superimposed images, or doubled images? We have learned something about visual attention—not only is it singular, but also it

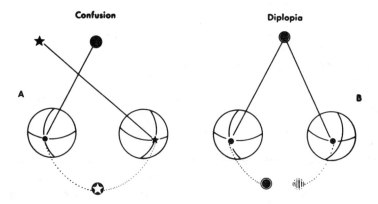

FIG. 7.9.   Confusion and Diplopia. In 'A', both foveas (which are represented by the intersection of the curved lines at the back of the schematic spheres) are turned on. Since the eyes are squinting (ie. mis-aligned) dissimilar images are superimposed.

In 'B', the fovea of one eye is "turned off" (suppression). Consequently the object in the line of regard of the squinting eye is not perceived, and instead a doubled and displaced image of the object in the line of regard of the nonsquinting eye is seen.

somehow regulates its own input. An electrophysiological correlate of this has been elegantly provided by Arden (1974), who has shown that the electrical response of the cortex during suppression is indeed depressed. Among other electrophysiological demonstrations that the *turn off* involves the cortical cells, is one in which an after-image effect was induced at some level (beyond the retina) in a suppressing eye, and its effects were transferred to the fixing eye (Blake & Lehmkuhle, 1976).

Suppression and Inattention are both *cortical* in that the cortex is demonstrated to participate in these phenomena but this participation does not *locate* the attentional process here. This point is emphasized at the conclusion of a recent paper on visual attention (Wurtz, Goldberg, & Robinson, 1982) who admit that an enhancement of response of cells in the posterior parietal cortex with attention '' . . . . . may accompany visual attention, just as an eye movement may, but not be part of the neural mechanism whose product is attention.'' These authors, in an ingenious series of experiments recording from single cells in the brains of conscious monkeys attending to spots of light, managed to differentiate between cells which had enhanced responses with visual attention to stimuli in the part of the visual field corresponding to their receptive field both when that attention was associated with eye movement, and when it was not. We have already described the fovea and the cortical magnification of the area dedicated to it, and we shortly discuss the movement of the eyes which brings the image of an attended object onto it. But nevertheless, *line of sight* and visual attention, although very often identical, are not necessarily so, as the expression *through the corner of the eye* testifies. It was only some cells in the posterior parietal cortex which showed enhanced response with visually attended stimuli and which did not, by their ingenious method, also evoke eye movement.

So now Suppression, Inattention, and Attention itself are all demonstrated to have a cortical correlate, but it is not the cortex at all which is usually considered in discussion of neural bases of attention. Subcortical structures are clearly implicated.

## SUBCORTICAL STRUCTURES

Nauta and Feirtag (1979) identify in the brain four structures whose input derives in one way or another from all (or most) of the neocortical expanse. These are the Limbic System, the Striatum, the Pons (and through it the cerebellum) and the Superior Colliculus. It is interesting to note that of these four, three infracortical structures mentioned above are also implicated in the control of eye movement.

The Lymbic system comprises the Hippocampus and the Amygdala, and both output to the hypothalamus, and perhaps to Septal nuclei. The hippocampus is found at the free edge of the cortex where that structure is rolled in on itself. Nauta describes it as the "end station of the neocortical march," the destination for sequential projections that span the neocortical sheet. The Amygdala has close connections with temporal and frontal cortex, and also directly from the olfactory cortex. Nauta conceives of the need for successive cortical stages of visual, auditory, and somaesthetic sensation as being, because *object constancy* is necessarily an abstraction, *three dimensional,* whereas smell is just intensity gradients. We saw, before, for vision that the association cortices were doing sophisticated image analyses. Somehow, they *get into* attention, here with the Amygdyla and Hippocampus. One should remember also the results of damage to these structures. The behavioral disturbances they produce are complex, severe, and intractable.

The Striatum receives projections directly from all parts of the brain, in a topographical fashion. Parts of its output, which is crucial for the initiation and patterning of motor programmes, curls back on itself to enter the ventro-medial nucleus of the thalamus.

The pons, comprising fibre tracts linking the cerebellar hemispheres and embedded reticular nuclei receives inputs from all parts of the neocortex and from there projects to the cerebellum. The reticular cells situated there and elsewhere in the brainstem and spinal cord are described by Nauta as "sitting with their dendrites—their cellular hands—spread across several millimeters, hoping it seems to catch any sort of message." We can note that in spite of this diffuse arrangement, usually identified with *arousal,* very important eye movement control centres are here.

Finally, the Superior Colliculus receives input from many cortical areas, and from the retina itself by a side branching of the optic tracts. It is implicated also in the control of eye movement. The remarkable accuracy in localizing visual targets achieved by some cortically blind people (blindsight) may have its anatomic locus here.

An economical model of the attentional process is provided by Pribram (1975). He identifies three classes of attentional systems, "arousal," "activation," and "effort," with references to the orienting reaction. He suggests that the fronto-amygdaloid system is concerned with *registering* a novel stimulus, and damage leads to inappropriate orienting. The Striatal system tells you what you latched on to and damage to it causes the *neglect*. The *effort* component he identifies with the Hippocampus. Figure 7.10 is a diagrammatic representation of these structures in situ. We noted before the homogeneous *modular* structure of the cortex, and can contrast this to the highly differentiated nature of the subcortical structures (although some, like the hypothalamus, also have a very homogeneous architecture). We know also that they are phylogenetically older. All this is compatible with the speculation that the core-brain structures are running the outfit, and that it is the cortex that is the data bank and computational matrix. Against this, it is often said that the human is sightless and senseless without the cortex, but this observation does not refute the other hypothesis and indeed would be the expected result in such a highly integrated system.

## EYE MOVEMENTS

From Retina, to Cortex, to Core in search of sight; and we have still yet not seen anything. For that, we have to look at it. There is one decision that we make about 100,000 times each day and that is the decision as to where to look next. The subject of the control of eye movements has an enormous literature, and there is one class of these movements, the *saccades,* which is under voluntary control, and thus can be considered to be informed by our Intentions. Intention can be economically defined as the process of organizing motor output, but this definition is not satisfactory in that it would include those compensatory movements, sometimes classed as reflexes, which simply maintain a status quo. In fact, there are five identifiable systems of eye movement control, and even the saccades can be argued to be largely a matter of reflexes. The literature itself shows a curious *neglect* phenomenon in regard to the discussion of attention. For example, Davson (1980), in his textbook on the physiology of the eye, says of the *fixation reflex* merely that if "the eyes are stimulated by a bright light in the peripheral field, Attention is aroused so that the eyes move and the images of the object approach the foveae . . . " (p. 428). This *attention* that can move the eye does not need to do so however.

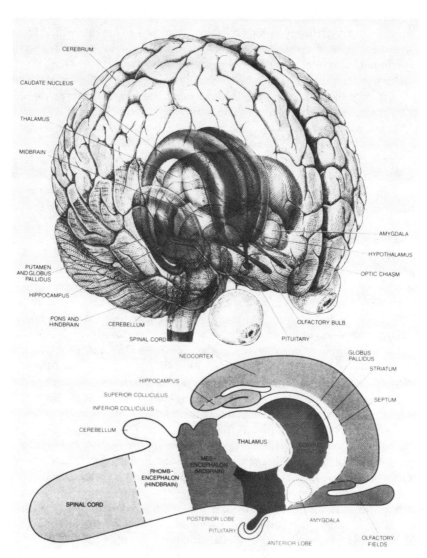

FIG. 7.10.   Schematic representation of core brain structures (from Nauta, *Scientific American*, Vol. 241 No. 3) Note the embedded core brain structures within the cortical mantle (cf. Fig. 7.12)

It remains a moot point whether, in the fixation reflex, it is really *attention* that is caught by something in the peripheral field, or whether attention moves the eye to capture something there. I chose the title of this chapter because of just such an ambiguity. However, the saccadic system is the only one which brings new objects to bear upon the fovea, unless they themselves stray across its projection. This system moves the eyes very rapidly about 200–700 degrees of visual angle per second, a rate which, if maintained, would at fastest make our eyes spin round in a complete circle about twice each second. Much has been written about the *ballistic* nature of these movements, and complex engineering models made of them. For a time, their resistance to modification once initiated led to a theory of *quantal sampling* which implied that the visual sensorium might only take in information in little chunks, and the timing of these coincided with the eye movements. We do know, however, that the saccadic movements are controlled from the frontal cortex, and that the fibres then descend to the para-median reticular formation, and the final common path of the occulo-motor nuclei. There is a reaction time of about 200 msec, before a saccade is made. These little quick movements are surely the ones that make eyes twinkle.

Quite separate from this and almost in competition with it is the Smooth Pursuit system, which appears to be controlled from the posterior cortex. Appearing only 6 weeks after birth, this system is very sensitive to the effects of drugs such as alcohol. It is much slower than the saccadic system, only managing to cover 45° of visual angle in one second—perhaps just good enough for watching tennis—and it is not *ballistic,* that is, the adjustments for the speed of the followed object are continuously graded. Rashbass (1971, p. 445) has compared the interaction of the saccadic and following systems as being like two drivers of the same car, one trying to keep the speedometer pointing at thirty m.p.h., the other trying to keep alongside another car also going at 30 m.p.h. There are situations when the position man must override the other, but ultimately they must work together.

The third system, the vergence system, is poorly understood, but similar to the above. This is the one that brings the eyes out of alignment to converge on something close. It is associated with the pupil aperture becoming smaller and the eye focusing in the *near triad.* The simple reflex of focus is a common synonym for attention, but to have something come into view in a way which makes detailed analysis possible entrains all the eye movement systems, and so perhaps this is a misplaced semantic identity.

The fourth system, the vestibul/ocular reflex, is just that, a reflex of great speed—about four msec latency as opposed to the 200 msecs of a saccade, and its neuronal links are confined to the brainstem. It is responsible for stabilizing the eye relative to inertial space and by means of it visual fixation upon the stationary world is automatically established during head rotation. There is another separate reflex system making eye position compensate for longer term postural changes. In fact, this most primitive of eye control systems is not at all irrelevant to students of interaction. They should note that this system adjusts eye position much faster than conventional frame by frame analysis can detect. When the head moves around in the fast and precise way that it does as people talk, much of the *expressive* effect of the eyes is achieved by this means. People with disorder of this system are often advised to wear specially squashy shoes to stop the world jumping about as they walk. It should also be noted that this system connects by a fiber tract in the brainstem and spinal cord—the medial longitudinal fasciculus—to muscles of neck and trunk so that they too contribute to the maintenance of visual stability.

The fifth system, which produces oculo-kinetic nystagmus, is the one which makes the eyes flick when someone is looking out of a train window at the outside environment. Many here will testify to a most interesting corollary effect which occurs when one is, in fact, stationary, and the *environment,* e.g., another train, is slowly moving. The overwhelming effect is of personal movement. It is thought that this system is mediated by the parietal association areas where there may be a kind of continuous *updating* of the personal context going on.

Finally, one should mention that superimposed on all these five systems is a continuous fine vibration of the eyes which keeps the otherwise stabilized image in slight movement against the detail of the actual retinal receptors. Without this, there is a fade out of the image, known as the *Troxler* phenomenon.

So we have five movement systems, one concerned with bringing objects onto the fovea, and the rest with keeping it there. The system appears dedicated to achieving *stability of the visual image,* and there are other mechanisms too which promote this. There is the *saccadic suppression* which turns off perception while a fast eye movement is in flight, and there is the supposed *corollary discharge* which is an entirely hypothetical feedback to the brain from the nerves governing eye movement, to tell it that nothing really moved after all. It is necessary to believe in this because if the eyes are moved artificially, the world does in fact seem to move. The source of it has never been discovered. The world we see, unless malfunctioning, has a stability independent of our own movements.

Before leaving eye movements, it is instructive to view some pictures of scan paths made by the eyes when viewing a scene, for example a picture. Figure 7.11 is taken from Yarbus (1976), who was able to reproject the targeting of eye movements back onto the scene surveyed using a cumbersome apparatus of suction caps applied to the eye. The study of scan paths too has an enormous literature, and modern techniques are a lot less invasive than that employed by Yarbus. Note that the dance of the eyes more or less outlines the object. In fact, the eye movement strategy employed varied according to the search task that the experimenter set the subject. In the saccadic system, therefore, intention modifies the trajectory of the glances; but there is no invariant pattern of scan which is followed for particular search tasks. There are statistical probabilities which can to some extent be generalized across subjects, yet each trajectory of glance is itself precisely programed. The dilemma is similar to that in the analysis of

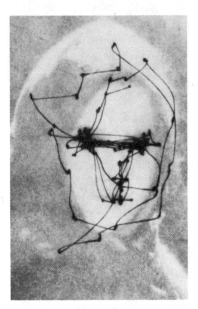

FIG. 7.11. From Yarbus, 1976. Scan Paths.

speech. One can enunciate certain rules which speech is likely to conform to, yet can never predict the precise form an utterance will take, or even if there will be an utterance. The microanalysis of interaction does demonstrate, however, that when speech and eye movement occur together, they are so precisely coordinated as to make it likely that they share a *timer.*

## EVOKED POTENTIAL STUDIES

The precisely timed phenomena of eye movements tell us something of the timings of cortical processes. There is another technique of investigation of attentional processes which purports to estimate them directly. This is the *Evoked Response,* or *Event-Related Potential.* There is an immense amount of work done on this (cf. Picton 1978, for a review). Effects studied included alterations in the *Contingent Negative Variation,* a potential change which precedes an action, changes in the "N 100" component, and changes in the "P 300" component. A word on Method is in order. Electrical recordings are taken from the scalp. The "P" and "N" refer to positive or negative respectively, and the numbers coming up after them refer to the latency in msec of the response after the stimulus. The stimulus in all these experiments has to be a very standard and simple one such as the detection of an unexpected configuration in an auditory or visual series which can be repeated. The repetition is necessary because of the technique itself which relies upon *response averaging,* the accumulation of a large number of responses to cancel out noise. The noise is present because of the remoteness of the signal from the recording electrode, and because so much else is going on in the head besides the response to the stimulus under investigation. Whereas before we could at least base our discussion on the neuro-anatomic and physiological substrata, this connection is less secure with event-related potentials, and so one is engaged in "black box" types of model building.

In auditory experiments, an "N 100" component has been identified which is thought to go with the activation of short-term memory processes relevant to the analysis of attended incoming information. The refractory period is about ten seconds. It has been suggested that this long refractory period might be homologous with the duration of the *conscious present.*

The most frequently studied of these waves, however, is the "P 300", a positivity occurring at 300 msec after the stimulus. Such a wave is said to be related to the subjective expectancy of the response, a kind of *information content* in the stimulus.

Another study found a large "P 300" with syntactic closure in utterances, a kind of resolution of temporal uncertainty (Picton, 1978, p. 455). It would seem that the kind of event that evokes large P 300s is an *ah-ha* experience, or as Picton et al. more densely put it, "the late positive component, being in some way associated with unequivocal task relevant information to its response in the context of the possible responses to that information.'' It is tempting to equate this timing with the movement of consciousness itself. Reaction time is also of this order (Donchin, Ritter, McCallum, & Cheyne, 1978). Certainly, we know from the existence of reaction time that quite complex situations can be understood and dealt with appropriately as fast as this. And we have seen from the timing of the saccade that this also is how long eyes take to twinkle. The evoked response studies fit very comfortably with timings of cerebral processes from these other sources.

## SOME TIMINGS

In an earlier paper (Mair, 1981) I caricatured the brain in a simple three dimensional line diagram which forms a simple conceptual summary of one interpretation of our knowledge. In it, we see three sets of paired plates *boxing in* a hooked central structure, and these represented the cortex and the core brain respectively. I imagined a cycle of activity in this device, one part of the loop being in the core brain, and its closure being action on the world, the results of which become incorporated and then transformed in the next action, and so on (see Fig. 7.12).

The model is designed to *generate text*, which is seen as an ordered concatenation of these cycles, each of which delivers a temporally stable *state of play*. This essay has given more detail of what goes on during such a cycle for vision, and we continue the speculative approach now by listing some of the timings which may be involved.

| Function | Time Taken |
|---|---|
| Nerve conduction, e.g., simple reflexes such as the vestibulo-ocular | msec |
| Fastest discriminatable visual impression Syllables, or phoneme clusters | 150 msec |
| Saccadic Eye Movements Reaction time Halliday's Tone Groups Late Positive Component (p300) | 200–300 msec |
| Short-term memory span Conscious present Text Episode | 10 sec |

I list the visual, auditory, and electrical phenomena in clusters together. Considered as separate phenomena they do appear to cluster in this way, and

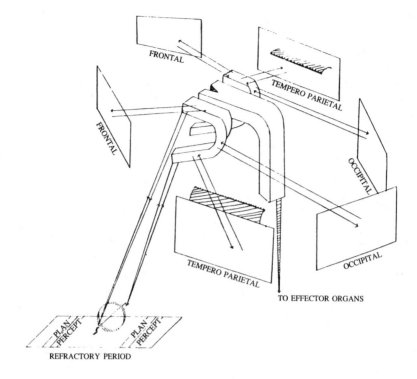

FRONTAL

TEMPERO PARIETAL

FRONTAL

OCCIPITAL

TEMPERO PARIETAL

OCCIPITAL

TO EFFECTOR ORGANS

PLAN
PERCEPT

PLAN
PERCEPT

REFRACTORY PERIOD

FIG. 7.12.   A Caricature of the Brain (a model of the text generator). Highly simplified schematic view of one possible interpretation of the cerebral realities.

microanalysis of videotape of spontaneous interaction also demonstrates *co-patterning* (Kendon, 1973). Kendon suggests perhaps a separate origin for the kinaesthetic/visual and auditory modes, but at least at the level of output they appear to share a *final common pathway*.

## CONCLUSION

In this final section, I would like to *bring it all together* as the brain itself must in so far as the brain product *is* coherent text. As Paul Bouissac once suggested, it could be that the workings of the mind are to some extent anarchic and do not make sense very well. In struggling to achieve a comprehensible model of the process of generating text we are inevitably engaged in the very process we seek to study and will have a very definite bias towards order and simplicity. We might thus be imposing a value judgment on our model, trying to make one which works well in producing something which is only one aspect of the activity of the generator—viz. the production of well-ordered, comprehensible text. Therein lies a joke. However, let us return to the project outlined at the beginning of this chapter. Can this model address the specter of the process of interaction revealed by the prolonged study of objective records of a half-hour-long conversation between two people? In what sense can it be said to *account for it?*

The digression into the physiology of vision shows something of the sort of operations the brain is completing for sight, and the time they take. The existence of synchronies in interaction, both in the sense of actually synchronously timed events and interweavings of timings (as if two beings shared a common timer) become comprehensible if the preconscious and conscious processes in those two beings are in fact intermeshed. The paradigm for this is that of two people working together in a visual scene, transforming it by their joint action. As they intersect with the timings in this scene, for example in catching an animal on the move, they are inevitably taking their timings from a common external source, and in so far as they are effective in working together, will continue to work in synchrony. By outlining a model for the text generator which is roughly in accord with its structure and functioning in the temporal aspect, one can follow into the brain how successful coordinated activity might be working.

For face-to-face interaction which involves speech, one might see a continuation of this process into the human virtual world which is dependent on the sign system of language. In this theory, the trajectories of vocal output are the manifestation of the interweaving cerebral processes as well as part of the means, and the shapes of them form the record of how the emerging outcomes were controlled (Mair, 1978, pp. 24, 34), in the same way that analysis of movement patterns in, say, physical combat, shows them to be the means and the record of the outcome.

The model of cyclical activity in the brain which becomes coordinated when working on a common scene which is either visual or virtual can follow the process, and in this sense render the brain *transparent*. There are many opaque areas in the model, but in principle it works, in terms of structure and timings, and is in accord with some of the anatomical and physiological realities. But it does not account for the actual form or content of any section of text, and I think that part of the reason for this might be that the model is four-dimensional, whereas an adequate model might need to employ five or more dimensions.

We saw that the three-dimensionality of the visual and somaesthetic world was seen as a problem for the brain which has its primary sensory surfaces as one-dimensional (hearing and smell) and two-dimensional (touch and vision). Nauta, and Hubel and Wiesel suggested that the complexity of cortical processing might in part be attributed to this difficulty of representing three dimensions on two-dimensional surfaces. We know also that the direct perception of depth in vision requires the subterfuge of disparate images from two eyes and it is at present unknown how three-dimensional perceptions are achieved from this. A movement shape is however four-dimensional, and it is these four-dimensional shapes which form the entities that the brain must work on in interpreting actions and gestures. We appear to be up against a limit of subjective comprehensibility in studying four-dimensional shapes. It appears that we can deal in them, and must do, when engendering four-dimensional text, but we cannot *stand aside* from them and manipulate them *at the same time*. We cannot even represent them, but must put ourselves through a chunk of experience in order to perceive them at all. This does not mean that five-or "n"-dimensional models cannot be constructed, but it might mean that a four-dimensional model of the process of text generation has no predictive value. Perhaps the Greeks were right, and brains do, in fact, project out through the eye.

## REFERENCES

Arden, G. B., Barnard, W. M., Mushin, A. S. (1974). Visual evoked responses in Amblyopia. *British Journal of Opthalmology, 58,* 190.

Blake, R., & Lehmkuhle, S. W. (1976). On the site of strabismic suppression. *Investigative Ophthalmology, 15,* 660.

Blakemore, C. (1977). *Mechanics of the mind* (p. 65). New York: Cambridge University Press.

Campbell, F. W. & Robson, J. G. (1968). Application of Fourier analysis to the visibility of gratings. *Journal of Physiology, 197* 551–566.

Condon, W. S., & Ogston, W. D. (1967). A segmentation of behaviour. *Journal of Psychiatric Research, 5,* 221–235.

Critchley, M. (1979). Modes of reaction to central blindness. In *The divine banquet of the brain* (p. 157). New York: Raven Press.

Davson, H. (1980). *Physiology of the eye.* London: Churchill Livingstone. Pp. 428.

Donchin, E. Ritter, W., McCallum, W. Cheyne (1978). Cognitive psychophysiology. In Callaway et al. (Eds.), *Event related brain potentials in man.* New York: Academic Press.

Fells, P. (1979). Confusion, diplopia and suppression. *Transactions of Ophthalmological Society of the U.K., 99,* 386–390.

Gibson, J. J. (1979). *The ecological approach to vision.* Boston: Houghton Mifflin.

Hubel, D. H., & Wiesel, T. N. (1979, Sept.). Brain mechanisms of vision. *Scientific American, 241,* No. 3.

Kendon, A. (1973). Studies in dyadic communication. In M. Van Cranach & I. Vine (Eds.), *Social communication and movement.* European Monographs in Psychology series.

Mair, M. W. (1978). *Steps towards principles of text regulation.* Toronto Semiotic Circle, Victoria University, Toronto. *2, 24, 34.*

Mair, M. W. (1981). A model of the text generator. In P. Perron (Ed.), *The neurological basis of signs in communication processes.* Toronto Semiotic Circle.

Mountcastle, V. B. (1979). An organising principle for cerebral function. In B. M. Edelman & V. B. Mountcastle (Eds.), *The mindful brain,* Cambridge: MIT Press.

Nauta, W. J. H., & Feirtag, M. (1979, Sept.). The organisation of the brain. *Scientific American,* Vol. 241, No. 3.

Perratt, S. I., Smith, P., Milner, D., Jeeves, M. A., & Rogers, B. J. (1982). Visual properties of temporal lobe neurons selectively receptive to the sight of faces. *Investigative Ophthalmology and Visual Science, 22,* supplement.

Picton. (1978). Neuropysiology of human attention. In J. Requin (Ed.), *Attention and performance VII. Lawrence Erlbaum Associates, Hillsdale, NJ.*

*Pratt-Johnson, J. A., & MacDonald, A. L. (1976). Binocular visual field in strabismus. Canadian Journal of Ophthalmology, 11,* 37.

Pribram, K. (1975). Arousal, activation and effort in the control of attention. *Psych Review, 82,* 116–149.

Rashbass, L. R. (1971). Second thoughts on smooth pursuit. In P. Bach y Rita et al. (Eds.), *The control of eye movements.* New York: Academic Press.

Wurtz, R. H., Goldberg, M. E., & Robinson, D. L. (1982, June). Brain mechanisms of visual attention. *Scientific American* Vol. *246,* No. 6.

Yarbus, A. L. (1976). *Eye movements and vision.* New York: Plenum Press.

Zeki, S. M. (1977). Colour coding in the superior temporal sulcus of rhesus monkey visual cortex. *Proceedings of the Royal Society of London (Biol.), 197,* 195.

# DEVELOPMENTAL THEORIES OF GESTURE

# 8 Form, Significance and Psychological Potential of Hand Gestures of Infants

Colwyn Trevarthen

## INTRODUCTION

*Since a great number of reflexes can be elicited in the young infant while 'higher' brain activity cannot yet be observed, the conclusion has been drawn that the infant's brain activity consists only of reflexes. This opinion does not at all do justice to the facts. At each stage of development there exist functions that occur without external stimulation . . . During their inactivity the centers have been charged and finally press for a discharge 'by themselves', i.e., without external stimulation. (Peiper, 1963, p. 248)*

Behind most efforts to explain the development of human gestures and symbolic expression lies the assumption that an infant must be born with no specific coordination of movements, no specific perceptual categories and no specific motivation for such culturally sensitive behaviors. Until recently, psychologists were confident that inherent brain anatomy could not have a blueprint for symbolic activities. However, for over 100 years, there has been evidence that speech, the principal symbolic behavior, is represented in the brains of most individuals with a strong asymmetry (Trevarthen, 1984a). Left hemisphere lateralization of the perception and production of speech in particular zones of the neocortex would seem to indicate that fundamental regulators of language activity are inherent. Nevertheless, it was assumed that cerebral asymmetry of language function or *cerebral dominance* is missing at birth. Recovery of speech communication after left hemispherotomy in infancy seemed to prove that the two halves of the brain are equipotential at birth. If so, as Lenneberg (1967) pointed out, it becomes difficult to explain the regular stages of language learning and eventual left hemisphere dominance. There must be some inherent morphogenetic principal for growth of the relevant brain systems. Now, of course, we have anatomical evidence that neocortical tissues are differently organized even in the brain of a 20-week fetus and some cortical cytoarchitectionic territories that are identified with language-related processes in adults tend to be larger in the left hemisphere at birth (Galaburda, 1983). It is also clear that data advanced in the past as evidence on the effects of early brain damage on language development have been inappropriate or misinterpreted. Recent studies show that lateralization is normally complete by age 5 (Carter, Hohenegger, & Satz, 1982) and that aphasic symptoms are not produced in young children by lesions restricted to the right hemisphere as had been claimed (Woods, 1980).

In infants, potentials evoked by speech sounds and the perceptual discrimination preferences they show for elements of speech both indicate that the left hemisphere is better adapted to process some features of speech input from soon after birth in most individuals (Trevarthen, 1983a, 1984a). This perceptual processing asymmetry is apparently linked with orientation sets that predispose infants to look to the right when they are attempting to respond to vocal signals (Studdert-Kennedy, 1983). Microdescription of television or film records of infants interacting with their mothers reveals behaviors in 2-month-olds that look like precursors of speech (Trevarthen, 1974, 1979a, 1983a, 1984d). Infants attracted to look at and listen to the affectionate expressive behaviors of their mothers respond with elaborately regulated expressions of their own that include vocalizations modulated to approach the range of speech sounds and lip-and-tongue movements that resemble speech articulation.

Accurate description of the arm and hand movements of neonates and infants reveals that the limbs, too, have a capacity for spontaneous activation and coordination (Trevarthen, 1974, 1984b). Their adjustment to the motions of objects further proves that the coordinative cerebral structures for hands are capable of being directed by perceptual representations of distal goals or targets. The two most remarkable forms of upper limb movement shown by infants under 3-months-of-age are *prereaching,* that can be aimed at nearby objects in motion, and expressive gestures, like the expressions adults make when they are talking, that are stimulated by engagement with the expressions of an affectionate mother (Trevarthen, 1974, 1977, 1979a).

The basic forms of these limb movements have now been described. They share a common pattern for the succession and synchronization of rotations about proximal and distal joints and have a similar time course and velocity profile. They differ in their choice of external goal or environmental situation, and show some differences in form (Trevarthen, 1984b). Prereaching movements have coordination with the infant's own head and eye orientations from birth. Expressive gesticulations are, at the same time, highly reactive to the flow of the mother's vocalizations and facial expressions. They are coordinated with their mutual eye contact and they are also affected by the emotional or motivational state of the infant, which is finely sensitive to the mother's emotional state. In other words, arm and hand movements of young infants are socially sensitive and they participate in emotional expression and the regulation of emotional engagement.

By the time a child is proficient in speech he or she is likely to have a clear manual dominance, and most children all over the world are right-handed, as most of their parents are. Even this has been explained as a consequence of social conditioning. Hildreth in the 1940s supported the astonishing theoretical position of most educators at that time, crediting innate anatomical structures with no part in the determination of human right-handedness. Preference for the right hand in communication arose as an established convention adhered to since prehistoric times out of convenience (Hildreth, 1949). Now it is accepted that some kind of genetic determination of an asymmetric cerebral anatomy is the cause of the distribution of manual preferences that has been remarkably consistent among humans since the Old Stone Age (Coren & Porac, 1977; Marshack, 1984).

Although handedness is usually assessed as a manipulative asymmetry, it is not hard to see that gesture and signing have a similar, if not identical, asymmetry (Kimura, 1973a, 1973b; Dalby, Gibson, Grossi, & Schneider, 1980). There has been a strong theoretical preference for *simple* explanations of how the common right-handedness originates, it being assumed that any innate asymmetry is confined to subcortical reflex postural systems or orientational biases. Such theories would deny infants any innate asymmetric coordinative systems for practical manipulation, for control of complementary actions of the two hands, or for expressive gesticulation. Correlations between the postural preferences or turning tendencies of sleeping or avoidant newborns and eventual manual dominance are presented as evidence in support of this position (Michel, 1981). Most attempts to measure manual preferences in young infants examine only prehension or manipulation of objects, as if the first asymmetry must be biomechanical. The most careful longitudinal studies find complex fluctuations in limb preference by this criterion (Gesell & Ames, 1947; Seth, 1973).

Current genetic theories of how hand preferences are inherited, like developmental studies, take data from a tally of which hand is chosen to handle a variety of objects, each subject receiving a handedness quotient. Asymmetries in expressive hand movement are taken to follow from some inequality in a single pair of hand controllers in the brain. The statistical data on genealogies of hand preference on this single continuum of *handedness* are so unclear that it has been concluded that the large phenotypic variance is caused by extragenetic cytoplasmic markers in the egg (Morgan & Corballis, 1978) or chance environmental factors modifying a single *right shift* genetic factor that is capable of determining right-handedness in 75% of the population (Annett, 1972; Corballis, 1983). Levy (1980) and Levy and Nagylaki (1972) argue that hand preferences, like cerebral organization for visual perceptual and linguistic processes, are under multiple genetic regulation. No one appears to have examined the theory that the hands may be moved by several different inherent motivating systems, each of which may have its own direction of asymmetry. The inheritance of hand preferences may be regulated by several factors that interact in the complex epigenesis of cerebral systems. The genetics of handedness must be as complex as the several motives, or mental strategies, that have evolved as alternative phenotypes for adaptive hand movement.

Here it is proposed that correlations between asymmetries in posture or reflex body coordination in newborns and voluntary hand use in older infants are due to asymmetric organization of innate motivational systems, incorporating widespread structures of the brain stem motor systems, diencephalic reticular formation, basal ganglia, thalamus and cortex that are preadapted to control of skilled manipulation. It is further proposed that, in early infancy, hand movements are also motivated by an emotional and communicative mechanism, possibly asymmetric, that seeks, even in the neonate period, to receive feedback regulation from other persons. One effective test of interpersonal regulation takes the form of demonstrations that infants can imitate hand movements (Maratos, 1973; Meltzoff & Moore, 1977), but lateral asymmetry in such reactions remains unexplored as yet.

Data are presented that suggest that the complex patterns of hand movement seen in infancy are due to the interaction of several cerebral coordinative systems with separate genetic regulation and epigenetic pathways to lateral asymmetry. These systems develop at different times and compete in the establishment of more elaborate coordinative structures and this produces swings in manual preference that may vary considerably in intensity and age of manifestation between different children.

## What Hand Movements Do

The motor possibilities of human upper limbs, and therefore demands for elaborate cerebral control, are very great, because the jointed lever system of arms, palms, and fingers has many degrees of freedom, and because cerebral programming of the combinations of rotation about the many joints is extremely refined and informed by many sensitive receptors. Hands can be projected from the body with high velocity to transmit large forces, moved with exquisite temporal and spatial programming and guidance in an extensive reaching field, and rotated to contact surfaces of objects with accuracy in any direction while responding to light touch. Fingers are extended or flexed in an infinite number of combinations to palpate, grasp, lift, push, poke, punch, pat, etc. These movements facilitate the perceptual function of the hands in attending to and identifying the *feel* of things. Moreover, the two hands cooperate, performing complementary mechanical work; to separate, join, remove, insert, hit together different objects or parts of objects. Hands are capable, as paws are in more primitive mammals, of helping in locomotion of the whole body, regulating balance, and attending to the stimulation, comfort, cleanliness, etc. of the surface of the body. By carrying food to the mouth, scratching itches, removing thorns, brushing off dirt, rubbing hot or cold parts, pulling on or off clothes, hands contribute to autonomic adjustment of body state. They also act to protect or shield the special sensors— eyes, ears, nose, and mouth, and to fend off blows.

All of the above remarkable array of actions of hands for transforming or feeling external objects or the body gain new psychological significance when they can be affected by another subject's consciousness. In primates, hand movements make important contribution to communication. For purposes of discussion we may classify human hand gestures into five kinds, differentiated by their communicative potential and psychological control. Ekman and Friesen (1969) have categorized hand movements in relation to other forms of expressive behavior and Kendon (1976, 1980) has discussed the relation of gesticulations to the processes that generate ideas for speech, with reference to microanalysis of the timing of hand movements that accompany speech.

1. When hands manipulate objects, an observer equipped with appropriate cognitive capacity can pick up information about the strategy of their owner's attention and interest, adding to conclusions that can be predicted from orientations of the observed person's whole body or the head and eyes. The level or intensity of motivation, as well as a more specific purpose or idea, may be detected in the effort of movement patterns. Whatever the psychological process involved, hand movements are certainly a particularly rich source of such information for humans. Often these communications are unintended, stolen by the observer, and yet they may be of vital importance in cooperative or competitive behavior. They can, of course, be performed deliberately, to show somebody how something can or should be done. These we may call *gratuitous* expressions of manipulation.

2. Movements of hands to comfort, protect or stimulate the body, including those to change input to the special sense organs, transmit information about motivation and regulation of the internal state of the person. *Self-regulating,* largely unconscious and unintended, movements form an undercurrent to any deliberate referential communication by speech or gesture. They are called "body focused" by Freedman and Hoffman (1972) and "self adaptors" by Ekman and Friesen (1969); (see also, Nespoulous & Lecours, this volume).

3. Hands are also capable of expressing emotion to evaluate and control the interpersonal contact itself. They can show how the presence and behavior of another is received. When hands move in specific ways with face expressions, eye movements and vocalizations to convey feelings to affect other persons, whether by imitation of conventional signs or in unconscious expression of

innate coordinations in an integrated affective signaling system, then these movements can be called *emotional*. This category of hand movements seems to have received only oblique attention by researchers and the specificity of their emotional content has not been defined.

4. When hands are added to attentional orienting, deliberately extended and aimed to show another person an object or place of interest in their common environment, they perform an *indicating* movement, directing attention and possibly action as well.

5. Finally, hand movements may be formed in patterns and sequences to construct graphical or symbolic representations of actions, events, objects, or situations. A full language of hand signs may be learned to express infinite subtleties of purpose, knowledge and feeling in a conventional vocabulary replacing speech. Though formed by arbitrary conventions, the latter signs of hand language are produced within a dynamic and spatial frame of hand activity that is shared with the spontaneous and universal or innate displays of motivation and emotion. The conversational *illustrators* of Ekman and Friesen (1969) grade into *emblems*. As Kendon (1976, 1980) has emphasized, gesticulations must be generated by a mechanism that is directly affected by the ideas being expressed in speech—often the gesticulations carry the idea sooner or more completely than the accompanying speech.

In summary, we have the following overlapping but reasonably clear classes of hand expression that communicate: gratuitous (given off in the course of manipulations, etc.), self-regulatory, emotional, indicating, and symbolic.

In natural conversation, and especially in hand signing language, all five levels of expression are combined, but all are clarified and articulated together by syntactic and semantic conventions of the language. The same kinds of expressive hand actions are variously combined in dance, drama, and musical performance (Birdwhistell, 1970).

We investigate infants to see how idea-communicating and symbolic hand movements come about. They are certainly rudimentary or absent at first. Children can start to make conventional hand signs to express protolinguistic ideas early in the second year. The hand-eye system can transmit true linguistic signals as early as the vocal articulatory one—especially if the child is deaf in an environment responsive to hand signs (Goldin-Meadow, 1978; Goldin-Meadow & Feldman, 1975; Preisler, 1983; Tervoort & Verbeck, 1967). This is weighty evidence for the existence of a general expressive mechanism in the brain that links oral, auditory, manual, and visual sensory and motor channels in such a way that they are complementary and equivalent for making ideas expressive in language. But much younger infants have elaborate facial and vocal expressions and they use these to regulate interactions with their caretakers or other persons from birth. We are led to ask in what ways are infants' hand movements related to the movements of their head, face, and vocal apparatus in the earliest interactions with other persons' expressions.

## Adaptive Advantages of Using One Hand

Acts to intercept objects or to grasp them could reasonably be expected to be bilaterally symmetric; simple prehensile, propulsive, or supportive aiming of the hands has no reason to be more useful to the left of the body than to the right. In contrast, both refined manipulative actions in a small space close to the body (focal hand activity) and expressive movements could well be asymmetric (Trevarthen, 1978).

Considering manipulation of objects first, once an object has been seized in one hand and then the manipulation has started to do something to the object with the other hand, there arises a difference of both sensory and motor functions in the two limbs. They may move at different times to different extents and with different strategies of reafferent control. Typically, one hand holds, steadies, and orients the ensemble in a favorable position, and the other does a discrete act or sequence of acts to part of it, or brings another object to operate on the first etc. The cerebral systems implicated in such complementarity of hand use are extensive and they lie outside the primary motor cortex (Trevarthen, 1978).

One set of theories on the evolution of manual asymmetry of function in humans departs from this basis. Hands are taken to have an inherent asymmetry of tasks or division of behavior in refined or complex manipulations, the one acting to fix a frame for finer more varied actions of the other *dominant* hand. The latter hand tends to make sequences of discrete movement at a higher tempo and in a smaller space. In Kimura's theory of manual praxis, backed by experimental measurement of speed and accuracy of performance of the two hands and studies of the effects of lesions in left and right cerebral hemispheres, the primary factor in evolution of lateral asymmetry of motor coordination in humans is the development of a coordinative mechanism for predictive motor sequencing in the left hemisphere (Kimura, 1979, 1982). The special properties of this hand movement programmer, which tends to give the right hand central place in the performance of complex strategic motor sequences, were later taken over for regulation of articulatory movements of speech. The theory of MacNeilage, Studdert-Kennedy, and Lindblom (1984) emphasizes the complementary logistical relationship between left context-framing hand action (right hemisphere) and the articulatory element-inserting action of the right hand controller in the left hemisphere. There is argument for concluding that the integrative controller for *both* hands may be in one hemisphere—and I found evidence that this was so for a skilled bimanual manipulation learned by baboons (Trevarthen, 1972, 1978).

Expressive hand movements that do no work on objects, and that may be emitted without aim towards any external physical object, are also free to be either unimanual or asymmetric, the two hands taking complementary roles in signaling to another subject. There may indeed be an important advantage in a genetic mechanism confining messages that carry a greater information or idea load to one hand, consistently. It might help the emitter get it right and help the receiving person to see the message. It is unnecessary (one might say *pointless*) to use two hands at once to point out something; why not consistently use one *message* hand wherever postural constraints and other concurrent hand activities permit? Once chosen for indicative signaling, the same hand would then be most effectively used to convey other more subtle signals about the quality and direction of interest by means of small movements.

Gestures in conversation and hand sign languages are, in fact, strongly asymmetric, most subjects preferring to use the right hand. However, the same is true for the performance of culturally significant skills that use tools to make symbolic or conventional artifacts, including written text. It is at least plausible that the intersubjective component, i.e., expressive movement of the hands for the sight of other persons, has evolved to be consistently asymmetric in humans, and it could be beginning to be so in some families of subhumans as well. Research to date on the signaling function of hand movements made naturally by monkeys or apes seems, with one or two exceptions, not to have provided relevant evidence on this point (Box, 1977; Brooker, Lehman, Heimbuch, & Kidd, 1981; Lehman, 1970; MacNeilage et al., 1984; Oyen, 1979; Trevarthen, 1978; Vauclair & Bard, 1983). Clearly Marshack (1984) is right in giving the evolution of bipedalism and freeing of the hands a great importance in connection with the development of symbolic imagination.

There is every reason to expect expressive *conversational* movements of the hands to share the same division of motoric or cognitive strategies as pertains for skilled manipulations—one hand acting as a context or frame-setter for the other. But we shall be looking at infant hand movements to discover if there is any asymmetry in expressive movements independently of the manipulative movements. Infants make expressive and emotional hand movements when they are too young to manipulate objects. Are these early gestures symmetrical?

## AN OUTLINE OF HAND ACTIONS IN INFANCY

We have found that, when they are responding to their mothers, 1- or 2-month-old infants impulsively carry their hands up away from the body, often with one or more fingers extended and palm supine or facing forwards. The hand movements are made in tight coordination with other expressions, particularly lip and tongue movements and vocalizations (Trevarthen, 1974, 1979a, 1984b). Similar hand gestures are made by newborns, but with less well-defined orientation to the expressions of the partner. Our recent data, discussed more fully below, indicate that a majority of infants make more of a large variety of expressions with their right hands.

The first functions of spontaneous hand movements in early infancy are emotional and self-regulatory. Prehensile and manipulative movements are rudimentary in the first 3 months. At about 15 weeks after birth, the infant shows increased interest in objects for reaching, as well as more exploration of the impersonal environment and its events, and this is accompanied by a rapid development in strength of head support and arm extension and control. By 20 weeks, most infants will eagerly track, reach for, and try to grasp any small object dangled in front of them. The beginning of controlled manipulation opens up a new channel of communication and mothers respond by play that assists and teases the infant's efforts to get hold of objects (Trevarthen, 1983b, 1984b, 1984c).

Mothers touch and grasp infants' hands from the first moments of birth and, as voluntary regulation of reaching and grasping markedly improves, after 3 months, they usually play more games involving holding and bouncing, patting or tickling the infant's hands while the mother chants or sings. We find evidence of infants taking particular interest in their mother's hands from 3 months, before they begin well-controlled manipulation of objects (Trevarthen, 1983b). Imitation experiments prove that the infant is capable of recognizing the equivalence of the hands of another person with the infant's own hands before 3 months (Maratos, 1973). This opens the possibility that infants can commence observational learning of movements of the hands and their use to manipulate objects before the infants are capable of performing acts of this level of complexity and control for themselves.

There appears to be a period of decline in freedom of hand movements after 2 months while the neuromotor system of the axial and proximal body segments is undergoing a growth spurt (Trevarthen, 1974, 1982, 1984b; von Hofsten, 1980, 1984). We shall examine this period carefully to see if there is any change in direction or strength of hand preference, because undoubtedly there is a change then in the balance of activity in central motor mechanisms of the brain. After 5 months, infants begin to imitate playful expressive hand games, such as clapping, and, by 7 months, many infants are imitating conventional gestures, including waving and pointing (see below). Many such movements are close to forms of expressive gesture that the infant emitted spontaneously in the first 2 months; but they are executed with more deliberate control by the older infant.

It is most interesting that expressive hand gestures develop along a course that closely parallels the maturation of vocal expression. We can find manual equivalents of babbling and other play vocalizations as the child enters protolanguage, at 9 or 10 months, fixing particular vocal forms to convey well-defined meanings (Halliday, 1975). Hand movements, too, are adapted more definitely at this age to the attentions and interpretations of other persons who are attempting to be partners in cooperative performance of a task, a game or an exchange of ideas (Hubley & Trevarthen, 1979; Trevarthen, 1979b). This is the time that deaf children in a signing home can acquire arbitrary hand signs to encode discrete meanings (Goldin-Meadow, 1978; Goldin-Meadow & Feldman, 1975).

In the second year, the meaningfulness of hand movements burgeons as the first words are uttered. Not only are manipulations of objects directed more obviously to the performance of recognizible and effective actions that are of interest to others, but gestural mannerisms of all kinds, including hand gestures, are used with increasing skill in social engagements. The developments certainly depend on more than the obvious increases in precision, speed, and variety of arm and hand movement, in finger dexterity and precision of grip, or in cognitive ability to represent objects from their felt, heard, or seen effects. The child gains awareness of the communicative value of all forms of actions, and use of the hands is increasingly either imitative or controlled by the reactions of other persons. This intersubjective aspect is present in the earliest interactions between mother and infant, as we have said, but it gains an entirely new range and power at the close of infancy. Shared meaningful purposes largely control what a toddler will do with his or her hands. Lateral preferences with respect to these kinds of hand movement can give valuable evidence as to inherent or acquired cerebral asymmetry of control for these functions (see below).

It does not follow that because lateral asymmetry in hand movements, or hand dominance, becomes increasingly apparent at the end of infancy, it is an imitated or socially reinforced acquisition as psychologists have long believed. Indeed, we shall discuss evidence that the asymmetry seen in expressive and emotional hand gestures of a given baby in the stage of primary intersubjectivity and the preferences that emerge in manipulation in the second 6 months are both directly related to the pattern of functional asymmetry seen in both hand signing and skillful use of cultural artifacts by the same child at 2 and 3 years.

In reporting data from our research we shall be investigating the following thesis: Already in early infancy the expressive function of the hands is distinct from their postural, locomotor, or object exploring and prehensile use (cf. Trevarthen, 1984e). Initially, the expressive function is nonsymbolic and automatic, but it includes *declarative* movements coupled to prespeech and vocalization and is, from early weeks, susceptible to modification by responses of a sensitive partner in interaction. Imitation studies show the direct response of hands to seen hand movement. But the spontaneous hand behaviors coordinated with the infant's vocalization, laughter etc. often in predictive relation to the others' behavior, show that indirect reaction of the hands to the total pattern of a partner's expressive signals is at least of equal importance as direct imitative shaping to match one expressive movement. The expressive movements of the baby's hands change with all reactions to the partner, i.e., they are coordinated with the quality or mood of interaction. Close coupling of the baby's expressive arm lifts and opening of the hands with prespeech emissions, both aimed to the attention of a partner, (Sylvester-Bradley, 1981; Trevarthen, 1974, 1984b, 1984d), indicates that these two kinds of expression are linked by a common motivation to form a complex *utterance*.

An important feature of gestural movements of hands is that, like vocalizations, they can be simultaneously monitored by the subject who is expressing and by the other who is receiving. Hand movements of the infant can be seen, and sometimes heard, by the infant as well as the mother. The infant can guide gestural patterns, therefore, by reafferent information from the ventral visual field, audition and somesthesis, as well as indirectly through monitoring of their effect on the other person. Visual self-monitoring of hand movements may be involved in the learning of communication gestures from others, as Baldwin proposed (Baldwin, 1894).

We need to clarify the communicative function of hand expressions that carry phatic and affective information (modality information) but not referential or representation information about objects or events that lie outside the behavior of the interactants (see Nespoulous & Lecours, this volume). Infants under 6 months certainly do not move their hands to represent absent topics, unless they spontaneously repeat movements that reproduce *tricks* for expression that have been learned as part of habitual games. We shall be on the lookout for such spontaneously repeated self-imitations.

The infant under 9 months is often wholly absorbed in actions on objects. He or she may interrupt exploration of an object to *play* with the mother or may gesture to her with an object in hand, but ready alternation of interest between object and mother, both orientations being integrated with action on object, does not exist before the beginning of Secondary Intersubjectivity at 9 months. Changes in the use of hand gestures as infants become capable of sharing a task and of attending to a mother's requests, instructions, etc. are of particular importance in our attempt to relate symbolic and manipulative hand use. Hand signs must be made with orientation towards the interests and wishes of another. But for making a useful reference this is not enough. The hand movements of a message must also describe some goal or topic. At the very least, the orienting to another must be unambiguously linked with deliberate performance of a discrete handling of a present object. Coordination of infant hand action with maternal speech and gesture, and with protolinguistic vocalizations of the infant addressed to the mother will give us evidence on the first stage of symbolic gesture.

## A PHOTOGRAPHIC CORPUS OF INFANT ACTIONS

In my laboratory, we have collected photographic and video material of mother-infant interaction covering mainly the first year. Recently, we have systematically studied sixteen mothers and infants at ages chosen to document important epochs in the development of communication before speech. The population is half male and half female and distributed across four social classes (Table 8.1a). Fourteen of these infants have been seen again at 2 and 3 years, playing with toys in the presence of their mothers, to obtain data on the development of imaginitive play, speech and handedness. Five of the latter were also seen at 19-months-of-age (see Table 8.4).

For the first year, each time they visited, mother and baby spent half-an-hour together interating in a variety of ways, the baby supported in a chair that allowed freedom to arm movement in front of the seated mother. First, they played together, face-to-face, the mother being given no more specific instructions than to *chat* with her infant. Then we asked the mother to try to elicit imitation of tongue protrusion and hand clapping. Next, we gave the mother a ball hanging on a piece of thread for the baby to track and reach after. For babies over 3 months we presented a toy truck with some wooden dolls on a table at the height of the baby's waist and instructed the mother to teach the baby to put the dolls in the truck. In two mildly stressful situations, the mother was asked to keep her face immobile and cease responding to the infant for 1–2 minutes. Then the mother left the room as a stranger took her place to chat with the baby for about 3 minutes. While the behavior of mother and baby were recorded on video, I observed through the viewfinder of a motor drive Nikon camera and took photographs from an adjacent darkened room, through a small window, attempting to sample all interesting forms of action. We have over 2000 photographs for the first 5 months, and over 1700 for the last half of the year. After eliminating unclear pictures, we have the corpus summarized in Table 8.1.

Toddlers were videotaped with their mothers in an uninstructed play situation, standing behind a table with interesting objects; again I took photographs of their play. Thus we have a further 4000 color photographs of the older children exploring and using toys and other objects in the presence of the mother. All the pictures with both age groups are taken with the camera in a standard position relative to the mother and infant, with constant lighting and camera settings.

While taking the photographs, I am aware that the babies are doing many complex things, as are the mothers. I note that babies are moving their hands continually while vocalizing, exploring, playing, and engaging in various tasks. The photographs are taken to record kinds of action that I feel are interesting, so they are not a random sample.

Gradually, as the study progressed, I came to realize that I was collecting material for a description of types of hand movements, both gesticulatory and exploratory or manipulative, that babies can make in different situations and when they're trying to do different things. I review these data in an attempt to relate the movements that are used for communicative purposes to those that are used for manipulatory or exploratory and performatory functions.

## Gesticulatory Behavior before Objects are Manipulated

To measure the balance between left- and right-hand activity, the photographs have been scored as left hand higher, right hand higher or both at the same level. This is a simple judgment made with almost perfect agreement by two scoreers separately. Of five infants photographed interacting face-to-face with their moth-

TABLE 8.1

Ages of Subjects, in Weeks, and (in Brackets) Numbers of Photographs Classified per Visit

(a) Subjects Under Six Months (Total Photos = 1972):

|  | LP (II) | SL (II) | LO (IV) | AH (I) | PL (II) | MT (IV) |
|---|---|---|---|---|---|---|
|  | *(FEMALE)* |  |  | *(MALE)* |  |  |
| F E M A L E | 4.5 (2) | 5 (54) | 5 (59) | 4 (1) | 4 (65) | 4 (22) |
|  | 6 (34) | 8 (14) | 8 (52) | 9 (34) | 6 (33) | 6 (45) |
|  | 8 (59) | 12 (79) | 12 (63) | 12 (88) | 9 (28) | 8 (6) |
|  | 12 (41) | 16 (79) | 16 (84) | 16 (88) | 12 (89) | 13 (40) |
|  | 16 (112) | 22 (74) | 20 (63) | 20 (118) | 15 (65) | 16 (82) |
|  | 20 (32) |  |  |  | 21 (105) | 20 (86) |
|  | 24 (76) |  |  |  |  |  |

Photos per subject

| LP | SL | LO | AH | PL | MT |
|---|---|---|---|---|---|
| 356 | 300 | 321 | 329 | 385 | 281 |

(b) Subjects Over Six Months (Total Photos = 1561):

|  | EB (IV) | EM (II) | CR (II) | BM (I) | JJ (IV) | AF (I) | PH (IV) | MS (II) | AS (II) | CK (IV) |
|---|---|---|---|---|---|---|---|---|---|---|
|  | 25 (35) | 29 (69) | 28 (71) | 46 (32) | 40 (32) | 28 (56) | 24 (37) | 30 (38) | 44 (12) | 40 (36) |
|  | 28 (68) | 32 (71) | 40 (60) | 48 (70) | 47 (41) | 32 (67) | 32 (70) | 41 (68) | 46 (45) | 45 (60) |
|  | 41 (67) | 40 (68) |  | 53 (68) |  | 40 (37) | 36 (70) |  | 49 (50) | 56 (47) |
|  |  |  |  | 56 (34) |  |  | 40 (82) |  |  |  |

Photos per subject

| EB | EM | CR | BM | JJ | AF | PH | MS | AS | CK |
|---|---|---|---|---|---|---|---|---|---|
| 170 | 208 | 131 | 204 | 73 | 160 | 259 | 106 | 107 | 143 |

Social Class is indicated; Registrar General's Classification, I, II and IV.

## Explanation for Tables 8.2 and 8.3

For each subject at a given age, left and right numbers on the top line indicate the number of photographs in which left or right hand, respectively, was higher (a) or actively feeling body or clothes (b). Numbers below the line indicate the total photographs collected in each visit for the specified condition. Significant asymmetry, as determined by a one-tailed Binomial Test, is indicated; $p < .05 =$ *, $p < .01 = $ **

TABLE 8.2
Hand Positions in Play Interaction With the Mother

| Age (Weeks) | LP | Female SL | LO | AH | Male PL | MT |
|---|---|---|---|---|---|---|
| **(a) Hand Raising** | | | | | | |
| 4-6 | 5  7 | 11  15 | 8  17* | | 4  24** | 1  7* |
|  | 29 | 34 | 42 | | 34 | 20 |
| 8/9 | | | 6  3 | 3  12** | | |
|  | | | 24 | 34 | | |
| 8+12 | 10  12 | 7  6 | | | 5  9 | 3  4 |
|  | 43 | 33 | | | 32 | 12 |
| 12 | | | 16**  2 | 1  11** | | |
|  | | | 36 | 13 | | |
| 16 | | 2  14** | 1  7* | 5  5 | | 10**  0 |
|  | | 29 | 11 | 11 | | 15 |
| 16+20 | 10  7 | | | | 5  6 | |
|  | 50 | | | | 42 | |
| 20 | | | 2  15** | 10  9 | | 7  4 |
|  | | | 23 | 28 | | 15 |
| 22 | | 0  20** | | | | |
|  | | 35 | | | | |
| 24 | 0  7** | | | | | |
|  | 17 | | | | | |
| **(b) Self-Touching** | | | | | | |
| 4-6 | 6*  0 | 7**  0 | 8**  0 | | 7**  0 | 3  2 |
|  | 7 | 8 | 12 | | 7 | 8 |
| 8-12 | 3  1 | 2  4 | 3  3 | 9*  1 | 3  1 | 2  0 |
|  | 4 | 16 | 8 | 14 | 20 | 2 |
| 16-20 | 2  0 | 10**  0 | 5  1 | 4  3 | 4  1 | 0  1 |
|  | 15 | 23 | 13 | 15 | 17 | 1 |
| 22-24 | 4  0 | 10**  2 | | | | |
|  | 12 | 21 | | | | |
| | 15  1 | 29  6 | 16  4 | 13  4 | 14  2 | 5  3 |
| | 38 | 68 | 33 | 29 | 44 | 11 |

ers at 4- to 6-weeks after birth (all except AH), four elevated their right hands more than their left (Table 8.2, Fig. 8.1). The fifth (MT) did the same on a first visit at 4 weeks. In a second visit, at 6 weeks, this infant's left hand was more often elevated, but he was excited and highly vocal, a state which, as discussed below, may have interfered with close coordination of expressive response to the mother's communication. He did not appear to be attending to her happily. In the second 8-week period the tendency to show a more active and more elevated right hand was weaker or reversed while the same three female and two male infants were interacting with their mothers. A third male (AH) who had not been photographed in the first 8 weeks was strongly right-handed at 9 and 12 weeks (Figs. 8.1 and 8.6). This boy was to show a pronounced left-handedness at 3 and 5 years and his interesting case is discussed in detail below. When males and females are compared, it appears that the three girls regained a strong right-handedness in response to the mother by 16 or 24 weeks, but the males all continued to raise both hands equally, or the left more, when last seen at 20 weeks. None of these infants were observed further in the first year.

While the 2-month-olds raised their right hands when apparently socially excited by their mothers, the left hand tended to touch their clothing, or the strap holding them to the chair, or to rest on their thighs more than the right hand (Table 8.2, Figs. 8.1 and 8.6). Thus they repeatedly showed a pattern of right hand reaching towards the mother while the left hand was held against the body or clothing and sometimes moved as if the infant sought self-stimulation. At 8 and 12 weeks the female infants no longer showed asymmetric self-touching, but this re-emerged in the fifth and sixth months. After 12 weeks most of the infants tended to hold their hands down or together in their laps, so the number of asymmetric postures is small. The left-handed male continued to touch his clothes more with the left hand at 9 and 12 weeks, but not at 16 and 20 weeks. The other two males showed no clear sidedness in self-touching after 8 weeks.

The evidence of these photographs suggests that a maturational process, possibly related to the growth of controlled reaching after 12 weeks, weakens or interferes with an asymmetric pattern of limb coordination for communicative expression that divides expressive and emotional or self-regulatory components between right and left hands asymmetrically before 3 months. This asymmetric expressive pattern re-emerged sooner in the females than it did in the males.

The nature of the motivation behind the lateralized expressive behaviors is clarified by details of the whole expressive behavior of the infant and its coordination with maternal behavior. As has been said, 1- and 2-month-olds frequently move one hand in synchrony with movements of the lips and tongue that resemble rudimentary attempts at speaking, or with "pleasure" vocalizations or coos that are modulated to approach the sound properties of speech (Fig. 8.1 and Trevarthen, 1974, 1979a, 1983a, 1984b and 1984d). They do these expressive outbursts after smiling at the mother. They appear to be excited by the mother's affectionate speech and the sight of her smiling and animated face to make a

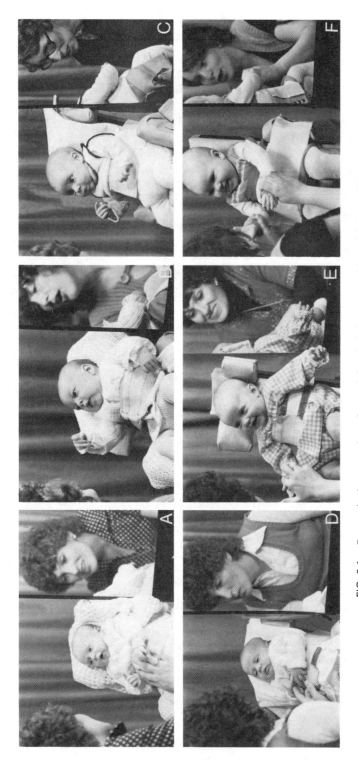

FIG. 8.1. Communicative expressions of young infants include gestures with the right hand: *A* LO, 4 weeks; *B* LP, 6 weeks; *C* AH, 9 weeks. When mothers play with infants they show preference for touching the right hand: *D* LO, 8 weeks; *E* LO, 20 weeks, mother is singing, "Round and Round the Garden, Like a Teddy Bear," tickling the infant's right hand; *F* EB, 28 weeks, mother, teasing infant, claps her own cheek with the infant's right hand, saying "Ah Boo!" Note, EB was already showing left-handedness in spontaneous and imitated gestures at this age (cf. Figs. 8.6, 8.7 and 8.8).

coordinated expressive response that includes one-sided hand activity, with varied lifting and opening of the hand, the movements resembling gestures that adults make subconsciously while speaking. At the same time the other hand may be actively grasping or touching clothing or the child's body or nearby objects while the infant keeps gaze fixed on the mother. It appears that spontaneous expressive behavior is most commonly of this complex form in young infants when they have been excited by the mother's affectionate stimulation.

## Changes with Development of Prehension

In a study of reaching after nearby moving objects with infants 1- to 19-weeks-of-age, von Hofsten (1984) has recently reported that extension of the hand while the infant is visually fixating the object declines at 7 weeks. It then rises slowly in frequency until, at 16 weeks, there begins a rapid improvement in aimed reaching. He confirms that 1- and 4-week-olds make visually directed prereaching movements and suggests that the fall in prereaching at 7 weeks may be related to the development of communication with the mother—infants both look more attentively at the mother's expressions and smile more in recognition after 6 weeks.

When the infants of the present study were photographed looking at or tracking a ball presented by the mother, they frequently moved their hands away from the body. In the first 2 months, occasional prereaching movements towards a visually fixated ball were observed (Fig. 8.2), but there is no evidence that either the left or the right hand was generally more likely to show this response which was coordinated with head and eye orienting that the mother could lead to right or left of the infant. It is certainly not the case that one-sided prereaching movements are inflexibly part of the so-called tonic neck reflex (TNR), because infants looking with head turned to a ball on one side may direct arm and hand of the opposite side across the body. In large populations of subjects there may be a correlation between eventual hand preferences and the TNR of a newborn lying on a mattress, or the postural asymmetries evident in active movements of the baby *in utero* or during birth, but no evidence for such a bias is evident in the photographs of any of our subjects when they were sitting up in the baby-chair and responding to a suspended ball. Subjects who showed a clear right hand preference in forthright gesturing with the mothers while oriented straight ahead or slightly to the left showed no bias in prereaching movements to the ball.

## Behavior in Distress

The infants' emotional regulations were tested in two mildly stressful situations:

1. After interacting playfully for 10 seconds or so the mother was given a signal to immobilize her face and remain silent for about 1 minute facing the infant, then she was signaled to smile and talk to her infant again (Fig. 8.3).

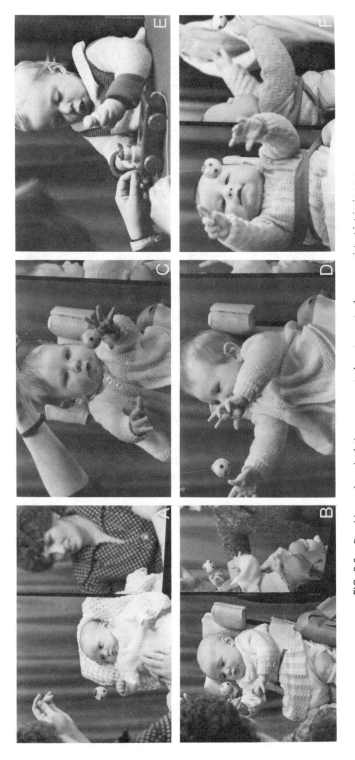

FIG. 8.2.  Reaching and manipulating movements do not seem to show a consistent intrinsic asymmetry. *A* LO, 4 weeks, prereaching to a ball presented near the right hand by the mother; *B* LO, 16 weeks, well-controlled reach with intent visual orientation; *C* and *D* AF, 28 weeks, efficient reaching and groping to either side by both hands; *E* AS, 44 weeks, holding up a doll to look at it; *F* PH, 36 weeks; infant, while reaching, shows learned pointing movements with dominant right hand (cf. Fig. 8.7).

2. The mother had been "chatting" with her baby and she left the room to be replaced by a stranger who was asked to be friendly but not to attempt to "win over" the infant too insistently (Figs. 8.4 and 8.5).

In both these situations we observed subtle signs of watchfulness and fear or sadness in even the 4-week-olds and developments in the quality of this unfriendly reaction occurred beyond 2 months (Trevarthen, 1984c, 1984d). Distinctive hand movements complemented facial expressions and vocalizations giving further evidence that the hands have emotion-signaling expressive functions from birth.

While the 1- and 2-month-old infants were withdrawn or distressed when the mother failed to respond, as has been described with other subjects (Murray & Trevarthen, 1984; Trevarthen, 1984c and 1984d), mixed emotions were evident after the infants were 12 weeks old; most vocalized more but in general 3- to 6-month-olds were contented or even playful while their mothers were silent. However, the positive expressions were unstable and infants frequently looked back at their mothers as if *checking* her strange behavior. With strangers, 1- and 2-month-olds were observant, unsmiling, or withdrawn (Fig. 8.4) and older infants showed rapid oscillations of emotion, swinging from friendly playfulness reaching out to the stranger to mistrustful staring or gaze-avoidance with scratching at clothing or surfaces in reach, wringing the hands, covering the eyes or mouth with the hands, and pouting or crying (Fig. 8.5).

Infants in these stressful situations tended to move their left hand more than the right to touch their bodies or to make large protesting or soliciting movements (Table 8.3). Two females (LP at 24 weeks, and LO at 20 weeks) were more expressive with their right hands when with an unresponsive mother or a stranger and they appeared more confident and friendly in these sessions. At 20 weeks, some of this younger group of subjects also showed a strange showing off of tricks they had learned in play with their mothers or other family members, both when left unresponded to by the still-faced mothers and when they were trying to communicate with a stranger, but such behaviors were commoner in the older group (see Fig. 8.7 below). In a majority of cases these movements, like more friendly expressive movements or gestures of approach or greeting to a responsive mother, were made with the right hand.

## Hands and Mouths

The youngest infants were capable of bringing their hands to their mouths to suck or chew them. Older infants also demonstrated an interesting kind of self-awareness in gestures towards their mouths when communicating with the mother and watching her speak. In the situation where mothers were asked to get the baby to imitate tongue protrusion, several infants gestured to their own mouths and, after 20 weeks, began to reach towards the mother's tongue (Fig. 8.6). Thus

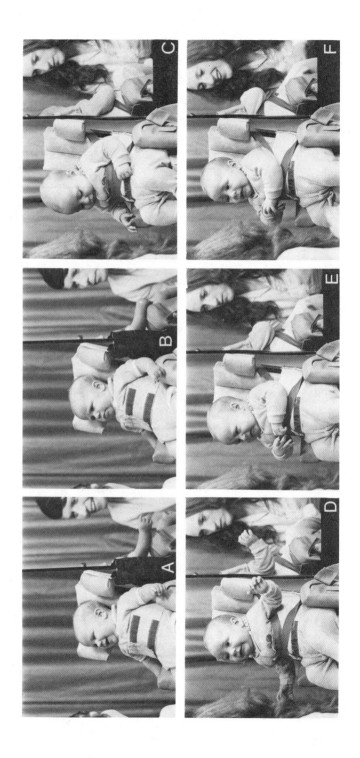

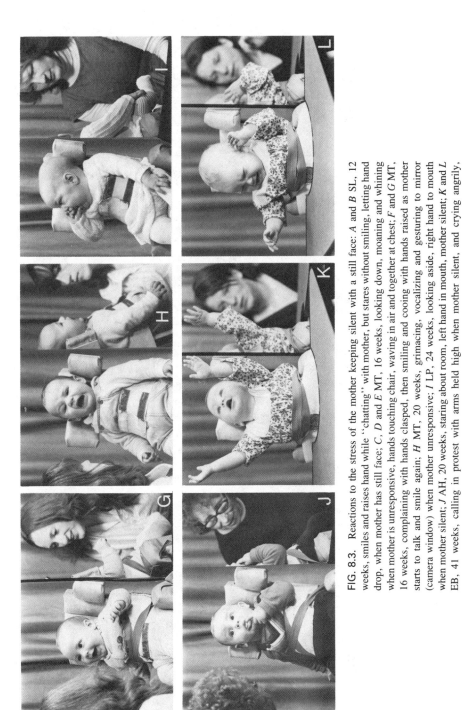

FIG. 8.3. Reactions to the stress of the mother keeping silent with a still face: *A* and *B* SL, 12 weeks, smiles and raises hand while "chatting" with mother, but stares without smiling, letting hand drop, when mother has still face; *C, D* and *E* MT, 16 weeks, looking down, moaning and whining when mother is unresponsive, hands touching chair, waving in air and together at chest; *F* and *G* MT, 16 weeks, complaining with hands clasped, then smiling and cooing with hands raised as mother starts to talk and smile again; *H* MT, 20 weeks, grimacing, vocalizing and gesturing to mirror (camera window) when mother unresponsive; *I* LP, 24 weeks, looking aside, right hand to mouth when mother silent; *J* AH, 20 weeks, staring about room, left hand in mouth, mother silent; *K* and *L* EB, 41 weeks, calling in protest with arms held high when mother silent, and crying angrily, touching ear with left hand.

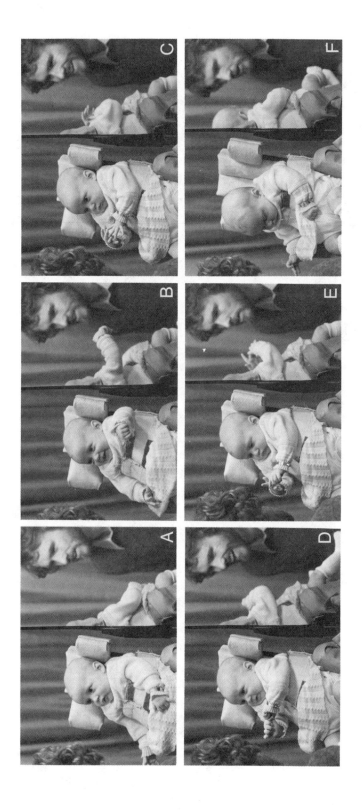

170

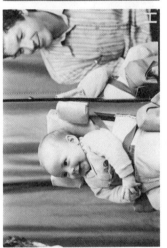

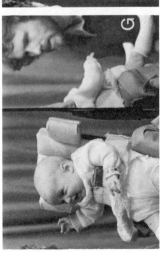

FIG. 8.4. Young infants reacting to strangers. *A* to *G LO*, 16 weeks, alternating fear/sadness and teasing playfulness with a wide variety of gestures, including hand regard and pulling at clothing; *H* and *I MT*, 16 weeks, clasping hands with teasing or defiant grin, hands to mouth with fearful look.

TABLE 8.3
Hand Positions in Stressful Interactions (Mother with Still Face, or Stranger)

| Age (Weeks) | Female | | | Male | | |
|---|---|---|---|---|---|---|
| | LP | SL | LO | AH | PL | MT |
| **(a) Hand Raising** | | | | | | |
| 4-6 | | | 0   5* | | 21  16 | |
| | | | 5 | | 44 | |
| 8-12 | 7** 0 | 3  1 | 7  7 | 4  31** | 9  5 | 2  2 |
| | 11 | 18 | 17 | 37 | 22 | 7 |
| 16-20 | 11** 2 | 3  1 | 8  25** | 25  19 | 10  16 | 15  14 |
| | 28 | 11 | 44 | 55 | 43 | 47 |
| 22-24 | 0  40** | | | | | |
| | 59 | | | | | |
| | 18  42 | 6  2 | 15  33 | 29  50 | 40  37 | 17  16 |
| | 98 | 29 | 66 | 92 | 109 | 54 |
| **(b) Self-Touching** | | | | | | |
| 4-6 | | | 0 | | 1  0 | |
| | | | | | 2 | |
| 8-12 | 0 | 5* 0 | 5  1 | 13** 0 | 1  1 | 0 |
| | | 10 | 9 | 13 | 12 | |
| 16-20 | 9* 1 | 0  0 | 9  4 | 2  11* | 0  9** | 3  3 |
| | 17 | 11 | 23 | 19 | 19 | 15 |
| 22-24 | 30** 1 | | | | | |
| | 42 | | | | | |
| | 39  2 | 5  0 | 14  5 | 15  11 | 2  10 | 3  3 |
| | 59 | 21 | 32 | 32 | 33 | 15 |

SL, while looking hard at her mother's tongue at 8, 12, and 16 weeks, made mouth movements accompanied by right hand movements as if she could feel the movements of her lips in her hand. Then, at 22 weeks, she reached out with her right hand to touch her mother's tongue. At the same ages LO behaved similarly, though she was not photographed touching her mother's tongue. The boy, AH, who later became left-handed, also raised his right hand at 12 weeks when his mother poked her tongue out. At 20 weeks, he seemed to be gesturing with his left hand and he was photographed touching his mouth with his left hand. At 12 and 16 weeks, PL touched his mouth with his right hand and at 20 weeks he chewed his right hand when faced with a stranger. At 8 weeks, MT raised his right hand when looking at his mother's tongue, but at 12, 16, and 20 weeks he raised both hands together in the same situation.

Hand biting and mouth touching seem to have an innate foundation in chimpanzees. Plooij (1979) has described hand biting by baby chimps about 6-weeks-of-age in the wild, and he presents evidence that playful biting, preceded by a *play face* grin, is responsible for stimulating the mother to play teasing games involving tickling the mouth or body of the baby who also touches the mother's mouth in play.

## Hand Play

Beyond 3-months-of-age infants show a sense of fun that stimulates mothers to tease and play games to make them laugh (Trevarthen, 1983b). Many of these games involve the hands, the child readily understanding the capacity of both his or her own hands and the mother's hands to act as if they had personal properties of purposefulness and emotional feelings. Hands become used for subtle affective interchanges in the same degree as faces and voices. Usually, games, chants, songs and body games control hand movements, touching etc. in synchrony with vocal shifts and large head and face signals. Repeated rhythmic patterns of hand waving, touching, tickling, clapping, etc. form the backbone of many games that cause infants over 3-months-of-age to laugh and vocalize. By 20 weeks infants often show eager anticipation of the development and denouement of much-practiced sociodramatic rituals in play (e.g., peek-a-boo; round and round the garden; clap-a-clap-a-handies) and start to invite their mothers to begin a game by extending their hands and vocalizing (Trevarthen, 1984b). The behavior of the infants shows every sign of being an intrinsically motivated form of expression that already existed before the games started and that has been changed into game form by emergence of a new complexity in emotional response to the mother and in imitative adaptation to her patterning of play. The fun of action and singing games is somehow related to the development of a power to predict the consequences of another person's actions and expressions, infants of the same age sharing a parallel development of interest in contingent events produced mechanically or electrically by their own movements (Papousek, 1967; Watson, 1977).

The basis for this sensitivity is to be found in the rhythm of engagements in the period of primary intersubjectivity, and before that in sensitive fitting in of movements between mother and newborn (Condon & Sander, 1974). It probably goes back to interactions that took place *in utero*. Our photographs show that mothers tend to favor the right hand in action games and they usually try to make the infants respond with their right hands (Figs. 8.1 and 8.2). Active play of infants, once they have achieved efficient voluntary control of hand movements, may counteract this favoring of the right hand if the infant is a left hander (Figs. 8.1, F and 8.7, B and C).

## Older Infants: Improved Manipulative Control and Imitated Gestures

Two other groups of infants were photographed after 20-weeks-of-age as shown in Table 8.Ib. Six of these were seen between 20 and 40 weeks and four between

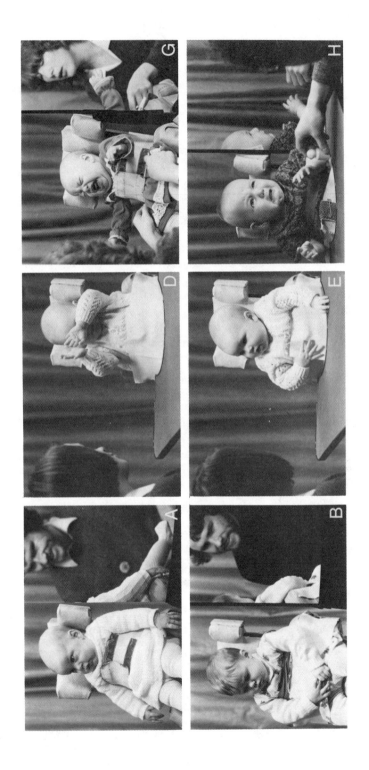

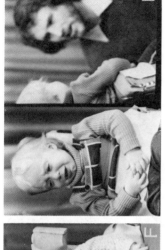
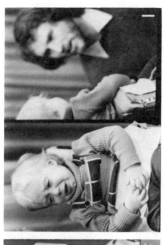
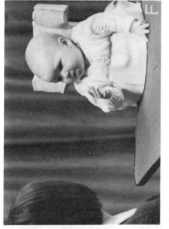

FIG. 8.5. Older infants showing fear of strangers. *A* LP, 24 weeks, staring with hands hanging down; *B* EM, 32 weeks, clasping hands and avoiding gaze; *C* PH, 40 weeks, staring with solemn face, hands hanging; *D*, *E* and *F*, EB, 25 weeks, covering eyes, scratching at restraining hand and gesture to mouth when about to cry; *G* LP, 16 weeks, crying in anger with mother, arms extended and flapping; *H* CR, 40 weeks, and *I* AS, 53 weeks, sad cry, hands tending to clasp, when these older infants are frightened by a stranger.

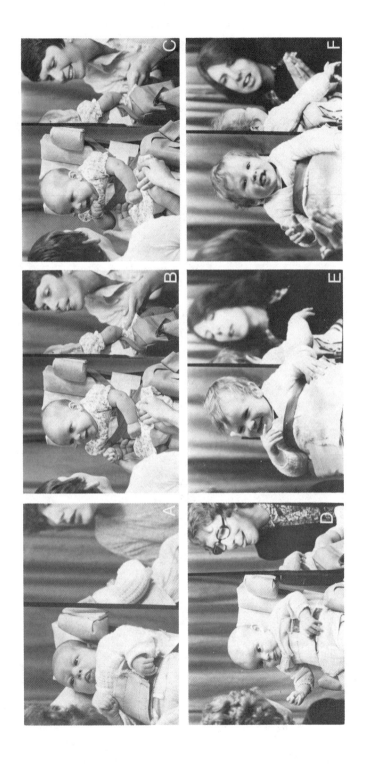

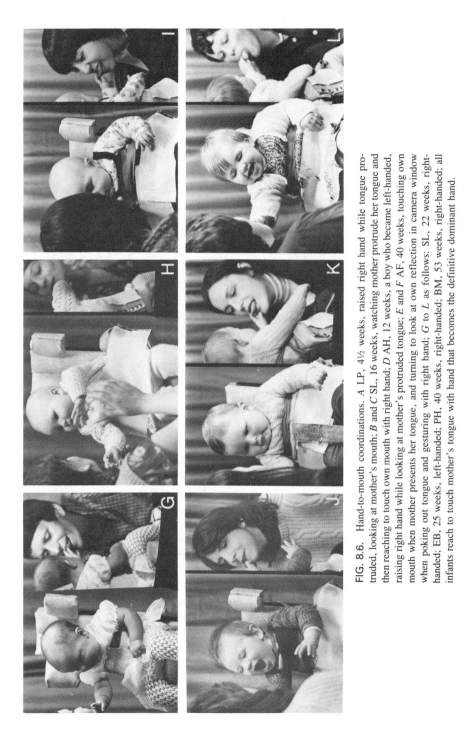

FIG. 8.6. Hand-to-mouth coordinations. *A* LP, 4½ weeks, raised right hand while tongue protruded, looking at mother's mouth; *B* and *C* SL, 16 weeks, watching mother protrude her tongue and then reaching to touch own mouth with right hand; *D* AH, 12 weeks, a boy who became left-handed, raising right hand while looking at mother's protruded tongue; *E* and *F* AF, 40 weeks, touching own mouth when mother presents her tongue, and turning to look at own reflection in camera window when poking out tongue and gesturing with right hand; *G* to *L* as follows: SL, 22 weeks, right-handed; EB, 25 weeks, left-handed; PH, 40 weeks, right-handed; BM, 53 weeks, right-handed; all infants reach to touch mother's tongue with hand that becomes the definitive dominant hand.

177

33 and 56 weeks. Subsequent observations at 2, 3, and 5 years as described below have established that one girl of these groups (EB) is strongly left-handed (see Figs. 8.6 to 8.9). The others are at least predominantly right-handed for acquired praxic skills and expressive or declarative gestures. The left-hander is of particular interest as she is both lively and clever, being the most advanced in language and other social skills of fourteen infants seen after 2 years. In a number of expressive and imitated actions she showed her left handedness before she was 30-weeks-of-age. For comparable actions all the other infants exhibited preferential use of the right hand.

We have described elsewhere how infants exhibit an important change in capacity to imagine their mother's intentions regarding objects and to share performance of manipulation tasks (Hubley & Trevarthen, 1979; Trevarthen & Hubley, 1978; Trevarthen, 1979b). This new insight into communication about objects, called Secondary Intersubjectivity, comes at a time when the hands are starting to show complementarity of manipulative action and when objects are used in combination by the two hands acting in coordination under visual guidance. We, and others, have drawn attention to the coincidence of the change in communicative function with development of a significant level of object permanence as brought out by Piagetian concealment and displacement tests with objects the infants want to grasp. However, it is clear that the quasi-symbolic gestural behavior in direct communication, both used by and understood by these infants towards the end of the first year, and the protolanguage functions emerging in their vocalizations (Halliday, 1975) cannot be explained as automatic consequences of a development in the infant's concept of physically described objects as entities separate and distinct from their bodies. Some specific motivation for cooperative interaction with the mother, some representation of mutual awareness requiring understanding of the communicative value of gestures, expressions and prosodic inflections of voice all together, is involved. The spontaneous use of the hands for expression gives interesting evidence on the cerebral structures that are incorporated in this important psychological development. Moreover, new kinds of imitated hand action emerge at this time. The child expresses a new level of intersubjectivity or "human sense" with hands, as well as with direction of looking, facial expressions, vocalizations, and various attitudes or posturings of the whole body.

The close coordination of expressive movements of one hand with mouth movements that was shown developing before 6 months was picked up immediately with the older group. These infants reached out with one hand to the mother's mouth or touched their own mouth while watching hers. Nine of the 10 infants used their right hands—the one exception is EB, the girl who from 25 weeks was increasingly left-handed in her communicative and imitated skills. She touched her own and her mother's mouth with her left hand (Table 8.4 and Fig. 8.6).

TABLE 8.4
Handedness of Infants in Second and Third Years

|  | Age in Months | Female | | | | | | | Male | | | | | | |
|---|---|---|---|---|---|---|---|---|---|---|---|---|---|---|---|
|  |  | SL | LO | EB* | EM | CR | BM | JJ | AH* | PL | MT | AF | MS | AS | CK |
| (a) Meaningful Actions | 19 | rl | rl |  |  |  |  |  | rl | Rl | rl |  |  |  |  |
|  | 25-28 | Rl | R | L | Lr | Lr | R | RL | Lr | R | Rl | R | R | R | RL |
|  | 36-39 | R | R | L | RL | R | R | Rl | L | R | Rl |  | R | R | Rl |
| (b) Storing | 19 | Lr | Lr |  |  |  |  |  | RL | L | Lr |  |  |  |  |
|  | 25-28 | LR | L | R | L | RL | L | R | Rl | LR | LR | L | L | Rl | Lr |
|  | 36-39 | L | L | R | L | Lr | L | L | R | L | R | L | L | Rl | L |

Meaningful actions are listed in Table 8.5. Storing refers to holding an object without paying attention to it, while activity is concentrated in the other hand. *EB and AH are left-handers.

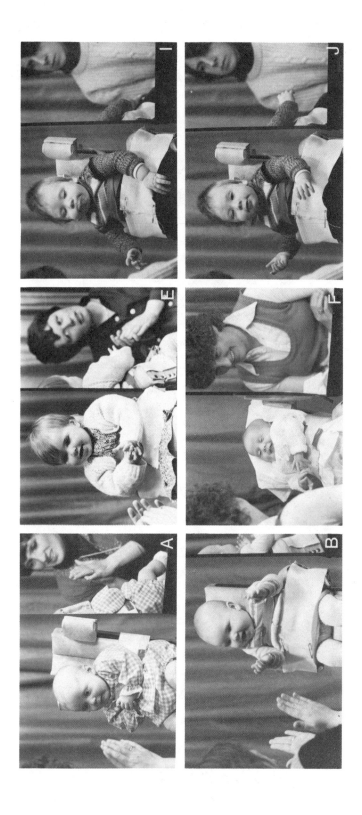

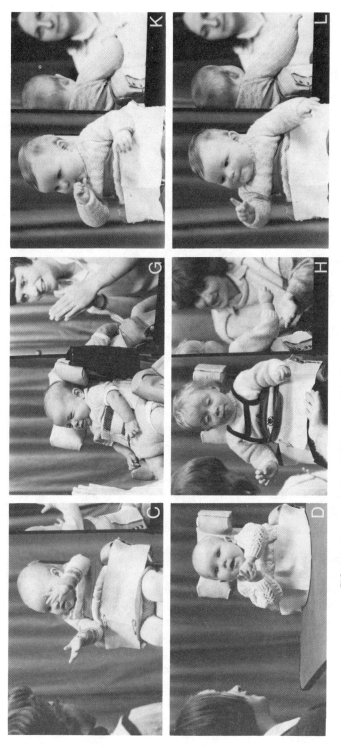

FIG. 8.7.   Learned tricks and "showing off". *A* LO, 20 weeks, imitating hand clapping, no sign of dominant hand; *B* and *C*, EB, 28 weeks, a left-hander, claps left hand over right when imitating her mother play a "Clappa, Clappa Handies" song, then in a "demonstration" to a stranger; *D*, EB, 25 weeks, another spontaneous "demonstration" to a stranger with left hand over right; *E* BM, 53 weeks, a right-hander, imitates her mother clap putting right hand onto left; *F* to *J* respectively; LO, 8 weeks; SL, 12 weeks; AS, 49 weeks; AF, 32 weeks; comical expressions with closed eyes and gestures, the older infants AS and AF, who were right-handed, make gestures with right hand; *K* and *L* PH, 36 weeks, when mother keeps her face still and remains silent, her infant performs a "trick" she has taught him, attempting to pop his right index finger in his mouth.

181

The most interesting imitated expressive hand activity took place in the situation where the mother was asked to teach her child to clap hands (Fig. 8.7). EB learned this trick earlier than the other infants and from the start she showed a tendency to clap like most left-handed adults do—with the prone left palm over the supine right palm. Both her parents are right-handed and her mother clapped in the most common way, with right hand over left. Several of the other infants showed a less clear right hand clapping—most being ambiguous in their rather clumsy attempts to imitate this under 1-year-of-age. Several of these infants reproduced imitated displays that they had learned previously, both to their mothers when the latter were keeping their faces immobile in the "Still Face" test, and to strangers, as if an awkward and embarrassing situation stimulated an impulse to self-assertion or a display of "cleverness." These displays were made with the habitually expressive hand, usually the right (Fig. 8.7).

Among the other right hand gesticulations of the over-6-month-olds was an interesting group that accompanied peculiar self-conscious displays that emerged in play—frequently while the infant was looking at his or her image reflected in the glass of the camera window (Figs. 8.6 and 8.7). These included raising of one overextended wrist with clasped and opposed fingers while the infant grimaced with tightly pursed lips, exaggeratedly raised (supercilious) brows and half-closed eyes.

Defensive and self-touching movements when the infants were avoiding or afraid with the stranger, or distressed and angry with their mothers, were made by both hands, but there appears to be a tendency for right-handers in positive expressive behavior to make self-comforting movements to the head, face or mouth with the left hand. Some defensive movements made with the expressively "dominant" hand, including EB's movement to hide her eyes from the stranger with her left hand (Fig. 8.5), may represent a movement adaptively motivated to show the other an expression of distress, rather than an entirely self-related defense. Ambiguity concerning the inner motives for hand movements is a real difficulty when the child is reacting with a mixture of fear and playfulness with a stranger.

The corpus of photographs does not reveal any lateral asymmetry or preference in the reaching and grasping to the ball (Fig. 8.2), behavior which became steadily more proficient and then highly playful after 6 months (Trevarthen, 1983b). (We may find asymmetries in these behaviors when we examine the videotapes more closely. Von Hofsten [1980] reports that infants 18- to 36-weeks-of-age show hand preference in intercepting moving objects.) Nor did we find any clear sidedness in the complex exploratory and manipulative actions of the hands with the dolls and truck before 9 months. Some infants who communicated well by 1 year, and who started to pay close attention to their mother's instructions about putting the dolls in the truck, simultaneously showed clear hand preference for the shared manipulation, using the dominant hand (i.e., the one that also made the above described expressive movements) to give and receive in joint performance of the task. Again, when we have completed detailed analysis of the videorecords of ball catching and the play with the truck and dolls manipulative asymmetries may come clear, but, in the photographs, the two hands reach about equally to catch the suspended ball, and with the dolls either hand is used to grasp, hold up and look at, bring to the mouth, or to hit against the table, as well as to put in and take out of the truck when not following directives of the mother.

A few imitated gestures revealed the growing capacity of infants under 9-months-of-age to identify with and return hand gestures of their parents. Subject PS learned before 36 weeks to imitate the movement to pop his right index finger in his mouth, though he could not make the sound (Fig. 8.7). He tended to extend his right index finger as a demonstrative gesture in other situations as well—e.g., when playing with the ball his mother was moving about and when trying to attract her attention when her face was immobile (Figs. 8.2,*F* and 8.7,*L*). He also held out one of the wooden men to her as if indicating it were interesting or offering it to his mother, though he was probably not intending anything so clear—merely expressing himself. EM used her right hand to bat the ball in play with her mother at 41 weeks, and EB (the early left-hander) used her then dominant left hand at 28 weeks to wipe a doll held in her right hand (Fig. 8.8). At 41 weeks EB again made this left-hand gesture, with no visible model, in immediate response to hearing her mother saying ''Dirty!'' in a disgusted tone of voice after E had put the doll in her mouth. The three wooden dolls had round holes about 5mm in diameter in their base and several of the infants discovered these. EB, at 28 weeks, held one doll upside down in her right hand and poked her left index finger in the hole. She was also seen to transfer objects to her left hand before holding them up to inspect them visually with care.

Hubley has noted that when infants over 40-weeks-of-age are collaborating with their mother in a joint task they frequently make vocalizations and gestures that acknowledge the partnership of interest that the task requires (Hubley & Trevarthen, 1979). Examples of a typical right-hand bias for cooperative actions and for gestures related to the instructions being passed on by the mother are shown in Fig. 8.8.

## THE CASE FOR AN INNATE PREVERBAL EXPRESSIVE SYSTEM WITH COMPOUND ASYMMETRY OF CONTROL

The behavior of the under-2-month-olds indicates that an asymmetric cerebral system coordinating expressive movements of vocalization and articulation with gestural movements of the hands can attain a minimal functional state before birth. The infant's hand movements are complex; elevation of the palm and supination of the wrist with various clasping and extension movements of the

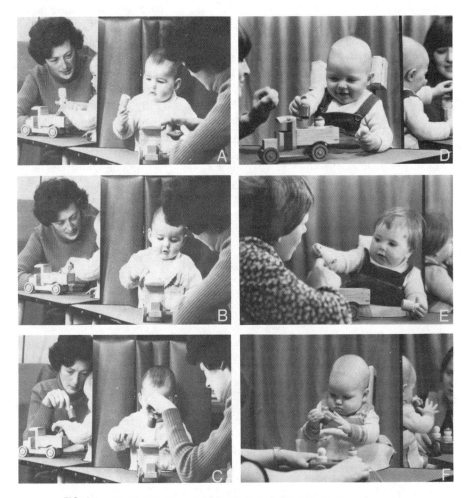

FIG. 8.8. *A* to *C* AW, 50 weeks, infant follows mother's instruction, given with a right index finger pointing to the truck, to put a wooden doll in the truck and, when the mother gives a second instruction, the infant points at the truck with the right hand before grasping the doll to obey the instruction (photos courtesy Penelope Hubley; see Hubley & Trevarthen, 1979); *D* JJ, 47 weeks, obeying the mother's message, and putting the doll in with the right hand; *E* BM, 56 weeks, mother points to the truck, infant holds out doll in right hand vocalizing a "request" for the mother to put the doll in herself. The mother complied; *F* EB, 28 weeks, mother says "Dirty!" in a disgusted voice when infant puts doll in own mouth, then infant wipes doll with left hand. EB is left-handed.

fingers, including index finger pointing. The whole emission or "utterance" appears to have a right orienting bias, the lifting of the right hand being frequently linked to shift of gaze away from the mother to the right as the infant vocalizes (Trevarthen, 1984d). Responses of this form of behavior to the mother's expressions of affect, speech, and touching show that the infant's motor coordinative structures are integrated with motivational and perceptual mechanisms that are specially adapted for communication (Trevarthen, 1984e). The infant has a control system that functions in interaction with the mother and the two of them can enter into two-way or reciprocal exchanges that have a "protoconversational" organization. Apparently, mother and infant move to closely similar internal beat of motivation and they share the same evaluation of emotions to adjust their behaviors to each other (Trevarthen, 1984b, 1984c).

The mother's behavior, her subtly regulated emotional tone, what she says and her gestures to touch the infant's hands or face show that she expects to perceive the infant's movements as expressions addressed to her. The occasional precise imitative or mirror responses made by the infant, or emissions synchronized with the mother's expressions, confirm that a motivational coincidence can be achieved by an accommodation on the infant's part. But imitations of the infant by the mother facilitate such exact counterpoint (Trevarthen, 1977, 1979a). The rapidity with which expressions and gestures are exchanged (inside a second) and the systematic development of engagements (over several seconds) demonstrate the openness and generative power of the motivational engagement, each partner seeking a right moment to assert an expressive utterance in relation to what the other is doing (Trevarthen, 1984c, 1984d).

This kind of positive and constructive interaction of Primary Intersubjectivity at 2 months or less, marked by signs of pleasure or *affiliative* emotion in both mother and infant, contrasts clearly with the situation where there is a breakdown of contact with the mother or where the infant is distressed by some painful internal stimulus, or by fatigue. Neonates have very clear displays of distress or displeasure that include vigorous cyclical threshing and pulling-in movements of arms and hands. The 2-month-olds also move their hands in characteristic manner when the interaction with the mother is perturbed. Our data suggest that self-touching movements directed to body or clothing, hand clasping, hand regard, touching of the face or side of the head, stretching out of the hands and occasional large flailing movements of one or both arms with partly closed or clenched hands are not random discoordinated motor activity or simple reflex approach and withdrawal responses, but adaptive expressions systematically linked to withdrawn, sad, or angry facial and vocal displays that solicit a particular pattern of care or comfort from the mother. The tendency for self-touching movements accompanying unsmiling avoidance to be made with the left hand seems to be evidence for a complementary motivational and expressive organization in which both positive affiliative and declarative kinds of impulse invoke right hand movements, while more withdrawn and self-directed or protesting, negative, avoidant states involve the left hand.

The reciprocal arm-hand patterns have some resemblance to the postural sets and reflex reactions well known to pediatric neurologists, but it must be emphasized that the movements are active coordinations to events remote from the body that are not elicited in reflex manner by discrete tactile, proprioceptive or vestibular stimuli—nor could they be formed by chains of reflexes triggered from within the infant's body. The positive expressions that coordinate face, voice, and hands so precisely are spontaneously emitted and guided by highly specific events emanating from the mother that are perceived in the main by visual and auditory means. I believe that the above described lateral asymmetries are an adaptive feature of goal-directed movements, and a product of genetic regulation of brain embryogenesis, not a trivial morphogenetic accident nor a consequence of fetal posture. Indeed, lateral asymmetries in the tonic neck reflex most clearly seen in sleeping infants below 3-months-of-age, or those in grasping and pulling-in reflexes, may be seen as a consequence or immature concomitant of structural asymmetries that show their function only when they are incorporated in the activity of a sentient and responsive infant in upright position and trying to control a specific event in the external world.

## Changes with Motor Development—Sex Differences

The apparent decline in asymmetric hand movements after 3 months, coincident with rapid growth in strength and control in the axial and proximal musculature and advances in exploratory and prehensile behaviors, is of great interest in the search for evidence on regional brain growth in infants. The dip in frequency of one-handed expressive movements, which accompanies reduction of cooing and prespeech, should be related to changes in prereaching that occur a few weeks earlier, and to the decline of neonatal stepping (Thelen, 1984). Von Hofsten (1984) has charted a sharp decline in aimed extensions of the arms to a visually fixated object at 7 weeks after birth. Thereafter, the pattern of arm and hand coordination for reaching and grasping that is clearly evident in neonates and coupled to conjugated head and eye orienting to an external goal undergoes partial disorganization and reintegration, before a more powerful and more versatile guidance of reaching develops after 4 months (Trevarthen, 1982, 1983b). Von Hofsten (1980) reports asymmetries in the reach and grasp movements after 15 weeks to intercept an object swinging rapidly past the infant. He proved that the infants perceive the velocity of the object and project their hand with accurate prediction in a repeated ballistic trajectory (with surges) to get ahead of and catch the target. Several of his subjects showed consistent preferences to catch with one hand, and they waited for the object to come by in a direction favoring that hand.

The photographs of under-6-month-olds reviewed here do not show any difference in frequency or form of left and right movements to reach for the ball on a string or in attempts to play with the wooden dolls and truck. All six subjects seemed to go through a period where gesticulatory behavior was diminished and lateral preferences vanished.

In this small population the girls were in advance of the boys in entering and leaving this delateralized phase. By 6 months all of the girls were again showing right hand preference for expressive gestures of a positive affiliative nature, but the boys were all then without evident asymmetry (the special case of AH is taken up below). Von Hofsten's data on prereaching suggest that his twelve girl subjects as a group showed an earlier, smaller, and briefer decline in arm responses than the eight boys (von Hofsten, 1984). He and Lindhagen also found girls to be in advance of boys in catching moving objects at 3- to 6-months (von Hofsten & Lindhagen, 1979). Held, Shimojo, and Gwiazda (1984) report that the rapid development of binocular stereoacuity at 5- to 6-months occurs a few weeks earlier in girls and they relate this to segregation of the ocular dominance territories in the visual cortex. They suggest that the delay in boys may be a consequence of a pulse in testosterone production which occurs only in boys between 2- and 15-weeks after birth (Forest, Cathiard, & Bertrand, 1973; Ratcliffe, 1984). Whether the sex hormone does have differential control over developments in the asymmetrically organized parts of the cerebral hemispheres or whether cerebral developments differing in males and females trigger the hormone production changes as a feedback system in a complex epigenetic neuro-humoral control loop remain questions to be resolved, but any sex differences in development of lateral asymmetry are potentially of importance in the search for the cellular mechanisms of hemispheric differentiation that relate to universal stages of psychological growth.

Leaving this issue for a moment, let us summarize the findings for the second 6 months after birth. In this period, infants develop precise manipulation under visual control and they exhibit a rapid development in conceptualization of the behavior and properties of objects and their affordances for bimanual use— including a capacity to represent nonpresent objects and events as having permanent existence and permanent identities. The corpus of photographs that has been reviewed reveals that, in this period, there are also large changes in the infant's communicative expression and imagination of other persons' states of mind. While the form of primary emotional expressions and their code or relationship to the quality of interpersonal contact remain the same (Trevarthen, 1984c), and while the hands regain an expressiveness close to that seen several months previously, many new forms of gesture and of sensitivity to the mother's expressions appear. Hand-to-mouth movements seem particularly interesting.

All but one subject reached to the mother's tongue (when she was trying to get the infant to imitate tongue protrusion) with their right hands. The exception, EB, later proved to be ahead of all other subjects, in rate of language development and in learning of conventional imaginative play, and she was an early left-hander. EB reached with her left hand to her mother's mouth at 25 weeks. She also clapped with the left hand above the right at 25 and 28 weeks. The other subjects, all less clear in this imitation than EB, were ambiguous or placed the right hand above the left in attempts to clap. A boy, PH, who clapped right-over-left at 24 weeks, had learned to imitate the movement of popping the finger in the mouth and he did this spontaneously with his right hand at 36 weeks, both to his mother and to a stranger (Figs. 8.2 and 8.7).

The reaching out and display movements favoring one hand when the infants, at 6- to 8-months, were engaging in friendly playful response to the mother or to strangers seemed to be clearly lateralized to the later-to-be-dominant hand. The few pointing movements during tracking of the ball, with the exception of PH's demonstrative (symbolic?) pointing, did not appear to show any lateral asymmetry and I think they should be seen as part of orienting and attending, in flexible response to the position of the ball round the body of the baby and in the field shared with the mother.

As infants gain in capacity to conceive a shared topic of interest and in the use of gestures to deliver a diectic message to the mother, cerebral control of pointing must change. At present, the evidence from rather artificial test situations as well as from more normal contexts is that the infant's understanding and following of the mother's pointing gestures may precede making pointing movements to show her something or to ask her about something (Bruner, 1976; Murphy & Messer, 1977; Murphy, 1978; Bates, Benigni, Bretherton, & Volterra, 1977; Scaife & Bruner, 1975; Leung & Rheingold, 1981). Nevertheless, it should be recalled that, in their spontaneous expressive responses to maternal attentions, even 1- and 2-month-olds may make a coordinated head and eye orientation and point in the same direction with an index finger even when there is no target to attract this orienting. The significant feature of the deliberate and/or imitated pointing for communication that emerges some time after 7 or 8 months will be in the control of the act with respect to the place and identity of surrounding objects of interest, and with respect to the mother's sharing of interest and action. Neonates and 2-month-olds make expressive waving, pointing, and finger clasping gestures as part of an interpersonal response and they may imitate hand movements (Maratos, 1973; Meltzoff & Moore, 1977), but they do not adapt them to circumstances or to the interests of the partner. Nine- to 12-month-olds begin to control the use of these gestures to deliver a familiar and recognizable message to a partner they trust, and they begin to combine the gestures with protolinguistic vocalizations, i.e., vocalizations with clarified illocutionary force.

Although few asymmetries were picked up in the still photographs of the under 12-month-old subjects reaching for or manipulating objects, there is evidence of consistent handedness in manipulation and for emergence of complementarity of hand action in this period, after 9 months. The majority view is that the left hand leads in prehension between 3- and 6-months for most infants, then the right hand becomes most active especially for finer more visually guided actions (Gesell & Ames, 1947; Seth, 1973).

The method Gesell and Ames (1947) used for testing hand preferences of infants had severe limitations: They dangled toys over a baby lying on its back in a cot, or they put objects that had no relation to an interactive context in standard positions on a table in front of the seated child. But they were undoubtedly right in insisting that handedness cannot be a single trait; it must be the outcome of intricate cerebral developments. They did not observe individuals in enough detail *longitudinally* to clarify the factors causing fluctuations in hand preference, and the same may be said for Seth (1973) who followed Gesell techniques. Gesell and Ames (1947) quote observations of vacillations of dominance by Giesecke (1936) and Lesne and Peycelon (1934) who reported "unidexterity" to be established by 10 or 11 months. Young, Lock, and Service (1985) have recorded frequencies of left and right "pointing," "holding an object out in the visual field of the mother" (i.e., possibly offering or showing) and "other gestures" (e.g., reaching to tug mother's clothes) as well as object-directed actions, between 8 and 15 months. They found no evidence that handedness changed in strength, but gestures (mostly pointing) increased after 10 months for the right hand but not for the left. There was an upsurge of right-handed offering and then pointing by mothers between 9 and 11 months—as we would predict from the development of infant participation in task sharing after 40 weeks (Hubley & Trevarthen, 1979; Trevarthen, 1983b). The cooperative/communicative significance of actions is not described by Young et al., though one of their situations was play with a box of assorted toys.

Bresson et al. (1977) studied upright, seated infants from 17 weeks to 40 weeks, offering a 2cm orange cube in the tips of fingers of one hand, on an extended palm, on a large blue cube, and on a flat white board. They traced developments from ballistic grabs before 21 weeks, reaching to the support only, to the support with the left hand and the object with the right hand, and sliding with one hand (usually the right) via the surface to the object. The ages at which successive levels of control emerged depended on the visuo-spatial features of the goal and its context, and they argued that the infant was developing better visual perception of the context for hand action, emphasizing, as did Seth (1973), that asymmetric reaching is collaborative, left hand stabilizing the relationship to the support and right-hand focusing on the discrete target. Bresson et al. suggest that this may express innate complementary functions of the cerebral hemispheres for visuo-motor control.

Among our subjects, BM, later a definite right-hander, transferred objects between the hands at 56 weeks. She seemed to favor use of the right hand for finer inspection of the object, or for putting it in her mouth.

The relationship between the development of bimanual coordination and division of labor between the hands for manipulation and the expressive function of the hands in communication remains to be elucidated. Ramsay (1980) has reported a fluctuation in hand preference for object prehension that is coupled to development of canonical babbling—early babblers show lateral asymmetry of reaching earlier, the asymmetry that appears at the onset of babbling being followed by a temporary disappearance of hand preference. Both sex differences and individual differences in rate of attainment of milestones in manipulative dexterity and protolanguage or speech will be of interest in this period leading into the second year.

A few instances photographed here of apparent complementary hand use seem to support the link with eventual manual dominance for skilled imitative use of objects, but it should be noted that these early actions all appear to have a potential or well-defined communicative significance as well. We do not know what, in fact, was motivating the infants to perform in the studies of Bresson et al. (1977) and Ramsay. It is likely that infants over 8-months-of-age will be inclined to construe any task that is presented ritually, as in an experiment, as some kind of play with communicative value. This issue grows to dominate the interpretation of asymmetries of gesture and object handling in the second and third years.

## GESTURE AND EUPRAXIS WITH THE DEVELOPMENT OF SPEECH

The video recordings in the second and third year show that our subjects were gaining not only in their capacities to understand and use speech with their mothers, but also in their awareness of the meaningfulness and usefulness of objects made for a purpose. They were gaining in culturally significant skills that defined instrumental functions and gave an agreed sense to things.

The four subjects seen around the end of the first year showed signs of increasing interest in their mothers' purposes and they started to share manipulation of the dolls and truck like those other subjects whose behavior has been studied longitudinally in detail by Penelope Hubley. A few interesting cases of right-hand gesture in this cooperative play lend support to the idea that the insight for Secondary Intersubjectivity and sharing a task is the outcome of a development in the same system as regulates expressive messages to another trusted companion earlier in infancy (Fig. 8.6; see Trevarthen & Hubley, 1978; Trevarthen, 1979b; Hubley & Trevarthen, 1979; Trevarthen, 1983b).

Five of the six infants studied in the first 6 months (Table 8.1) were also observed at 18- to 19-months-of-age. Their hand activities, with those of the larger group who came to the laboratory at 2- and 3-years-of-age, are summarized in Table 8.5. Examples of their actions with the objects are shown in Fig. 8.9.

In a preliminary analysis of the videotapes and photographs of these sessions we have noted all the actions of the infants as they played with a set of toys

TABLE 8.5
Meaningful Actions with Unfamiliar Laboratory Toys and Dolls in Free Play

### At 19 Months

| | | |
|---|---|---|
| Holding cup to drink | Pouring teapot | Pushing train, truck |
| Cup to mother, doll | Stirring "tea" with spoon | Using baby bottle as |
| Baby bottle to self | Spooning "sugar" or "food" | screwdriver |
| Baby bottle to doll | Brushing hair (self, doll, mother) | Using brush to clean truck |
| | | Hugging, cuddling doll |

### New Actions After 2 Years

| | |
|---|---|
| Feeding self "food" | Washing dishes |
| Putting lid on teapot, sugar bowl | Drying dishes |
| Cutting with knife, eating with fork | Scraping plate clean* |
| Putting "food" in cup, plate | Wiping bath |
| Holding hot "tea" to blow and cool it | Mopping up spilt "milk" |
| Wiping doll's face with sponge | Turning bath taps on, off |
| Wiping own face with sponge | Placing and tucking in blankets |
| Pulling clothes off doll | on bed |
| Drying doll on table, chair | Drawing (3 years) |
| Putting doll in bed, bath | Laying out cutlery* |
| Waving to doll | Dealing cards* |
| | Cradling doll to give bottle* |

* For scraping the plate, dealing cards and laying out cutlery the subdominant hand held the plate, or stored and the dominant hand scraped, or laid down cards or cutlery. The doll was cradled in the subdominant hand while the bottle was held in the dominant hand. Quotation marks indicate imagined items.

resembling objects that they would be likely to recognize. Pointing did not emerge as a consistently lateralized behavior, but the intention to use an instrument "properly" appeared to favor activity of a dominant hand by 2 years, or earlier. We were indeed surprised that the purposes of several of the objects, actually never seen before, were recognized by the 19-month-olds, apparently without help from their mothers. At this age, the children were characteristically independent of their mothers' ideas about what to do (it is Spitz' period of "No!") and although they heard and understood some names of things and acted accordingly, it must be admitted that many of their actions were meaningless *sensorimotor* behaviors exploring the affordances of things, their feel, noisiness, etc. Attempts made to do some *proper* actions are listed in Table 8.5, and the lateral preferences for such actions are summarized in Table 8.4. (A more detailed report is in preparation.) The youngest showed manipulative preferences for short periods, but on the whole they were unnervingly ambidextrous. Subject PL demonstrated a clear right-handedness, however. Further analysis will be needed to decide if the others were expressing consistent asymmetries for some of their purposes. An underlying difference between the hands was seen in the tendency of four subjects, all eventually right-handed, to keep (store) objects that they were not attending to in the left hand. The fifth child, who was definitely left-handed by 2 years, used his right hand more frequently to store.

The results for 2 and 3 years show that while the children differed in rate of development of a stable hand preference, ten already showed the direction in which they were heading for at 2 years (Fig. 8.9). Two of these, AH and EB, are

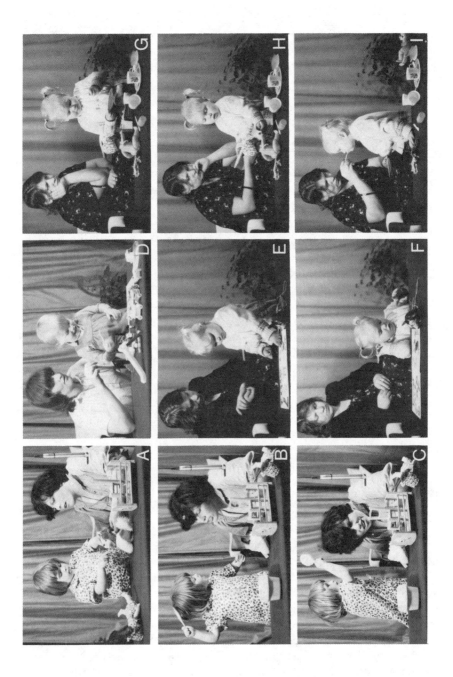

left-handers at 5 years. Of the remaining four, CK and CR appear to be late right-handers and EM and JJ are more ambidextrous.

A definite link was detected between the development of speech and the emergence of dominance in conventional manual praxis within the limits of our infrequent sampling. As each child gained a clear and consistent hand preference his or her speech became richer in vocabulary and clearer in articulation. More significantly, the slow developers in speech also had uncertain handedness for longer. At 3 and 5 years, AH was speaking less clearly and less fluently than the other children. We are following this lead to check an impression that lateralization of hand use is defined *before* the vocabulary starts to grow rapidly. Many 2-year-olds worked busily with their dominant hands while silent or speaking very little.

When a child grows into a left-hander in a family of right-handers there is clearly some powerful internal determinant of which hand will be preferred for actions to be shared with others. EB, a first child with right-handed parents exhibited her left-handedness at 6 months and she resisted all efforts to make her do things with her right hand. AH at 19- and 29-months was, in contrast to EB, in considerable conflict—possibly this relates to his much less independent personality. At 2, he kept changing from left to right preference, especially when approaching his right-handed mother or being led by her in exploration of the objects. He had toys (e.g., a crank-handle music box) that did not work properly if he used his left hand as he repeatedly tried to do. He has two older sisters who are strongly right-handed. The difficulty for a child in this position is that one's impulses to make symbolic actions make one's behavior part of others' consciousness—they can decide if it is working as communication or not, and they can try to change it.

## Differences in Language Development and Epigenetics of Handedness

Our population is too small to justify generalizations about the occurrence of normal and pathological forms of development, but the individual data on changes with age can demonstrate the complexity of factors affecting use of the hands to perform socially meaningful actions. The boy, AH, who had high socioeconomic advantages, was slow to develop a clear hand preference, was more left-handed at 3, expressed himself awkwardly in speech and was less inclined at 2 and 3 to take initiative in using objects for conventional purposes.

---

FIG. 8.9.    Two-year-olds play with their mothers, using objects with imagination for their 'proper' functions. *A, B* and *C* BM, 26 months, a right-hander, feeds a toy dog, brushes own hair and brushes mother's hair, all with right hand; *D* JJ, 25½ months, a right-hander, puts piece in jigsaw puzzle with right hand; *E* to *I* EB, 27 months, a left-hander, counts pennies from right hand to place them with left hand, gestures with left hand while counting, scrapes plate and feeds doll with left hand. Mother uses right hand to "feed" EB.

His mother maintained a gentle but insistent and somewhat insensitive control and, though he eventually asserted his independence, it appears as though there is a link between his hesitation over which hand to use, his slow grasp of symbolic initiatives including speech and his mother's highly controlling, protective approach to their play together. When he was 19-months-old, she seemed to bring his attention to rather meaningless, self-gratifying behaviors, and perhaps she felt she was helping his communication. Now 5½, he is firmly left-handed. He is regarded as intelligent and well-adjusted socially but is causing some concern in his speech development. His first efforts at writing show many reversals of letters.

Subject EB, the other left-hander, was entirely different. From 6 months, she showed a precocious initiative in performance of imitated gestures and activities and her mother and father encouraged her to master many performances for the pleasure of others. She was strongly left-handed in imitative clapping at 6 months, before any of the other subjects had learned a comparable play action. At 18 months, she was in advance of the others in speech and in adaptation to the meaningful objects. She maintained this lead in handedness, skill in using familiar objects and speech, demonstrating a considerable repertoire of nursery songs at 2 and is now, at 6, recognized as a bright, self-possessed and fluent primary school girl in spite of a very unfavorable socioeconomic status. (She came from our poorest working-class family and lives on the edge of a poor neighborhood with high unemployment where she goes to school.)

Unfortunately, EB was not seen before 6 months, so we have no information on her gestural asymmetry in the stage of Primary Intersubjectivity. The fact that AF was more strongly and more persistently right-handed with his expressive gestures than other subjects in early months indicates that early and late handedness may be the result of different psychological processes and different cerebral developments. His early manifest right-handedness is part of intense effort at expression when he was reacting positively to another person. His late developing left-handedness was a part of his slowly maturing competence for sharing understanding of the conventional meanings and uses of things.

Development of hand preferences in the rest of the population studied, including those with an early and strong right-handedness, and relatively fast development of speech, as well as less certain right-handers or ambidextrous subjects, some of whom appear to have difficulty in accepting conventional strategies for their manipulation of objects in the second and third years, fits the principle that hand preferences develop with communication from near the end of the first year onwards. Both hand preference for gesture and speech appear to develop in consequence of maturation in cerebral mechanisms that integrate inherent capacities for identifying with and complementing the purposeful behaviors of other persons. This development allows the child to find interest in the shared meanings of a language community, while his or her manipulative and object-conceiving skills are growing. The degree of privacy or sharing of these latter object-related activities seems to depend on the ease and speed with which two types of motive or representation, an intersubjective one and a privately subjective one, are integrated together in the child's mind. Some children make this step more quickly than others.

If I may be permitted some anatomical speculations, I would suggest that in addition to the well-supported concepts of Kuypers and his colleagues concerning parallel central motor systems for regulating proximal and distal musculature in the limbs (Kuypers, 1973), these central motor systems having differential maturation rates in infancy (Kuypers, 1962), we must consider mechanisms that couple hand movement to expressive communication. Kuyper's functional anatomy, confirmed by split-brain research (Brinkman & Kuypers, 1973; Trevarthen, 1968, 1984a), suggests ways of explaining both the development of arm and hand control and developments in perceptual acuity concerned with control of movements of different scale and different degrees of focal concentration on manipulative targets. It is also relevant to considerations of movements that are emitted as signals to be seen by another subject.

In evolution of primate communication, with increasingly visual reception of emotional signals in interactions, forelimb control systems have teamed up with the facial, oral, and vocal mechanisms, possibly by evolutionary making over of hand to mouth movements for feeding that appear in amphibia and reptiles but that become richly elaborated in primates. The spontaneous gesture-like movements of infants accompanying prespeech may be due to activity of subcortical systems of the basal ganglia and thalamus that have evolved along with new cortical mechanisms for communication, but that mature earlier than the cortex. Galaburda (1983) reviews recent evidence, from studies of fetal and postnatal developments in cerebral hemispheres of monkeys and from the distribution of anomalous clumps of neurones in the brain of a dyslexic boy, that cortex in the dorsal temporal lobe and temporo-parietal junction, important in humans for language, may have been formed of a particular contingent of cell population that multiply in a growth point called the "ganglionic eminence." At one point in time, about the middle of fetal development, this germinal region of the hemisphere wall injects neuroblasts into the basal ganglia and diencephalic nuclei on both sides as well as into the neocortex in the left hemisphere. It is possible that cells produced together and migrating apart become selectively connected when axons are produced and synaptic arrays form in late fetal or early postnatal stages. The dyslexic shows pathological cell clumps up and down the system responsible for reading.

It is possible that the spontaneous movements of arms and hands of infants under 3-months-of-age are patterned in the basal ganglia, possibly in association with supplementary motor cortex. The initiation and sensory guidance of these affectively modulated movements may be regulated from orbital and medial frontal cortex, as well as from anterior temporal/limbic cortices and mediodorsal thalamus. The complementary asymmetries observed, with the right hand being more expressive in positive interaction and the left more self-directed or self-regulatory, may have been set up in the early fetus in these anterior parts of the forebrain limbic and striatal systems.

The obscuring of these lateral asymmetries with emergence of controlled reaching in the fourth postnatal month suggests that proximal motor control, which requires information from specific proprioceptive and exproprioceptive systems implicating the posterior thalamus, parietal cortex, and cerebellum, is equally represented in both halves of the central nervous system, and/or that the proximal musculature and its sensory fields are bilaterally represented in each of the two halves of the brain. As refined manipulation develops, with its require-ments of high acuity focal visual guidance, sensitive somesthetic input from the hand and more direct pyramidal motor control from the precentral motor cortex, cerebral asymmetry of hand control reappears and this must be associated with large-scale functional advances in parietal cortex. I think it is likely that areas of cortex in the rear half of the brain, including the parieto-temporal junction (inferior parietal lobule), then begin their differentiation and become involved in perceptual guidance and programming of hand movement strategies that have communicative significance. This development may be closely coordinated with development of imitative speech, that would invoke the auditory perceptual functions of the temporal planum.

In the first year, handedness for object prehension and manipulation tends to disappear or moves to the left limb then shows right dominance for precise grasping with bimanual complementarity for object holding, the left hand sup-porting and the right hand selecting more precise goals. This progress would seem to indicate either emergence of a cerebral division of labor, each hand controlled by the opposite half-brain, and the two hemispheres coordinated through the corpus callosum or in subcortical structures, or development of control of the two hands in a system of one hemisphere that has overall domi-nance for purposeful, skilled manipulative praxis of both hands. Lateral asym-metry of hand control, probably more related to a phase of differentiation in lateral parietal cortex can, it would seem from AH's case, form a hand domi-nance that is of opposite direction to the earlier manifested asymmetry in ex-pressive hand movements for affiliative response to the mother. The emergence of firm and final hand preference in toddlers seems closely tied to the maturation of cerebral systems that reassert and elaborate the communicative purposes of hand movements. Evidently, the process involves integration (or reintegration) of systems in different parts of the cerebrum that may not agree in direction of lateral asymmetry for hand control.

To learn culturally approved and useful ways of employing objects (tool use) a child must take account of how others behave. However, the evidence suggests that the impulse to choose a particular hand for signing, as well as for doing meaningful tasks, is not itself imitated. At least some children firmly follow their own internal asymmetry of hand motivation for these skills, some strong left-handers, like EB, learning symbolic left-hand movements from right-handed adults more quickly than most right-hand children learn to be the same as their parents, and such strong left-handers may learn language more quickly too (Annett, 1970). Not agreeing with one's parents about which hand to use for communication does not have to be an obstacle to development of shared human intelligence. Nevertheless, the correlations in the case of some subjects between weaker left-handedness and slowed or even abnormal language development, especially for slow learning of reading and writing, would suggest that the process of brain development in late infancy can reflect confused and at least initially inefficient sorting of cerebral circuits linking speech with hand action. Since nearly all right-handers and most left-handers retain stronger representation of speech comprehension and production in the left half of the brain, the difficulties seem to arise from the way in which a reverse mechanism for hand dominance and visual and tactile control of socially important actions with the hands becomes reintegrated with already developed left hemisphere mechanisms for expressive use of voice under predominantly auditory control.

I cannot accept the proposition that the genetics of this developmental scenario is anyway as simple as either the widely accepted single allele hypothesis or the hypothesis of a somatic (extragenetic) source of left-right differences would claim (Annett, 1972; Corballis, 1983). Sex differences, male children being more often left-handed, with, especially in the weakly left-handed boys, slow language development or dyslexia, and the fact that makes one more often autistic than females, indicate an important epigenetic process in the sorting of inner-directed controls for communicative hand movement, and this process must relate to the possibly very indirect effects of sex linked genes on brain growth (Gillberg & Wahlström, 1985). The rare Rett's syndrome (autism/childhood psychosis) in which girls show retardation of language development, affective disturbances, and bizarre gesticulatory behaviors with loss of purposeful hand movements in the second or third year, a disease correlated with a fragile X chromosome anomaly, fra(X) (p22), indicates how the genetic system can have a devastating voice at the stage that hand preferences normally become fixed (Hagberg et al., 1983).

Why are there sex differences in development of communication? Males are more muscular with a greater chance of developing both visuo-spatial and mathematical skills to an exceptional degree. With regard to mathematical thought, Einstein said his mathematical invention came to awareness in the form of sensations of bodily movement, or visual images, and he stressed that the ideas were only symbolized later by an effortful process for the sake of communication or further processing in thought (Hadamard, 1945). It may be that development of body-related limb control and representation of a visuo-kinesthetic personal action space is stimulated by production of testosterone in males. This line of thought, generated by recent research of Geschwind and colleagues, merits careful attention (Geschwind & Behan, 1983; Geschwind & Galaburda, 1985a & b). Just before males show a more prolonged suppression of expressive right-handedness in early infancy, and again in early adolescence when differences in spatial and verbal ability appear between boys and girls, there are peaks of testosterone production. However, if testosterone is the trigger substance for asymmetries in brain mechanisms of communication and thought, its effects on brain development are prolonged and elaborate. It is just one component of the epigenetic mechanism that governs sex differences in brain development.

In most human cultures, where religious or political conceptions do not deliberately reshape behaviors contrariwise, females are more involved than males in interpersonal responsibilities and communication important in assisting early child development and males are more active in constructive invention and discovery. These psychological specializations may justify the evolutionary retention of the more difficult and risky male pattern of development, which may be closely paralleled in the development of some females as well. The sex differences in brains may help keep intact the complex balance of private self-discovery, exploration of nature, leadership, cooperation, communication, and imitation that vitalizes human communities and makes culture possible.

Study of patterns of hand preference in development can give us valuable evidence on this intriguing problem. The strangely conflicted strategy of development for manual skills of culture makes sense only if we recognize that human hands are motor organs for many cerebral systems, serving expressive communication, display of emotion, both exploratory and creative handling of objects and manufacture. Symbolic hand movements concentrated to a dominant hand unite all these functions for the first time some time near the end of infancy. From this point, hands are at the ready disposal of spoken language and their movements are primed to be cultivated in early childhood into a visible language that represents, or even replaces, speech. No wonder we cannot decipher development of hand control by counting which hand an infant uses to grasp at a meaningless object dangled on a string or placed in a standard midline position on a table top!

## ACKNOWLEDGMENTS

This research was supported by the Social Science Research Council of the U.K. and the Spencer Foundation of Chicago. I am indebted to Rhona Fraser for help in preparing the manuscript. My colleague Katerina Logotheti generously helped code hand positions.

## REFERENCES

Annett, M. (1970). The growth of manual preference and speed. *British Journal of Psychology, 61*, 545–558.

Annett, M. (1972). The distribution of manual asymmetry. *British Journal of Psychology, 63*, 343–358.

Baldwin, A. (1894). *Mental development in the child and the race.* New York: Macmillan.

Bates, E., Benigni, L., Bretherton, I., & Volterra, V. (1977). From gesture to the first word: On cognitive and social prerequisites. In M. Lewis & L. A. Rosenblum (Eds.), *Interaction, conversation and the development of language* (Ch. 11). New York: Wiley.

Birdwhistell, R. L. (1970). *Kinesics and context: Essays on body motion communication*. Philadelphia: University of Pennsylvania Press.

Box, H. O. (1977). Observations of spontaneous hand use in the common marmoset (*Callithrix jacchus*). *Primates, 18*, 395–400.

Bresson, F., Maury, L., Pieraut Le Bonniec, G., & Schonen, S. de (1977). Organization and lateralization of reaching in infants: An instance of dissymetric functions in hands collaboration. *Neuropsychologia, 15*, 311–320.

Brinkman, J., & Kuypers, H. G. J. M. (1973). Cerebral control of contralateral and ipsilateral arm, hand and finger movements in the split-brain rhesus monkey. *Brain, 966*, 653–674.

Brooker, A. S., Lehman, R. A. W., Heimbuch, R. C., & Kidd, R. K. (1981). Hand usage in a colony of Bosmet monkeys, *Macaca radiata*. *Behavior Genetics, 11*, 49–56.

Bruner, J. S. (1976). From communication to language—a psychological perspective. *Cognition, 3*, 225–287.

Carter, R. L., Hohenegger, M. K., & Satz, P. (1982). Aphasia and speech organization in children. *Science, 218*, 797–799.

Condon, W. S., & Sander, L. W. (1974). Neonate movement is synchronized with adult speech: Interactional participation and language acquisition. *Science, 183*, 99–101.

Corballis, M. C. (1983). *Human laterality*. New York: Academic Press.

Coren, S., & Porac, C. (1977). Fifty centuries of right-handedness: The historical record. *Science, 198*, 631–632.

Dalby, J. T., Gibson, D., Grossi, V., & Schneider, R. D. (1980). Lateralized hand gesture during speech. *Journal of Motor Behavior, 12*, 292–297.

Ekman, P., & Friesen, W. V. (1969). The repertoire of nonverbal behavior: Categories, origins, usage and coding. *Semiotica, 22*, 353–374.

Forest, M. G., Cathiard, A. M., & Bertrand, J. A. (1973). Evidence of testicular activity in early infancy. *Journal of Clinical Endocrinology and Metabolism, 37*, 148–151.

Freedman, N., & Hoffman, S. P. (1972). The analysis of movement behavior during Clinical Interviews. In A. Seigman & B. Pope (Eds.), *Studies in dyadic communication*, Elmsford, NY: Pergamon Press.

Galaburda, A. M. (1983). Definition of the anatomical phenotype. In C. L. Ludlow & J. A. Cooper (Eds.), *Genetic aspects of speech and language disorders* (pp. 71–84). New York: Academic Press.

Geschwind, N., & Behan, P. (1983). Left-handedness: Association with immune disease, migraine, and developmental learning disorder. *Proceedings of the National Academy of Sciences (Psychology), 79*, 5097–5100.

Geschwind, N., & Galaburda, A. M. (1985a,b). Cerebral lateralization. Biological mechanisms, associations and pathology: A hypothesis and a program for research. *Archives of Neurology, 42*, Part I, 428–459; Part II, 521–552.

Gesell, A., & Ames, L. B. (1947). The development of handedness. *Journal of Genetic Psychology, 70*, 155–175.

Giesecke, M. (1936). The genesis of hand preference. *Monographs of the Society for Research in Child Development*, Vol *1*, part 5.

Gillberg, C., & Wahlström, J. (1985). Chromosome abnormalities in infantile autism and other childhood psychoses: population study of 66 cases. *Developmental Medicine and Child Neurology, 27*, 293–304.

Goldin-Meadow, S. (1978). Structure in a manual communication system developed without a conventional language model: Language without a helping hand. In H. Whitaker & H. A. Whitaker (Eds.), *Studies in neurolinguistics, 4*, New York: Academic Press.

Goldin-Meadow, S., & Feldman, H. (1975). The creation of a communication system: A study of deaf children of hearing parents. *Sign Language Studies, 8*, 225–236.

Hadamard, J. (1945). *The psychology of invention in the mathematical field*. New Jersey: Princeton University Press.

Hagberg, B., Aicardi, J., Dias, K., & Ramos, D. (1983). A progressive syndrome of autism, dementia, ataxia and loss of purposeful hand use in girls. Rett's syndrome: Report of 35 cases. *Annals of Neurology, 14,* 471–79.

Halliday, M. A. K. (1975). *Learning how to mean: Explorations in the development of language.* London: Arnold.

Held, R., Shimojo, S., & Gwiazda, J. (1984). Gender differences in the early development of human visual resolution. Proceedings of the ARVO Meeting, April–May, 1984, Abstract No. 90. *Investigative Opthalmology and Visual Science, 25,* 220.

Hildreth, G. (1949). The development and training of hand preferences. *Journal of Genetic Psychology, 75,* 197–220.

Hofsten, C. von (1980). Predeictive reaching for moving objects by human infants. *Journal of Experimental Child Psychology, 30,* 369–382.

Hofsten, C. von (1984). Developmental changes in the organization of prereaching movements. *Developmental Psychology, 20,* 378–380.

Hofsten, C. von, & Lindhagen, K. (1979). Observations on the development of reaching for moving objects. *Journal of Experimental Child Psychology, 28,* 158–173.

Hubley, P., & Trevarthen, C. (1979). Sharing a task in infancy. In I. Uzgiris (Ed.), *Social Interaction During Infancy, New Directions for Child Development, 4,* 57–80.

Kendon, A. (1976). Gesticulation, speech and the gesture theory of language origins. *Sign Language Studies, 9,* 349–373.

Kendon, A. (1980). Gesticulation and speech: Two aspects of the process of utterance. In M. R. Key (Ed.), *The relationship of verbal and nonverbal communication.* The Hague: Mouton Publishers.

Kimura, D. (1973a). Manual activity during speaking: I Right handers. *Neuropsychologia, 11,* 45–50.

Kimura, D. (1973b). Manual activity during speaking: II Left handers. *Neuropsychologia, 11,* 51–55.

Kimura, D. (1979). Neuromotor mechanisms in the evolution of human communication. In H. D. Steklis & M. J. Raleigh (Eds.), *Neurobiology of communication in primates* (pp. 742–775). New York: Academic Press.

Kimura, D. (1982). Left-hemisphere control of oral and brachial movements and their relation to communication. *Philosophical Transactions of the Royal Society of London, 298,* 135–149.

Kuypers, H. G. J. M. (1962). Cortico-spinal connections: Postnatal development in the rhesus monkey. *Science, 138,* 678–680.

Kuypers, H. G. J. M. (1973). The anatomical organizations of the descending pathways and their contributions to motor control, especially in primates. In J. E. Desmedt (Ed.), *New developments in E. E. G. and clinical neuropsychology (Vol. 3).* Basel: Karger.

Lehman, R. A. W. (1970). Hand preference and cerebral dominance in 24 rhesus monkeys. *Journal of the Neurological Sciences, 10,* 185–192.

Lenneberg, P. (1967). Biological foundations of language. New York: Wiley.

Lesne, M., & Peycelon, (1934). A quel age un enfant cesse-t-il d'etre ambidextre pour devenir droiter? *Bulletin de la Societe de Pediatrie, Paris, 32,* 436–439.

Leung, E. H. L., & Rheingold, H. L. (1981). Development of pointing as a social gesture. *Developmental Psychology, 17,* 215–220.

Levy, J. (1980). Cerebral asymmetry and the psychology of man. In M. C. Wittrock (Ed.), *The brain and psychology* (pp. 245–321). New York: Academic Press.

Levy, J., & Nagylaki, T. (1972). A model for genetics of handedness. *Genetics, 72,* 117–128.

MacNeilage, P. F., Studdert-Kennedy, M. G., & Lindblom, B. (1984). Functional precursors to language and its lateralization. *American Journal of Physiology, 246* (Regulatory Integrative Comparative Physiology, 15), R912–R914.

Maratos, O. (1973). *The origin and development of imitation in the first six months of life.* Doctoral thesis, University of Geneva.

Marshack, A. (1984). The ecology and brain of two-handed bipedalism: An analytic, cognitive and evolutionary assessment. In H. L. Roitblat, H. S. Terrace, & T. G. Bever (Eds.), *Animal cognition.* Hillsdale, NJ: Lawrence Erlbaum Associates.

Meltzoff, A., & Moore, M. K. (1977). Imitation of facial and manual gestures by human neonates. *Science, 198,* 75–78.

Michel, G. F. (1981). Right-handedness: A consequence of infant supine head-orientation preference? *Science, 212,* 685–687.

Morgan, M. J., & Corballis, M. C. (1978). On the biological basis of human laterality, II The mechanisms of inheritance. *Behavioural and Brain Sciences, 1,* 270–277.

Murphy, C. M. (1978). Pointing in the context of a shared activity. *Child Development, 49,* 371–380.

Murphy, C. M., & Messer, D. J. (1977). Mothers, infants and pointing. In H. R. Schaffer (Ed.), *Studies in mother-infant interaction: The Loch Lomond symposium* (pp. 227–270). London: Academic Press.

Murray, L., & Trevarthen, C. (1984). Emotional regulation of interactions between two-month-olds and their mothers. In T. Field & N. Fox (Eds.), *Social perception in infants.* Norwood, NJ: Ablex.

Oyen, O. J. (1979). Tool-use in free-ranging baboons of Nairobi National Park. *Primates, 20,* 595–597.

Papousek, H. (1967). Experimental studies of appetitional behaviour in human newborns and infants. In H. W. Stevenson, E. H. Hess, & H. L. Rheingold (Eds.), *Early behaviour, comparative and developmental approaches* (pp. 249–277). New York: Wiley.

Peiper, N. (1963). *Cerebral functions in infancy and childhood* (p. 248). New York: Consultants' Bureau.

Plooij, F. (1979). How wild chimpanzee babies trigger the onset of mother-infant play—and what the mother makes of it. In M. Bullowa (Ed.), *Before speech: The beginnings of interpersonal communication* (pp. 223–243). London: Cambridge University Press.

Preisler, G. (1983). *Deaf children in communication.* Laholm: Trydells Tryckeri.

Ramsay, D. S. (1980). Beginnings of bimanual handedness and speech in infants. *Infant Behavior and Development, 3,* 67–77.

Ratcliffe, S. G. (1984). Klinefelter's Syndrome in Children: A longitudinal Study of 47, XXY boys identified by population screening. In H.-J. Bandmann & R. Breit (Eds.), *Kleinfelter's syndrome* (pp. 38–47). Berlin: Springer.

Scaife, M., & Bruner, J. S. (1975). The capacity for joint visual attention in the infant. *Nature, 253,* 265–266.

Seth, G. (1973). Eye-hand co-ordination and "handedness": A developmental study of visuo-motor behaviour in infancy. *British Journal of Educational Psychology, 43,* 34–49.

Studdert-Kennedy, M. (1983). On learning to speak. *Human Neurobiology, 2,* 191–195.

Sylvester-Bradley, B. (1981). Negativity in early infant-adult exchanges and its developmental significance. In P. Robinson (Ed.), *Communication in Development* (pp. 1–37). London: Academic Press.

Tervoort, B., & Verbeck, A. J. A. (1967). *Analysis of communicative structure patterns in deaf children.* Groningen: Vocational Rehabilitation Administration, Project R.D.467-64-65.

Thelen, E. (1984). Learning to walk: Ecological demands and phylogenetic constraints. In L. P. Lipsitt & C. Rovee-Collier (Eds.), *Advances in Infancy Research, Vol. 3* (pp. 213–250). New York: Academic Press.

Trevarthen, C. (1968). Two mechanisms of vision in primates. *Psychologische Forschung, 31,* 299–337.

Trevarthen, C. (1972). Brain bisymmetry and the role of the corpus callosum in behaviour and conscious experience. In J. Cernáček & F. Podovinsky (Eds.), *Cerebral interhemispheric rela-*

*tions*. Proceedings of an International Colloquium held in Smolenice, June 1969 (pp. 319–333). Bratislava: Slovak Academy of Sciences.

Trevarthen, C. (1974). The psychobiology of speech development. In E. H. Lenneberg (Ed.), *Language and Brain: Developmental Aspects Neurosciences Research Program Bulletin, 12*, 570–585.

Trevarthen, C. (1977). Descriptive analyses of infant communication behaviour. In H. R. Schaffer (Ed.), *Studies in mother-infant interaction: The Loch Lomond symposium* (pp. 227–270). London: Academic Press.

Trevarthen, C. (1978). Manipulative strategies of baboons and the origins of cerebral asymmetry. In M. Kinsbourne (Ed.), *The asymmetrical functions of the brain*. New York and London: Cambridge University Press.

Trevarthen, C. (1979a). Communication and cooperation in early infancy. A description of primary intersubjectivity. In M. Bullowa (Ed.), *Before speech: The beginnings of human communication*. London: Cambridge University Press.

Trevarthen, C. (1979b). Instincts for human understanding and for cultural cooperation: Their development in infancy. In M. von Cranach, K. Foppa, W. Lepenies, & D. Ploog (Eds.), *Human ethology* (pp. 530–571). Cambridge: Cambridge University Press.

Trevarthen, C. (1982). Basic patterns of psychogenetic change in infancy. In T. Bever (Ed.), *Dips in learning*. Hillsdale, NJ: Lawrence Erlbaum Associates.

Trevarthen, C. (1983a). Cerebral mechanisms for language: Prenatal and postnatal development. In U. Kirk (Ed.), *Neuropsychology of language, reading and spelling* (pp. 48–50). New York: Academic Press.

Trevarthen, C. (1983b). Interpersonal abilities of infants as generators for transmission of language and culture. In A. Oliverio & M. Zapella (Eds.), *The behaviour of human infants* (pp. 145–176). London and New York: Plenum.

Trevarthen, C. (1984a). Hemispheric specialization. In S. R. Geiger et al. (Eds.), *Handbook of physiology (Section 1, The Nervous System); Volume 2, Sensory Processes* (pp. 1129–1190). (Section Editor, Darian-Smith, I.) Washington: American Physiological Society.

Trevarthen, C. (1984b). How control of movements develops. In H. T. A. Whiting (Ed.), *Human motor actions: Bernstein reassessed* (pp. 223–261). Amsterdam: Elsevier (North Holland).

Trevarthen, C. (1984c). Emotions in infancy: Regulators of contacts and relationships with persons. In K. Scherer & P. Ekman (Eds.), *Approaches to emotion* (pp. 129–157). Hillsdale, NJ: Lawrence Erlbaum Associates.

Trevarthen, C. (1984d). Facial expressions of emotion in mother-infant interaction. *Human Neurobiology, 4*, 21–32.

Trevarthen, C. (1984e). Biodynamic structures, cognitive correlates of motive sets and development of motives in infants. In W. Prinz & A. F. Saunders (Eds.), *Cognition and motor processes* (pp. 327–350). Berlin-Heidelberg-New York: Springer Verlag.

Trevarthen, C., & Hubley, P. (1978). Secondary intersubjectivity: Confidence, confiding and acts of meaning in the first year. In A. Lock (Ed.), *Action, gesture and symbol* (pp. 183–229). London and New York: Academic Press.

Vauclair, J., & Bard, K. A. (1983). Development of manipulations with objects in ape and human infants. *Journal of Human Evolution, 12*, 631–645.

Watson, J. S. (1977). Perception of contingency as a determinant of social responsiveness. In E. B. Thoman (Ed.), *Origins of the infant's social responsiveness* (pp. 33–63). Hillsdale, NJ: Lawrence Erlbaum Associates.

Woods, B. T. (1980). Restricted effects of right hemisphere lesions after age one: Wechsler test data. *Neuropsychologia, 18*, 65–70.

Young, A., Lock, A. J., & Service, V. (1985). Infants' hand preferences for actions and gestures. *Developmental Neuropsychology, 1*, 17–21.

# 9 Some Implications of Lateralization for Developmental Psychology

Sidney J. Segalowitz

Infants communicate with their mothers very soon after birth. Sometimes this communication involves subtle reciprocating body movements (e.g., of the tongue, eyes, mouth, fingers), and sometimes it involves exchanges of vocalizations. The intentionality of these interactions is evidenced by their regularity and by the negative reaction shown by the infant when the chain is broken (Bretherton & Bates, 1979; Fafouti-Milenkovic & Uzgiris, 1979; Trevarthen, 1977). What can be said of the cerebral organization of such communicative skills? How does such a psychobiological basis relate to particular theoretical positions concerning the development of thought? In this section, we will focus on these related issues, the first concerning evidence for cerebral specialization of functions related to communication in infancy, the second focusing on the implication of this evidence for theories of cognitive development.

## CEREBRAL ORGANIZATION OF COMMUNICATION IN INFANTS

### Brain Organization for Communication in Adults

The most obvious relation between brain structures and the communicative function in humans is that the left hemisphere is responsible for language. It is well-established that in the vast majority of people, language is disrupted significantly from damage to particular regions of the left hemisphere (Kertesz, Lesk, & McCabe, 1977; Segalowitz, 1983a). Despite considerable individual differences that exist in the exact sites of the left hemisphere that subserve certain aspects of language, there is no doubt that it is the left hemisphere that is critical for language (Ojemann, 1983; Millar & Whitaker, 1983). The aspects of language functions most closely studied in aphasia research are disruption of phonological, syntactic, and semantic processing (Blumstein, 1981). Other aspects to *communication* do exist, however, and this broader term includes the study of intonation pattern, the discourse demands of the situation, the appreciation of nonexplicit factors in discourse such as implied humor and sarcasm, social status differences between the conversants, the distinction between new versus old information, the emotional state of the other discussant including the appreciation of nonverbal body and facial expressions, and so on. The extent to which the left hemisphere has a dominance over these skills is not as well studied, but we suspect that the right hemisphere plays a large role in the representation of these activities (Foldi, Cicone, & Gardner, 1983; Segalowitz, 1983b).

There is a vast literature on the relative superiority of the right hemisphere in dealing with certain types of information, especially when visually coded (Bryden, 1982; Hécaen, DeAgostini, & Mozan-Montes, 1981) or emotional in content (Galin, 1974; Bryden & Ley, 1983). Faces have been extensively tested in visual half-field paradigms, indicating that both the recognition of the face and the appreciation of the emotional expression in a face is superior when presented in the left visual half-field, suggesting a right hemisphere superiority on these tasks (see Bryden & Ley, 1983, for a review). This does not imply necessarily that there is a special mechanism for facial recognition residing only in the right hemisphere, for prosopagnosia (facial agnosia) usually results from bilateral damage, although right hemisphere involvement seems more important than left (Hécaen & Albert, 1978). Rather, there probably is some perceptual mechanism, for which the right hemisphere is superior, that is especially employed in facial recognition tasks in the visual half-field paradigm (e.g., Sergent & Bindra, 1981). Whatever the source, it is probably the case that facial apprehension engages right hemisphere processes especially, if not exclusively, both because of some visual-spatial property and because of the emotional information of such importance in the task.

There is also now considerable evidence from clinical (Albert, Sparks, & Helm, 1973; Bogen & Gordon, 1971; Heilman, Scholes, & Watson, 1975; Mosidze, 1976; Ross & Mesulam, 1979) and experimental (Blumstein & Cooper, 1974; Ley & Bryden, 1982) studies that intonation pattern is especially appreciated by the right hemisphere. The right hemisphere seems to be better at recognizing and producing melodic contour in the voice and of pairing such patterns with the intended emotion. These are aspects to communication that do not concern the linguistic functions traditionally examined in aphasia research. Yet, these factors are important in considering the wider meaning of communication in adults and especially in children (Anderson, Garrison, & Anderson, 1979).

## Cerebral Asymmetries in Infants

As indicated in the foregoing summary, evidence for cerebral asymmetries in adults depend on a variety of factors that contribute separately to lateralized behavior. The study of cerebral asymmetries in infancy is complicated by a further two factors: (1) the behavior patterns of infants are notoriously less stable than older children or adults; and (2) an experimenter is never sure that infants, possessing different cognitive structures from older people, are dealing with the stimuli in the expected way. However, careful study has shown that there are reliable motor asymmetries in the neonate (Liederman, 1983; Michel, 1981; Young, Segalowitz, Corter, & Trehub, 1983). These differences correspond to what could be expected from the child literature, e.g., that degree of right-sided preference correlates with parental right-handedness (Liederman & Kinsbourne, 1980). Of course, some motor patterns are more stable than others, and the areas of the greatest control reflect the most asymmetry (Liederman, 1983; Michel, 1983).

There is also a small, but growing, literature on cerebral asymmetries in neonates related to perceptual processing of verbal versus nonverbal stimuli. Although neonates cannot process speech the way adults do and cannot have the same language knowledge, it is quite reasonable to think that children do have some processes of perceptual discrimination for these modalities and that these processes may depend on asymmetrically organized tissue. For example, young infants can discriminate speech categories in ways similar to adults (Walley, Pisoni, & Aslin, 1981). This ability, which may be lateralized, may be based on processes that are not speech-specific (Jusczyk, Pisoni, Reed, Fernald, & Myers, 1983), just as it was suggested earlier that the lateral asymmetry in facial recognition may be based on some general perceptual process not limited to faces. These general processes, of course, are good candidates for lateralized representation. The difficulty with laterality work with infants is that since it is often not known what meaning a stimulus has for an infant, it is hard to predict what perceptual/cognitive processes are being engaged in the task, and therefore what activity is producing behavior, whether asymmetric or not.

Nevertheless, when cerebral asymmetries are found in neonates, they are in the expected direction—speech related processes in the left hemisphere, visual-spatial related processes in the right (Segalowitz & Gruber, 1977; see Segalowitz, 1983c). As an aside, it should be noted that in the few instances of cerebral asymmetries reported in animals, the communicative functions are linked to the left hemisphere (Nottebohm, 1979; Petersen, Beecher, Zoloth, Moody, & Stebbins, 1978) and emotional effects are linked to the right hemisphere (Denenberg, 1981).

## Is Infant Communication a Left or Right Hemisphere Affair?

Given these two conclusions—that infants show a right-side of body preference and have brains asymmetrically associated with various perceptual-cognitive processes—it is tempting to draw a further analogy with the adult literature. Adults, when engaging in speech processes, show a tendency to make right-sided movements. This is manifested in rightward eye movements (Kinsbourne, 1974), more disruption of an independent right-hand motor task while speaking (Kinsbourne & Cook, 1971; Kinsbourne & Hicks, 1978), and more spontaneous related right-handed gestures and movements while engaged in a verbal activity (Hampson & Kimura, 1984; Kimura, 1973). The link between right-hand movement and language processes is a natural one—both are based on left hemisphere activity. Should it be expected, then, that the early communication attempts of infants be accompanied by right-hand movements, i.e., does the activation model of hemisphere asymmetries (e.g., Kinsbourne, 1975, and this volume) apply in this circumstance? Trevarthen (1982) has suggested that excitatory movements of the right hand during mother-infant interactions indeed reflect the asymmetric organization of the communicative function in the child, i.e., that right-hand movements are linked to left hemisphere activation for communication. This is interesting since from the foregoing discussion, we would predict that, if anything, the activation model would suggest the opposite: that communication in infancy is a right hemisphere affair. The logic behind this rests on an examination of the communicative function in infants—a great deal of visual searching, emotional interplay, and facial examination. All these processes suggest a right hemisphere basis, not a left hemisphere one.

Besides these right hemisphere processes being intimately involved in infant communication, the infant is listening to and producing various vocal sounds. In the normal communicative context, much of the emphasis is on the intonation pattern of the vocalizations, in as much as the syllable formations do not yet carry semantic weight for the listening party (Fernald & Simo, 1984). It is the intonation and stress pattern that communicates, and this has been linked consistently to right hemisphere activity.

When these factors are taken together, one would expect an increase in left hand activity during communication between the mother and the young infant. However, the right hand and arm of the infant has been shown to be stronger and more agile the left (Caplan & Kinsbourne, 1976). It can reasonably be expected that these factors will produce more movement on the right side, especially when excited during interactions with mother. This is not because of a specific hemispheric activation, but because of a generally raised activity level. What is implied here is that brain laterality for communicative functions in infants and asymmetry of hand use are separate functions, not interacting causally (Segalowitz, 1983d). That is, hand movement in infancy, while fascinating, is probably not at all indicative of asymmetrical representation of the communicative function. Rather, there are a number of psychological and psychomotor processes at work during communication, each of them with their own neuropsychological basis.

## CEREBRAL ASYMMETRIES AND THE DEVELOPMENT OF THOUGHT

### Differentiation Versus Integration

Fifty and 60 years ago, developmental psychologists were very concerned with whether or not organisms begin life with uncoordinated, independent reflexive motor patterns that gradually integrate into useful behavior patterns over time. The contrasting view of this "integration" approach is a "differentiation" one, where an organism's global activity patterns become differentiated into individually manipulable elements (Carmichael, 1970). This controversy, although now seen to be somewhat simplistic with respect to motor development, still has considerable import for work in cognitive development. If the differentiation view is accepted, then we must place our energies in finding out what processes children use to differentiate their environments, for development is a series of such processes. Such a "perceptual learning" approach does not emphasize the acquisition of facts from the environment nor the integration of knowledge into hierarchical structures (Gibson & Gibson, 1955). This view prompts us to look for activity patterns, such as gestures, well-integrated into communication skills at a very early age, and to consider the child's growth patterns as a refining of these patterns. The child learns to be more specific with his gestures, differentiating facets of the communicative act not previously distinguished in his mind or behavior.

Alternatively, with the integration approach, we should focus on the mental apparatus needed to integrate previously separate, uncoordinated ideas and actions. With this approach, we would predict that the movements associated with communicative acts are coincidental, perhaps simply as a byproduct of overall activity levels (Kinsbourne, this volume). In this perspective, development for the child is seen as a gradual accretion of motor and thought patterns to the growing communicative skills. These two positions can be extended to theories of general cognitive development, as found in the contrast between the differentiation and the integration views of the child's mental development, a contrast seen in the developmental psychologies of E. J. Gibson and Jean Piaget. Gibson (1969; Gibson & Gibson, 1955) suggests that the child's initial mental skills (especially perceptual ones) are integrated and that the task the child faces is not to learn to perceive new facts about the world, but to learn to differentiate and make use of what already is within his grasp. Bower (1966, 1982) takes this

theory further and suggests that the child is born with considerable mental equip-
ment—that the child appreciates size constancy, some properties of 3-dimen-
sional objects and that the rudiments of hand-eye coordination exist at birth or
very shortly thereafter.

In contrast to this view of development is that of Piaget (1952), who emphasizes the way the baby learns to coordinate his actions. In the fourth substage of
the sensorimotor period, according to Piaget's theory, the child begins to assimi-
late action schemes to other action schemes, i.e., to coordinate previously separate action patterns, such as developing coordination of hand and eye, or of arm
movements and vocalization. Similarly, the child's mental development consists
of assimilating old ideas to new concepts, such as the application of familiar
ideas, objects, and actions to new concepts of classification, reversibility or
compensation. Thought and action have a common developmental thread here—
that of gradual integration. Piaget also emphasizes differentiation, in that the
child develops variations of an action scheme to apply to different contexts. For
example, sucking a nipple is different from mouthing a blanket, sucking a finger,
etc. Thus the child both integrates and differentiates according to this theory. The
lateralization literature can be related to this issue directly. The existence of
neural tissue specialized for psychological functions suggests that mental structures are separable. In the adult, the fact that brain structures for linguistic,
visual-spatial and emotional functions are somewhat separable indicates that
these functions are not well-integrated. In fact, various neuropsychological theorists divide adult mental activity into domains that interact poorly with each other
relative to the information transfer within the domain. It can therefore be said
that people have several "selves"—verbal, emotional, perceptual, etc. These
divisions of the psyche can be accounted for on the basis of cerebral asymmetries
of function (Bogen & Bogen, 1969; Galin, 1974; Gazzaniga & LeDoux, 1978).
Thus, the adult can be seen as an organism that could bear some integration of
mental functions.

Whether this stage is seen as a not-yet-completed integration or as a late stage
of differentiation depends entirely on whether or not the young infant is considered less or more lateralized than the adult. It may be that children are not less
differentiated than adults and that the division applies to them as well. Although
it was presumed for some time that lateralization was a gradual process of
development (e.g., Krashen, 1973; Lenneberg, 1967), more recent work has
suggested that the young infant's brain, while more likely to show "plasticity"
in recovery from damage to the cerebral cortex, is nevertheless specialized for
mental functions so far attained (Segalowitz, 1983c; Segalowitz & Gruber, 1977)
and may even be more asymmetric in function than adults (Segalowitz, 1980;
Witelson, 1977). It is thus plausible that the brain does not differentiate in
functioning over time. There is also evidence that integration does take place, at
least during early childhood: The myelin sheaths aiding neuronal transmission of
electrical impulses continue developing until middle childhood at least, es-

pecially those in the corpus callosum. Anatomical evidence (Yakovlev & Lecours, 1967) and functional evidence (Galin, Johnstone, Nakell, & Herron, 1979) support the notion that communication between the hemispheres increases until this period. This situation suggests that the verbal system is a poor entree into the visual-spatial and emotional domains in adults, but even more so in children. One could argue, then, that integration of separate schemes waits for neurological as well as cognitive maturation.

We could speculate that cognitive differentiation takes place within hemispheres or within functional subsystems (language, emotions, etc.), and that knowledge within a domain that is poorly differentiated mentally is also less differentiated neurologically. For example, a poorly learned second language is disrupted by electrical stimulation applied to the surface of the cortex in a wider area of the left hemisphere than a more fluent second language (Ojemann, 1983). As an activity becomes more practised, it may require less neural tissue to sustain it (cf. Goldman, Crawford, Stokes, Galkin, & Rosvold, 1974). Thus, differentiation may take place within a hemisphere while integration develops between hemispheres or functional areas. That both processes may coexist even within a single mental domain is not a problem for developmental theory, since they have been integrated into a single theory, both in the psychobiological domain (Gottlieb, 1976) and cognitive theory (Werner, 1957).

## Unitary Versus Multiple Cognition

Another developmental issue that can be related to lateralization is the question of whether there is a general, unitary cognitive growth, affecting all aspects of structured thought, or whether each modality or cognitive domain has its own developmental schedule and path of development. Piaget opts for the former position. He sees the child's development involving a gradual lessening of the totally egocentric viewpoint the baby has at birth. This decentration is an intellectual ability that pervades all domains of the child's thinking. Whether the content involves visual-perceptual stimuli, emotional relationships, numerical concepts, or just simple action sequences, the child's ability to handle the information with particular mental transformations depends on the degree to which he or she has decentered cognitively. Of course, there will be some differences between domains. The child may be relatively more advanced with one context compared to another, presumably due to extra experience the child has gained in that domain. For example, children of potters have been found to have a precocious sense of weight conservation. These children have particularly relevant experiences since they carry the clay before and after shaping (Adjei, 1977; Price-Williams, Gordon, & Ramirez, 1969). But these differences are, according to Piaget, relatively minor and attributable to individual differences in cultural background (Piaget, 1972).

An alternative approach, recently explored by Fodor (1983) and Gardner (1983), is that the human brain and mind consist of various subcomponents that function and develop somewhat independently. If the neural substrate for linguistic skills, spatial-perceptual skills, musical skills, and emotional relations are functionally separated to some extent, it makes sense to consider the notion that each has its own developmental schedule and that the ability to perform complex mental transformations in one domain may not extend to another. It may even be the case that the mental transformations and their schedule suggested by Piaget may apply only to the spatial-mathematical domain Piaget uses to test the requisite skills. It may be that the musical genius shown by a prodigy is not necessarily of the same sort as that of a mathematical sophisticate. If the many domains of development do not integrate with maturation, this may be because they involve different brain tissue with separately maturing functions (Gardner & Wolf, mimeo). This "heterogeneity" of the mind is well-supported by current work in neuropsychology, and is having some influence on child development theory (Flavell, 1982).

## SUMMARY

We can relate the existence of cerebral asymmetries in infancy to a number of general issues in developmental psychology. (1) The brain base for infant communication, taken in its broad sense, may shift as the task changes with age. Although the young infant has some phonological perceptual skills (Molfese, 1977; Walley, Pisoni, & Aslin, 1981) there is no evidence that they aid in communication at this stage. Other, less linguistically-oriented communicative skills may be more critical. (2) Lateralized behavior in infants has more than one source. Asymmetric hand use may not always be related to hemisphere activation induced by communicative activites. (3) Differentiation and integration of perceptual and motor patterns may have correlates in brain maturation, and thus have a physiological basis besides their behavioral ones (Gottlieb, 1976; Werner, 1957). Once a great deal more is known about the growth of communicating fibres (i.e., the increase in myelination and synaptic connections) in the early years, it may become possible to examine this relationship more directly. (4) Different facets of intellectual development may have different developmental schedules for psychobiological reasons, in that they are based on different brain tissue with possibly different organizational properties or rates of development. It may be that intellectual maturation in verbal, visual-spatial, and musical modalities are somewhat independent of each other. In addition, emotional development may have a physiological substrate overlapping with, yet functionally somewhat independent from, these three other domains (cf. Cowan, 1978).

# REFERENCES

Adjei, K. (1977). Influence of specific maternal occupation and behavior on Piagetian cognitive development. In P. R. Dasen (Ed.), *Piagetian Psychology*. New York: Gardner Press.

Albert, M. L., Sparks, R. W., & Helm, N. A. (1973). Melodic intonation therapy for aphasia. *Archives of Neurology, 29*, 130–131.

Anderson, P. A., Garrison, J. P., & Anderson, J. F. (1979). Implications of a neurophysiological approach for the study of a nonverbal communications. *Human Communication Research, 6*, 74–89.

Blumstein, S. E. (1981). Neurolinguistic disorders: Language-brain relationships. In S. B. Filskov & T. J. Boll (Eds.), *Handbook of clinical neuropsychology*. New York: Wiley.

Blumstein, S., & Cooper, W. E. (1974). Hemispheric processing of intonation contours. *Cortex, 10*, 146–158.

Bogen, J. E., & Bogen, G. M. (1969). The other side of the brain III: The corpus callosum and creativity. *Bulletin of the Los Angeles Neurological Societies, 34*, 191–217.

Bogen, J. E., & Gordon, H. W. (1971). Musical tests for functional lateralization with intracarotid amobarbital. *Nature, 230*, 524–525.

Bower, T. G. R. (1966). The visual world of infants. *Scientific American, 215*, 80–92.

Bower, T. G. R. (1982). *Development in infancy* (second edition). San Francisco: W. H. Freeman.

Bretherton, I., & Bates, E. (1979). The emergence of intentional communication. *New Directions for Child Development, 4*, 81–100.

Bryden, M. P. (1982). *Laterality: Functional asymmetry in the intact brain*. New York: Academic Press.

Bryden, M. P., & Ley, R. G. (1983). Right-hemispheric involvement in the perception and expression of emotion in normal humans. In K. M. Heilman & P. Satz (Eds.), *Neuropsychology of human emotion*. New York: Guilford Press.

Caplan, P., & Kinsbourne, M. (1976). Baby drops the rattle: Asymmetry of duration of grasp by infants. *Child Development, 47*, 532–534.

Carmichael, L. (1970). Onset and early development of behavior. In P. H. Mussen (Ed.), *Manual of child psychology*. New York: Wiley.

Cowan, P. A. (1978). *Piaget: With feeling*. New York: Holt, Rinehart & Winston.

Denenberg, V. H. (1981). Hemispheric laterality in animals and the effects of early experience. *Behavioral and Brain Sciences, 4*, 1–49.

Fafouti-Milenković, M., & Uzgiris, I. C. (1979). The mother-infant communication system. *New Directions for Child Development, 4*, 41–56.

Fernald, A., & Simo, T. (1984). Expanded intonation contours in mothers' speech to newborns. *Developmental Psychology, 20*, 104–113.

Flavel, J. H. (1982). On cognitive development. *Child Development, 53*, 1–10.

Fodor, J. A. (1983). *The modularity of mind: An essay on faculty psychology*. Cambridge, MA: MIT Press.

Foldi, N. S., Cicone, M., & Gardner, H. (1983). Pragmatic aspects of communication in brain damaged patients. In S. J. Segalowitz (Ed.), *Language functions and brain organization*. New York: Academic Press.

Galin, D. (1974). Implications for psychiatry of left and right cerebral specialization. *Archives of General Psychiatry, 31*, 572–573.

Galin, D., Johnstone, J., Nakell, L., & Herron, J. (1979). Development of the capacity for tactile information transfer between hemispheres in normal children. *Science, 204*, 1330–1332.

Gardner, H. (1983). Frames of mind: The theory of multiple intelligences. New York: Basic Books.

Gardner, H., & Wolf, D. (date). *Waves of human symbolization*. Harvard University. (Mimeo)

Gazzaniga, M. S., & LeDoux, J. E. (1978). *The integrated mind*. New York: Plenum Press.

Gibson, E. (1969). *Principles of perceptual learning and development.* New York: Appleton-Century-Crofts.

Gibson, J. J., & Gibson, E. (1955). Perceptual learning: Differentiation or enrichment? *Psychological Review, 62,* 32–41.

Goldman, P. S., Crawford, H. T., Stokes, L. P., Galkin, T. W., & Rosvold, H. E. (1974). Sex-dependent behavioral effects of cerebral cortical lesions in the developing rhesus monkey. *Science, 186,* 540–542.

Gottlieb, G. (1976). Conceptions of prenatal development: Behavioral embryology. *Psychological Review, 83,* 215–234.

Hampson, E., & Kimura, D. (1984). Hand movement asymmetries during verbal and nonverbal tasks. *Canadian Journal of Psychology, 38,* 102–125.

Hécaen, H., & Albert, M. L. (1978). *Human neuropsychology.* New York: Wiley.

Hécaen, H., DeAgostini, M., & Monzon-Montes, A. (1981). Cerebral organization in left-handers. *Brain and Language, 12,* 261–284.

Heilman, K. M., Scholes, R., & Watson, R. T. (1975). Auditory affective agnosia: Disturbed comprehension of affective speech. *Journal of Neurology, Neurosurgery, and Psychiatry, 38,* 69–72.

Jusczyk, P. W., Pisoni, D. B., Reed, M. A., Fernald, A., & Myers, M. (1983). Infant's discrimination of the duration of a rapid spectrum change in nonspeech signals. *Science, 222,* 175–177.

Kertesz, A., Lesk, D., & McCabe, P. (1977). Isotope localization of infants in aphasia. *Archives of Neurology, 34,* 590–601.

Kimura, D. (1973). Manual activity during speaking. I. Right-handers. *Neuropsychologia, 11,* 45–50.

Kinsbourne, M. (1974). Direction of gaze and distribution of cerebral thought processes. *Neuropsychologia, 12,* 279–281.

Kinsbourne, M. (1975). The mechanism of hemispheric control of the lateral gradient of attention. In P. M. A. Rabbitt & S. Dornic (Eds.), *Attention and performance V.* New York: Academic Press.

Kinsbourne, M., & Cook, J. (1971). Generalized and lateralized effects of concurrent verbalization on a unimanual skill. *Quarterly Journal of Experimental Psychology, 23,* 341–345.

Kinsbourne, M., & Hicks, R. E. (1978). Functional cerebral space: A model for overflow, transfer and interference effects in human performance: A tutorial review. In J. Requin (Ed.), *Attention and performance VIII.* Hillsdale, NJ: Lawrence Erlbaum Associates.

Krashen, S. D. (1973). Lateralization, language learning, and the critical period: Some new evidence. *Language Learning, 23,* 63–74.

Lenneberg, E. H. (1967). *Biological foundations of language.* New York: Wiley.

Ley, R. G., & Bryden, M. P. (1982). A dissociation of right and left hemispheric effects for recognizing emotional tone and verbal content. *Brain and Cognition, 1,* 3–9.

Liederman, J. (1983). Mechanisms underlying instability in the development of hand preference. In G. Young, S. Segalowitz, C. M. Carter, & S. E. Trehub (Eds.), *Manual specialization and the developing brain.* New York: Academic Press.

Liederman, J., & Kinsbourne, M. (1980). Rightward motor bias in newborns depends upon parental right-handedness. *Neuropsychologia, 18,* 579–584.

Michel, G. (1981). Right handedness: A consequence of infant supine head-orientation preference? *Science, 212,* 685–687.

Michel, G. F. (1983). Development of hand-use preference during infancy. In G. Young, S. Segalowitz, C. M. Carter, & S. G. Trehub (Eds.), *Manual specialization and the developing brain.* New York: Academic Press.

Millar, J. M., & Whitaker, H. A. (1983). The right hemisphere's contribution to language: A review of the evidence from brain-damaged subjects. In S. Segalowitz (Ed.), *Language functions and brain organization.* New York: Academic Press.

Molfese, D. L. (1977). Infant cerebral asymmetry. In S. J. Segalowitz, & F. A. Gruber (Eds.), *Language development and neurological theory*. New York: Academic Press.

Mosidze, V. M. (1976). On the lateralization of musical function in man. [in Russian] In V. P. Kaznacheyev, S. F. Semyonov, & A. P. Chuprikov (Eds.), *Functional asymmetry and adaptation in man*. Moscow: Moscow Psychiatric Research Institute.

Nottebohm, F. (1979). Origins and mechanisms in the establishment of cerebral dominance. In M. S. Gazzaniga (Ed.), *Handbook of behavioral neurobiology* (Vol. 2). New York: Plenum Publishing.

Ojemann, G. A. (1983). Brain organization for language from the perspective of electrical stimulation mapping. *The Behavioral and Brain Sciences, 6,* 189–230.

Petersen, M. R., Beecher, M. D., Zoloth, S. R., Moody, D. B., & Stebbins, W. C. (1978). Neural lateralization of species-specific vocalizations by Japanese macaques (Macaca fuscata). *Science, 202,* 324–327.

Piaget, J. (1952). *The origins of intelligence in the child*. New York: International University Press.

Piaget, J. (1972). Intellectual evolution from adolescence to adulthood. *Human Development, 15,* 1–12.

Price-Williams, D. R., Gordon, W., & Ramirez, M. (1969). Skill and conservation. *Developmental Psychology, 1,* 769.

Ross, E. D., & Mesulam, M. M. (1979). Dominant language functions of the right hemisphere? *Archives of Neurology, 36,* 144–148.

Segalowitz, S. J. (1980). *Developmental models of brain lateralization*. (Mimeo). Brock University, St. Catharines, Ontario.

Segalowitz, S. J. (Ed.). (1983a). *Language functions and brain organization*. New York: Academic Press.

Segalowitz, S. J. (1983b). *Two sides of the brain*. Englewood Cliffs, NJ: Prentice-Hall.

Segalowitz, S. J. (1983c). Cerebral asymmetries for speech in infancy. In S. J. Segalowitz (Ed.), *Functions and brain organization*. New York: Academic Press.

Segalowitz, S. J. (1983d). How many lateralities are there? In G. Young, S. J. Segalowitz, C. M. Carter, & S. E. Trehub (Eds.), *Manual specialization and the developing brain*. New York: Academic Press.

Segalowitz, S. J., & Gruber, F. A. (Eds.). (1977). *Language development and neurological theory*. New York: Academic Press.

Sergent, J., & Bindra, D. (1981). Differential hemispheric processing of faces: Methodological considerations and reinterpretation. *Psychological Bulletin, 89,* 541–554.

Trevarthen, C. (1977). Descriptive analysis of infant communicative behavior. In H. R. Schaffer (Ed.), *Studies in mother-infant interaction*. New York: Academic Press.

Trevarthen, C. (1982). *Form, significance and psychological potential of hand gestures of infants*. Symposium on Gestures, Cultures and Communication, May 27–29, 1982, University of Toronto.

Walley, A. C., Pisoni, D. B., & Aslin, R. N. (1981). The role of early experience in the development of speech perception. In R. N. Aslin, J. R. Alberts, & M. R. Petersen (Eds.), *Development of perception, Vol. 1*. New York: Academic Press.

Werner, H. (1957). The concept of intelligence from a comparative and organismic point of view. In D. B. Harris (Ed.), *The concept of development*. Minneapolis: University of Minnesota Press.

Witelson, S. F. (1977). Early hemisphere specialization and interhemispheric plasticity: An empirical and theoretical review. In S. J. Segalowitz, & F. A. Gruber (Eds.), *Language development and neurological theory*. New York: Academic Press.

Yakovlev, P. I., & Lecours, A. R. (1967). The myelogenetic cycles of regional maturation in the brain. In A. Minkowski (Ed.), *Regional development of the brain in early life*. Oxford: Blackwell.

Young, G., Segalowitz, S. J., Corter, C., & Trehub, S. (Eds.). (1983). *Manual specialization and the developing brain: Longitudinal research*. New York: Academic Press.

# 10 The Impact of Visual-Spatial Information on the Development of Reading Proficiency in Deaf Children

Cheryl Gibson
Sidney J. Segalowitz

Despite normal nonverbal intelligence, deaf children generally do not achieve a reading profiency beyond a fourth grade level. Attempts to account for this deficit point to reduced vocabulary and delayed language acquisition. We explore the possibility that it is the biological constraints of a nonauditory language environment which could create a counterproductive bias which, in turn, interferes with their ability to read. When deaf children attempt to learn a language system, the visual modality carries the most consistent and compelling information. This is true for speech reading, sign language, pantomime, and gesture but we will restrict our discussion primarily to sign language because sign language is a highly efficient system for transmitting a visual language and as such probably represents an optimal model for a discussion of visual information processing. Two readily identifiable components of sign language that may have an important influence on the development of competence in the verbal language system are the symbolic dimension, which provides language information, and the spatial component, which carries this information in a modality specific manner. The spatial component may promote a dependence on or initial strategy for a mode of processing that conflicts with the procedures required for efficient reading of written text. We see these conflicts directly represented in the modes preferred by each cerebral hemisphere. Deaf, as opposed to hearing children may use right hemisphere processes in reading, producing a restriction on the development of reading skills.

## BIOLOGICAL BASIS OF LANGUAGE

Children gradually acquire a complex rule-governed system to communicate their thoughts feelings, moods, and images to others. Language appears to be an automatic ordering and naming of objects and relationships which unfolds in a somewhat predetermined pattern, another of the maturational process displayed by the child (Lenneberg, 1970). One way of understanding this process is to see language and speech as independent components. As Vygotsky (1962) suggested, speech and thought may have different developmental roots and mature separately; eventually these streams meet and "thought becomes verbal and speech rational" (p. 44). In deaf children, however, speech may or may not develop and the hands and thought may merge to create a language system characteristically different from a verbal one in some respects.

For many deaf children, who have little or no auditory input during infancy, the eyes and hands provide the child with a basis for a linguistic communication system built on different perceptual characteristics. This, in turn, suggests the language system used by deaf children may have elements in common with a verbal language and other elements which are unique. There is evidence that American Sign Language (ASL) is an autonomous linguistic system which did not develop from verbal language (Bellugi, 1983). It does however possess many of the same underlying details of verbal language, with two levels of organization which are comparable to the grammar and lexicon of a spoken language. For example, American Sign Language has both grammatical markers which serve as inflectional morphemes and sublexical elements which have systematic restrictions on the way they are used (Bellugi, Poizner, & Zurif, 1982). These characteristics are principles which appear to be common to all language development. Some language learning principles exist in sign language in much the same way they exist in a verbal language, presumably because there are some universal perceptual and cognitive constraints on the acquisition system. Language, as a biological capacity, shows some invariance and reflects the necessity of the organism to deal with and communicate complex symbols and relationships.

While the biological capacity for language may be identical in deaf and hearing children in terms of an ability to store, retrieve, and manipulate complex symbols, the unique elements of a nonverbal language may also influence the development of a language system. Language conveys syntactical and semantic information which is embedded in the dominant perceptual system. For example, the temporal-sequential pattern of auditory stimuli is embedded in a verbal language, whereas parallel or simultaneous patterns are available to the deaf child whose linguistic channels are the visual and haptic systems.

Because a verbal language involves rapid changes in temporal sequence, children need strategies to decode this information which are consistent with auditory perceptual input. For example, two strategies that have been postulated are (1) to pay attention to the ends of words, and (2) to pay attention to the order of words. These strategies seem to be effective for processing auditory information because these properties are more perceptually salient in verbal material (Slobin, 1971). If a child is exposed to both auditory and visual forms of language, it could be that other stategies are appropriate. If this hypothesis is correct, the acquisition of a nonverbal language should reflect both normal linguistic characteristics and the influence of visual-spatial characteristics. While the order of acquisition appears to be similar in both verbal and sign language, Schlesinger (1978) found that perceptual salience did influence the acquisition of some linguistic markers. Using hearing-impaired children exposed to speech and sign language, she found that the information which is regular and perceptually salient will appear first in the modality which is more important for the child. Thus a child with little residual hearing could develop a construction in sign before it is apparent in speech and could develop the auxiliary *is* before the inflection *ing* because *is* will be more salient in sign. For example, a child with some residual hearing used the inflected form first in speech (as in the word *feeling*). With his degree of hearing loss, the *ing* was salient through the auditory channel and he was able to ''pay attention to the end of words'' the way a normal hearing child would. In a child with less hearing, the order of acquisition was *is sleep* which one year later became *is sleeping*. In sign language, *is* stands out clearly as a separate and distinctive morpheme while *ing* tends to blend in with the word and may be easily disregarded and inconsistently expressed. Thus a child with a greater hearing loss may not pay attention to the ends of words because it is not perceptually salient in that modality.

Therefore language systems based on the auditory or visual modality will have some basic principles in common but there will be other characteristics which are unique to each system. The biological constraints of each system will affect the encoding and decoding of language information. This, in turn, could have implications for the reading process.

## BIOLOGICAL CONSTRAINTS AND THE READING PROCESS

The language of deaf and hearing children may be equivalent in terms of the capacity to deal with similar levels of complexity. It may still be difficult, however, for a deaf child to learn to read. Hearing children are confronted with the task of learning a phoneme-grapheme correspondence and must translate visual information into previously acquired auditory information. All of the knowledge they have acquired in 6 years of listening is brought to the reading process. An average deaf child starts to learn to read not only with an impoverished vocabulary but also little or no information about the characteristics of auditory information which hearing children have previously absorbed.

Deaf children typically encounter difficulties in the reading process at many levels. For example, the printed word could be decoded by the child using an articulatory, a fingerspelling or a sign-based code. For some deaf children, the articulatory code is the preferred mode and yet when these children are matched with a group of hearing children with equal ability on a test of articulatory coding, the deaf children still have significantly lower reading scores (Conrad, 1979). Thus the code that a deaf child uses should not be considered in isolation from other variables. In addition to the code, the deaf child is often deficient in a knowledge of syntax and vocabulary. Thus, an 18-year-old deaf person could be functioning as a 10-year-old when measured on syntactic ability (Quigley, 1982). It has been suggested that deaf and hearing children bring a very different knowledge of language to the reading process (Parasnis & Samar, 1982). Thus, deaf children usually are unable to make inferences about information in a story and fail to interact efficiently with the text (Wilson, cited in Quigley, 1982). Many factors will influence the success with which a child will learn to read including vocabulary, knowledge of linguistic structure, ability to decode efficiently, etc. Everything from phonetic decoding to metacognitive strategies militates against this being a successful endeavor for the deaf child.

In addition to the previously mentioned difficulties, there are characteristics of speech which appear to influence reading directly. Brooks (1978) discussed the importance of the rhythmic characteristics of speech which are inherent in verbal languages. She points out that the language process is guided by "a program that has rhythmic, relative time determinants." This rhythmic aspect of speech allows people to focus on important information and at the same time provides periods of quiet in the system during which minimal information is being transmitted. During these quiet periods, previous information is processed. This rhythmic quality, which is inherent in speech, appears to provide a good information processing strategy.

Brooks further points out that the timing or rhythmic patterning of speech may have important implications for reading. For normal children, she suggests, learning to read involves referring visual symbols to a phonologically based system which maps onto the speech perception apparatus. What children focus on in a text is preprogrammed by their knowledge of linguistic and speech rules. In addition, knowledge of the rhythmic structure of speech allows the reader to search for and integrate information efficiently by allowing the reader to ignore less important parts of the sentence. Therefore, one problem the deaf have when learning to read is an inability to chunk information efficiently and anticipate meaning because their knowledge of the linguistic rules and timing parameters of speech is limited and not easily accessible. An example of an inappropriately driven reading system is found in the abnormal eye movement patterns of deaf children during reading (Beggs & Breslaw, 1982).

In addition to accessibility and perceptual salience there may be another aspect of auditory information which is important in learning to read. Hearing children develop a bias toward processing sequential information in general which allows them to understand the sequential information inherent in English. Deaf children, at the same age, do not appear to have developed a similar bias. For example, on a task which presented numbers in a sequential order and could be reported in a sequential or spatial pattern, hearing children invariably used the sequential pattern. Deaf children, however, were just as likely to pick a random or spatial pattern. In addition, deaf children appear to have smaller attention spans for ordered sequences than hearing children (Lake, 1981). However, Lake suggests that the efficiency with which children are capable of processing sequential information also affects the reading process of deaf children. A deaf child may think of the syntactical rules of a verbal language as a largely arbitrary exercise; reading, then, exists without any logical framework within which the information can be organized and accessed. If this is the case then the child's ability to process syntactic information will be limited by sequential memory efficiency. Thus, Lake sees both efficiency and bias as determinants of reading ability in the deaf child.

The possibility that deaf children use different coding strategies in reading tasks has also been advanced by Hung, Tzeng, & Warren (1981). They used a sentence-picture verification task in which the deaf subjects read a sentence where the truth value and syntactic structure could vary and subjects were required to match the sentence to a picture. For example, the sentence could read "star is above plus," "plus is not above star" or "plus is below star." It has previously been demonstrated that "below" sentences take longer than "above" sentences. A deaf group also had reaction times for "above" sentences that were faster than for "below" sentences when these sentences were signed. This relationship was not obtained, however, when the sentences were written. Similarly, if one uses a linguistic coding strategy in this task, it takes about 4 times as long to process a negative sentence as a mismatch (Clarke & Chase, 1972). The ratio for the deaf subjects was 1.379. When these same sentences were signed to a different group of deaf subjects the ratio was much closer to 4 (3.314). In addition, order of difficulty for true affirmative, true negative, false affirmative and false negative sentences did not match the expected linear model proposed by Carpenter and Just (1975). Hung et al. concluded that English may be processed using a visual-imagery strategy rather than a linguistic coding strategy. When the task was presented explicitly as a sign language task, the subjects appeared to use a linguistic code; in other words, the order of difficulty matched the Carpenter and Just linear model.

Thus, characteristics of a language based initially on a visual system (including speech reading and sign language) could influence the reading process directly. Hearing children generally attempt to map the grapheme system onto a phonemic system. Since deaf children find spatial information generally more salient and temporal order considerably less so, they could be attempting the task of reading as a grapheme-to-morpheme correspondence. The morpheme, however, exists as a hand movement in space. Thus, deaf children not only miss the temporal, rhythmic information available in the phonemic system, they also may develop a bias to process spatial rather than temporal information when attempting to read. For example, they may ignore the syntactic information in the sentence "John was hit by Bill" and conclude that "John hit Bill," interpreting all sentences as a subject-verb-object logographic unit.

## NEUROPSYCHOLOGY AND LANGUAGE

Although it may be theoretically interesting to attribute reading difficulties to the salience of visual information, there are a number of problems which make research in this area difficult. In general, it is difficult to distinguish the cause and effect when there is a difference between deaf and hearing children on the same task, i.e., do the deaf children do poorly because they are deaf or because they can't read? It is important to consider the cognitive demands of the task, the biological constraints of the organism and the perceptual characteristics of the stimuli when attempting to unravel the complex interrelationship of deafness and its effect on language and reading. Cerebral asymmetry research can be used to focus the attention on some specific biological issues mentioned previously. This model not only provides a variety of techniques with which one may investigate the relationship between brain activity and cognitive processes, it also incorporates a dichotomous model of behavior as an integral part of its structure. Thus, it is possible to use this model to investigate the parameters of temporal and spatial information and their relationship to cerebral organization. In general, this literature suggests that language and speech appear to be primarily mediated by the left hemisphere and nonverbal visual-spatial skills are mediated by the right hemisphere in the normal population (Bryden, 1982; Segalowitz, 1983).

A number of attempts have been made to investigate the issue of laterality and deafness using techniques developed in the lateral asymmetry literature (see Appendix). To summarize, the investigation of hemispheric asymmetries using deaf and hearing subjects with a visual technique has suggested that deaf subjects tend to be less lateralized than hearing subjects. While hearing subjects consistently display a left hemisphere advantage for verbal material, deaf subjects tend to show reduced or reversed asymmetries (Phippard, 1977; McKeever, Hoemann; Florian, & VanDeventer, 1976; Scholes & Fischler, 1979; Ross, Pergament, & Anisfeld, 1979; Kelly & Tomlinson-Keasey, 1981; Boshoven, McNeil, & Lane, 1979; Kelly & Tomlinson-Keasey, 1981; Boshoven, McNeil, & Harvey, 1982). On nonverbal visual tasks, the hearing generally show a right hemisphere advantage and the deaf are inconsistent (Manning, Goble, Markman, & LaBreche, 1977; Neville, 1977; Neville & Bellugi, 1978; Phippard, 1977; Virostek & Cutting, 1979; Poizner & Harvey, 1982). Sign language and fingerspelling have been used in visual studies with very mixed results (McKeever et al., 1976; Virostek & Cutting, 1979; Poizner & Lane, 1979; Poizner, Battison & Lane, 1979; Boshoven, McNeil, & Harvey, 1982). However, the use of a visual technique to investigate lateral asymmetries in the deaf has been questioned because the deaf appear to have abnormal eye movement patterns. Others have investigated lateral asymmetries using a tactual technique. Cranney & Ashton (1980) and LaBreche, Manning, Goble, & Markman (1977) have reported finding no difference between hearing and deaf subjects. Gibson & Bryden (1984) have reported a reversal of the normal laterality effect in deaf children. Using a concurrent verbal and fingertapping task, Ashton and Beasely (1982) reported an interference for the right hand of both deaf and hearing subjects.

There have been several reports of EEG studies with deaf subjects, Neville (1977), Neville & Bellugi (1978) and Neville, Kutas, & Schmidt (1982) have reported reversals of normal laterality using evoked potentials in deaf subjects. Suter (1982) has reported no lateral asymmetry effects in deaf subjects using alpha asymmetry as a measure of cerebral involvement. Samar (1983) reported normal laterality in deaf subjects. Overall, deaf subjects do not appear to exhibit the same pattern of cerebral organization as hearing subjects with the same consistency (see Appendix).

The literature dealing with aphasic deaf patients yields additional information about the lateralization of cerebral function. Osgood and Miron (1963) reviewed five cases of deaf aphasics and reported that left hemisphere lesions caused disturbances of sign language. Kimura, Battison, and Lubert (1976) also reported a left hemisphere lesion in a deaf subject who was subsequently impaired in sign language; however, they attributed this deficiency to impaired motor sequencing. Underwood and Paulson (1981) reported sign language disturbance in a deaf left-handed male who had a left hemisphere lesion. Kimura, Davidson, & McCormick (1982) reported no evidence of sign language impairment in a deaf right hemisphere stroke patient. Bellugi (1983) recently reported 3 cases in which left hemisphere lesions influenced the fluency of sign language. Poizner, Bellugi, and Iraqui (1984) reported language disturbance in a series of left hemisphere stroke patients and a visuo-spatial deficit in a right hemisphere stroke patient.

Generally, the deaf aphasic literature indicates the possibility of left hemisphere control over some components of sign language. The perceptual research suggests that deaf children and adults may be processing visually presented information inappropriately or inconsistently. The tactual technique, which may be more appropriate, tends to indicate a reversal of the normal pattern. The EEG literature also suggests a reversal of the normal organization. The inability to process verbal and nonverbal information in the *normal* manner on these laterality tasks may well indicate that deaf subjects are using a right hemisphere rather than a left hemisphere mechanism for information processing, even though some components of sign language may be primarily mediated through the left hemisphere. While these statements appear to be contradictory they are, in fact, addressing different issues. Deaf children appear to have access to linguistic codes with the same neurological substrate as a verbal language. When confronted with a reading task, these linguistic codes are not necessarily accessed.

The reading tasks require different strategies which seem to involve a right hemisphere bias. For the deaf, language and reading are not complementary tasks.

In summary, if the early environment of the deaf is predominantly visual-spatial; if the right hemisphere in the normal population is generally involved in visual-spatial perception; and if the perceptual characteristics of the language interact with the biological constraints of the cerebral structure, it suggests that the deaf may be tuned into inappropriate information when attempting to read. That is, deaf children will not only be restricted in the facilitation usually provided by a rhythmic phonetic linguistic system, but may also make use of a counterproductive bias for inaproriate characteristics of linguistic information. In addition, the capacity of the right hemisphere for language mediation has traditionally been viewed as limited, and restricted to semantic rather than syntactic processes. If the deaf are, in fact, using the right hemisphere to mediate the reading process, it may place an upper limit on their reading ability.

If it is possible to bypass the phonetic system, would reading ability improve? This question has been considered in the past. Sperling (1978) discussed the possibility of deaf children using ideographs (similar to Chinese characters) to learn to read. He suggested that Ameslan could be transcribed to provide a reading and language based code based on a system common to both. This idea has a great deal of appeal but so far has not been tested extensively.

## SUMMARY

In general, it has been suggested that the hand and eye are capable of mediating, storing, retrieving and manipulating complex images and relationships as well as the ear and voice. Both verbally mediated and spatially mediated languages achieve similar levels of complexity and as such reveal the underlying neurological characteristics of the human language system. However, the perceptual characteristics of each system dictate what becomes the most salient characteristic for the organization of information. This, in turn, permits access to a particular form of information retrieval during the reading process which may be counterproductive for deaf children. This issue is relevant both at the theoretical level in the discussion of the relationship between thought and language and at the practical level of improving the reading ability of deaf children. It also suggests a dissociation between language and reading in, at least some, deaf children.

## REFERENCES

Ashton, R. & Beasely, M. (1982). Cerebral laterality in deaf and hearing children. *Developmental Psychology, 18,* 2, 294–300.

Beggs, W. D. A., & Breslaw, P. I. (1982). Reading, clumsiness, and the deaf child. *American Annals of the Deaf, 127(1),* 32–37.

Bellugi, U. (1983). Language structure and language breakdown in American Sign Language. In M. Studdert-Kennedy (Ed.), *Psychobiology of Language*. Cambridge, MA: MIT Press, 152–176.

Bellugi, U., Poizner, H., & Zurif, E. B. (1982). Prospects for the study of aphasia in a visual-gestural language. In M. A. Arbib, D. Caplan, & J. C. Marshall (Eds.), *Neural models of language processes*. (pp 271–292). New York: Academic Press.

Boshoven, M. M., McNeil, M. R., & Harvey, L. O. (1982). Hemispheric specialization for the processing of linguistic and nonlinguistic stimuli in congenitally deaf and hearing adults: A review and contribution. *Audiology, 21*, 509–530.

Brooks, P. H. (1978). Some speculations concerning deafness and learning to read. In L. S. Liben (Ed.), *Deaf children: Developmental perspectives*. New York: Academic Press.

Bryden, M. P. (1982). *Laterality: Functional asymmetry in the intact brain*. New York: Academic Press.

Carpenter, P. A., & Just, M. A. (1975). Sentence comprehension: A psycholinguistic processing model of verification. *Psychological Review, 82*, 45–73.

Clark, H. H., & Chase, W. (1972). On the process of comparing sentences against pictures. *Cognitive Psychology, 3*, 472–517.

Conrad, R. (1979). *The deaf schoolchild*. London: Harper and Row.

Cranney, J., & Ashton, R. (1980). Witelson's dichaptic task as a measure of hemispheric asymmetry. *Neuropsychologia, 18*, 95–98.

Gibson, C., & Bryden, M. P. (1984). Cerebral laterality in deaf and hearing children. *Brain and Language*, 1–12.

Hung, D., Tzeng, O., & Warren, D. (1981). A chronometric study of sentence processing in deaf children. *Cognitive Psychology, 13*, 583–610.

Kelly, R., & Tomlinson-Keasey, C. (1981). The effect of auditory input on cerebral laterality. *Brain and Language, 13*, 67–77.

Kimura, D., Battison, R. & Lubert, B. (1976). Impairment of nonlinguistic hand movements in a deaf aphasic. *Brain and Language, 3*, 566–571.

Kimura, D., Davidson, W., & McCormick, C. W. (1982). No impairment in sign language after a right hemisphere stroke. *Brain and Language, 17*, 359–362.

Klima, E. S., & Bellugi, U. (1979). *The signs of language*. Cambridge, MA: Harvard University Press.

LaBreche, T. M., Manning, A. A., Goble, W., & Markman, R. (1977). Hemispheric specialization for linguistic and nonlinguistic tactual perception in a congenitally deaf population. *Cortex, 13*, 184–194.

Lake, D. (1981). *Syntax and sequential memory in hearing impaired children*. Unpublished Ph.D. Dissertation, University of Waterloo.

Lenneberg, E. H. (1970). What is meant by a biological approach to language? *American Annals of the Deaf, 15*, 67–72.

Manning, A. A., Goble, W., Markman, R., & LaBreche, T. (1977). Lateral cerebral differences in the deaf in response to linguistic and nonlinguistic stimuli. *Brain and Language 4*, 309–321.

McKeever, W. F., Hoemann, H. W., Florian, V. A., & VanDeventer, A. D. (1976). Evidence of minimal cerebral asymmetries for the processing of English words and American Sign Language in the congenitally deaf. *Neuropsychologia, 14*, 413–423.

Neville, H. (1977). Electroencephalographic testing of cerebral dominance in normal and congenitally deaf children: A preliminary report. In S. Segalowitz & F. A. Gruber (Eds.), *Language development and neurological theory*. New York: Academic Press.

Neville, H., & Bellugi, U. (1978). Patterns of cerebral specialization in congenitally deaf adults: A preliminary report. In P. Siple (Ed.), *Understanding language through sign language research*. New York: Academic Press.

Neville, H. Kutas, M., & Schmidt, A. (1982). Event-related potential studies of cerebral specialization during reading. *Brain and Language, 16*, 300–315.

Osgood, C. E., & Miron, M. S. (1963). *Approaches to the study of aphasia*. Urbana: University of Illinois Press.

Parasnis, I., & Samar, V. J. (1982). Visual perception of verbal information by deaf people. In D. Sims, G. Walter & R. Whitehead (Eds.), Deafness and communication: Assessment and training. Baltimore: Williams & Wilkins.

Phippard, D. (1977). Hemifield differences in visual perception in deaf and hearing subjects. *Neuropsychologia, 15,* 555–561.

Poizner, H., Battison, R., & Lane, H. (1979). Cerebral asymmetry for American Sign Language: The effects of moving stimuli. *Brain and Language, 7,* 351–62.

Poizner, H. Bellugi, U., & Iragui, V. (1984). Apraxia and aphasia in a visual-gestural language. *American Journal of Physiology.* June, 246(6-2), R868–83.

Poizner, H., Lane, H. (1979). Cerebral asymmetry in the perception of American Sign Language. *Brain and Language, 7,* 210–226.

Quigley, S. P. (1982). Reading achievement and special reading materials, *The Volta Review, 84,*(5), 95–106.

Ross, P., Pergament, L., & Anisfeld, M. (1979). Cerebral lateralization of deaf and hearing individuals for linguistic comparison judgments. *Brain and Language, 8,* 69–80.

Samar, V. (1983). Evoked-potential and visual half-field evidence for task-dependent cerebral asymmetries in congenitally deaf adults. *Brain and Cognition, 2,* 383–403.

Sarno, J. E., Swisher, L. P., & Sarno, M. T. (1969). Aphasia in a congenitally deaf man. *Cortex, 5,* 222–230.

Schlesinger, H. (1978). The acquisition of a signed and spoken language. In L. S. Liben (Ed.), *Deaf children: Developmental perspectives.* New York: Academic Press.

Scholes, R. J., & Fischler, I. (1979). Hemispheric function and linguistic skill in the deaf. *Brain and Language, 7,* 336–350.

Segalowitz, S. J. (1983). *Language functions and brain organization.* New York: Academic Press.

Slobin, D. I. (1971). Developmental psycholinguistics. In W. O. Dingwall, *A survey of linguistic science.* Maryland, University of Maryland.

Suter, S. (1982). Differences between deaf and hearing adults in task-related EEG asymmetries. *Psychophysiology, 19,* 124–8.

Underwood, J. K., & Paulson, C. J. (1981). Aphasia and congenital deafness: A case study. *Brain and Language, 12,* 285–291.

Virostek, S., & Cutting, J. E. (1979). Asymmetries for Ameslan handshapes and other forms in signers and nonsigners. *Perception and Psychophysics, 26,* 505–508.

Vygotsky, L. S. (1962). *Thought and Language,* Cambridge, MA: MIT Press.

# APPENDIX

Summary of cerebral asymmetry studies with deaf subjects. LH = left hemisphere; RH = right hemisphere; SL = sign language; VHF = visual half-field; RVF = right visual field; LVF = left visual field; adv = advantage; RT = reaction time; adol = adolescents; ERP = event-related potentials.

| Task/Stimuli | Author | Subjects | Results |
|---|---|---|---|
| *Clinical* | | | |
| | Osgood & Miron (1963) | 5 deaf stroke patients | LH lesion interferes with SL |

*(continued)*

| Task/Stimuli | Author | Subjects | Results |
|---|---|---|---|
| *Clinical* | | | |
| | Sarno, Swisher, & Sarno (1969) | LH deaf stroke patient | Interference with SL |
| | Kimura, Battison, & Lubert (1976) | LH stroke deaf patient | Interference with SL & complex nonlinguistic hand movements |
| | Underwood & Paulson (1981) | LH stroke left-handed patient (deaf) | SL disturbance |
| | Kimura, Davidson, & McCormick (1982) | RH stroke patient (deaf) | no interference in SL |
| | Bellugi (1983) | 3 LH stroke patients (deaf) | SL disturbance |
| | Poizner, Bellugi, & Iraqui (1984) | as in Bellugi (1983) and 1 RH patient (deaf) | SL disturbance in LH patients; visuo-spatial skills disrupted in RH patient |
| *EEG* | | | |
| ERP—pictures | Neville (1977) | children (9–13 yrs) deaf and hearing | RH response for hearing children. LH response for signing deaf children. No asymmetries for nonsigning deaf children. |
| ERP—words | Neville, Kutas, & Schmidt (1982) | adults, deaf and hearing | LH response in hearing RH response in deaf |
| alpha—letter writing | Suter (1982) | adults, deaf and hearing | LH activation in hearing No asymmetries in deaf |
| alpha—signed story | Suter (1982) | adults, deaf and hearing | LH activation in hearing No asymmetries in deaf |
| ERP—words | Samar (1983) | deaf adults | RVF adv; ERPs predict asymmetries |
| ERP—line orientation | Samar (1983) | deaf adults | LVF adv; ERPs predict symmetries |
| *Behavioral* | | | |
| *VHF* | | | |
| words | McKeever, Hoemann, Florian, & VanDeventer (1976) | adults, deaf and hearing | RVF adv in hearing No asymmetry in deaf |
| words | Phippard (1977) | adol, hearing and deaf | RVF adv in hearing LVF adv in oral deaf No asymmetry in signing deaf |
| words | Manning, Goble, Markman, & LaBreche (1977) | adol, hearing and deaf | RVF adv in hearing RVF adv in deaf |
| picture-word match | Scholes & Fischler (1979) | adol, hearing and deaf | RVF adv in hearing No asymmetry in deaf |

(*continued*)

| Task/Stimuli | Author | Subjects | Results |
|---|---|---|---|
| *Behavioral* | | | |
| letters | Ross, Pergament, & Anisfeld (1979) | adults | RVF adv in hearing |
| | | | No asymmetry in deaf |
| words | Poizner, Battison, & Lane (1979) | adults, deaf and hearing | RVF adv in deaf |
| | | | RVF adv in hearing |
| words | Kelly & Tomlinson-Keasey (1981) | children (8–10 yrs) deaf and hearing | LVF adv in deaf with high imagery words |
| | | | RVF adv in hearing with low imagery words |
| words | Boshoven, McNeil & Harvey (1982) | adults, deaf and hearing | LVF adv in deaf |
| | | | LVF adv in hearing |
| signs | McKeever, Hoemann, Florian, & VanDeventer (1976) | adults, deaf and hearing | LVF adv in hearing |
| | | | No asymmetry in deaf |
| signs | Neville & Bellugi (1978) | adults, deaf and hearing | RVF adv in deaf |
| signs (using RT) | Poizner & Lane (1979) | adults, deaf and hearing | LVF adv in deaf |
| | | | LVF adv in hearing |
| signs | Poizner, Battison, & Lane (1979) | deaf adults | LVF adv for static signs and no asymmetry for moving signs |
| finger-spelling | Virostek & Cutting (1979) | deaf and hearing adol and adults | RVF adv in deaf |
| | | | RVF in hearing |
| signs | Boshoven, McNeil, & Harvey (1982) | adults, deaf and hearing | RVF adv in deaf |
| | | | RVF adv in hearing |
| shapes | Manning, Goble, Markman, & LaBreche (1977) | adol, deaf and hearing | No asymmetry in either group |
| lines | Phippard (1977) | adol, deaf and hearing | LVF adv in hearing |
| | | | LVF adv in oral deaf |
| | | | No asymmetry in signing deaf |
| faces | Phippard (1977) | adol, deaf and hearing | No asymmetry in either group |
| pictures | Neville (1977) | children, deaf and hearing | No asymmetry in either group on a behavioral task |
| dot localization | Neville & Bellugi (1978) | adults, deaf and hearing | LVF adv in hearing |
| | | | RVF adv in deaf |
| shapes | Poizner & Lane (1979) | adults, deaf and hearing | No asymmetry in either group |
| pictures (using RT) | Kelly & Tomlinson-Keasey (1981) | children (8–10 yrs) deaf and hearing | LVF adv in deaf |
| | | | No asymmetry in hearing |
| pictures | Boshoven, McNeil, & Harvey (1982) | adults, deaf and hearing | LFV adv in deaf |
| | | | RVF adv in hearing |
| dots | Boshoven, McNeil, & Harvey (1982) | adults, deaf and hearing | LVF adv in deaf |
| | | | LVF adv in hearing |

(*continued*)

| Task/Stimuli | Author | Subjects | Results |
|---|---|---|---|
| *Tactile* | | | |
| letters | LaBreche, Manning, Goble, & Markman (1977) | adol, deaf and hearing | No asymmetry in either group |
| letters | Gibson & Bryden (1984) | children (10 yr), deaf and hearing | RHand adv in hearing LF adv in deaf |
| shapes | LaBreche, Manning, Goble, & Markman (1977) | adol, deaf and hearing | RHand adv in hearing No asymmetry in deaf |
| shapes | Cranney & Ashton (1980) | children (8–11 yr) deaf and hearing | No asymmetries in either group |
| shapes | Gibson & Bryden (1984) | children (10 yr) deaf and hearing | LHand adv in hearing No asymmetry in deaf |
| concurrent tapping with verbal task | Ashton & Beasely (1982) | children (5–12 yr) deaf and hearing | RHand tapping interference in both groups |
| concurrent tapping nonverbal task | Ashton & Beasely (1982) | children (5–12 yr) deaf and hearing | No interference with either hand in hearing Equal interference in both hands in deaf |

# IV

## THE PATHOLOGICAL MANIFESTATIONS OF GESTURAL BEHAVIOR

# 11 Standard Teaching on Apraxia

André Roch Lecours
Jean-Luc Nespoulous
Pierre Desaulniers

This chapter deals with a somewhat renewed conception of apraxia. The subject matter has long been and, to a large extent, remains classical *standard teaching on apraxia*. In a preliminary section, we summarize a not-so-standard although equally classical conception of human motility and its neuroanatomical substratum, and thereafter define apraxia by reference to this conception. Also as a preliminary, and in order to define what apraxia is not (at least in the context of this chapter), we briefly discuss the various forms of motility disorders that can be observed in clinical neurology. The last and main section bears on apraxia, more precisely on upper limbs apraxia.

Most of us can conceive of the world as having two sides, the right one and the left one, which can be apprehended because we have two eyes, two ears, and so forth, and upon which we can act because we have two hands (among other reasons), the right one and the left one, the clever one and the clumsy one. And most of us also agree that there are two halves to the human brain, an assertion which one can choose to consider in either of two manners. On the one hand, one might state that there are the anterior or prerolandic, as opposed to the posterior or retrolandic halves: and one might thereafter insist that the former is the executive half and the latter the cognitive one. Or else, on the other hand, one might state that there is the left or dominant half or hemisphere ("dominant" because it governs language behaviors as well as the activities of the clever hand), as opposed to the right or nondominant half: and one might thereafter insist that each constitutes the biological substratum of one of two modes of human cognition, the analytic or deductive mode for the left hemisphere, and the holistic or inductive mode for the right one.

The above perhaps corresponds to reality of a sort and, up to a point, it is related to our subject matter; nonetheless, the rest of this chapter deals with threes rather than twos: we thus successively invoke three ''brains'' and three types of motility, three families of motor disorders resulting from various brain lesions, and three labels which, somewhat indiscriminately, have been used over the years in discussions on apraxia from either of three—the clinical, the psychological, and the anatomical—points of view.

## THREE BRAINS AND THREE TYPES
## OF MOTILITY

Our first threes come as a pair and they are borrowed from Paul Yakovlev's teachings (Yakovlev, 1948, 1964, 1968, 1970, 1972) (Fig. 11.1). Between the third and the fourth week of human gestation, a holosphere begins to appear at the rostral end of the neural tube. This holosphere is the anlage of the *rhinic brain,* to which Yakovlev refers as *telencephalon impar* since it is embryologically ablateral. Around the seventh or eighth week, a pair of evaginations starts to form laterally to the holosphere. These represent the anlage of the *limbic brain,* to which Yakovlev refers as *telencephalon semipar* since, embryologically, it is paired only in part. Still later, around the eleventh or twelfth week, a second pair of evaginations begins to develop dorsolaterally to the first one. These represent the anlagen of the *supralimbic brain,* to which Yakovlev refers as *telencephalon totopar* since, embryologically, they stem from entirely lateralized sources. Growth of the supralimbic brain will thereafter be such that the other two brains will soon be crowded on the midline and near it; it should also be noted that, of the three brains, the supralimbic is not only the one whose ontogenesis begins the latest but also the one whose biological maturation will last the longest (Yakovlev, 1962; Yakovlev & Lecours, 1967). Furthermore, it should be noted that those movement disorders which are collectively designated as *apraxia* in the present context all result from supralimbic lesions and dysfunctions. The latter fact has been established through the correlative study of brain lesions and their resulting clinical disorders, that is, through application of the *anatomo-clinical method.*

Arguing from both the phylogenetic and the ontogenetic points-of-view, Yakovlev (1948, 1964, 1968, 1970, 1972) establishes a priviliged although not exclusive link between each of his three brains and one of three types of human motility. Thus, *endokinesis*—movement within the body, cell-bound movement—is linked to the rhinic brain, to telencephalon impar: This corresponds to the motility of visceration, for instance to peristaltis. Likewise, *ereismokinesis*—body-bound movement—is linked to the limbic brain, to telencephalon semipar: This corresponds to emotional (e-motion-al) motility, for instance to facial ex-

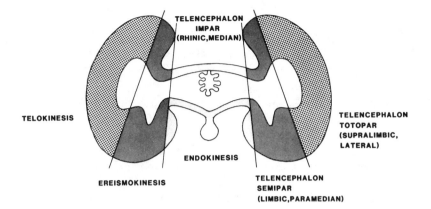

FIG. 11.1.

pressions and vocalizations (articulated or otherwise) accompanying pleasure, fear, surprise, etc. And *telokinesis*—object-bound movement—is linked to the supralimbic brain, to telencephalon totopar: This corresponds to motility targeted on objects and events outside the body, to manipulation of tools for instance, as well as to the production of propositional language. It should be emphasized that those movement disorders which are collectively designated as *apraxia* in the present context are, specifically, disorders of telokinesis.

## THREE FAMILIES OF MOTOR DISORDERS
## OF THE LIMBS

There are several ways in which acquired lesions of the cerebral hemispheres can interfere with human limbs motility. Without aiming at exhaustiveness in this respect, we now identify three families of such motor disorders. The commonest and most elementary such disorders interfere with muscle strength and tone; the archetype is *hemiparesis* or *hemiplegia,* a form of paralysis impairing both ereismokinesis and telokinesis, although not necessarily to the same degree. There also exists a less frequent and more puzzling type of motor disorder to which neurologists will sometimes refer as *motor neglect* and which might be defined as an absence of, or an immediately evident reduction in spontaneous use of a nonparalyzed limb; it is our impression that this disorder, whether or not a primarily motor one, also interferes with both ereismokinesis and telokinesis. The third family is that of the *apraxias*: These specifically involve telokinesis, i.e., they are disorders interfering with voluntary movements, those the mastery of which has been acquired through learning.

## APRAXIA

Stating that the apraxias specifically interfere with learned voluntary movement is about as far as one can go in way of a positive definition of this particular type of motor disorder. As a matter of fact, it is easier to focus on what the apraxias are not than it is to formulate a definition in positive terms others than the above: The apraxias do not result from muscle weakness, dystonia and so forth, and neither are they the result of primary sensory deprivation; moreover, the apraxias do not belong with the group of disorders known as "pathological reflexes" (grasp, avoidance, and so forth), nor with that of "involuntary movements" (tremor, adiadochocinesis, and so forth) that can be observed in various diseases of the central nervous system; finally, the apraxias do not witness to a disorder in language comprehension, nor are they to be interpreted as witnessing to lack of cooperation on the part of the tested subject. The apraxias are something else.

Given the lack of a precise definition, it should be kept in mind that the apraxias, or at least those we are discussing here, are disorders which occur in people who could previously produce normal voluntary gestures and who, as the result of an acquired supralimbic lesion, have an impaired gestural behavior. Furthermore, it is useful to know that apraxic disorders—just like other neuro-psychological disorders—are inconsistent: When an apraxic subject is observed at one point to be unable to execute a given gesture on command, he may well turn out to be able to do so the next minute. As a matter of fact, a useful clinical procedure to show that an abnormal gesture indeed testifies to the existence of apraxia is to demonstrate that the subject cannot execute this gesture in a certain set of circumstances but can do it in another. For instance, the subject who is requested to "make a fist," who understands this request but does not succeed after several attempts, might be observed to close his fist without the slightest anomaly nor hesitation when handed an object in a manner favoring fist closing. Obviously, this dissociation in motor behavior demonstrates the integrity of the primary sensorimotor pathways involved in making a fist and it shows that the disorder stems from dysfunction at a higher level of neural integration.

## History

Who coined the word apraxia? Nielsen (1946), on the one hand, as well as Signoret and North (1979), on the other, note that it is often claimed in the literature that it was Gogol (writing in German) who created this term in 1873. Yet, these authors also mention that Steinthal used the same word, in 1871, to designate a clinical condition which was perhaps apraxia and perhaps not. Before the word was coined, however, facts had been described, for instance by Hugh-

lings Jackson in 1866, which in retrospect can be identified as clear cut cases of limb apraxia.[1]

Although he had predecessors, Hugo Karl Liepmann (above) was (and remains) the great man of "apraxiology." Liepmann was born in Berlin, on April the 9th, 1863, and he committed suicide in the same city, on May the 6th,

---

[1]Although we have chosen to center the present chapter on limb apraxia, we might mention that, in 1897, Von Monakow published his observations on two patients who would nowadays be considered as typical cases of buccofacial apraxia: Neither patient could blow on command but the first could blow ashes out of a tray while the second, a professional clarinetist, was still capable of playing his instrument. As a matter of fact, and although subtle clinical demonstrations remained to be defined, similar dissociations had long intrigued physicians when von Monakow published these observations: Dax the father, for instance, quoted, in 1836, and posthumely published, in 1865, a passage that he had excerpted from a book edited in 1585, by Schenkius, who was himself quoting another scientist by the name of Atheus: *"Observatum a me est plurimos, post apoplexiam, aut lethargum, aut similes magnos capitis morbos, etiam non praesente linguae paralysi, loqui non posse quod memoriae facultate extincta verba proferanda non succurant."*

1925 (Haymaker & Schiller, 1970; Signoret & North, 1979). His interest in apraxia lasted from 1900 to 1920 and, during this period, he published a great deal on the topic (Liepmann, 1900, 1902, 1905a, 1905b, 1905c, 1906, 1907a, 1907b, 1907c, 1908, 1913, 1920; Liepmann & Maas, 1907). Indeed, it can legitimately be claimed that most of contemporary standard teachings on apraxia can be traced back to Liepmann's work. He published his first observation in 1900: a case of unilateral apraxia involving the right limbs in an ambidextral syphilitic imperial counselor:[2] obviously, one should not dwell further on this princeps since it was upon Liepmann's subsequent research that doctrine was later to consolidate.

## Three Labels

Liepmann's taxonomy of the apraxias[3] was already defined in his 1907 publications (as summarized by Rose, 1907). This taxonomy recognizes the existence of three types of apraxia of the limbs (of the upper limbs, essentially): *melokinetic apraxia, ideokinetic apraxia,* and *ideatory apraxia.* It should be noted that the term *ideomotor apraxia* was deliberately avoided in this taxonomy because Pick (1905) had used it a few years earlier to label cases that Liepmann considered as typical of the motor disorder to which he referred as ideatory apraxia. As things turned out, clinicians to come were to retain Pick's label and Liepmann's views, i.e., the term "ideomotor apraxia" has persisted in the vocabulary of neurology but it is not used in line with Pick's acception but rather to designate the conditon that Liepmann recognized as "ideokinetic apraxia," which is a rather typical example of the terminological tangles which researchers interested in aphasia, apraxia, and agnosia have lovingly engendered, generation after generation, and thereafter attempted to live with. In view of Kleist's (1906, 1907, 1912, 1922, 1934) and Pick's (1902, 1905) contributions to the study of apraxia, Signoret and North (1979) have a terminological suggestion of their own, which they think might help to disentangle this particular skein: their suggestion is to designate— by reference to Liepmann's terminology—melokinetic apraxia as *Kleist's apraxia,*[4] ideokinetic apraxia as *Liepmann's apraxia,* and ideatory apraxia as *Pick's apraxia;* we like this idea and shall thereafter occasionally comply.

---

[2]As far as we can tell, no other such case has ever been reported since. Now, consider Leborgne, Broca's first case in 1861. Would this case, in 1985, be considered as prototypical of Broca's aphasia?

[3]If "buccofacial apraxia" and "gaze apraxia" are excluded from the present discussion on the ground of our chosen subject matter, that is, apraxia of the limbs, other clinical entities such as those currently labeled as "constructional apraxia," "apraxia for dressing," and so forth, are excluded because, in our opinion, their kinship to apraxia is one in terms rather than nature.

[4]Which would sanction an already established custom, anyway.

## Three Points of View

Resorting as a rule to Liepmann's labels and founded for a major part on his conceptions, standard teaching on apraxia usually unfolds under three main headings, respectively related to the clinical, psychopathological, and anatomopathological aspects of the problem.

### The Clinical Point of View

Clinical neuropsychology perforce defines deviant behavior by reference to normal behavior: For instance, a phonemic paraphasia can only be identified as such by reference to a presumed target utterance. In line with this necessity, clinicians have developed a basic lexicon to evoke normal telokinesis. One thus opposes, for example, *transitive* to *intransitive* gestures. The former are defined as acts oriented towards the external world and actually involving object manipulation (e.g., hammering a nail, lighting a candle). The notion of intransitive gesture is more composite: It refers to both gestures that naturally require no object manipulation (e.g., waving good-bye, pointing, describing a spiral staircase) and mimicry of transitive gestures (e.g., pretending to be hammering a nail, pretending to be washing one's teeth).

Other lexical oppositions of this type are currently used in clinical work: For instance, one might speak of *reflexive* versus *nonreflexive* gestures, the first refering to telokinetic movements in which one part of the body has to be put in relation with another (e.g., making a military salute, pretending to be brushing one's teeth) and the second to movements in which no such relation is established (e.g., scolding with the index finger, throwing a stone). Or one might speak of *conventional* or *symbolic* versus *arbitrary* gestures, the former bearing a sharable semantic charge (e.g., making a military salute, rubbing tips of thumb and index finger to represent money) and not so the latter (e.g., rubbing tips of thumb and little finger). Or again, one might speak of gestures which are naturally *unilateral* (e.g., using a small brush) as opposed to those which are naturally *bilateral* (e.g., using a broom with a long handle).

The pairs of opposite terms in the above lexicon are overlapping to such an extent that one wonders about their utility. Their emergence in the vocabulary of clinicians is no doubt related, on the one hand, to lack of an appropriate classification of telokinetic movements (in this respect, see Chapter 2 of this volume) and, on the other hand, to the fact that clinicians have observed pathological dissociations—cases in which one type of gesture was believed or observed to be more impaired than another—which they have attempted to characterize at best. Be this as it may, three types of apraxic productions are said to be identifiable by reference to one aspect or another of this lexicon.

One might refer to the first type as *clumsiness in purposive movement*. The patient's gestures are incomplete or else slowed, hesitating, laborious; the intentionality related to the command given to the patient is nonetheless recognized. This behavior is typically limited to a single upper limb and it impairs telokinesis as a whole although it can be more obvious in unilateral transitive actions requiring more precision (e.g., drawing, buttoning one's shirt). If convinced that this is not witnessing to very mild or residual hemiparesis, which is not always easily decided, in particular when there exists no other evidence of apraxia, clinicians abiding by classical teachings will label the subject's condition as Kleist's or melokinetic apraxia.

The second type of abnormal purposive movements can be designated as *parapraxis*. In intransitive mimicry, the patient assimilates a part of his body to an object (e.g., the index finger becomes a tooth brush, the fist becomes a hammer, fingers are fanned and act as a comb): In our opinion, the anomalous nature of this behavior, especially among children and elderlies, becomes obvious only when the disorder is unilateral. In reflexive symbolic gestural production, for instance, a requested action can be replaced by another (e.g., required to thumb his nose, a subject makes the closed-fist-thumb-up approbation sign); this often corresponds to a phenomenon of perseveration, which in certain cases can be partial (e.g., requested to make a military salute after having correctly thumbed his nose, a subject retains the hand position of nose thumbing and brings the tip of his thumb to his forehead). Combined or not with clumsiness, this behavior is usually considered by clinicians as ideomotor or ideokinetic apraxia; Signoret and North (1979) would identify it as Liepmann's apraxia.

Although this is not a canonic term, the third (and the most spectacular) type of apraxic behavior observed in clinical neuropsychology can be designated as a *disorder in the '"syntax" of gestures*. Manifestations are bilateral and the perturbation is best observed in relatively complex transitive telokinesis. A common clinical test is, for instance, to hand the patient a box of matches and a candle and to ask him to light the latter. A typical behavior might then be the following: The patient opens the box, picks a match out of it, closes the box (or not); he then takes the candle and strikes it on the side of the box, or else tries to light the match by striking it alongside the candle; he thereafter presents the unlighted match at the wick of the candle (sometimes at the wrong end) and may look puzzled when realizing that it does not work. Usually if not always coexisting with parapraxis, this very characteristic behavior—in which each kinemic component of a relatively complex transitive action could be considered as normal while sequential arrangement between the various components is obviously perturbated—is labeled by most clinicians as ideatory apraxia; Signoret and North (1979) would identify it as Pick's apraxia.

### The Psychological Point of View

The psychopathology of apraxia has been the topic of numerous and often abstruse publications (for a review, see de Ajuriaguerra & Hecaen, 1960). In line with the title of the present chapter, we limit our comments on this subject to the tenets of classical (associationist) teaching, that is, essentially, to Liepmann's views as summarized by Rose (1907) and by Signoret & North (1979).

In Liepmann's psychology, telokinesis depends, beyond purely executive mechanisms, (a) on a particular memory specialized in the retention of kinetic and kinesthetic traces, (b) on a global action programming mechanism, and (c) on a system of associations between the special memory and the programming mechanism (two boxes and one arrow).

According to Liepmann, the perturbation leading to melokinetic apraxia interferes with the special mnestic traces, usually with a subset of these traces related to particular segments of the body. One readily sees how close this notion is to that of Wernicke's (1874) Bewegungsvorstellungen ("movements and changes in the state of the musculature give rise to sensations, memory images of which . . . remain in the cerebral cortex"). Ideatory apraxia, on the other hand, occurs when there exists a perturbation of the programming mechanism, and ideomotor apraxia when the system of associations between the mnestic and the programming components is impaired.

### The Anatomical Point of View

In 1905(a), Liepmann published one of the first major series in neuropsychology. His paper reported on 89 patients with unilateral brain lesions whom he had tested for their purposive movement abilities. Among these, 42 had right hemisphere lesions: None of these showed apraxia. The remaining 47 subjects had left hemisphere lesions; 41 of these presented and six did not present right hemiplegia. None of the latter showed apraxia. Among the 41 subjects with right hemiplegia, 20 showed and 21 did not show apraxia of their left upper limb (right upper limb telokinesis could not be tested in view of the primary motor disorder). Among the 20 subjects with right hemiplegia and left upper limb apraxia, fourteen were aphasic and six were not; among the 21 subjects with right hemiplegia but without left upper limb apraxia, only four were aphasic whereas 17 were not. One could thus conclude that there exists left cerebral dominance for (upper) limbs telokinesis; as Broca had done in 1865 concerning left cerebral dominance for language, Liepmann (1905a) insisted that left dominance for telokinesis depends on an innate biological predisposition characteristic of the human species. Moreover, one could also conclude that the neuroanatomical substratum of upper limbs telokinesis and that of articulated language are close to but remain distinct from one another (on the one hand, apraxia was more frequent when aphasia was present but, on the other hand, apraxia was observed without aphasia and vice versa).

In 1907, Liepmann committed himself further as to the localization of lesions responsible for the three types of apraxia that he recognized. In rather cautious terms, he then attributed melokinetic apraxia to lesions of "the cortex of the central convolutions and possibly some part of the immediately adjacent (frontal) cortex," ideomotor apraxia to "an anatomical isolation of the central convolutions from the . . . inferior parietal lobes," and ideatory apraxia "to diffuse lesions . . . particularly of the left hemisphere and, in the left hemisphere, to lesions involving particularly the parieto-occipital junction." Also in 1907, Liepmann and Mass reported a case of unilateral left-sided limb (ideomotor?) apraxia resulting from a lesion of the callosal genu: Obviously, this was also interpreted, given left hemisphere dominance for limb telokinesis, in terms of disconnection. As reviewed and corrected by Norman Geschwind (1965a; 1965b) in his famous "Disconnexion" papers, Liepmann's conception of the neuroanatomical substratum of purposive action remains, in 1985, the basis of standard—i.e., associationist—teaching on the subject: The special memory and the programming device each have found a particular cortical seat; the former is linked to the latter and each is linked to other parts of the homolateral and controlateral brain by particular connections.

Standard teaching on apraxia is no doubt coherent. To what extent does it correspond to reality is another question. If the clinical typology on which it is founded probably remains the best we have so far, one has to admit that it is built on the observation of clinical pictures some of which are indeed so very infrequent that one wonders why they should be taken as a valid basis for generalization. As to the psychological and psychopathological typology, it leaves clinical differences (as well as inconsistency in apraxic behavior) unaccounted for, at least with regard to the manifestations of ideomotor versus ideatory apraxia, and, above all, it is almost totally devoid of heuristic value (unless one considers, for instance, that it is an explanation to say, after observing ideatory apraxia, that this behavior testifies to the existence of a programming mechanism, and that dysfunction of this programming mechanism will lead to ideatory apraxia). Finally, with the possible exception of anterior callosal lesions, the anatomical and anatomopathological typology, whether or not one adheres to Liepmann's original teachings or to the Boston revision, remains most uncertain (for instance, given this typology, conduction aphasia and ideomotor apraxia should hardly ever occur one without the other, which as far as we know is not the case). Well, apraxiology has remained somewhat static since the turn of the century.

## REFERENCES

de Ajuriaguerra, J., & Hecaen, H. (1960). *Le cortex cerebral: Etude neuro-psycho-pathologique,* Paris: Masson.

Broca, P. (1861). Remarques sur le siege de la faculte du langage articule, suivies d'une obsevation d'aphemie. *Bulletin de la Societe Anatomique, 2,* 330–357.

Dax, M. (1865). Lesions de la moitie gauche de l'encephale coincidant avec l'oubli des signes de la pensee: Lu au Congres meridional tenu a Montpellier en 1836. *Gazette Hebdomadaire de Medecine et Chirurgie, 2,* 259–260.

Geschwind, N. (1965a). Disconnexion syndromes in animals and man (Part I). *Brain, 88,* 237–294.

Geschwind, N. (1965b). Disconnexion syndromes in animals and man (Part II). *Brain, 88,* 585–644.

Haymaker, W., & Schiller, F. (1970). *The founders of neurology*, Springfield, IL: Thomas.

Kleist, K. (1906). Uber Apraxie. *Monatsschrift fur Psychiatrie und Neurologie, 19*, 269–290.

Kleist, K. (1907). Kortikale (innervotarische) Apraxie. *Jahrbuch fur Psychiatrie und Neurologie, 28*, 46–112.

Kleist, K. (1912). Der Gang und der gegenwartige Stand der Apraxie-Forschung. *Ergebnisse der Neurologie und Psychiatrie, 1*, 342–252.

Kleist, K. (1922). Die psychomotorischen Storungen und ihr Verhaltnis zu den Mobilitatsstorungen bei Erkrankungen der Stammganglien. *Monatsschrift fur Psychiatrie und Neurologie, 52*, 253–268.

Kleist, K. (1934). *Gehirnpathologie*, Leipzig: Barth.

Liepmann, H. K. (1900). Das Krankheitsbild der Apraxie ('Motorischen Asymbolie') auf Grund eines Falles von einseitiger Apraxie. *Monatsschrift fur Psychiatrie und Neurologie, 8*, 15–44, 102–132, 188–197.

Liepmann, H. K. (1902). Uber Apraxie mit Demonstration des makroskopischen Gehirnbefundes das im Marz 1900 Vorgestellen einseiting Apraktischen, sowie eines zweiten Falles von Apraxie. *Neurologisches Centralblatt, 21*, 614–617.

Liepmann, H. K. (1905a). *Uber storungen des handelns bei gehirnkranken*, Berlin: Karger.

Liepmann, H. K. (1905b). Die linke Hemisphare und das Handeln. *Munchner Medizinische Wochenschrift, 48*, 2321–2326.

Liepmann, H. K., (1905c). Der weitere Krankheitsverlauf bei dem einseitig Apraktischen und der Gehirnbefund auf Grund von Serienschnitten. *Monatsschrift fur Psychiatrie und Neurologie, 17*, 289–311.

Liepmann, H. K. (1906). Der weitere krankheitsverlauf bei dem einseitig apraktischen und der gehirnbefund auf grund von serienschnitten. *Monatsschrift fur Psychiatrie und Neurologie, 19*, 217–243.

Liepmann, H. K. (1907a). Kleine hilfsmittel bei der untersuchung von gehirnkranken. *Deutsche Medizinische Wochenschrift, 38*, 1492–1494.

Liepmann, H. K. (1907b). Beitrage zur aphasie und apraxielehre. *Neurologisches Centralblatt, 26*, 473–474.

Liepmann, H. K. (1907c). Apraxie. *Neurologisches Centralblatt, 26*, 934–937.

Liepmann, H. K. (1908). *Drei aufsatze aus dem apraxiegebiet*, Berlin: Karger.

Liepmann, II. K. (1913). Motorische aphasie und apraxie. *Monatsschrift fur Psychologie, 35*, 485–494.

Liepmann, H. K. (1920). Apraxie. In *Real-Encyclopadie der gesamten heilkunde*, Berlin and Vienna: Urban & Schwarzenberg.

Liepmann, H. K., & Maas, O. (1907). Klinisch-anotomischer Beitrag zur lehre von der Bedeutung der linken hemisphare und des balkens fur das handeln. *Berliner Klinische Wochenschrift, 1*, 757–758.

Nielsen, J. M. (1946). *Agnosia, apraxia and aphasia*. New York: Hoeber.

Pick, A. (1902). Zur psychologie der motorischen apraxie. *Neurologisches Centralblatt, 21*, 994–1000.

Pick, A. (1905). *Studien uber motorische apraxie und ihr nahestehende erscheinungen*, Leipzig and Vienna: Deuticke.

Rose, F. (1907). De l'apraxie. *L'Encephale, 2*, 510–545.

Signoret, J.-L., & North, P. (1979). *Les apraxies gestuelles*, Paris: Masson.

Wernicke, C. (1874). *Der aphasische symptomenkomplex*, Breslau: Cohn et Weigert.

Yakovlev, P. I. (1948). Motility, behavior and the brain: Stereodynamic organization and neural co-ordinates of behavior. *Journal of Nervous and Mental Diseases, 107*, 313–335.

Yakovlev, P. I. (1962). Morphological criteria of growth and maturation of the nervous system in man. *Mental Retardation, 39*, 3–46.

Yakovlev, P. I. (1964). Telokinesis and handedness: An empirical generalization. In J. Wortis (Ed.), *Recent advances in biological psychiatry (Vol. VI,* pp. 21–30). New York: Plenum Press.

Yakovlev, P. I. (1968). Telencephalon 'impar', 'semipar' and 'totopar': Morphogenetic, tectogenetic and architectonic definitions. *International Journal of Neurology, 6,* 245–265.

Yakovlev, P. I. (1970). The structural and functional 'trinity' of the body, brain, and behavior. *Current Research in Neurosciences, 10,* 197–208.

Yakovlev, P. I. (1972). A proposed definition of the limbic system. In C. H. Hockman (Ed.), *Limbic system mechanisms and autonomic function* (pp. 241–283). Springfield, IL: Thomas.

Yakovlev, P. I., & Lecours, A. R. (1967). The myelogenetic cycles of regional maturation of the brain. In A. Minkowski (Ed.), *Regional development of the brain in early life '(pp. 3–70). Oxford and Edinburgh: Blackwell.*

# 12

# New Perspectives on Apraxia and Related Action Disorders

Eric A. Roy

Apraxia involves a disruption in the performance of gestures, both transitive (with objects) and intransitive (without objects), and/or more complex sequential motor acts, such as putting a letter into an envelope. In examining this disorder we do not describe the traditional classifications (e.g., ideational, ideomotor, and limb-kinetic apraxias) as these are fully described in this volume and elsewhere (Heilman, 1979; Roy, 1982). Rather, consideration is given to the types of errors observed and the four major views as to the nature of apraxia. Discussion then focuses on the work by Roy (1978, 1981, 1982, 1983) and others (Luria, 1980), which considers that apraxia results from a disruption to a functional neurobehavioural system.

## ERRORS IN PERFORMANCE

In performing actions errors may be observed in sequences of action or in single gestures. For movement sequences errors involve omissions, repetitions, misordering of movements in the sequence, a difficulty in terminating movements when required, and in coordinating the limbs in time and space. Errors involved in performing the movement elements which form the sequence have been described by Kimura and Archibald (1974) and Heilman (1979) as clumsiness. Movement loses its smoothness and becomes jerky and ataxic-like: fine finger control may be particularly affected (Heilman, 1975).

With regard to single gestures movements may be performed in a clumsy, ataxic-like fashion; the movement may be misaligned in space so that it is in the wrong plane or, when using an implement (e.g., a saw), it may be grasped in a spatially incorrect way (e.g., cutting edge of the saw facing up rather than down). In demonstrating how to use an object, the patient may use a body part as the object (e.g., clenched fist as a hammer), or he may perform a motion that is associated with the required action. Perseverations may also be observed in which the patient may repeat the previous gesture or perform the subsequent gesture using some of the same spatiotemporal characteristics as before (e.g., in the same spatial plane as the previous gesture). Finally, the patient may exclaim that he knows what the object is used for or where it is used but is unable to demonstrate how to use it. Also, in some parts of the examination although he is asked not to pick up the object, he may do so anyway and examine it with a puzzled look in an apparent attempt to use the sight and feel of it to provide him with information as to how to use it.

## MECHANISMS OF APRAXIA

In an attempt to understand the nature of the apraxias several mechanisms have been postulated. One of the oldest notions of apraxia was that it was representative of a more general disorder termed asymbolia—the inability to understand or express symbols. One line of investigation here reasoned that if apraxia is a symbolic disorder, it should be related to the incidence of aphasic disorder to the language/speech system, which does involve the use of symbols. Findings from studies which have examined this relationship do not necessarily support the notion that apraxia is a symbolic disorder; rather, they imply that there may be some general comprehension-conceptual disorder which underlies both apraxia and language (see Roy, 1982 for a discussion).

Another approach suggests that if apraxia is a symbolic disorder, apraxics should perform symbolic gestures more poorly than nonsymbolic (meaningless) ones. Kimura (Kimura & Archibald 1974, 1977) indicates, however, that apraxics perform poorly on both types of gesture, implying that the disorder in apraxia may not be symbolically based.

Although evidence does not strongly support the notion that apraxia is a symbolic disorder, some evidence does point to a subtle- type of comprehension deficit which may underlie some forms of apraxia (Heilman, 1979; Roy, 1982, 1983). It would seem important to continue investigations into apraxia and other related disorders with the aim of more clearly delineating such subtle comprehension deficits (see Roy, 1983).

Another view of the mechanisms underlying apraxia is that the disorder may result from a disconnection between control centers within the cerebral cortex. Liepmann (cited in Brown, 1972) envisaged that the disconnection of a praxic control center in the parietal lobe of the left hemisphere from the anterior motor control areas in that hemisphere (ideomotor apraxia) or from the homologous areas in the right hemisphere (sympathetic apraxia) resulted in apraxic disorders (see also Heilman, Rothi, & Valenstein, 1982). This disconnection view of apraxia was adopted by Geschwind (1975). In contrast to Leipmann, however, disconnection of the speech reception areas (Wernicke's area) as opposed to the praxic control area were seen to be important in eliciting apraxia (see Kimura, 1979, and Roy, 1982 for a consideration of this viewpoint).

Apraxia has also been viewed as a disruption in spatial orientation. De-Ajuriaguerra and Tissot (1969) and others (e.g., Luria, 1980 and Roy, 1978) have alluded to this type of deficit in apraxia. It is unclear precisely what the nature of the spatial deficit might be; however, while some view the problem as involving disruptions at a relatively low (sensory) level, others consider it a disturbance to higher level integrative processes or to a distorted body image. Most recently, Kimura (1979) has proposed that apraxia may result from a disruption to an internal (body-centered) spatial reference system.

The most pervasive view is that apraxia is a disorder to the perceptual-motor processes involved in movement organization or execution. Liepmann (cited in Brown, 1972), the first to suggest that apraxia was a movement disorder, proposed that the critical region for the control of limb praxis was in the left supramarginal gyrus. Limb or oral movements involving a minimum of visual guidance were thought to be controlled from this region, with damage resulting in ideational apraxia. In this apraxia the ideational outline, an idea of the body parts as well as the rhythm, speed, and sequence of movements to be used. was thought to be disturbed.

In elaborating upon this position, Kimura (Kimura & Archibald, 1974, Kimura, 1977, 1979, 1982) suggested that the supramarginal region of the left hemisphere involves a system which controls the selection and/or execution of limb positions/postures bilaterally. This control is not exerted over the sequence of positions/postures in an action, but rather over the transition from one position to another. This postural selection mechanism is considered to be used within an egocentric (body-centered) spatial reference system in which external (visual primarily) guidance is thought to be minimal, controlling movements in which the external constraints are unvarying (i.e., the environmental demands do not change). Such a system, would, she suggests, be important in traditional limb praxis tasks (the use of common objects), where the movements involved are characterized by unvarying external constraints.

Heilman (1979) also argues for the importance of the supramarginal region of the left hemisphere. Damage to this area results in apraxia due to the destruction of visuokinesthetic engrams. Heilman's emphasis on the importance of damage to the posterior regions of the left hemisphere in apraxia concurs with Kimura's viewpoint, however, the mechanism he describes may be different in that the sequencing of movements and external (visual) guidance seem to be features of his scheme.

Heilman (1975) also describes a mechanism which is concerned with the finesse with which movements are performed. On a rapid finger-tapping task, his quantification of finesse or clumsiness, he found that the average rate of tapping was significantly lower in his apraxic patients than in his nonapraxic patients, suggesting that clumsiness may be an important mechanism in apraxia. Others (e.g., Haaland, Porch, & Delaney, 1980; Kimura, 1979) have also addressed this problem of the clumsiness of apraxic patients, but their results have not concurred with those of Heilman, finding no differences between apraxics and nonapraxics in various measures of fine motor control. With these findings in mind Kimura suggested that while such poor fine finger control would undoubtedly affect the apraxic patient's ability to use objects (i.e., he would be clumsy), this observed clumsiness may not be the result of ineffective control by the praxis system in the left hemisphere.

Haaland et al. (1980) examined the performance of left-brain damaged apraxics and nonapraxics on a series of manual dexterity tasks. While the patient groups did not differ on a simple repetitive finger-tapping task, there were large differences in favor of the nonapraxic group on more complex tasks (maze coordination and grooved pegboard). These results related to differing demands in the two types of task. The tapping task involved repeating (sequencing) the same response. The other more complex tasks required sequencing different responses. The apraxic patients, having incurred more anterior brain damage than that in the nonapraxics, possibly involving the premotor cortex, would, they argue, have very likely experienced more difficulty with the latter more complex tasks, since according to Luria (1980) damage to the premotor area leads to disruption of movements which require the sequencing of *different* responses as opposed to the *same* response over time. This idea that apraxics experience particular problems with tasks which require the performance of a series of different responses is reminiscent of Kimura's (1977) proposal. In this case, however, the neural control center seems to be anterior, while Kimura's view of the control center is more posterior.

It is apparent, then, that apraxia may accrue from damage to the posterior and possibly the anterior regions of the left cerebral hemisphere. Luria (1980) and Roy (1978), however, suggest that the contribution of these two regions to the control of limb praxis may be somewhat different. According to this view the cerebral cortex is like a highly differentiated but interacting system of zones, with complex functions, such as limb praxis, being organized as functional systems which may be disturbed by lesions in any link among these systems.

Elaborating on Luria's views, Roy (1978) described apraxia as involving disturbances to one or more functions in a cognitive, information-processing system. Damage to the frontal or parietal-occipital areas disrupted planning, although in somewhat different ways, while damage to the premotor and sensorimotor regions disturbed the smooth execution of actions, either in terms of the serial order of several movements (premotor damage) or control over isolated movements in a sequence (sensorimotor damage).

This notion that disruptions to limb praxis may arise from damage to different brain regions is supported by the work of Basso and Roland. In her research comparing the CT scans of apraxics with those of nonapraxics Basso showed that apraxia may result from damage in a number of regions in the left hemisphere (Basso, Luzzati, & Spinnler, 1980). Roland has examined the contribution of various brain areas to motor performance using the regional cerebral blood flow technique (Roland, Larsen, & Lassen 1980). When repetitive tapping of the index finger and thumb was the task, the primary motor area was found to be most active. When a more complex sequence of finger/thumb appositions was required, both this primary motor area and a region in the premotor area of the cortex, the supplementary motor area, were active. In a third task the same type of complex sequence of positioning responses was required, the action was performed using the whole arm. In this case both the supplementary motor area (anterior) and areas in the parietal lobe (posterior) were active. These findings support the notion that different regions of the brain contribute somewhat differently to motor performance, depending on the nature of the task. The need for an interface between information on area of brain damage and the nature of the task is demonstrated in this approach to the study of disorders to limb praxis (see Roy, 1983).

Kelso and Tuller (1981) offer one of the most recent accounts of apraxia as a movement disorder. The notion that the motor system is organized heterarchiacally (i.e., there is no one executor or controller) and involves a coalitional style of control based on a dynamic interface between the performer and the environment is central to their approach (see Turvey, Shaw, & Mace, 1978). One of the key concepts of this view of the motor system is that of tuning: supraspinal influences bias brainstem and spinal organization to provide the postural context in which a circumscribed class of movements may arise. Apraxia may result, in their view, from brain insults which disturb these supraspinal influences, preventing the patient from specifying the appropriate postural context for actions he is requested to perform.

## CONSIDERATIONS OF THE NATURE OF THE ACTION SYSTEM

These various perspectives as to the nature of apraxia have led to a greater awareness of the possible neurobehavioural mechanisms underlying apraxia. Nevertheless, a full understanding of the nature of the disorder continues to evade us. In order to more clearly comprehend apraxia one needs to conceptualize how the action system is organized. A careful study of the types of errors made by apraxic patients within this framework may foster such an understanding.

*Principles of Organization.*    Roy (1978, 1982, 1983) has developed a model
of the action system which encompasses two major subsystems: a conceptual and
a production system. The conceptual system is thought to represent knowledge of
actions and includes three types of knowledge: that relevant to the use of objects,
that relevant to actions (e.g., cutting) into which objects (e.g., scissors, a knife)
may be incorporated and that relevant to the serial ordering of actions in a
sequence. Each of these aspects of knowledge is thought to have both linguistic
and perceptual referents (see Roy, 1983 for details),

The production system is concerned with generating the action itself. Links
between the conceptual and production systems are envisaged such that at the
highest level the conceptual system may drive the production system in a top-
down fashion. Attention is required at key choice points in the unfolding action
to ensure that successive actions in the sequence are correct (Norman 1981; Roy,
1982). Between these key points control is exerted by action programs which are
not as attention demanding as the processes alluded to earlier. These programs
are generalized in that they may be applied to any one of a number of effectors so
as to produce the desired action. For example, one can write one's name with the
pen held in the mouth, the hand, or between the toes. While these programs
control the general spatiotemporal pattern of the actions represented, the details
of motor control are carried out at a lower level through the operation of intact
neuromotor systems involving muscle collectives and synergies (see Roy, 1982;
Turvey et al., 1978).

Through the operations or the conceptual system or action programs, then, the
production system may be directed in this type of top-down fashion. This system
may also be directed in a bottom-up fashion, however, through links between the
environment and the performer. Perceptual referents (visual and tactual features
of an object which relate to its function) and contextual referents (the time or
place at which actions are performed) for actions provide environmental information which relates to action. If the performer does not attend at the key choice
points described above, unintended actions may arise through the intrusion of
this environmental information. The environment then can direct the selection of
actions to be performed.

The production system, then, involves not one system but a nubmer of parallel systems in which control may migrate from one level of control to another. As
Roy (1982) and others (e.g., Keele, 1980, Reason, 1979) have suggested performing actions efficiently requires a delicate balance between processes of
higher levels which demand attention and those observed at lower levels which
involve more autonomous operations.

*Disorders to the Action System.*    Considering the organization and operation
of the action system how might these observations be used to understand disorders in apraxia? In apraxia one of the more common observations is that while
the patient can indicate what an object is used for, he is unable to demonstrate

how to use it appropriately. This observation is indicative of a knowledge-mechanism dualism which seems to support the distinction made between the conceptual and the production systems. That the patient is able to indicate the function of the object or tool would seem to indicate that the conceptual system is intact.

Work by Caramazza (Whitehouse, Caramazza, & Zurif, 1978) and Good glass (Goodglass & Baker, 1976), however, suggests that posterior aphasics are unable to use functional information in structuring lexical items. The problem these patients have with naming may be accounted for by this difficulty in integrating perceptual and functional information. Since many apraxics are also aphasic with similar posterior damage, some of the problems they encounter with demonstrating actions may accrue because of a similar inability to use functional information. There may be a disruption to what Roy (1982, 1983) has referred to as action fields.

We have developed two tasks to investigate the integrity of this functional information. In one task the patient is requested to point to objects which are used for particular functions named by the examiner (e.g., Show me the object used for driving nails). In this task the perceptual referents for the objects pertaining to their function (e.g., the long handle and asymmetrical head of a hammer) are available as rather direct information about the use of the object. In the other task, this perceptual information is much less apparent since the patient is required to evaluate the functional properties of objects which may not look alike. As one example the patient must indicate which one of four objects, a hammer, a feather, a shoe, and a pencil, might be used to drive a nail into wood. To answer correctly (the shoe and the hammer) the patient has to understand the functional properties of the objects involved and, in the case of the shoe, go beyond its usual function. While there is not substantial data as yet using these tasks, findings to date indicate the apraxics have little difficulty with the first task but frequently make errors on the second, suggesting some disruption in knowledge of object functions.

Considering knowledge of actions, the second knowledge component in the conceptual system, several investigators have investigated patients' knowledge about actions by having them observe an action and then indicate whether it depicts a particular action (e.g., Is he hammering?) or point out a particular movement depicted in a picture (Heilman, 1979; Heilman et al., 1982). We have been investigating this knowledge of action component in apraxics in a number of ways. Preliminary findings reveal near perfect accuracy in apraxic (96%) and nonapraxic (98%) left-hemisphere-damaged patients in identifying action-object relationships when asked to point to one or three objects associated with an action depicted on videotape. Apraxics, then, are aware of the appropriate action, although in most cases they are unable to demonstrate it themselves.

In several other conditions an object (e.g., a comb) was placed in front of the patient and he was shown four different pantomimed actions: one which is correct for the object shown, one which is totally inappropriate (e.g., an action depicting hammering), one which depicts a body part as the object (e.g., running the fingers through the hair like a comb) or one which depicts the correct action but which is spatially misaligned. The results here indicate that virtually all of the patients endorsed the correct action and rejected the inappropriate one as being appropriate for the object presented. In the remaining conditions, all of the nonapraxic patients indicated that the body-part-as-object action and the spatially incorrect action were inappropriate for the object or tool presented, while the apraxics often endorsed the body-part-as-object action as being appropriate. Thus, while the apraxics clearly know what action is appropriate and quite inappropriate for each tool, they do not recognize the inappropriateness of actions which involve using a body part as the object.

These preliminary findings relate quite well to the types of errors seen in apraxia. The apraxic very seldom makes a wholly inappropriate action when asked to demonstrate the use of an object. In agreement with the finding here these patients recognize the inappropriateness of unrelated actions. The most frequent types of error are ones in which a body part is used as the object or in which the action is spatially misaligned. The knowledge-of-action results seem to fit with these observations as the apraxics endorse body-part-as-object actions as being appropriate. In part, then, these patients may produce these types of inappropriate actions because they conceptualize these actions as being correct.

While much more work is required here, these initial findings suggest that the apraxic's problem with object use may, in part, be due to a conceptual as opposed to a motor or production disorder. That these patients do apparently know that spatially inappropriate actions are indeed incorrect implies that the errors involving spatially misaligned actions are due to production rather than conceptual problems (see Roy, 1983).

Using an action sequencing task, Roy (1981, 1983) has further examined disruptions to the conceptual system. In this case disturbances to knowledge of the elemental actions in a sequence and to the serial order of actions in the sequence were examined. Basically, these studies have shown, particularly for the left-hemisphere patients who also aphasic, that some of the difficulty in performing action sequences relates to a poor knowledge of the constituent elements in the sequence as well as the serial order of these elements in the sequence.

While disruptions to the conceptual system have been one focus of study, Roy has also studied disorders which affect the production system. Using a task which required the patient to learn a sequence of four actions, Roy (1981) showed that fewer left- than right-hemisphere patients learned to correctly sequence the actions, and, for those who were able to learn the sequence, significantly more trials were taken to do so. In examining various types of errors it was apparent that the left-hemisphere patients made more perseverative errors. For the nonaphasics analyses of the serial position of the point of origin of these perseverations indicated that they originated an equal number of times from each position in the sequence, and these patients tended to repeat an action only once. On the other hand, the aphasics made many higher order perseverations in which an action was repeated twice or even three times (the maximum number in this task). As a result perseverative errors originated at the first two positions more frequently in this group.

Further insight into these perseverative errors was provided by comparing performance in the action sequencing task to one in which the conceptual as opposed to the motor (action) component was emphasized. In this task requiring the patient to place a series of action-word cards in the appropriate sequence, the left-hemisphere patients made a number of sequencing errors comparable to that observed in the action sequencing task, while perseverations were markedly reduced, suggesting that perseverations were apparently not conceptual in origin: The patient did not repeat actions due to a persistence of the idea of the previous action. Rather, perseverations appeared to be a motor phenomenon, since they were apparent almost exclusively when action was involved.

What do these errors in action sequencing, then, indicate about the production system? The disorder in producing actions in the correct sequence seems, in part, to be related to a problem in the conceptual system. The internal (top-down) driving of the production system which provides a type of higher level feedforward control (through processes such as verbal mediation) may be disrupted. If this level control is not exerted the patient may find it difficult to direct attention at the key choice points in the sequence, thus leaving the production system under the control of lower level systems.

When the system is under the control of these lower levels, factors such as degree of familiarity or learning, recency and degree of association with the current action may determine the action subsequent to the current one in the sequence which is selected and produced (see Roy, 1982). For example, when asked to light a candle the patient may begin by striking the match but rather than lighting the candle he may blow out the match. One might envisage an initial choice point occurring after the first action of lighting the match. A number of actions are possible at this point: lighting the candle (the correct one), lighting a cigarette, or blowing out the match. The error may have arisen because the patient was not monitoring his performance at this critical point. The sequence was, then, diverted into an action (blowing out the match) which was associated more strongly with match lighting or which was performed more recently than the correct action.

This work provides a framework within which to examine apraxia and action sequencing disorders, suggesting important considerations for further work. In examining limb praxis one must be careful to evaluate both the conceptual and production aspects of action. Considering the three types of knowledge alluded to above the conceptual basis for praxis should be assessed with reference to knowledge of object functions, knowledge of actions associated with various functions and knowledge of the serial order of actions in a sequence. With regard to the production system it is important to examine various dimensions of performance in order to acquire a view of the extent of the deficits in limb praxis. Further, careful analyses of the types of errors observed as well as the conditions under which they occur is essential to an understanding of the nature of the underlying disorder. With regard to sequences of actions Roy (1981) and others (e.g., Kimura, 1977, 1982) have provided such a description. For single gestures we have begun to examine such error patterns under various performance conditions (e.g., to verbal command, to imitation). Other implications of this approach to the study of apraxia have been discussed by Roy (1983) and include the nature of the motor task (e.g., complexity), the dependent measures employed to assess performance (e.g., accuracy vs timing performance), and the role of context in facilitating performance in the apraxic patient.

## ACKNOWLEDGEMENT

Preparation of this manuscript was supported through grants from NSERC and NHRDP.

## REFERENCES

Basso, A., Luzzatti, C., & Spinnler, H. (1980). Is ideomotor apraxia the outcome of damage to well-defined regions of the left hemisphere? *Journal of Neurology, Neurosurgery and Psychiatry, 43,* 118–126.

Brown, J. W. (1972). *Aphasia, apraxia & agnosia: Clinical and theoretical aspects.* Springfield, IL: CC Thomas.

DeAjuriaguerra, J., & Tissot R. (1969). The apraxias. In P. J. Vinken & G. W. Bruyn (Eds.), *Handbook of clinical neurology, Volume 4, Disorders of speech, perception and symbolic behavior.* Amsterdam: North-Holland.

Geschwind, N. (1975). The apraxias: Neural mechanisms of disorders of learned movement. *American Scientist, 63,* 188–195.

Goodglass, H., & Baker E. (1976). Semantic field, naming and auditory comprehension in aphasia. *Brain Language, 3,* 359–374.

Haaland, K. Y., Porch, B. E., & Delaney, H. D. (1980). Limb apraxia and motor performance. *Brain and Language, 9,* 315–323.

Heilman, K. M. (1975). A tapping test in apraxia. *Cortex, 11,* 259–263.

Heilman, K. M. (1979). Apraxia. In K. M. Heilman & E. Valenstein (Eds.), *Clinical neuropsychology.* New York: Oxford University Press.

Heilman, K. M., Rothi, L. J., & Valenstein, E. (1982). Two forms of ideomotor apraxia. *Neurology, 32,* 342–346.

Keele, S. (1980). Behavioural analysis of motor control. In V. Brooks (Ed.), *Handbook of physiology, motor control.* Washington, D.C.: American Physiology Society.

Kelso, J. A. S., & Tuller, B. (1981). Towards a theory of apractic syndromes. *Brain and Language, 12,* 224–245.

Kimura, D. (1977). Acquisition of a motor skill after left hemisphere damage. *Brain, 100,* 527–542.

Kimura, D. (1979). Neuromotor mechanisms in the evolution of human communication. In H. D. Steklis & M. J. Raleigh (Eds.), *Neurobiology of social communication in primates* New York: Academic Press.

Kimura, D. (1982). Left hemisphere control of oral and brachial movements and their relations to communication. *Philosophical Transactions of the Royal Society of London.* 135–149.

Kimura, D., & Archibald, Y. (1974). Motor functions of the left hemisphere. *Brain, 97,* 337–350.

Luria, A. E. (1980). *Higher cortical functions in man.* New York: Basic Books.

Norman, D. A. (1981). Categorization of action slips. *Psychological Review, 88,* 1–15.

Reason, J. T. (1979). Actions not as planned. In G. Underwood & R. Stevens (Eds.), *Aspects of consciousness.* London: Academic Press.

Roland, P. E., Larsen, B., & Lassen, W. (1980). Supplementary motor area and other cortical areas in the organization of voluntary movement. *Journal of Neurophysiology, 43,* 118–136.

Roy, E. A. (1978). Apraxia: A new look at an old syndrome. *Journal of Human Movement Studies, 4,* 191–210.

Roy, E. A. (1981). Action sequencing and lateralized cerebral damage: Evidence for asymmetries in control. In J. Long & A. Baddeley (Eds.). *Attention and performance IX.* Hillsdale, NJ: Lawrence Erlbaum Associates.

Roy, E. A. (1982). Action and performance. In A. Ellis (Ed.), *Normality and pathology in cognitive function.* New York: Academic Press.

Roy, E. A. (1983). Neuropsychological perspectives on apraxia and related action disorders. In R. Maqill (Ed.). *Advances in psychology, Volume 12, Memory and motor control.* Amsterdam, North-Holland.

Turvey, M. T., Shaw, R. E., & Mace, W. (1978). Issues in the theory of action: Degrees of freedom, coordinative structures and coalitions. In J. Requin (Ed.), *Attention and performance VII.* Hillsdale, NJ: Lawrence Erlbaum Associate.

Whitehouse, P., Caramazza, A., & Zurif, E. (1978). Naming in aphasia: Interacting effects of form and function. *Brain and Language, 6,* 63–74.

# 13 Central Communication Disorders in Deaf Signers

Yvan Lebrun
Chantal Leleux

## INTRODUCTION

So far a dozen cases of communication disorders following cerebral injury in adult deaf people have been reported. What do the symptoms noted in these cases tell us about the ways communicative skills can be disturbed by brain damage in deaf signers? And does our knowledge of aphasia in hearing subjects help us understand the pathophysiology of acquired disorders of communication in deaf people? The present paper proposes to examine these issues.

## REVIEW OF PUBLISHED CASES

*Unilateral Disturbance.* The first known description of communication disorders in a deaf signer after brain damage is the brief report by Grasset (1896) of a congenitally deaf man who had learned to fingerspell, read, and write. As a result of what Grasset thought to be progressive ischemic softening of the left hemisphere, the patient lost the ability to write and to fingerspell with the right hand, while retaining the ability to fingerspell, and probably also to write, with the left hand. His right upper extremity was paretic but not to such an extent as to account for the inability to fingerspell and to write. Apparently he had no apraxia and he is said to have had no comprehension disorder.

This case has been construed by Poizner and Battison (1980) as an instance of peripheral pathology on the ground of its being unilateral. However, unilateral agraphia (e.g., Pitres, 1884; Yamadori, Osumi, Ikeda, & Kanasawa, 1980) may certainly be caused by cerebral damage. There is no reason, therefore, to question Grasset's diagnosis of a central disorder in his patient.

Kimura (1981) regards Grasset's case as an instance of fine motoric impairment resulting most probably from a lesion of the lateral corticospinal system. However, Grasset himself insisted that though the patient's right upper extremity was paretic, the motor deficit was not severe enough to account for the inability to write and to fingerspell.

Sarno, Swisher, & Taylor Sarno (1969) are of the opinion that Grasset's "description suggests limb apraxia rather than aphasia." In fact, the French neurologist pointed out that his patient could shake hands, eat, pour himself a glass of water . . . , all with his right hand. The patient, therefore, does not seem to have been apraxic for everyday actions. What he had lost was the ability to perform with his right hand the learned movements which produce written or signed letters. He resembles Pitres' patient (1884) who following left brain damage could no longer write with his right hand, although this hand was neither paralyzed nor apraxic; this man then had a selective impairment of writing movements. Grasset's case shows that in literate deaf people who are familiar with the finger alphabet, writing and fingerspelling may be both affected while other manual actions are undisturbed; moreover, this disorder may be unilateral.

*Unresponsiveness.*    In 1905, Charles Burr reported the case of a deaf woman with massive right-sided hemiplegia and akinesia of the left limbs, who remained unresponsive to written and signed messages, although she had been fully conversant with both written and signed language before falling ill. She would follow with the eyes an object moved in her left visual field and withdraw her left extremity when pricked with a pin. No other movements were observed. She did swallow food put in her mouth, but otherwise remained inert in her bed. She was incontinent. Her condition remained unchanged until she died. At autopsy an infiltrating tumor was found in the superior and mesial part of the left frontal lobe. It was surrounded by an area of softening which involved almost the entire white matter of the hemisphere. The softening was due in part to hemorrhage and in part to thrombosis. In view of the anatomicopathologic findings the symptomatology may be interpreted in two different ways. The patient may have had frontal aspontaneity with akinesia, indifference, and lack of communicative drive. This condition is not infrequent when the superior and mesial parts of the left frontal lobe are injured. In such a case, comprehension does not seem to be completely obliterated, although due to akinesia it is often difficult to ascertain to what extent the patient understands the messages he is addressed. Another possibility is that Burr's patient had lost all of her communicative skills, in much the same way as global aphasics have. This second diagnosis seems less likely, however, as global aphasics usually are not akinetic and often attempt to react, however clumsily and inadequately, to verbal stimulation.

*Differential Disturbance of Fingerspelling and Writing.*    In 1938, Critchley described a patient who had been well until the age of 7, when he gradually lost his hearing. As his disability steadily increased, he was taught fingerspelling and later on lipreading. To what extent he also learned sign language is not documented in the paper. When aged 42 he sustained a stroke in the left hemisphere which caused a right-sided paralysis and, apparently, total loss of communicative abilities. Improvement occurred in the ensuing weeks. Eventually he was found to have recovered from his motor deficit, but there was still hemi-hypesthesia. He could again understand dactylology but had difficulty in lipreading. Although he was not apraxic, he made errors when fingerspelling. There were sign confusions. Moreover, his finger movements appeared more erratic and more jerky than before the stroke. His sentences were "short, telegrammatic and ungrammatical," and there were sign omissions. On the other hand, "tests with writing . . ., word-building with cards, typing and reading were executed pretty well on the whole."

Although rather vague, this description indicates that fingerspelling was noticeably more disturbed than writing. The difference can hardly have been due to an impairment of finger motricity, since the right-sided hemiplegia is said to have cleared up. The impairment of fingerspelling cannot have been an orthographic problem either, since it did not show in writing, which was "executed pretty well on the whole." It would appear, therefore, that Critchley's patient had a selective disorder of dactylology, maybe an apraxia affecting fingerspelling but sparing graphomotricity. Is this hypothesis compatible with the observation that the patient's fingerspelled sentences were "short, telegrammatic and ungrammatical"? It would seem that this question can be answered in the affirmative. If as a result of a specific praxic impairment the patient had difficulty in forming individual signs and in sequencing them flexibly, it is conceivable that he should have used short sentences and should have dropped function words and grammatical endings. At any rate, Critchley's case shows that fingerspelling and writing may be effected differently by brain damage in deaf people. This conclusion generally agrees with the findings of Tureen, Smolik, and Tritt (1951) which are discussed later.

*An Equivalent of Sensory Aphasia.*    In 1943, Leischner published a detailed description of a 64-year-old congenitally deaf Czech who had been taught sign language. He had acquired a number of spoken words as well, which he used to utter while making the corresponding signs. Articulation was defective, but the words were usually recognizable. In addition, the patient had learned to read and write in two languages: Czech and German. Following repeated strokes in the left hemisphere he to a large extent lost the ability to communicate effectively. To be sure, he would sign, but some of his gestures did not belong to sign language or were ill-formed, or else the concatenations of signs which he produced did not make sense. Also, he superfluously repeated many signs. More-over, he showed a tendency to perseveration, signs used previously being sub-stituted for the appropriate ones. Such errors also occurred in the imitation of signs but were less numerous: reproduction was better than spontaneous produc-tion. It was further noted that the patient was more "talkative" than before: he would give longer answers than he used to. Also, the words he uttered while signing did not always correspond to the signs he was making. When there was a dissociation between sign and word, the former was usually appropriate, while the latter was not. However, the wrong word was often semantically akin to the word that should have been used, as when he signed *February* and said *April*. In addition to the output disorder, there was impaired comprehension. The patient had difficulty in understanding sign language, and many sentences had to be repeated several times before he could grasp their meaning. Reading was also impaired, and more so in German than in Czech. Copying of written words was paragraphic. Translation of signs into written words was faulty. Occasionally the patient mixed up Czech and German. Translation of written words into signs was equally disturbed.

This symptomatology seems to run parallel with what is commonly observed in hearing subjects with Wernicke's aphasia. Sign substitutions as they occurred in Leischner's case, may be compared to verbal paraphasias, which are frequent in sensory aphasia. Formational errors in signs resemble phonemic paraphasias in aphasic speech, and nonsense signs are reminiscent of neologisms. Iterations and perseverations are as frequent in sensory aphasia as they were in the signed output of Leischner's patient.

Dissociation between two expressive language modalities may occasionally be observed in Wernicke's aphasia. As in the case reports by Lhermitte and Derouesné (1974), oral naming of ordinary objects may be considerably more anomalous than written naming of the same objects. One of our patients with severe sensory aphasia (M.W.) used many paraphasias and even neologisms in oral naming but would make few mistakes if he had to perform the task in writing. Indeed, this discrepancy could still be observed when he had to perform the oral and written naming tasks simultaneously: He would often write the correct word but say another word. This, of course, very much resembles what was noted in Leischner's case: The patient frequently made the appropriate sign but said a word that did not correspond to it.

As is the rule in sensory aphasia, Leischner's patient had difficulty in under-standing verbal messages. In addition, he showed so-called "polyglotte Reak-tionen." This symptom, which is often observed in multilinguals with Wer-nicke's aphasia, consists of the mixing up of two or more languages.

Sensory aphasia in hearing subjects generally results from a left temporal lesion. Interestingly enough, at autopsy it was found that the superior part of the left temporal lobe was damaged in Leischner's case. To be sure, the patient had several other cerebral lesions, but his temporal lesion was the largest.

*Differential Disturbance of the Reception and Production of Written vs. Fin-gerspelled Language.*  In 1951, Tureen, Smolik, and Tritt described a con-genitally deaf man who had learned to fingerspell, lip-read, read, and write and who had achieved the equivalent of a high school education. He could say a few words. At 43-years-of-age he started to have Jacksonian convulsions on the right side with transient motor disturbances in the right upper extremity. During these periods he would fingerspell with his left hand. A pneumoencephalography precipitated a right-sided hemiplegia and total loss of communicative skills. After a week or so, the patient recovered the ability to understand written lan-guage and, to some extent, the ability to lip-read. He had marked difficulty in using dactylology both receptively and expressively, and he could not write. His left hand was not apraxic, though. A left fronto-parietal craniotonomy was performed and hemorrhagic tumoral tissue underlying the posterior halves of the second and third cerebral convolutions was removed together with the cortex of the posterior part of the second frontal gyrus. Immediately after surgery the patient was totally unable to communicate. Then he gradually recovered the ability to read, to utter a few words, and to use fingerspelling. However, when expressing himself by means of the finger alphabet he was not as fluent as he used to be (He had to use his left hand to fingerspell as his right upper extremity was paralyzed). In addition, he had agraphia: He could no longer write. With the recurrence of convulsions a few months later, his condition deteriorated rapidly and he soon died.

Immediately before he was operated upon, this patient could understand writ-ten language better than fingerspelling although both are visual and are based on the same system of orthography. There may be several reasons why he found reading easier than the decoding of fingerspelled messages. To begin with, when you read, you can proceed at your own speed, while in deciphering dactylology you are dependent on the signer's rate of sign production; and the speed at which messages are delivered may influence their understanding by brain-damaged subjects (Albert & Beer, 1974). Second, when trying to grasp the meaning of a written text, you may re-read phrases or sentences several times if you do not understand them at first glance. Fingerspelled sentences, on the contrary, are evanescent and cannot be scanned repeatedly. Finally, comprehension of fin-gerspelled messages probably taxes short-term memory more than reading does, as you have to remember the letters that are successively formed in order to identify the words intended by the signer.

On the other hand, after the operation, the patient of Tureen et al. appeared to have more difficulty in writing than in fingerspelling. Indeed, he gradually recovered the ability to use the finger alphabet (although less fluently than before he fell ill) but remained unable to write with his left hand (the right hand was paralyzed). Since he could spell in the air with his left hand, it is to be assumed that he still knew orthography. Furthermore, as he could perform everyday actions with his left hand, it may be presumed that this hand was not so clumsy as to be unable to trace letters. Accordingly, the patient appears to have had a selective impairment of writing movements: While he had recovered the ability to make dactylological signs, he no longer knew how to produce written letters. The cases reported by Critchley (1938) and by Tureen et al. (1951) show then that writing and fingerspelling comprise sets of learned movements which may be selectively disturbed by cerebral damage despite the fact that both sets of movements are performed by the same limbs and have the same symbolic values. In a paper on aphasia in signers to be discussed later, Sarno, Swisher, and Taylor Sarno (1969) ask: "Is there a basic difference between the motor acts of moving a pen to produce a series of letters and manipulating one's fingers to produce the same letters?" It is not quite clear what *basic difference* means in this question, but it appears that, in some signers at least, writing movements and dactylology movements are sufficiently distinct to be differently affected by brain injury.

*Differential Disturbance of Sign Language, Dactylology, Spoken and Written Language.*   In 1959, Douglass and Richardson described a right-handed, congenitally deaf woman who early in life had been raised by deaf siblings. Later she attended an elementary school for the deaf. She could both fingerspell and write but was more proficient in the former than in the latter skill. She also knew sign language and was able to read. Her spoken vocabulary was very limited and of such poor quality that "it was considered of no practical communicative value." When she was 21-years-old she suffered a postpartum stroke which resulted in a right-sided pyramidal syndrome. Eventually she was left with paresis of the right leg, spastic paralysis of the right upper extremity, some sensory loss on the right side, and a central communication disorder. She could still understand short written messages but not longer ones. She could identify individual finger positions but was unable to recognize fingerspelled words. Understanding of sign language was also impaired. With her left hand she could copy written material but could no longer express herself in writing. She had difficulty in imitating dactylological finger positions. She could not express herself by means of fingerspelling, her attempts at doing so being faulty or perseveratory. Similar difficulties were observed in the use of sign language. Morever, "she was not capable of accurately translating from printed script to dactylological signs, nor could she translate from fingerspelling to printed forms." With the passing of time, the patient's neurolinguistic condition improved: After some time she was again able to express herself in writing and by means of the finger alphabet, but her production was not errorless. She also recovered the active use of sign language, but to a lesser extent than writing and fingerspelling. Her comprehension of sign language was also inferior to that of written language and dactylology, which was almost normal.

Initially then, reading was less impaired than the understanding of dactylology. The reasons for this difference may have been the same as in the earlier case reported by Tureen, Smolik, and Tritt.

In 1969, Sarno et al. described a right-handed, congenitally deaf male who was conversant with sign language, fingerspelling, and written language, and who could lip-read. He had also learned to speak and would produce short sentences, "frequently without phonation but with much articulation." When addressing his wife, whose hearing had become severely impaired when she was 10-years-old, he would use a combined means of communication: His utterances included spoken words, signs, and fingerspelled segments. At 69-years-of-age this man suffered a cerebro-vascular injury in the left hemisphere which entailed paresis of the right leg, spastic paralysis of the right upper extremity, and a central communication deficit. He could no longer speak or write, and he made many errors of omission, substitution, reversal, and perseveration when fin-gerspelling with his left hand. The use of sign language was less impaired. He could reproduce single letters fingerspelled by the examiner and could copy single written words. The left upper extremity was not apraxic for everyday movements. The patient was moderately impaired in reading, more so in sign language comprehension, and understanding of fingerspelling and lipreading were drastically reduced. After some time, improvement was noted. He could speak a few words and he made less mistakes when fingerspelling. Communica-tion by sign language showed the greatest improvement.

The next case was reported by Kimura, Battison and Lubert in 1976 and by Poizner and Battison in 1980. The patient was a right-handed male who became deaf when he was 6-years-old. He attended residential schools for the deaf where he acquired sign language and dactylology and learned to read and write. He received an academic education and as an adult was considered a skilled signer and writer. At age 70 he suffered left middle cerebral artery thrombosis which caused a right-sided hemiparesis and a central communication disorder. Three years later, his motor deficit had almost completely disappeared. His commu-nicative impairment remained, however. His verbal comprehension is not de-scribed in the two papers but there is the suggestion in the paper by Kimura et al. (1976) that it was not intact. His expressive difficulties, on the contrary, are reported in some detail by Poizner and Battison (1980). Speaking, signing, fingerspelling, and writing are all said to have been "dysfluent, with hesitations, substitutions, formational errors, and perseverations." The different modalities were not affected to the same degree, however. Sign language was less disturbed than writing and fingerspelling. One of the errors he made in sign language was that when producing a bimanual sign he would occasionally invert the right-handed and the left-handed roles, thus signing like a left-hander, or else he would transfer only part of the role from one hand to the other, thus making a hybrid sign. Also, he would sometimes revert to a dialect form of a sign which he had learned early in life and deny knowledge of the more standard form, which he had known and used for years. When communicating in signs and speech simul-taneously, the patient would often produce the correct word and an incorrect sign, thus presenting the reversal of what had been noted in Leischner's case (see

above). Although fingerspelling was more impaired than sign language, he
sometimes attempted to fingerspell when he could not find the appropriate sign.
A somewhat similar strategy can sometimes be observed in hearing aphasics,
who try to spell aloud the words they cannot speak.

*7. Reading Skills More Resistant to Cerebral Damage*    In 1979, Meckler,
Mack, and Bennett reported the case of a 19-year-old left-handed hearing man
who had been raised by deaf-mute parents and hearing grandparents and was
conversant with spoken, written, and signed language as well as with fingerspelling. Following traumatic cerebral contusion he had a right-sided hemiparesis
with hypesthesia. At first he could use none of the codes he was familiar with,
neither receptively nor expressively. Eventually understanding of spoken, written, and signed language returned, spoken and written languages being recovered
better than sign language and fingerspelling. His expressive skills improved too,
but to a much lesser extent: His output was sparse and the few words or signs he
used were not always correct, except in well-routinized sequences, like his own
name. He could copy written words and repeat spoken or signed language items
better than he could use them spontaneously. His preferred left hand, which he
used for signing and writing, was not apraxic. Moreover, the patient could
imitate complex nonsymbolic hand and finger movements on the left side.

In this case then, as in the cases reported by Critchley (1938), by Tureen et al.
(1951), by Douglas and Richardson (1959), by Sarno et al. (1969), and possibly
also in the cases described by Kimura et al (1976) and by Poizner and Battison
(1980), reading was, if only temporarily, the least affected verbal skill. In their
paper, Sarno, Swisher, and Taylor Sarno (1969) express the view that "there is
no hierarchy among the various methods of communication employed by . . .
deaf aphasics" and further "that variations in deficit severity among communication modalities result from differences in the location and severity of neuronal damage." The relative preservation of reading skills in the cases reviewed
above suggests, however, that there might be some hierarchy among the various
communicative modalities used by deaf people, with reading being generally
more resistant to cerebral damage than other verbal skills. Interestingly, no case
has ever been reported of a deaf-born subject who would have selectively lost the
ability to read (and possibly to understand dactylology) while retaining the ability
to express himself in writing and by fingerspelling. In other words, *pure* alexia
has not yet been observed in congenitally deaf people.

*The Left Hemisphere Dominant for Sign Language Also.*    The patient of
Meckler et al. was left-handed. Following injury to his left cerebral hemisphere
he became unable to use any of the verbal codes he knew. His left hemisphere
therefore appears to have been dominant for each of his communicative skills,
including spoken, written, signed, and dactylological language. The situation
was different in a case briefly described by Poizner and Battison in 1980. Their

patient was a prelingually deafened man who was left-handed but who had been compelled by his schoolteachers to write with his right hand. He was also familiar with sign language and fingerspelling. Following a cerebro-vascular accident in the right hemisphere, he had left hemiparesis. In addition, both comprehension and production of written, signed and fingerspelled languages were disturbed. Poizner and Battison's is the only case reported so far of communication disorders following right brain damage in a deaf patient. To be sure, in some of the cases reviewed earlier the right hemisphere may not have been fully intact. (In Leischner's patient we know for sure that it was also injured.) But the main lesion or lesions were in the left hemisphere. It may therefore be concluded that in deaf signers, as in hearing subjects, communication disorders result far more frequently from damage to the left than from damage to the right hemisphere. Indeed, Kimura, Davidson, and McCormick (1982) recently noted the absence of communication disorders in a right-handed signer with right brain damage. Even in left-handed signers the dominant hemisphere seems to be more frequently the left hemisphere, since only one lefthanded deaf patient with right hemisphere damage and communication disorders has been reported so far (Poizner & Battison) as opposed to two left-handers with left cerebral injuries (Meckler et al., and Underwood & Paulson, discussed below).

Kimura (1979) has proposed that the left hemisphere is not specialized for symbolic representation per se, but for the programming of complex self-generated movements. This class of movements includes vocal, graphic, and manual symbol productions since these require series of swift, complex, varied (= non-repetitive) and finely timed displacements of body parts. In other words, the left hemisphere is responsible for *praxis,* which comprises the use of language in its oral, written, and signed forms.

*The Motor Theory of Speech Perception.*    There are difficulties with this unified view of the role of the left hemisphere. To begin with, the theory fails to account for the comprehension difficulties which a lesion of the left hemisphere so often entails. If aphasic symptoms are construed as movement disorders, how are we to explain the disturbances of understanding that can be observed in so many patients with central communication disorders following left brain damage? To be sure, there exists a motor theory of speech perception which implies that the listener has to repeat in himself what he has just heard, before he can understand it. One of the main proponents of the theory, Alvin Liberman, stated in 1957: "Speech is perceived by reference to articulation—that is, that the articulatory movements and their sensory effects mediate between the acoustic stimulus and the event we call perception." Liberman, however, was of the opinion that in the adult listener the articulatory movements need not be overt: rather they "occur in the brain without getting out into the periphery."

Applied to sign language, the motor theory of speech perception implies that the onlooker mentally reproduces the movements that are being made by the signer: this cerebral motor activity and its sensory consequences (to use Liberman's words, 1957) make possible the decoding of the perceived signs. If the onlooker is apraxic and therefore cannot properly reproduce the signs he perceives, he will not be able to understand them.

Unfortunately, the motor theory of speech perception is not borne out by clinical facts, as Lebrun (1967) and more recently Fourcin (1975) and Ammon (1978) showed. Experimental evidence has also been adduced that does not accord with the theory (Ammon, 1978; Denes, 1967). As a consequence, Liberman and coworkers (1968) have felt obliged to loosen their hypothesis, nearly to the point of vacuity:

> Reference to production provides a pathway for perception, but not one that is obligatory—that is, the existence of this pathway does not preclude direct auditory processing of speech patterns by the same means that are used for recognizing animal cries, traffic noises, and the like. The *special* pathway *would be used,* we *suppose,* whenever it facilitates percept as it would in recovering linguistic units that lack invariant acoustic counterparts, but when it is not needed, it may not be used'' (emphasis added).

Because it is so vague and so uncertain the motor theory of speech perception cannot give real support to Kimura's hypothesis that apraxia, as a movement control deficit, lies at the root of aphasia.

*Disturbance of Symbolic vs. Nonsymbolic Movements.*    It is fair to say that Kimura herself has not resorted to the motor theory of speech perception to strengthen her theory. Rather, she seems to have ignored the comprehension problem and to have concentrated so far on the difficulty aphasics have in producing nonverbal oral movements and on the difficulty signers with left brain damage have in imitating meaningless manual movements. In the paper she wrote with Battison and Lubert (see Kimura et al., 1976) she emphasized that the patient, although he could handle objects appropriately and could demonstrate how to use various objects (without the object being present), yet was deficient in the imitation of nonverbal complex hand and finger movements. According to Kimura et al., this defect was primarily one of motor control. The case therefore is said to corroborate the thesis "that the left hemisphere is specialized primarily for certain types of motor control, and that its important role in language functions is derived from the former." In other words, signing disorders are based on manual apraxia just as speech aphasia is based on oral apraxia (Kimura, 1981).

In the paper co-authored by Battison and Lubert, Kimura points out that the complex hand and finger movements which the patient found difficult to imitate, were deemed by four deaf signers to be meaningless body-part displacements not resembling actual signs. Interestingly enough, Chiarello and colleagues' deaf patient who is described below could imitate real Ameslan signs as well as nonsense signs that conformed to the phonology of Ameslan. She had difficulty, however, in imitating both nonsense signs that did not obey the phonological rules of Ameslan and the complex hand and finger movements devised by Kimura. Conversely, in the case reported by Meckler et al. (1979), "although sign language expression was quite deficient, (the patient) was able to imitate complex hand and finger movements with the nonparetic left hand." Indeed, Meckler et al. point out that the patient was consistently more successful in tests using nonverbal material. These various observations strongly suggest that there is a fundamental difference between movements that are, or could be, symbolic signs and novel extraneous movements. In other words, movements that belong to the subject's stock of verbal signs or could be easily incorporated into it, are treated by the brain differently from movements which do not belong to that stock and are not deemed capable of being included in it. This conclusion is confirmed by a fact pertaining to aphasia in hearing subjects. Anarthria, or apraxia of speech, has been shown to be—as its English name implies—an apraxia of articulatory movements (Lebrun, 1982a). It does not, however, result from oral apraxia. As a matter of fact, apraxia of speech may occur without oral apraxia (Lebrun, 1976b), and when both impairments obtain simultaneously, they generally evolve differently: one may disappear while the other remains, and vice versa (Tissot, Rodriguez, & Tissot, 1970). Since oral apraxia is the inability to perform voluntary oral movements (such as sticking out one's tongue or inflating one's cheeks) which are different from articulatory movements, the dissociation between apraxia of speech and oral apraxia stresses the distinction which the brain makes between articulatory, i.e., verbal, movements, and non-verbal displacements of oral structures. This corroborates the view that at the cerebral level movements belonging to the patient's code of communication and movements that could belong to this code but happen not to be used, are treated differently from movements which due to their structure could not be part of the patient's vocabulary. It follows that there is as little reason to hold signing disorders to be a consequence of manual apraxia as there is to consider apraxia of speech (or aphasia, for that matter) to result from oral apraxia. Communicative disorders in hearing and in deaf persons cannot be accounted for in terms of disturbed praxis; they do not fall under the category of motor disorders. They are quite specifically disturbances of symbolic formulation.

*Ribot's and Pitres' Laws.* In 1981, Underwood and Paulson described a left-handed male who had presumably been deaf from birth. He knew sign language, which was his preferred mode of communication. He knew fingerspelling also but did not use this system as frequently as sign language. In addition he had some command of written language and minimal lipreading ability. He occasionally uttered words but these were generally unintelligible. Following thrombosis of the left middle cerebral artery he had right flaccid hemiplegia and communication disorders. Sign-finding difficulties, sign substitutions, perseverations, and jargon were observed in his verbal output. For instance, he once fingerspelled *shoe* for *pencil,* and *konil* for *shoe.* Although before his stroke he used signing more frequently than fingerspelling, he now made less mistakes when fingerspelling. Searching posturing behavior was often observed when he was unsuccessfully attempting to fingerspell a word. Occasional letter substitutions were made which approximated the intended letter. For instance, he confused *s, a,* and *e,* all of which have similar finger positions. (This kind of confusion was also observed in Douglass and Richardson's case, which was discussed earlier.) In the naming task the patient would perform better if given the initial letter of the name to be produced. Imitation of signs and of fingerspelled words was better than spontaneous production. And semi-automatized language, like telling from 1 to 10 or reciting the Lord's Prayer, was preserved. Paragraphias and jargon appeared in his writing. In addition, the patient had sign language and fingerspelling comprehension difficulties. At first he could not read, but he seemed to recover some reading ability with the passing of time. It should be noted that before the stroke he did not have full command of written language.

Because they adhere to the view "that the most recently acquired functions are the last to be recovered in aphasic patients," Underwood and Paulson (1981) find it difficult to account for the fact that in their case fingerspelling was less impaired than signing, although there is no indication that the former was acquired before the latter. Not only did their patient most probably learn to sign before he learned to fingerspell, but before the stroke he used signing more frequently than fingerspelling. This case therefore does not conform either to what is known in aphasiology as Ribot's rule (the more recently acquired functions are the more impaired following brain damage) or to what goes by the name of Pitres' rule (the language which polyglot aphasics used the most frequently is the least impaired). That neither of the two rules applies need not surprise us unduly, however. Study of aphasia in hearing polyglots (Lebrun, 1976a, 1982b) has shown that Ribot's and Pitres' rules do not always hold true. Occasionally, psychological or sociolinguistic factors modify the hierarchy that existed before the onset of illness. This alteration is usually temporary when the cause is psychological, but it may be permanent when the cause is sociolinguistic. Whether the same applies to congenitally deaf subjects is not known, due to the limited number of available observations.

*Differential Disturbance of the Two Hands.*    In 1982, Chiarello, Knight, and Mandel described a right-handed, prelingually deaf woman who had first been taught fingerspelling and later Ameslan and normal written English. As an adult, however, she was more fluent in sign language than in fingerspelling. At age 66 she developed a right-sided pyramidal syndrome of sudden onset, with hemi-paresis, hemi-hypesthesia and a severe disorder of communication: She could hardly express herself and her understanding of signed and written messages was limited to simple utterances. CAT scan revealed a low parietal lesion in the left hemisphere. At two weeks post-onset, the patient was able to imitate single signs but not two-sign sentences. When signing spontaneously she made frequent formational errors. Some 4 weeks later it was found that the patient could imitate single Ameslan signs as well as movements that could have been ASL signs but in fact were not. Two-word sentences in Ameslan could be reproduced correctly, but imitation of longer sentences was incomplete and garbled. Naming of objects and of colors on confrontation was possible. The patient could correctly form short sentences including two or three signs specified by the examiner. Her spontaneous signing, though generally intelligible, contained formational errors. Pointing to objects or colors named in ASL by the examiner was correct. Her score on the Spreen and Benton version of the Token Test, however, indicated a comprehension deficit at the level of the sentence, especially when redundancy was low. Reading paralleled comprehension of ASL with impairment appearing at higher levels of linguistic complexity. The patient's performances when fingerspelling were somewhat inferior to those in Ameslan. The most frequent errors were misspellings and perseverations. In writing she made even more mistakes.

Because her right hand was paretic, the patient signed, fingerspelled, and write with her left, i.e. her nonpreferred, hand. Is this likely to have influenced her performances? The following clinical findings suggest that it may not be a matter of indifference which hand is used after cerebral damage.

Leischner (1983) has reported on five aphasic patients who despite their right-sided hemiplegia were able to trace letters with their right hand using a writing aid. All of them made less errors when writing dictated words with their handicapped right hand than with their valid left hand.

The notion that in brain-injured subjects linguistic output may be qualitatively different according to the hand being used seems to apply also to deaf signers. As a matter of fact, Poizner and Battison (1980) in the case discussed earlier of a right-handed deaf male with left cerebral thrombosis noted that the ''right vs. left-handed unimanual fingerspelling productions appeared dissimilar in quality: right hand productions appeared to be fluent nonsense, while left hand productions tended to be dysfluent but communicative.''

As was noted above, central communication disorders in right handed signers result far more frequently from a left-sided than from a right-sided cerebral lesion. If this lesion involves the motor cortex or the fibres underlying it, there is a concomitant contralteral hemiplegia. In such a case, the patient cannot use one of his hands for signing. Bellugi, Poizner and Klima (1983), in what is probably the latest publication on the subject, claim that ''the fact that a deaf signing patient may have use of only one hand does not itself produce a language impairment.'' Indeed, one of the three patients they describe was ''right hemiplegic and performed all tests using her non-dominant hand.'' The observations made by Leischner (1983) and confirmed by Brown et al. (1983) and the case reported by Poizner and Battison (1980) indicate, however, that it may not be indifferent whether the patient is signing with his right of left hand. Accordingly, caution should be used when one examines a brain-injured subject who is prevented from using his preferred hand for signing or fingerspelling: The patient may make mistakes that would not have occurred, had he been able to use his preferred hand. Conversely, when either hand can be used, double testing seems desirable, as verbal output produced with the nonpreferred hand may be more intelligible than that produced with the dominant hand.

## CONCLUSIONS AND SUMMARY

In summary, review of acquired central communication disorders in deaf signers shows that:

1. writing and fingerspelling may in the same brain-injured patient be disturbed differently;
2. reading is often the least impaired, or the best recovered, verbal skill;
3. the expressive modality which is the best preserved is often, but need not necessarily be, the earliest or the preferred means of expression of the patient premorbidly;
4. in right-handed signers acquired disorders of communication are conspicuously more frequent after left than after right cerebral injury, just as is aphasia in hearing people;
5. like aphasic impairments, signing disorders can hardly be said to result from apraxia, as Kimura's theory would have it;
6. caution should be used when a brain-injured signer is tested who uses his nonpreferred hand to communicate because his dominant hand is paralyzed: this necessary use of the nonpreferred hand may influence the quality of his signed output.

## REFERENCES

Albert, M., & Bear, D. (1974). Time to understand, *Brain, 97,* 373–384.
Ammon, K. (1978). Patholinguistische und experimentelle Befunde gegen die Motor-Theorie der Sprachwahrnehmung. In G. Peuser (Ed.), *Brennpunkte der Patholinguistik* (pp. 27–34). Munich, Fink.
Bellugi, U., Poizner, H., & Klima, E. (1983). Brain organization for language: Clues from sign aphasia. *Human Biology, 2,* 155–170.
Brown, J., Leader, B., & Blum, B. (1983). Hemiplegic writing in severe aphasia, *Brain and Language, 19,* 204–215.
Burr, C. (1905). Loss of the sign language in a deaf mute from cerebral tumor and softening. *New York Medical Journal, 81,* 1106–1108.
Chiarello, C., Knight, R., & Mandel, M. (1982). Aphasia in a prelingually deaf woman. *Brain, 105,* 29–51.

Critchley, M. (1938). Aphasia in a partial deaf-mute. *Brain, 61,* 163–169.

Denes, B. (1967). On the motor theory of speech perception. In W. Wathen-Dunn (Ed.), *Models for the perception of speech and visual form* (pp. 309–314). Cambridge, MA: MIT Press.

Douglass, E., & Richardson, J. (1959). Aphasia in a congenital deaf-mute. *Brain, 83,* 68–80.

Fourcin, A. (1975). Language development in the absence of expressive speech. In E. Lenneberg, *Foundations of language development* (Vol. II, pp. 263–268). New York: Academic Press.

Grasset, J. (1896). Aphasie de la main droite chez un sourd-muet. *Le Progrès Médical, 4,* third series, 44.

Kimura, D. (1979). Neuromotor mechanisms in the evolution of human communication. In H. Stekelis & M. Raleigh (Eds.), *Neurobiology of social communication in primates* (pp. 197–219). New York: Academic Press.

Kimura, D. (1981). Neural mechanisms in manual signing. *Sign Language Studies, 33,* 291–312.

Kimura, D., Battison, R., & Lubert, B. (1976). Impairment of nonlinguistic hand movements in a deaf aphasic. *Brain and Language, 3,* 566–571.

Kimura, D., Davidson, W., & McCormick, W. (1982). No impairment of sign language after right-hemisphere stroke. *Brain and Language, 17,* 359–362.

Lebrun, Y. (1967). Clinical evidence against the motor theory of speech perception. In *Sixth International Congress of Phonetic Sciences.* Prague, Academic Publishing House of the Czechoslovak Academy of Sciences, pp. 531–534.

Lebrun, Y. (1976a). Recovery in polyglot aphasics. In Y. Lebrun & R. Hoops (Eds.), *Recovery in aphasics,* (pp. 96–108). Lisse: Swets & Zeitlinger.

Lebrun, Y. (1976b). Neurolinguistic models of language and speech. In H. Whitaker (Ed.), *Studies in neurolinguistics 1.* (pp. 1–30). New York: Academic Press.

Lebrun, Y. (1982a). Aphasie de Broca et anarthrie. *Acta Neurologica Belgica, 82,* 80–90.

Lebrun, Y. (1982b). L'aphasie chez les polyglottes. *La Linguistique, 18,* 129–144.

Leischner, A. (1943). Die Aphasie der Taubstummen. *Archiv für Psychiatrie und Nervenkrankheiten, 115,* 469–548.

Leischner, A. (1983). Side differences in writing to dictation of aphasics with agraphia: A graphic disconnection syndrome. *Brain and Language, 18,* 1–19.

Lhermitte, F., & Derouesné, J. (1974). Paraphasie et jargonaphasie dans le langage oral avec conservation du langage écrit. *Revue Neurologique, 130,* 117–123.

Liberman, A. (1957). Some results of research on speech perception. *Journal of the Acoustical Society of America, 29,* 117–123.

Liberman, A., Cooper, F., Studdert-Kennedy, M., Harris, K., & Shankweiler, D., (1968). On the efficiency of speech sounds. *Zeitschrift für Phonetik, Sprachwissenschaft und Kommunikationsforschung, 21,* 21–32.

Meckler, R., Mack, J., & Bennett, R. (1979). Sign language aphasia in a non-deafmute. *Neurology, 29,* 1037–1040.

Pitres, A. (1884). Considérations sur l'agraphie. *Revue de Médecine, 4,* 855–873.

Poizner, H., & Battison, R. (1980). Cerebral asymmetry for sign language: Clinical and experimental evidence. In H. Lane & F. Grosjean (Eds.), *Recent perspectives on American Sign Language.* (pp. 79–101). Hillsdale, NJ: Lawrence Erlbaum Associates.

Sarno, J., Swisher, L., & Taylor Sarno, M. (1969). Aphasia in a congenitally deaf man. *Cortex, 5,* 389–414.

Tissot, A., Rodriguez, J., & Tissot, R. (1970). Die Prognose der Anarthrie im Sinne von Pierre Marie. In A. Leischner (Ed.), *Die Rehabilitation der Aphasie in den romanischen Ländern* (pp. 20–43). Stuttgart, Thieme.

Tureen, L., Smolik, E., & Tritt, J. (1951). *Aphasia in a deaf mute. Neurology, 1,* 237–244.

Underwood, J., & Paulson, C. (1981). Aphasia and congenital deafness: A case study. *Brain and Language, 12,* 285–291.

Yamadori, A., Osumi, Y., Ikeda, H., & Kanazawa, Y. (1980). Left unilateral agraphia and tactile anomia. *Archives of Neurology, 37,* 88–91.

# 14 Deficits in Facial Expression and Movement as a Function of Brain Damage

Joan C. Borod
Elissa Koff
Marjorie Perlman Lorch
Marjorie Nicholas

## INTRODUCTION

Everyday experience and scientific study suggest that the face is a primary organ for communication of emotional expression. It is well known that among the animals, the human being has the most extensively developed facial musculature and is heavily dependent on facial behavior to facilitate social interaction (Roberts, 1966) and emotional communication (LoCastro, 1972; Mehrabian & Wiener, 1967). Much attention has focused recently upon the neuro-psychological mechanisms involved in the facial expression of emotion (Borod & Koff, 1984; Rinn, 1984). While the majority of studies in this area have used normal adult subjects, investigators recently have begun to examine facial behaviors in brain-damaged populations. Studies of facial emotion in patients with unilateral focal brain damage provide an opportunity to illuminate brain/behavior relationships underlying the emotional processing system in the human being. In this chapter, we describe our program of research which has investigated multiple aspects of emotional facial expression in a group of focal lesion patients with right or left hemisphere pathology and in normal matched controls (Borod & Koff, 1982; Borod, Koff, & Buck, in press; Borod, Koff, Perlman [Lorch], & Nicholas, 1983, 1984, 1985, in press; Perlman, Borod, Nicholas, & Koff, 1984).

A special role for the right hemisphere has been recently suggested for both the perception and expression of facial emotion (for review, see Borod, Koff, & Caron, 1983). In normals, perception studies have demonstrated left visual-field (i.e., right hemisphere) advantages for perceiving emotional expression (Hansch & Pirozzolo, 1980; Ley & Bryden, 1979; McKeever & Dixon, 1981; Strauss & Moscovitch, 1981; Suberi & McKeever, 1977). Expression studies have documented that, compared to the right, the left side of the face ("hemiface") moves more extensively (Borod & Caron, 1980; Borod, Caron, & Koff, 1981a; Borod, Koff, & White, 1983; Moscovitch & Olds, 1982) and appears more intense (Campbell, 1978; Heller & Levy, 1981; Rubin & Rubin, 1980; Sackeim & Gur, 1978) during emotional expression. This appears to be the case during both posed and spontaneous expression (Borod, Koff, & White, 1983; Dopson, Beckwith, Tucker, & Bullard-Bates, 1984; but see also Ekman, Hager, & Friesen, 1981). We define *posed* expression as deliberate or volitional movements clearly intended by an individual or requested of him or her, and *spontaneous* expression as involuntary movements which are unintended reactions to appropriately evocative emotional situations (after Myers, 1976). The greater involvement of the left hemiface in emotional expression suggests a dominant role for the right cerebral hemisphere in emotional expression. This speculation is based on the fact that the face, and particularly the lower portion, is predominantly innervated by the contralateral hemisphere (DeJong, 1979; Kuypers, 1958). While the bulk of the evidence suggests an overall right hemisphere dominance for emotion (for reviews, see Borod, Koff, & Caron, 1983; Ley & Bryden, 1982; Tucker, 1981), recent studies have speculated about right hemisphere dominance for negative emotions and left hemisphere or bilateral involvement for positive ones (Ahern & Schwartz, 1979; Borod, Caron, & Koff, 1981b; Borod & Koff, 1984; Bruyer, 1981; Davidson, Schwartz, Saron, Bennett, & Goleman, 1978; Dimond, Farrington, & Johnson, 1976; Karlin, Weinapple, Rochford, & Goldstein, 1979; Reuter-Lorenz & Davidson, 1981; Sackeim, Greenberg, Weiman, Gur, Hungerbuhler, & Geschwind, 1982).

Clinical studies have suggested that defects in the perception of facial emotion are associated primarily with right-sided brain damage and this research has been well described in the literature (e.g., Benowitz, Bear, Rosenthal, Mesulam, Zaidel, & Sperry, 1983; Borod, Koff, Perlman, & Nicholas, 1983; Cicone, Wapner, & Gardner, 1980; Heilman, Bowers, Speedie, & Caslett, 1983; Heilman, Scholes, & Watson, 1975). Studies of the expression of facial emotion in brain-damaged patients are fewer in number, and often these have been in the form of anecdotes or case reports (Ross & Mesulam, 1979) focusing on spontaneous, rather than posed, expression. For example, Buck and Duffy (1980) found that spontaneous expressions of emotion were less likely to occur in right brain-damaged patients, relative to left brain-damaged patients and hospitalized normal controls. Since posed and spontaneous expression are considered to reflect separate and possibly independent neuroanatomical origins and pathways (Damasio & Maurer, 1978; Geschwind, 1975; Kahn, 1964; Miehlke, 1973; Tschiassny, 1953), it could be illuminating to study both types of expression in brain-damaged patients. Pyramidal control and cortical sites have been implicated in posed, or volitional, facial movement while nonpyramidal control and presumably subcortical sites have been suggested for spontaneous expression.

One purpose of this chapter was to describe the effects of unilateral brain damage on the facial expression of emotion under both posed and spontaneous elicitation conditions. The dimension of emotional valence was included by examining both positive and negative emotions in order to test the speculation in the literature concerning normals that negative emotion is primarily associated with the right hemisphere and positive emotion with the left hemisphere or with both hemispheres. Prior to our work (Borod & Koff, 1982), this notion had not been experimentally tested with brain-damaged patients. If there are indeed valence differences between the hemispheres, right brain-damaged patients might show a selective impairment regarding negative emotion and left-damaged patients regarding positive emotion. To assess patients' performance on tasks of facial emotional expression, we examined the behavioral parameters of accuracy (Borod, Koff, Perlman [Lorch], & Nicholas, 1983 in press) and asymmetry. An accuracy measure was used specifically to address the clinical observation in the literature that right hemisphere pathology can produce disturbances in emotional expression. Facial asymmetry was measured to test the finding in normals that the left hemiface is more active than the right in facial expression. It was hypothesized that patients with right hemisphere pathology would show less striking facial asymmetry during emotional expression than those with left-sided pathology or normal controls.

Another purpose of this chapter was to describe the contribution of other aspects of facial movement control to the expression of facial emotion. Such variables include buccofacial apraxia (Kimura, 1982), nonemotional hemiface mobility (Koff, Borod, & White, 1981), and facial paralysis (Gordon & Friedberg, 1978). Brain damage typically produces impairments in these behaviors, and it is conceivable that these impairments could confound a patient's ability to execute tasks of facial emotion. Measures of facial emotion (accuracy, asymmetry) were correlated with measures of related facial behaviors (facial paralysis, hemiface mobility, bucco-facial apraxia). The relationship among the separate measures of emotional expression and among those of facial movement was also determined, reasoning that a lack of correlation might suggest that these aspects of facial emotional expression and movement are relatively separate and independent of each other.

Finally, we have explored the relationship between facial emotional expression and variables that have been documented to affect patient performance on other neuropsychological tasks (Borod, Goodglass, & Kaplan, 1980; Lezak, 1983). These included months post onset, age, education, occupation, general intellectual functioning, and auditory comprehension (among the left hemisphere aphasics). We also examined the relationship of the facial expression variables to the patients' affective history and presence or absence of clinically determined visual field neglect. Visual field neglect has been reported to be a relevant factor in studies of brain damage and affective deficits (for review, see Ruckdeschel-Hibbard, Gordon, & Diller, 1984).

## METHOD

### Subjects

Twelve males with unilateral right (RBD) and 15 males with unilateral left (LBD) brain damage served as subjects; 16 normal males (NC) served as controls. Patients were recruited from the neurology wards of the Boston V.A. Medical Center. All subjects were right-handed by self-report or familial-report; the three groups did not differ on formal assessment of lateral dominance (Coren, Porac, & Duncan, 1979), with the majority of subjects right-footed (86%) and right-eyed (86%). The three subjects groups did not differ significantly on demographic variables, with an overall mean age of 57 years (S.D. = 8.1), 13 years of education (S.D. = 2.8), and an occupational level of 3.9 (S.D. = 1.5) as measured by the Hollingshead–Redlich Scale (Hollingshead & Redlich, 1958). The typical socioeconomic occupational level was that of a middle-class white collar worker.

Patients were tested at least 1 month post onset of illness (median = 9 months); the two patient groups did not differ significantly in number of months post onset. Patients were only included for study if their lesions were the result of a cerebrovascular accident, e.g., occlusion, embolism, thrombosis, hemorrhagic infarct, and if there was a negative history of psychiatric disorder, psychotropic drug treatment, or secondary neurological disorder (e.g., epilepsy, dementia). Evidence of the unilateral and focal nature of the lesion was confirmed by CT scan in all but two cases, where clinical data from neurological examination were used. Fourteen (i.e., 63%) of the patients had lesions restricted to the cortex and/or subcortical white matter, while the remainder had lesions which extended to subcortical grey matter structures (e.g., basal ganglia, thalamus). The patient groups were similar with regard to the distributions of their lesions. The percentages of patients with lesions in a particular region, for RBDs and LBDs respectively were: frontal—58%, 60%; parietal—92%, 67%; temporal—58%, 67%; occipital—17%, 7%; subcortical white matter—83%, 60%; and subcortical grey structures—50%, 27%. At the time of testing, the majority of each patient group had clinically determined deficits on the side contralateral to their lesion. These deficits were hemiplegia (58% of RBDs, 60% of LBDs); facial paralysis (75% of RBDs, 80% of LBDs); and visual field loss (58% of RBDs, 47% of LBDs).

Although all of the LBDs were aphasic (3 Broca's, 2 Mixed Nonfluents, 2 Globals, 2 Conductions, 4 Wernicke's, 2 Unclassifieds), all had adequate auditory comprehension (mean Boston Diagnostic Aphasia Examination [Goodglass & Kaplan, 1972] z-score = -0.88, S.D. = .7) and cognitive functioning (mean WAIS Performance IQ [Wechsler, 1958] = 94, S.D. = 16) to perform the experimental tasks. All subjects had sufficient visuo-perceptual skill, as assessed by ability to correctly describe two practice slides, Thematic Apperception Test card 3GF (Murray, 1938) and a scene from a kindergarten classroom (Buck, 1978).

## Facial Emotional Expression

## Procedures

*Spontaneous condition.* Slides designed to elicit expressions of positive (pleasant) and negative (unpleasant) emotion (Buck, 1978) were presented on a Singer Caramate projector positioned directly in front of the subject and slightly below eye level (Borod, Koff, Perlman [Lorch], & Nicholas, 1983, 1985, in press). Ten pleasant and six unpleasant slides were shown to each subject. Pleasant slides showed, for example, a little baby picking flowers, or a nude couple embracing, or a sunset, and unpleasant slides, for example, a surgical procedure, or a victim of starvation. The order and orientation (original and mirror-reversed) of the slides were counterbalanced across subjects. Subjects were seated facing a one-way mirror covered with a screen, behind which was a videocamera for recording their facial expressions. The examiner sat next to the subject and side of subject was counterbalanced. A headrest was used to keep the subject's head upright and relatively immobile to ensure that the camera could record the full face for later ratings. Each slide was presented for 6 seconds, after which the subject was requested to describe his feelings about and reactions to the slide. The slide was then left on the screen for 10–15 seconds during which time the subject talked about these feelings. After describing his feelings, the subject was asked to respond to the question—"Does this picture make you feel good or bad (or neutral)?" Following this was a 3 second intertrial interval, to allow the subject's face to return to a neutral expression, to check the headrest position, and to advance to the next slide, using the remote control cord from the Caramate.

*Posed condition.* There were two posed subconditions, verbal and visual, in which positive (happiness, surprise, sexual arousal) and negative (sadness, anger, confusion, fear, disgust) expressions were studied (Borod, Koff, Perlman [Lorch], & Nicholas, 1983, in press). In the posed-verbal subcondition, subjects were requested to pose each of the nine expressions to oral command, e.g., "Look happy." If the subject was unable to pose to command, contextual coaching was used to facilitate a response, e.g., "Show me how you'd look if you found a large sum of money and were very happy." In the posed-visual subcondition, subjects were shown slides (Ekman & Friesen, 1975) of prototypical facial emotional expressions on the Caramate projector, and required to pose each expression in turn. Subjects were instructed, e.g., "Look happy, like the man in the picture looks." They were told that a direct imitation of the poser's facial pattern was not essential. Both auditory verbal and visual nonverbal instructions were used to avoid selectively priming one hemisphere through the input modality.

To facilitate deliberate control over the expressions produced in the posed condition, subjects were first required to practice each expression. During actual filming, they were requested to make each expression immediately following a command of "Ready, go," to make one complete expression, and then to return to a neutral baseline.

*Emotional Valence.* The stimulus slides used during the spontaneous condition were classified as positive or negative based on findings from an earlier study of normal adults (Borod & Koff, 1983; Borod, Koff, & White, 1983). Facial expressions in response to these slides were rated by trained judges for the degree of pleasant versus unpleasant affect on a 7-point Likert scale. A significant majority (71%) of the responses to the "positive" slides were rated as pleasant, and a significant majority (78%) of the responses to the "negative" slides were rated as unpleasant. The expressions examined during the posed conditions in the current study were classified as positive or negative based on findings from earlier studies (Borod & Koff, 1983; Borod, Koff, & White, 1983) in which posed expressions (to verbal command and to visual imagery) were rated for degree of pleasantness. A significant majority of the posed positive expressions were rated as pleasant (98% for happiness, 92% for sexual arousal), and a significant majority of the posed negative expressions were rated as unpleasant (91% for sadness, 82% for confusion, 90% for disgust).

## Scoring and Analysis

Two judges viewed the videotapes of the experimental sessions and rated each facial expression for accuracy and asymmetry. For the spontaneous condition, the tape was run from the onset of each slide until the occurrence of the first complete facial expression, determined by rater consensus. For the posed condition, the expression that was made following the "Ready, go" command was rated. Each tape segment was played through and reviewed several times to identify the point at which maximum or peak expression occurred; ratings were made at that point. Half of the videotapes were viewed under normal conditions and half were viewed under mirror-image conditions on a TV monitor especially modified to reverse the video image. This was done in order to rule out the possibility that the ratings might be affected by a bias on the part of the perceiver to attend preferentially to the left hemiface (e.g., Campbell, 1982; Gilbert & Bakan, 1973; Heller & Levy, 1981).

For accuracy ratings, each expression was scored as accurate/successful (score = 1) or unsuccessful (score = 0). To be rated as accurate, an expression had to be appropriate to the stimulus. Asymmetry ratings measuring the relative degree of muscular involvement or the extent of expression in the lower face were made on a 7-point scale, from 1 (extreme left-sided) to 7 (extreme right-sided), with 4 representing symmetry.

The judges were trained for the rating of accuracy as follows. For the *spontaneous* task, judges were familiarized with the slides used in the actual experiment and shown a training tape containing the facial responses of two adult subjects who had responded appropriately to the slides. During rating, they were asked to determine whether or not the response to each slide was appropriate. For the *posed* task, the judges examined the series of stimulus photographs used during the posed-visual subcondition. In addition, they were familiarized with exemplars of prototypical expressions of happiness, surprise, sadness, anger, fear, and disgust published by Ekman and Friesen (1975, pp. 112, 45, 127, 96–97, 62, 76, respectively) and by Izard (1971, pp. 328–330).

Interrater agreement was determined on a subsample of initial findings. Since interrater agreement was high (complete agreement = 91% for asymmetry [563 observations] and 95% for accuracy [184 observations]), a mean score of the two raters was used for each variable for each expression. Expressions were pooled according to valence. Subjects were assigned mean scores for positive, and for negative, emotions, in both the spontaneous and posed (visual and verbal combined) conditions.

## Bucco-Facial Apraxia

### Procedures

Tasks were developed to examine the ability of brain-damaged and normal subjects to make movements of the upper and lower face to verbal command (Perlman, Borod, Nicholas, & Koff, 1984). Both intransitive and transitive commands were employed. For the intransitive task, three movements were specific to the upper face, and three movements to the lower face. The six commands were: (1) close one eye, (2) lift your eyebrows, (3) lower your eyebrows, (4) put your tongue out, (5) raise the corners of your mouth, and (6) pucker your lips. For the transitive task, four items were selected from a standard clinical test of apraxia (Goodglass & Kaplan, 1972); these items were: (1) suck through a straw, (2) blow out a match, (3) sniff a flower, and (4) lick an envelope. Subjects' responses were videotaped for rating at a later time.

### Scoring and Analysis

Two judges viewed the videotapes and rated each response with respect to criterial elements and motoric execution. The elements rating was based on the features of location, shape, and direction of the movement. A 4-point scale was developed where a score of 0 signified no recognizable features, a 1 indicated one correct feature, a 2 indicated two correct features, and a 3 indicated three correct features. In pilot testing, two things became apparent: (1) the only single element which was produced correctly by itself was location—correct shape or movement always appeared in combination with another element, and (2) at least one of these elements could be identified in each response. Since it appeared that the three elements were neither orthogonal nor equiprobable, we redesigned our elements ratings, giving full weighting to location (1) and partial weighting (.5) to shape and to movement, thus producing a 3-point scale (1, 1.5, and 2). The execution rating was designed to assess the motoric quality (i.e., clumsy or smooth) of the performance. A 3-point scale was developed, ranging from poorly executed (a score of 1) to well executed (a score of 3). There were ten instances of no response (1% of the total of 688 responses) which were dropped from the analyses.

Interrater reliability was computed for the ratings on a sample of eight subjects (four LBDs, two RBDs, two NCs), based on a total of 80 observations. For execution ratings, the percent of complete agreement was 84%. For the elements ratings, there was 100% complete agreement for each of the two tasks. The mean rating of the two judges was used for each movement. Ratings for individual movements were averaged to form total scores for each subject. For the intransitive condition, there were two elements scores (upper face, lower face), and two execution scores (upper face, lower face). For the standard transitive condition, there were elements and execution scores for each of the movements.

## Hemiface Mobility

### Procedures

Subjects were instructed to make four unilateral facial movements, three involving mouth (lower face) and one involving eye (upper face), using procedures developed by Koff, Borod, and White (1983). Three angles of mouth movements were required, approximating angles of 45, 90, and 135° with respect to the vertical midline. Instructions were to "move the corner of your mouth up towards your eye" (45°) to "pull your mouth straight out to the side" (90°) to "pull your mouth down while lowering your jaw" (135°), and to "close one eye." Two methods of assessment were used: undirected and directed. Subjects were first asked to attempt each one of the four movements (undirected assessment) to determine which side was preferred spontaneously. After all four movements were tried, subjects were instructed to make each movement five times in succession on each side of the face, with the examiner specifying on which side of the face to begin (directed assessment). Photographs of an adult model making these movements were provided as a visual cue. The order in which these movements were requested was fixed, but the side on which subjects began each movement was randomized and counterbalanced.

### Scoring and Analysis

For the undirected assessment, the side of the face used spontaneously by the subject was recorded (left, both, right) and transformed to a 3-point scale where a score of 1 was used for left, a score of 2 for equal, and a score of 3 for right. For the directed assessment, facial movements were videotaped and later rated by two observers for hemiface mobility asymmetry on a 5-point scale (only left side, better on the left, equal, better on the right, only right side). In addition, for hemiface mobility adequacy, each hemiface was rated on a 3-point scale (inadequate, partially adequate, adequate). Since the two raters were in agreement for 97% of the movements (N = 65) on asymmetry and for 83% of the movements on adequacy (N = 80), each score represented the average for the two raters. Each subject received separate scores for the lower and the upper face for undirected asymmetry, directed asymmetry, and directed adequacy.

## Facial Paralysis

### Procedures

Facial paralysis in the upper and lower face was examined from neutral poses on the videotapes, using techniques adapted from Devriese (1972), Gordon and Friedberg (1978), Miehlke (1973), and van Gelder (1981). For the upper face, the following three parameters were used: (1) wrinkles in the forehead, (2) position of eyebrow, and (3) size of eyelid. For the lower face, the parameters used were: (1) depth of the nasolabial fold, (2) position of the corner of the mouth, and (3) direction to which the middle of the mouth is pointing.

### Scoring and Analysis

A rating from 1 to 3 was made for each parameter where 1 signified more paralysis in left hemiface, 2 signified no difference between left and right hemifaces, and 3 signified more paralysis in right hemiface. For example, a subject would receive a rating of "3" for each of these six parameters if there were fewer wrinkles on the right forehead, the right eyebrow was lower than the left, the right eyelid was wider than the left eyelid, the right nasolabial fold was shallower than the left fold, the right corner of the mouth was lower than the left corner, and the middle of the mouth was directed away from the right side of the face. Ratings of paralysis were made for the normal control, as well as the brain-damaged, subjects.

Two raters made independent ratings; since interrater reliability was high across all ratings (84% complete agreement on a sample of 67 observations), the mean of the two ratings was used. Each subject received a facial paralysis asymmetry score (direction) for the upper and the lower face. In addition, a facial paralysis performance score (degree) for the upper and the lower face was determined by computing the absolute value of the "direction" rating; this provided a measure of the extent, regardless of the side, of paralysis.

## RESULTS

For the following analyses, the facial emotional expression and facial movement variables were categorized as measures of performance or asymmetry. Performance measures indicate the overall level of performance; asymmetry measures indicate the hemiface (left, right, or both) most involved in the behavior. There is one measure of facial expression performance (i.e., accuracy) and one measure of facial expression asymmetry. Facial movement performance measures include praxis intransitive (execution, elements), praxis transitive (execution, elements), directed mobility (adequacy), and paralysis (degree). Facial movement asymmetry measures include directed mobility, undirected mobility, and paralysis (direction).

### Analysis of the Emotional Expression Variables

We conducted a series of repeated measures analyses of variance (ANOVAs) on each of the emotional expression variables of accuracy (Borod, Koff, Perlman [Lorch], & Nicholas, 1983, in press) and asymmetry. For each variable, the effects of Group (RBD, LBD, NC), Condition (posed, spontaneous), and Valence (positive, negative) were examined. The Newman-Keuls multiple comparison procedure (Winer, 1971) was used for post-hoc tests. Table 14.1 presents a summary of the ANOVA findings. As can be seen in Table 14.1, almost all main effects of the Group variable were significant.

### Accuracy

The three-way ANOVA conducted on the accuracy scores (Borod, Koff, Perlman [Lorch], & Nicholas, 1983, in press) yielded a significant main effect of Group (F = 4.89; df = 2,40; $p \leq .01$). Using post-hoc tests, the RBDs ($\bar{X}$ = 0.49) were significantly ($p < .05$) impaired in the expression of facial emotion as compared to LBDs ($\bar{X}$ = 0.62) and NCs ($\bar{X}$ = 0.67). A significant Group by Valence interaction (F = 3.33; df = 2,40; $p < .05$) suggested that this was especially the case for positive emotions. There was also a significant main effect for Condition (F = 23.98; df = 1,40; $p < .001$), such that subjects produced more accurate expressions during the posed ($\bar{X}$ = 0.73) than the spontaneous ($\bar{X}$ = 0.46) conditions. Finally, a significant Condition by Valence interaction (F = 12.39; df = 1,40; $p < .005$) suggested that positive emotions were more accurately expressed than negative ones in the posed condition while negative emotions were more accurately expressed than positive ones in the spontaneous condition.

TABLE 14.1

Significant Findings for ANOVAs on Facial Emotional Expression Variables

| Dependent Variable | Main Effects | | | Interactions | | | |
|---|---|---|---|---|---|---|---|
| | Group | Condition | Valence | Group, Condition | Group, Valence | Valence, Condition | Group, Valence, Condition |
| Performance (accuracy) | * | * | | | * | * | |
| Asymmetry | * | | | | | | |

*$p \leq .05$

## Asymmetry

The three-way ANOVA conducted on the asymmetry scores yielded a significant main effect of Group (F = 3.94; df = 2.26; $p < .05$) such that asymmetry scores were right-sided for RBDs ($\bar{X}$ = 4.36) and left-sided for LBDs ($\bar{X}$ = 3.38) and NCs ($\bar{X}$ = 3.79). Using post-hoc tests, only the two brain-damaged groups differed significantly ($p < .05$).

## Analysis of the Facial Movement Variables

We conducted a series of repeated measures analyses of variance for each of the facial movement variables, i.e., praxis (execution and elements) mobility (adequacy and asymmetry), and paralysis (degree and direction). For each variable, the effects of Group (RBD, LBD, NC) and Face Part (Upper, Lower) were examined. Table 14.2 presents a summary of these ANOVA findings. As can be seen in Table 14.2, the majority of main effects for the Group variables were significant.

## Praxis

*Intransitive.*    Separate two-way ANOVAs were conducted on the execution and elements scores for the intransitive task. There was a significant main effect

TABLE 14.2
Significant Findings for ANOVAs on Facial Movement Variables

| Dependent Variable | Main Effects | | Interactions |
| --- | --- | --- | --- |
| | Group | Facepart | Group X Facepart |
| PERFORMANCE | | | |
| Praxis Intransitive | | | |
|   Execution | * | | |
|   Elements | * | | |
| Praxis Transitive | | | |
|   Execution | * | NA | NA |
|   Elements | * | NA | NA |
| Mobility Adequacy | | | |
|   Directed | * | * | |
| Paralysis Degree | | * | |
| ASYMMETRY | | | |
| Mobility Asymmetry[a] | | | |
|   Directed | * | | |
|   Undirected | * | | |
| Paralysis Direction | * | | |

[a] The hemiface variable, as well as Group and Facepart were included in this ANOVA, and a significant interaction for Group and Hemiface also emerged.

$^*p \leq .05.$

NA signifies nonapplicable.

of Group (F = 17.67; df = 2.40; $p$ < .001) on the execution ratings. Post-hoc tests revealed that LBDs ($\bar{X}$ = 2.19) were significantly ($p$ < .01) more impaired than either RBDs ($\bar{X}$ = 2.70) or NCs ($\bar{X}$ = 2.80). When the elements scores were examined, again, there was a significant main effect of Group (F = 7.89; df = 2,40; p < .005), such that LBDs ($\bar{X}$ = 1.66) were significantly (p < .01) more impaired than RBDs ($\bar{X}$ = 1.82) or NCs ($\bar{X}$ = 1.88).

*Transitive.* Separate one-way ANOVAs were conducted to examine the effects of Group on the execution and elements scores for the transitive task. (Since all four transitive items involved the lower face only, a mean score was computed and used as the dependent variable in these analyses.) For the execution score, there was a significant main effect of Group (F = 8.73; df = 2,40; p < .001). Using post-hoc tests, LBDs ($\bar{X}$ = 2.57) were significantly ($p$ < .05) more impaired than RBDs ($\bar{X}$ = 2.80) or NCs ($\bar{X}$ = 2.91). For the elements score, there was also a main effect of Group (F = 6.05; df = 2,40; $p$ < .005), and again, using post-hoc tests, LBDs ($\bar{X}$ = 1.78) were significantly ($p$ < .01) more impaired than RBDs ($\bar{X}$ = 1.97) or NCs ($\bar{X}$ = 1.95).

## Mobility, Directed

*Adequacy.* A three-way ANOVA was conducted to examine the effects of Group, Facepart, and Hemiface on the adequacy scores for directed mobility. Overall, there was a main effect of Group (F = 5.05; df = 2,40; $p$ ≤ .01), such that RBDs ($\bar{X}$ = 2.37) and LBDs ($\bar{X}$ = 2.21) were significantly ($p$ < .05) impaired relative to NCs ($\bar{X}$ = 2.70). There was also a significant Group by Hemiface interaction (F = 9.67; df = 2,40; $p$ < .001). Post-hoc tests demonstrated that the left hemiface ($\bar{x}$ = 2.47) was less impaired than the right hemiface ($\bar{x}$ = 1.95) among LBDs while the right hemiface ($\bar{x}$ = 2.61) was less impaired than the left hemiface ($\bar{x}$ = 2.13) among RBDs; there were no differences between the right ($\bar{x}$ = 2.71) and left ($\bar{x}$ = 2.70) hemifaces among NCs. Finally, there was a main effect for Facepart (F = 6.43; df = 1.40; $p$ < .05) such that lower face mobility ($\bar{x}$ = 2.30) was less adequate than upper face mobility ($\bar{x}$ = 2.56).

*Asymmetry.* A two-way ANOVA was conducted to examine the effects of Group and Facepart on the asymmetry scores for mobility. Overall, there was a main effect of Group (F = 14.30; df = 2.40; $p$ < .001). Post-hoc tests revealed that all possible group comparisons were significant ($p$ < .01), such that asymmetry scores were right-sided for RBDs ($\bar{x}$ = 3.76), left-sided for LBDs ($\bar{x}$ = 2.44), and symmetrical for NCs ($\bar{x}$ = 3.10).

## Mobility, Undirected

A two-way ANOVA was conducted to examine the effects of Group and Facepart on the asymmetry scores for undirected mobility. Overall there was a marginally significant effect for Group (F = 3.05; df = 2,40; $p$ = .059). Using post-hoc tests, LBDs ($\bar{x}$ = 1.87) and RBDs ($\bar{x}$ = 2.46) differed significantly ($p$ < .05) from each other as to which side of the face was preferred but not from NCs ($\bar{x}$ = 2.07).

## Paralysis

*Direction.*    A two-way ANOVA was conducted to examine the effects of Group and Facepart on the paralysis direction scores. There was a significant main effect for Group (F = 3.73; df = 2.40; $p$ < .05). When post-hoc tests were conducted, the only significant ($p$ < .05) difference was between the RBDs ($\bar{x}$ = 1.85) and LBDs ($\bar{x}$ = 2.25); the mean score for NCs was 2.04.

*Degree.*    A two-way ANOVA was conducted to examine the effects of Group and Facepart on the paralysis degree scores. There was no ($p$ = .17) significant difference between scores for LBDs ($\bar{x}$ = .71), and RBDs ($\bar{x}$ = .66), and NCs ($\bar{x}$ = .52). There was a significant main effect for Facepart (F = 5.92; df = 1.40; $p$ < .05), such that there was more paralysis in the lower ($\bar{x}$ = .68) than the upper ($\bar{x}$ = .57) face.

## Correlations Between Facial Variables

### Relationships Within Categories

Prior to examining the effect of the facial movement variables on the emotional expression variables, we intercorrelated the variables separately by category for each of the three subject groups. Spearman rank order correlations were computed. Based on the findings from the ANOVAs reported above, the condition (posed, spontaneous) and valence (positive, negative) distinctions were preserved for both the emotional expression performance and asymmetry variables, and the facepart distinction (upper, lower) was preserved for the movement asymmetry variables. For the movement performance variables, data were combined across factors, except for directed mobility adequacy. In that case, the unaffected hemiface was examined for each group, that is, the left hemiface for LBDs, the right hemiface for RBDs, and both hemifaces combined for NCs.

*Expression performance vs. expression performance.*    Among the 18 correlations computed (6 rhos X 3 subject groups), only three were significant, which is only slightly more than would be expected by chance.

*Expression asymmetry vs. expression asymmetry.*    Among the 18 correlations computed (6 × 3), eight were significant. There were significant positive correlations between posed positive and spontaneous positive asymmetry scores for all three subject groups, and between posed negative and spontaneous negative scores for all groups.

*Movement performance vs. movement performance.* Among the 45 correlations computed (15 × 3), only five were significant. While this is twice the number expected by chance (N = 2.3), no systematic patterns emerged, except for the positive correlations between praxis transitive elements and praxis transitive execution for LBDs (rho = .61) and for NCs (rho = .77).

*Movement asymmetry vs. movement asymmetry.* Among the 18 correlations computed (6 × 3), there were four significant findings. For the upper face, directed mobility was correlated with undirected mobility for LBDs (rho = .53) and RBDs (rho = .49). For the lower face, the direction of paralysis was inversely correlated with directed (rho = .53) and undirected (rho = −.31) mobility for RBDs.

## Relationship Between Expression and Movement Variables

Since there were relatively few significant correlations within the four categories, except for expression asymmetry, individual variables were maintained throughout the analyses to follow. For expression asymmetry, the ratings for the four scores were averaged.

*Expression performance vs. movement performance.* Among the 72 correlations computed (24 × 3) there were five significant correlations, not more than would be expected by chance.

*Expression asymmetry vs. movement asymmetry.* For this analysis, only the movement scores for the lower face were used since the original asymmetry ratings for emotional expression were made for the lower face only. As can be seen in Table 14.3, many of the correlations (6 of 9) between expression and

TABLE 14.3

Significant Spearman Correlation Rhos Between the Asymmetry Measure of Emotional Facial Expression and Asymmetry Measures of nonemotional Facial Movement for the Lower Face

| Subject Group | Paralysis Direction | Mobility Directed | Undirected |
|---|---|---|---|
| RBD | −.66* | +.64* | +.68* |
| LBD | −.31 | +.75 | +.64* |
| NC | −.26 | −.59* | −.39 |

*p ≤ .05

movement asymmetry variables were significant. For the mobility variable, there were positive correlations with expression asymmetry for the brain-damaged patients and inverse correlations for the NCs. For the paralysis variable only one of the correlations was significant.

## Effects of Demographic and Cognitive Variables on Facial Expression Performance

We examined the effect of a range of variables on facial expression ability. The demographic variables included: months post onset (for the patients), age, education, and occupation. Cognitive variables included the WAIS Performance IQ (for LBDs and RBDs) and the BDAE comprehension z-score (for LBDs). These six variables were correlated with the four expression accuracy scores. For the demographic variables, only two of the 36 correlations were significant, not more than would be expected by chance. For months past onset, three of the eight correlation coefficients were significant: posed negative (rho = .60) for LBDs, and spontaneous negative (rho = .59) and spontaneous positive (rho = .72) for RBDs. While none of the eight correlations with the WAIS Performance IQ score were significant, there was one significant correlation with the auditory comprehension z-score (−.56 with spontaneous negative), and one trend (p = .06) (−.53 with spontaneous positive).

## Effects of Visual Neglect and Affective History on Facial Expression Performance

We wanted to determine the possible effects of visual neglect and abnormal affective history on emotional expression impairments among the RBDs. There were seven RBDs with abnormal affective history (ascertained from the patients' medical charts) and seven with visual neglect. For each of the four expression accuracy variables, the median score for the RBDs was determined, and separate contingency tables were constructed for affective history, and for visual neglect. A subject's placement with respect to the median score (above or below) and the presence or absence of abnormal affective history or visual neglect were entered into these tables. The fact that none of the Chi Square tests were significant suggests that deficits in facial emotional expression may not be related to the presence of neglect. Further, those RBD patients whose affect was described by medical and nursing staff as abnormal (i.e., inappropriate or flat) did not necessarily show more impairment on our experimental task of emotional expression than those patients whose affective history was unremarkable.

## DISCUSSION

In this chapter, we have described our systematic assessment of the effects of brain damage on the expression of facial emotion. In light of recent literature suggesting right hemisphere dominance for emotional expression (for reviews, see Borod, Koff, & Caron, 1983; Ley & Bryden, 1982; Tucker, 1981), it was hypothesized that patients with unilateral lesions of the right hemisphere would be more impaired on tasks of emotional expression than either patients with lesions of the left hemisphere or demographically-similar normal controls. We found (Borod, Koff, Perlman [Lorch], & Nicholas, 1983, in press) that patients with right hemisphere pathology were more impaired in their expression of facial emotion than either of the other two groups. Further, these findings were independent of elicitation condition (spontaneous, posed). While these data do not lend support to the speculation that the right hemisphere mediates negative emotion and the left hemisphere positive emotion, there were some differences as a function of valence.

We also measured facial asymmetry while subjects were expressing emotion. Past research with normal adults (see Borod & Koff, 1984, and Rinn, 1984, for reviews) has demonstrated greater left than right hemiface involvement during emotional expression. We had hypothesized that right brain-damaged patients would deviate from the typical pattern of facial asymmetry while left brain-damaged patients would resemble normal controls. When facial asymmetry was measured, there were significant differences between the groups, with greater left hemiface involvement for LBDs and NCs, and greater right hemiface involvement for RBDs.

We were also interested in determining the effect of nonemotional aspects of facial movement (i.e., apraxia, mobility, paralysis) on the facial expression of emotion. The literature has long suggested that the left hemisphere is dominant for the execution of praxic commands (Geschwind, 1975; Nathan, 1947), and this indeed was the case for our subjects (Perlman, Borod, Nicholas, & Koff, 1984). The patients with left hemisphere pathology were significantly impaired in the facility and accuracy with which they carried out bucco-facial commands. This was the case on tasks involving both intransitive items (e.g., raise the corners of your mouth) developed for experimental purposes and transitive items (e.g., sniff a flower), adapted from a standardized clinical battery (Goodglass & Kaplan, 1972). Using a less conventional procedure (i.e., the assessment of hemiface mobility), both brain-damaged groups, relative to NCs, were shown to be significantly impaired in the adequacy with which they carried out unilateral movements with either the paretic or nonparetic hemiface.

We also examined asymmetry ratings for facial paralysis and hemiface mobility. Using the experimental measures of facial paralysis that were developed for this project, paralysis was greater on the right hemiface for LBDs, the left hemiface for RBDs, and neither hemiface for NCs. When directed and undirected mobility were examined, there was greater facility of the left hemiface for LBDs, the right hemiface for RBDs, and neither hemiface for NCs. For the brain-damaged groups, the findings were not surprising in light of the facial paralysis results; that is, the LBDs had more paralysis in their right hemiface and the RBDs in their left hemiface. For the normals, however, the absence of a hemiface advantage was not parallel to findings from earlier studies with normal subjects. In the one study which examined undirected hemiface mobility (Borod & Koff, 1983), young adults were significantly right-sided, and in several studies of directed hemiface mobility (Borod & Koff, 1983; Campbell, 1982; Chaurasia & Goswami, 1975; Ekman, Hager, & Fiesen, 1981; Koff, Borod, & White, 1981), subjects were strikingly left-sided. The discrepancy among these findings may be a function of methodology, since in most of these studies, subjects were instructed by verbal command; in the current study, photographs were shown as well. Another possible interpretation may relate to the fact that our normal subjects had a mean age of 59, making this the first examination of hemiface mobility in an older population. Three of the studies cited above used college-aged subjects (approximate mean age of normal controls = 20); Ekman et al. studied children; and Chaurasia and Goswami reported only that their right-handed subjects ranged in age from 17- to 40-years and their left-handers from 10- to 25-years. The findings from the normal control subjects in the current study raise the possibility that directed hemiface mobility and facial expression, reputed to reflect right hemisphere functioning, become less asymmetrical with age. This possibility is consistent with the recent literature suggesting that right hemisphere specialization may diminish with age, thus reducing the degree of lateralization for some functions (Brown & Jaffe, 1975; Borod & Goodglass, 1980.

Another purpose of this chapter was to describe the influence of performance and asymmetry variables of facial movement (i.e., praxis, mobility, paralysis) on performance and asymmetry measures of facial emotional expression. In preparing for the analysis between categories, correlations were first computed within categories. Among the performance measures for both emotion and movement, the majority of the correlations were nonsignificant, suggesting that these measures tap separate aspects of facial behavior. While we cannot make the claim that these behaviors are orthogonal, there does seem to be some evidence for independence. For facial movement asymmetry, the direction of facial paralysis of the lower face was significantly (inversely) correlated with both directed and undirected mobility only for RBDs. It is of some interest to note that, while both brain-damaged groups had a significant amount of contralateral facial paralysis, it was only for RBDs that the direction of paralysis related to the direction of hemiface mobility. While there was no quantitative relationship between paralysis and mobility for LBDs, that does not override the fact that among LBDs the left hemiface was more paretic and the right one more mobile.

When we examined the influence of performance measures of facial movement on the performance measure of facial emotional expression, almost all correlations were nonsignificant. These results have implications for future performance studies of facial emotional expression among brain-damaged populations. It does not seem to be the case that the ability accurately produce facial emotional expressions is mediated by such factors as degree of facial paralysis and the ability to carry out bucco-facial praxis tasks.

A different picture emerged when we examined the relationship between the two sets of asymmetry measures. Facial mobility for both directed and undirected movement was positively correlated with expression asymmetry for both brain-damaged groups. For NCs, there also was one significant correlation between facial mobility and expression asymmetry but this one was inverse. Among the brain-damaged subjects, the hemiface with the greater muscular mobility was the one to move more extensively during emotional expression; just the opposite occurred for normal controls.

Finally we examined various characteristics of our subject population and their relationship to performance on tasks of facial emotional expression. For the most part, correlations were nonsignificant. Neither visual field neglect, affective history nor demographic factors mediated performance on these emotional tasks. There was, however, a significant positive relationship between months post onset and the patients' performance, suggesting that the more time past since the stroke, the more accurate the patient's expression of emotion. Another interesting finding was an inverse relationship between auditory comprehension and facial expression accuracy for LBDs, suggesting that the more impaired the aphasic's comprehension, the more emotionally expressive he was. Similar inverse correlations have been reported between aphasia severity and nonvocal communication (Borod, Fitzpatrick, Helm-Estabrooks, & Goodglass, 1984) and between aphasia severity and functional communication (Helmick, Watamori, & Palmer, 1976). Such findings may have implications for therapeutic remediation.

In summary, we have described our studies of a number of different aspects of facial behaviors in a brain-damaged population suffering from right or left hemisphere cerebrovascular accidents. Both brain-damaged groups had substantial facial paralysis and impairment in muscular mobility on the hemiface contralateral to their site of lesion. Subjects were videotaped while undergoing experimental procedures designed to examine both emotional facial expression and nonemotional facial movement. In general, patients with right hemisphere pathology were impaired in their expression of facial emotion relative to patients with left hemisphere pathology or normal controls. Patients with left hemisphere pathology, however, were impaired on tasks of buccofacial apraxia relative to the patients with right hemisphere pathology. These results lend support to the notion that the right hemisphere is dominant for expressing facial emotion while the left hemisphere is dominant for executing facial movements to verbal command. These findings suggest the existence of two separate systems for emotional and nonemotional facial movement; the lack of significant correlation between these different types of facial behaviors may be interpreted as additional support for these notions.

## ACKNOWLEDGMENTS

This chapter reports research conducted over the past few years at the Aphasia Research Center, Department of Neurology, Boston University School of Medicine, and the Boston V. A. Medical Center.

This work was supported, in part, by USPHS Grant No. MH37952 to New York University School of Medicine, USPHS Grant No. NS06209 to Boston University School of Medicine, and Bio-Medical Research Support Grant 1-S07RR 07186-02 to Wellesley College. Portions of this chapter were presented at the annual meetings of the International Neuropsychology Society in 1982, 1983, and 1984, and at the Academy of Aphasia in 1984. We are grateful to Errol Baker and Dr. Mary Hyde for assistance in statistical analysis, to Jerry Martin and Karen Olsen for assistance in videotaping, to Dr. Ross Buck for assistance on the project, and to Christine Padovan and Scott Sparks for assistance in manuscript preparation. We are especially grateful to the Medical Research Service of the Boston V.A. Medical Center.

## REFERENCES

Ahern, G. L., & Schwartz, G. E. (1979). Differential lateralization for positive versus negative emotion. *Neuropsychologia, 17,* 693–698.

Benowitz, L. J., Bear, D. M., Rosenthal, R., Mesulam, M., Zaidel, E., & Sperry, R. W. (1983). Hemispheric specialization in nonverbal communication. *Cortex, 19,* 5–11.

Borod, J. C., & Caron, H. S. (1980). Facedness and emotion related to lateral dominance, sex, and expression type. *Neuropsychologia, 18,* 237–242.

Borod, J. C., Caron, H. S., & Koff, E. (1981a). Asymmetry of facial expression related to handedness, footedness and eyedness: A quantitative study. *Cortex, 17,* 381–390.

Borod, J. C., Caron, H. S., & Koff, E. (1981b). Asymmetries in positive and negative facial expressions: Sex differences. *Neuropsychologia, 19,* 819–824.

Borod, J. C., Fitzpatrick, P., Helm-Estabrooks, N., & Goodglass, H. (1984), October. *A scale for the evaluation of nonvocal communication in aphasic patients.* Paper presented at the Annual Meeting of the Academy of Aphasia, Los Angeles, California.

Borod, J. C., & Goodglass, H. (1980). Lateralization of linguistic and melodic processing with age. *Neuropsychologia, 18,* 79–83.

Borod, J. C., Goodglass, H., & Kaplan, E. (1980). Normative data on the Boston Diagnostic Aphasia Examination, Parietal Lobe Battery, and Boston Naming Test. *Journal of Clinical Neuropsychology, 2,* 209–215.

Borod, J., & Koff, E. (1982, February). *Facial asymmetry and lateral dominance in normal and brain-damaged adults.* International Neuropsychology Society, Pittsburgh.

Borod, J. C., & Koff, E. (1983). Hemiface mobility and facial expression asymmetry. *Cortex, 19,* 355–361.

Borod, J. C., & Koff, E. (1984). Asymmetries in affective facial expression. In N. Fox & R. Davidson (Eds.), *The psychobiology of affective development.* Philadelphia, PA: Lawrence Erlbaum Associates.

Borod, J., Koff, E., & Buck, R. (in press). The neuropsychology of facial expression in normal and brain-damaged subjects. In P. Blanck, R. Buck & R. Rosenthal (Eds.), *Nonverbal communication in the clinical context.* University Park: Pennsylvania State University Press.

Borod, J. C., Koff, E., & Caron, H. S. (1983). Right hemispheric specialization for the expression and appreciation of emotion: A focus on the face. In E. Perecman (Ed.), *Cognitive processes in the right hemisphere.* New York: Academic Press.

Borod, J. C., Koff, E., Perlman, M., & Nicholas, M. (1983, February). *Expression and appreciation of facial emotion in brain-damaged patients.* Paper presented at the International Neuropsychology Society Meeting, Mexico City.

Borod, J., Koff, E., Perlman, M., & Nicholas, M. (1984, February). *Channels of emotional communication in patients with focal lesions.* Paper presented at the International Neuropsychology Society Meeting, Houston.

Borod, J., Koff, E., Perlman Lorch, M., & Nicholas, M. (1985). Channels of emotional expression in patients with unilateral brain damage. *Archives of Neurology, 42,* 345–348.

Borod, J. C., Koff, E., Perlman Lorch, M., & Nicholas, M. (in press). The expression and perception of facial emotion in patients with unilateral brain damage. *Neuropsychologia.*

Borod, J. C., Koff, E., & White, B. (1983). Facial asymmetry in posed and spontaneous expressions of emotion. *Brain and Cognition, 2,* 165–175.

Brown, J. W., & Jaffe, J. (1975). Hypothesis on cerebral dominance. *Neuropsychologia, 13,* 107–110.

Bruyer, R. (1981). Asymmetry of facial expression in brain damaged subjects. *Neuropsychologia, 19,* 615–624.

Buck, R. (1978). The slide viewing technique for measuring non-verbal sending accuracy: A guide for replication. *Catalogue of Selected Documents in Psychology, 8,* 62.

Buck, R., & Duffy, R. J. (1980). Nonverbal communication of affect in brain-damaged patients. *Cortex, 16,* 351–361.

Campbell, R. (1978). Asymmetries in interpreting and expressing a posed facial expression. *Cortex, 14,* 327–342.

Campbell, R. (1982). Asymmetries in moving faces. *British Journal of Psychology, 73,* 95–103.

Chaurasia, B. D., & Goswami, J. K. (1975). Functional asymmetry in the face. *Acta Anatomica, 91,* 154–160.

Cicone, M., Wapner, W., & Gardner, H. (1980). Sensitivity to emotional expressions and situations in organic patients. *Cortex, 16,* 145–158.

Coren, S., Porac, C., & Duncan, P. (1979). A behaviorally validated self-report inventory to assess four types of lateral preferences. *Journal of Clinical Neuropsychology, 1,* 55–64.

Damasio, A. R., & Maurer, R. G. (1978). A neurological model for childhood autism. *Archives of Neurology, 35,* 777–786.

Davidson, R. J., Schwartz, G. E., Saron, C., Bennett, J., & Goleman, D. (1978, September). *Frontal versus parietal EEG asymmetry during positive and negative affect.* Paper presented at the Society for Psychophysiological Research, Madison, Wisconsin.

DeJong, R. N. (1979). *The neurologic examination: 4th Ed.* Hagerstown, MD: Medical Department of Harper & Row.

Devriese, P. P. (1972). *Experiments on the facial nerve.* Amsterdam: North-Holland Publishing Company.

Dimond, S. J., Farrington, L., & Johnson, P. (1976). Differing emotional response from right and left hemisphere. *Nature, 261,* 689–691.

Dopson, W. G., Beckwith, B. E., Tucker, D. M., & Bullard-Bates, P. C. (1984). Asymmetry of facial expression in spontaneous emotion. *Cortex, 20,* 243–252.

Ekman, P., & Friesen, W. (1975). *Unmasking the face.* Englewood Cliffs, NJ: Prentice-Hall.

Ekman, P., Hager, E., & Friesen, W. V. (1981). The symmetry of emotional and deliberate facial actions. *Psychophysiology, 18,* 101–106.

Geschwind, N. (1975). The Apraxias: Neural mechanisms of disorders of learned movement. *American Scientist, 63,* 188–195.

Gilbert, C., & Bakan, P. (1973). Visual asymmetry in perception of faces. *Neuropsychologia, 11,* 355–361.

Goodglass, H., & Kaplan, E. (1972). *The assessment of aphasia and related disorders.* Philadelphia: Lea and Febiger.

Gordon, A. S., & Friedberg, J. (1978). Current status of testing for seventh nerve lesions. *Otolaryngologic Clinics of North America, 11,* 301–324.

Hansch, E. C., & Pirozzolo, F. J. (1980). Task relevant effects on the assessment of cerebral specialization for facial emotion. *Brain and Language, 10,* 51–59.

Heilman, K. M., Bowers, D., Speedie, L., & Caslett, H. B. (1983). The comprehension of emotional and nonemotional prosody. *Neurology (supplement 2), 33,* 241.

Heilman, K. M., Scholes, R., & Watson, R. T. (1975). Auditory affective agnosia: Disturbed comprehension of affective speech. *Journal of Neurology, Neurosurgery, and Psychiatry, 38,* 69–72.

Heller, W., & Levy, J. (1981). Perception and expression of emotion in right-handers and left-handers. *Neuropsychologia, 19,* 363–372.

Helmick, J. W., Watamori, T. S., & Palmer, J. M. (1976). Spouses' understanding of the communication disabilities of aphasic patients. *Journal of Speech and Hearing Disorders, 41,* 238–243.

Hollingshead, A. B., & Redlich, F. C. (1958). *Social class and mental illness.* New York: Wiley.

Izard, C. D. (1971). *The face of emotion.* New York: Appleton-Century-Crofts.

Kahn, E. A. (1964). Facial expression. *Clinical Neurosurgery. 12,* 9–22.

Karlin, R., Weinapple, M., Rochford, J., & Goldstein, L. (1979). Quantitated EEG features of negative affective states: Report of some hypnotic studies. *Research Communications in Psychology, 4,* 397–413.

Kimura, D. (1982). Left-hemisphere control of oral and brachial movements and their relation to communication. *Philosophical Transactions of the Royal Society, 298,* 135–149.

Koff, E., Borod, J., & White, B. (1981). Asymmetries for hemiface size and mobility. *Neuropsychologia, 19,* 825–830.

Ley, R. G., & Bryden, M. P. (1979). Hemispheric differences in processing emotions and faces. *Brain and Language, 7,* 127–138.

Ley, R. G., & Bryden, M. P. (1982). Consciousness, emotion, and the right hemisphere. In R. Stevens & G. Underwood (Eds.), *Aspects of consciousness.* New York: Academic Press.

Lezak, M. (1983). *Neuropsychological assessment.* New York: Oxford University Press.

LoCastro, J. (1972). *Judgment of emotional communication in the facial-vocal-verbal channels.* Unpublished Ph.D. Thesis, University of Maryland, College Park, Maryland.

McKeever, W. F., & Dixon, M. F. (1981). Right-hemisphere superiority for discriminating memorized from nonmemorized faces: Affective imagery, sex, and perceived emotionality effects. *Brain and Language, 12,* 246–260.

Mehrabian, A., & Wiener, M. (1967). Decoding and inconsistent communications. *Journal of Personality and Social Psychology, 6,* 109–114.

Miehlke, A. (1973). *Surgery of the facial nerve.* Philadelphia, PA: W. B. Saunders.

Moscovitch, M., & Olds, J. (1982). Asymmetries in spontaneous facial expression and their possible relation to hemispheric specialization. *Neuropsychologia, 20,* 71–81.

Murray, H. A. (1938). *Explorations in personality.* New York: Oxford University Press.

Myers, R. F. (1976). Comparative neurology of vocalization and speech: Proof of a dichotomy. *Annals of the New York Academy of Sciences, 280,* 745–757.

Nathan, P. W. (1947). Facial apraxia and apraxic departhria. *Brain, 70,* 449–478.

Perlman, M., Borod, J., Nicholas, M., & Koff, E. (1984, October). *Facilitation effect of emotional context on bucco-facial apraxia.* Paper presented at the Annual Meeting of the Aphasia Academy, Los Angeles, CA.

Reuter-Lorenz, P., & Davidson, R. (1981). Differential contributions of the two cerebral hemispheres to the perception of happy and sad faces. *Neuropsychologia, 19,* 609–613.

Rinn, W. B. (1984). The neuropsychology of facial expression: A review of the neurological and psychological mechanisms for producing facial expression. *Psychological Bulletin, 95,* 52–77.

Roberts, L. (1966). Central brain mechanisms in speech. In E. C. Carterette (Ed.), *Brain function: Speech, language and communication.* Berkeley: University of California Press.

Ross, E. D., & Mesulam, M. (1979). Dominant language functions of the right hemisphere? Prosody and emotional gesturing. *Archives of Neurology, 36,* 144–148.

Rubin, D. A., & Rubin, R. T. (1980). Differences in asymmetry of facial expression between left- and right-handed children. *Neuropsychologia, 18,* 373–377.

Ruckdeschel-Hibbard, M., Gordon, W., & Diller, L. (1984). In S. Filskov & T. Boll (Eds.), *Handbook of neuro-psychology, Volume 2.* New York: Wiley.

Sackeim, H., Greenberg, M., Weiman, A., Gur, R., Hungerbuhler, J., & Geschwind, N. (1982). Functional brain asymmetry in the expression of positive and negative emotions: Lateralization of insult in cases of uncontrollable emotional outburst. *Archives of Neurology, 19,* 210–218.

Sackeim, H., & Gur, R. C. (1978). Lateral asymmetry in intensity of emotional expression. *Neuropsychologia, 16,* 473–481.

Strauss, E., & Moscovitch, M. (1981). Perception of facial expressions. *Brain and Language, 13,* 308–332.

Suberi, M., & McKeever, W. F. (1977). Differential right hemisphere memory storage of emotional and nonemotional faces. *Neuropsychologia, 15,* 757–768.

Tschiassny, K. (1953). Eight syndromes of facial paralysis and their significance in locating the lesion. *Annals of Otology, Rhinology and Laryngology, 62,* 677–691.

Tucker, D. M. (1981). Lateral brain function, emotion, and conceptualization. *Psychological Bulletin, 89,* 19–46.

Van Gelder, R. (1981). *Facing the facial nerve.* Unpublished manuscript. Amsterdam: Interfaculteit Lichamelijke Opvoeding, Vrjie Universiteit.

Wechsler, D. (1958). *The measurement and appraisal of adult intelligence.* Baltimore: Williams and Wilkins.

Winer, B. J. (1971). *Statistical principles in experimental design.* New York: McGraw-Hill.

# 15

# Shrugging Shoulders, Frowning Eye-Brows, Smiling Agreement: Mimic and Gesture Communication in the Aphasic Experience

Dominique Labourel

## INTRODUCTION

In work dealing with aphasic patients, the usual approach to aphasia consists in testing patients in order to assess their linguistic competence. Insofar as our point of view is ethological, we have analyzed videotaped recordings of several such patients. However, studying mimics and gesture on a screen is somewhat like looking at T.V. in a foreign country or like looking at someone gesticulating in a telephone booth; body movements are the cues to what is being said.

Oral communication is, by far, the most developed aspect of language. Yet, speaking cannot express everything. When we speak, more than words are being exchanged and when we do not speak a great deal can also be exchanged without a word being said. From the moment two individuals get together, they communicate. The various attitudes of each of the interlocutors, their gestures and mimics mean something. But a look, a face, a gesture, a countenance, an intonation, a silence have no meaning if they are analyzed separately. They only convey meaning when a person's behavior is considered globally in a communicative situation.

Exchange between individuals, each of them having a particular status, is located at a given place, at a given moment and refers to their past relationship. This exchange is a function of a particular context and of the requirements of the situation. We can easily imagine that if one of the modes of communication is modified, the exchange strategy and its content will therefore be modified. Are compensations possible? And if so, of what type are they? Do they cover all deficits? In other words, when ''language'' itself is disturbed, can we communicate in a different manner? And what do we communicate? Does aphasia cover only the verbal aspect of language? What about mimics and gestures?

Our observations of six patients presenting different types of aphasia seem to indicate that, in order to assess their communicative competence, it is important to consider not only their linguistic behavior but also their nonverbal means of communication (that is mimics and gestures).

## MATERIAL AND OBSERVATION METHODS

### The Patients Observed

The six patients observed present different semiological aspects of aphasia (Fig. 15.1). As we had known them for quite some time previous to this study, they accepted being filmed at home. With the exception of patient #6 (a case of jargon aphasia), all the subjects showed a stable set of symptoms for more than 18 months. We could therefore expect relative stability in their communication behavior.

For all the patients the lesions were severe and their symptoms obvious. The first three patients (#1, 2, and 3) were classified as "nonfluent" patients with predominant deficits in expression, the other three as "fluent" patients with predominant deficits in comprehension (see Figs. 15.1 and 15.2).

### Corpus Analysis

We observed these patients' gestural behavior in three different situations: language assessment with a neuropsychologist; a group therapy session with other aphasic patients; a family meal.

All the recording sessions lasted about 45 minutes. Each recording was transcribed as a polygraph: The text (that is, what was said by the patient and his various interlocutors) was presented in chronological order together with mimic and gestural elements. Various parts of the body were pinpointed: the head (eyebrows, eyes and mouth), the hands, the chest. The movements observed were described as behavioral features. For example: "he raises his left hand, he frowns, he leans sideways."

After this transcription, each gesture or mimic was interpreted according to its possible functions in each of the three situations mentioned above. The results of this analysis will not be presented in detail.

## THE FUNCTIONS OF MIMOGESTUALITY

Jakobson's communication diagram (Jacobson, 1963) offered a useful working basis in classifying the various functions (their use) of gestures and mimics.

TABLE 15.1

The Patient Biographical and Neurological Status

| | Age in 1978 | Profession | Duration of the Aphasia | Initial Aspect of the Aphasia | Etiology | Laterality |
|---|---|---|---|---|---|---|
| Patient 1 Mr. M.S. | 52 | agricultural engineer | 10 years August, 1968 | global aphasia plus hemiplegia | left intern- al carotid thrombosis | right handed |
| Patient 2 Mr. C.R. | 35 | industrial draftsman | 1 year and a half September, 1976 | global aphasia plus hemiplegia | left sylvian embolism | right handed |
| Patient 3 Mr. M.L. | 40 | architect | 3 years May, 1975 | global aphasia plus deafness and anarthria | left sylvian artery thrombosis | right handed |
| Patient 4 Mr. B.L. | 57 | lawyer | 6 years July, 1972 | WERNICKE aphasia with verbal deaf- ness plus phono- logical | left intern- al carotid thrombosis | right handed |
| Patient 5 Mr. M.R. | 45 | supermarket managering | 2 years and a half December, 1975 | WERNICKE aphasia | head trauma left temporo parietal fracture | left handed (writing) |
| Patient 6 Mr. P.R. | 61 | housing development director | 6 months October, 1977 | WERNICKE aphasia plus jargon | left carotid stenosis | left handed (writing) |

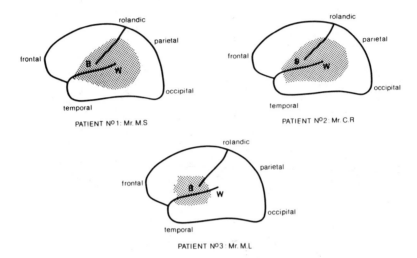

FIG. 15.1.    Lesion sites in the three nonfluent patients.

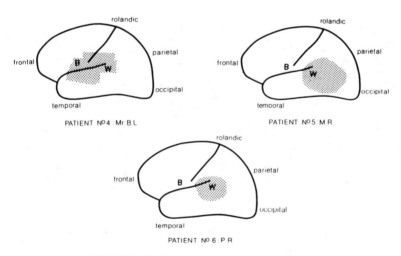

FIG. 15.2.    Lesion sites in the three fluent patients.

In Jakobson's diagram, the notion of a metacommunicative function is implicitly linked to the code, though never explicitly stated. We decided to emphasize this function in order to insist on the importance, not of the code itself, but of the way the code is used.

The aphasic person must judge his own speech acts as well as those of the interlocutor. The interlocutor must do the same. But, the gestures and mimics we

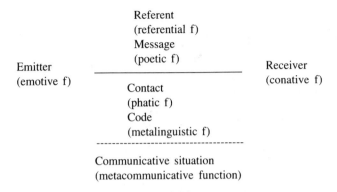

studied often combined several functions at the same time. Yet, sometimes, it was quite difficult to determine the criteria which led one gesture to be classified as referential rather than conative, expressive or metalinguistic. The difference was often a slight one depending on the context. Another reason lies in the fact that the perception of mimics and gestures is partly subjective. The final aim of a gesture in communication, that is, its function, is the result of several requirements. The gestures we make, as well as the words we use, give us information, help us to perform social acts and to regulate interindividual homeostasis. The modalities used according to the different communication situations vary from one moment to another and from one individual to another.

Keeping in mind these remarks, we shall examine to what extent the movements observed are successful regarding the different communicational functions mentioned above. Referring back to Jakobson's diagram, we are not able to find any clear-cut example of poetic messages in the mimics and gestures of the aphasic patients observed, though this function cannot be exluded a priori. Other elements of behavior corresponding to homeostatic functions (scratching, rubbing, smoking, etc.) seem to have a specific status and are classified separately.

## The Referential Function

This can be defined as the illustrative function of a gesture accompanying or replacing speech. It can either be mimetic, deictic or symbolic.

(a) *A gesture is mimetic (imitative)* when there is some isomorphic relation between if and the referent. A gesture can mime one or several features of an object or it can mime an action. For example, patient #6 during the meal, refers to big mountains where he goes on vacation with his family. We considered this gesture as mimetic (Fig. 15.3).

(b) *A gesture is deictic (designative)* when there is a relation, whether precise or vague, with the referent: the referent being present or imagined, the speaker designates an object, a place or a person with his hand, with his eyes or his head.

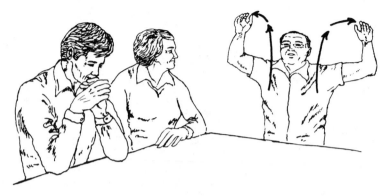

FIG. 15.3. Mimetic gesture: "Big mountains."

(c) *A gesture is symbolic* when it refers to a cultural or personal code. The relationship with the referent is arbitrary and conventional. According to the context, some mimetic, deictic or symbolic gestures have a quasi-linguistic value and can be analyzed with no danger of ambiguity.

For example, when patient #1 is presented with a text whose sentences are to be read (Fig. 15.4, he makes a symbolic gesture with his left hand meaning he does not understand what is written; at the same time, his face expresses his feelings about the difficulty of the task. In my observations referential gestures seem to be linked to the moment of speech output. They also vary from one patient to another, from one communicational instance to another.

—Deictic gestures seem more frequent than others. They are often redundant as they accompany speech and show that communicative behaviour integrates the immediate environment. They seem to provide a rather small amount of information.

FIG. 15.4. Symbolic gesture and expressive mimic.

—Mimetic gestures prove to be different according to the patient's personality and to whether or not he has a motor handicap (many gestures require both hands).

Some patients are not able to mime an object or an action in order to replace a word they cannot remember; likewise they do not use mimetic gestures to reinforce their speech. For these patients we can say there is a "lack of gestures" in the same way we say there is a "lack of words." Symbolic gestures are often used, to comment either on the utterance or on the situation. Some of them belong to the cultural code, but others can be decoded only in relation to the verbal context and are a specific code for each patient.

## The Communicational Functions

Gestures and mimics refer to the situation and to the interlocutors involved. They can have an expressive function, a conative function or a phatic function.

*Expressive or Emotive Function.*    Within this category, gestures and mimics refer to the speaker. They express an emotion, a feeling, a personal attitude. The person expresses something about himself, in relation to another person and to the communicative situation. This function is not necessarily well perceived by the receiver. The intention underlying an expression and its interpretation depends on the relation between the emitter and the receiver; it depends on their respective emotional states (that is, smiles, making faces, gestures of impotence).

*Conative Function.*    These mimic and geture signals are directly aimed at the receiver. They can express a question, a call, a protest, an order, an answer. For

FIG. 15.5.   Conative gesture.

instance, patient #4 making a gesture with his index finger shows the doctor that he has not understood (Fig. 15.5).

Several parts of the body are used according to the intention and the intensity of the message:

—the look, first, whether modulated or not by the eyebrows.
—leaning forward either with the entire upper half of the body or just the head.
—using a hand or an arm.

Some gestures are considered to be conative only because of the response of the other person. In this case, it is made obvious that there is a difference between the function given to the gesture by the emitter, that is, in relation to his intention, and the function given by the receiver, that is, the meaning he gives to it.

*Phatic or Regulating Function.*    Without being directly aimed at the other person, many signals are used in order to maintain contact so that communication can continue. These signs indicate to what extent the interlocutor implicates himself in the situation. Contact between the emitter and the receiver is maintained through looks, smiles, movements of the head or the body. Such signals show that contact is established. The receiver uses them to encourage and support the emitter. There can also be negative signals, signs of poor communication: frowns, making faces and the body shrinking away. These mimics and gestures, sometimes unconsciously performed by the receiver, can be perceived by the emitter so that something must happen: Either he modifies his message using other signals or the conversation falters.

Now let us examine how aphasics use these communicative gestures. For each of the six patients, there are a great many communicative gestures, especially during the meal situation where a lot of conative gestures occur. The patients try to influence their surroundings. The phatic function is predominant for all the patients. One example was given by patient #1 during a meal (Fig. 15.6). He did not completely agree when his wife imitated him calling his dog.

## Metalinguistic Functions

Because aphasics have difficulties nuancing what they want to say, it is very important for them to use gesture to compensate. These gestures help them to make their message more subtle, giving them some liberty of expression. They modalize what is often said in an unsatisfactory way. For instance, the emitter shrugs his shoulders when he mispronounces a word or the receiver frowns when he hears an incorrect word.

Metalinguistic gestures are quite frequent in all the patients observed, especially during the test situations and the group therapy session. Yet, the numer-

FIG. 15.6.    Opening and closing with independent finger movements.

ous commentary gestures are linked to the quality of speech output. The patients evaluate themselves with respect to what they say (in particular concerning the coherence of what they say) and also to what others say (that is, what they understand); gestures which are prosodic movements correlate with the amount of speech output. In some cases, they play a very important part in the articulation efforts made by aphasics. Moreover, some patients use mimics and gestures redundantly to back up and reinforce the inadequate utterance.

## Homeostatic Functions

Other gestures can be classified in a fourth category; nondirectly communicative gestures act as a homeostatic function. They set free tension that would otherwise disturb a given message and these gestures are more or less consciously perceived by the participants. They help to create a balance and can occur in a rhythmic pattern. Examples are gestures of comfort or discomfort, adjusting the position of the body (crossing legs, shrinking-away movements, resting the chin in the hand). They are gestures centered on the body (scratching one's head, adjusting clothes, placing a finger on the mouth); they are also diversion activities: fidgeting with an object, or making certain body movements, for example.

There are a great number of gestures that have a homeostatic function (Dahan & Cosnier, 1977). They are observed in all situations, but in various proportions, and vary according to the number of difficult moments encountered during communication. It is not patients having difficulty speaking who use the greatest number of homeostatic gestures; but rather those having serious problems in comprehension. Each patient has his own personal stock: one of them coughs and taps his fingers, another touches his paralyzed hand, a third fiddles with his glasses. It must be stated that the doctor who examines the patient uses a lot of homeostatic gestures too: particularly with patient 2 and 6, it seems difficult to be able to put up with the noninformative speech output of the former and the jargon of the latter.

## VARIABLES AFFECTING MIMOGESTUALITY

The number of gestures observed varies greatly from one patient to another (Table 15.2). This variation does not seem to be clearly correlated to the fluent or non-fluent characteristic of the type of aphasia. It also appears that the patients are more active during the actual medical examination than during the other filmed situations. During the medical examination, they are continually stimulated THOUGH they are seldom free to actually start the conversation. One might add that the main function of mimics and gestures also varies from one patient to another. The family environment, with its implicit elements, certainly helps some of them (Table 15.3). Communication seems easier for these and gives them better opportunities to speak. On the other hand, other patients are particularly ill at ease in the family situation because they are unable to deal with their children. When several people are speaking at the same time, comprehension difficulties appear. This has the effect of isolating them from the situation.

For the patients who actively participate in group therapy sessions, this type of situation seems to be a favorable environment for relatively efficient and spontaneous communication. How the patient adapts his behavior during the medical examination does vary from one patient to another and is modified throughout the examination. As a rule, they rarely initiate a conversation, and most of the time they merely answer the doctor's questions. Nevertheless, some do show a good sense of humor (cracking jokes) and make personal comments. To a certain extent, the most verbally handicapped patients are the ones who take charge of the communication by their conative mimics and gestures.

We tried to evaluate the changes in mimics and gestures within a given situation, comparing the number of gestures and the amount of mimics observed

TABLE 15.2
Total Number of Gestures Observed in Each Situation

|  | Meal | Group | Examination |
|---|---|---|---|
| Patient 1 | 278 | – | 464 |
| Patient 2 | 159 | 208 | 344 |
| Patient 3 | 239 | 297 | 314 |
| Patient 4 | 121 | 128 | 295 |
| Patient 5 | 109 | 325 | 435 |
| Patient 6 | 340 | – | 552 |

TABLE 15.3
The Different Functions per Patient and per Situation
The Most Important Function is Underlined

|             | Referential Function | Communicational Function | Metalinguistic Function | Homeostatic Function |
|-------------|:---:|:---:|:---:|:---:|
| MEAL        |     |     |     |     |
| Patient 1   | 19  | 27  | 35  | 19  |
| Patient 2   | 12  | 38  | 36  | 13  |
| Patient 3   | 16  | 44  | 16  | 23  |
| Patient 4   | 10  | 41  | 22  | 26  |
| Patient 5   | 34  | 34  | 20  | 12  |
| Patient 6   | 17  | 26  | 50  | 6   |
| GROUP       |     |     |     |     |
| Patient 2   | 32  | 12  | 48  | 8   |
| Patient 3   | 14  | 25  | 31  | 30  |
| Patient 4   | 2   | 30  | 42  | 26  |
| Patient 5   | 49  | 13  | 24  | 13  |
| EXAMINATION |     |     |     |     |
| Patient 1   | 23  | 20  | 37  | 10  |
| Patient 2   | 28  | 14  | 53  | 5   |
| Patient 3   | 8   | 27  | 30  | 34  |
| Patient 4   | 14  | 15  | 49  | 22  |
| Patient 5   | 24  | 16  | 32  | 28  |
| Patient 6   | 19  | 19  | 53  | 9   |

at three different moments (the first 5 minutes, 5 minutes in the middle of the recording and the last 5 minutes). Once again, some modifications are observed according to the situations and patients. The quantity of mimics and the number of gestures are more or less constant during mealtime. In the group therapy session these correspond to the length of the time they speak. But, during the medical assessment, all the patients (and the doctor) make fewer gestures after the first 30 minutes. Yet, among the various gestures, there is a particularly noticeable drop in the number of metalinguistic gestures. For the nonfluent patients, this drop is accompanied by a drop in the number of utterances; on the contrary, for the fluent patients (as well as for the doctor) there is no change in the number of verbal exchanges.

## SOME DISCUSSION ELEMENTS

Studying gestures in relation to speech led us to consider two specific areas: apraxia, and the question of gesture laterality and brain dominance.

1. Regarding apraxia, it can be said that pathology of communicative gestures is, by far, more complex and difficult to evaluate than the usual ideomotor or ideatory apraxia. One may wonder if adults, having speech difficulties, can use a more primitive means of communication such as the "preverbal" mimogestual

language of children. Very early in development, a child relates directly to his space environment. When he speaks about something, he shows it: his gesture is above all a sign. Yet, the aphasics studied use a lot of deictic gestures; they use the immediate space as a significant element and force the receiver to discover the meaning of their message from their common space. But sometimes a patient's deictic gestures are too vague and the referred object too far away for the interlocutor. Because of their egocentrism or because of their inability to express subtle meaning, some aphasics reduce their "semantic domains" to personal connotations and are not capable of using more abstract and general rules. The "over-there" beyond the windows often means something that is only known to the patient. In order to mime one object or an action, one must know its essential distinctive features and restructure them through one's own body. Here, mental imagery has a prominent role to play. There also exists individual variation in the use of symbolic gestures. A particular code must be known. Many ritualized signs are used according to the situation. A misuse as well as a misinterpretation of conventional signs can lead to serious disturbances in individual exchanges. Some of the illustrative gestures just mentioned always occur within a specific verbal and situational context. During the medical exam the patient is asked to make some of these same gestures. But they are "performed" "in vacuo," that is, out of their natural context. We all know the phenomenon of automatic–voluntary dissociation. Some gestures and mimics are performed automatically and are closely linked to the situation. In particular, many symbolic and conventional gestures, such as gestures of politeness, were observed in ritualized social situations. They correspond to set phrases such as "how do you do" used by most of the patients even when their verbal production is severely limited.

The assessment of the patient's apraxia essentially tests the referential function of the gesture, and has no relation with the communication situation. However, other functions of gestures can be affected, although it is difficult to observe and to isolate them. There is often a reorganization of the communication strategy, used to balance the exchange. In addition, what is emitted by the patient can be more easily evaluated than what he receives. It is possible that nuances and subtle elements which accompany and enrich language escape the patient's comprehension, as he only globally understands the message. There undoubtedly exists other less obvious parameters which are affected and which are not generally taken into account during the neuropsychological assessment. The patient should be placed in a language situation which would induce the use of mimogestuality in relation to verbal speech; in other words, incite the use of the body.

2. Concerning the question of gestures and cerebral dominance: it has been difficult to find a definitive relationship between aphasia and the laterality of the gesture studied. Some of the patients are also hemiphlegic and can only use the left side, others have a somato-sensory deficit on the right side and tend to neglect it in daily-life gestures. Among the patients studied who have no motor

or somato-sensory deficit, one of them is ambidextrous and the other is left-handed. We might add that the three doctors (observed by means of a second camera) often make gestures with their left hands though none of them is left-handed!

## CONCLUSION

The functional analysis of gestures and mimics points to their obvious ambiguities. One has to adopt different levels of interpretation.

Two hypotheses should be considered. Either the aphasic can compensate for his verbal deficit thanks to a preserved mimogestuality, or the deficit is global and involves the verbal and the nonverbal production. There is no simple answer. Clearly, we have to consider both the type of gesture and the particular patient studied.

An ethological approach, taking into account the patient as a whole, demonstrates that the gestural deficit in most cases is not as serious as the VERBAL deficit. Thanks to nonverbal communication, patients can act upon their interlocutors by expressing their feelings and emotions, and situating themselves with respect to verbal speech. However, they rarely use gestures to transmit information with referential functions.

Using verbal fluency as the sole criterion in classifying aphasia does not account for the fact that speech is only one aspect of communication. Communication can be effective without speech. Indeed, some of the patients compensate for their verbal deficit by using mimics and gestures. For some of them, a paradigmatic choice is possible. The analysis of the gestures and mimics of these six patients observed in several communication situations led us to believe that the aphasic's mimogestuality should be analyzed according to three criteria:

—the function of the gestures in a communicating situation,
—the patient's personality.
—whether or not praxic disorders are present.

Speech and mimogestuality cannot be dissociated. The aphasic's expression and comprehension capabilities must be analyzed in relation to the communication situation. These fundamental remarks should be applied to the therapeutic approach taken for each patient. Language is produced through interaction between the locutors; speaking is not merely responding to a series of exercises which test linguistic competence. Communication is partly due to verbal exchange and partly due to mimogestuality.

The language assessment of an aphasic patient by a doctor is one particular communication situation in which their roles are defined, but it could be made more natural if nonverbal elements accompanying or replacing speech were taken into account. It must also be noticed that the doctor's behavior has an influence upon the performance of the patient opposite him. The speech therapy session is also a very particular situation. Here too, nonverbal elements of communication should play an important role, in order to give the patient a chance to rediscover his capacity for expression and to help him find his place in everyday life. The therapist must put the patient in a situation which incites verbal language and he must also encourage him to use nonverbal cues to compensate for his verbal deficit in order to communicate effectively.

## REFERENCES

Dahan, G., & Cosnier, J. (1977). "Sémiologie des quasi-linguistiques français." *Psychologie Médicale, 9*(11), 2053–2072.

Jakobson, R. (1963). *Essais de linguistique générale.* Paris: Editions de Minuit.

# Author Index

Pages with full reference citations occur at the end of each chapter.

# Subject Index